MUSEUMS AND COMMUNITIES

CHANGING DYNAMICS

DEBORAH TRANTER

MUSEUMS AND COMMUNITIES

CHANGING DYNAMICS

DEBORAH TRANTER

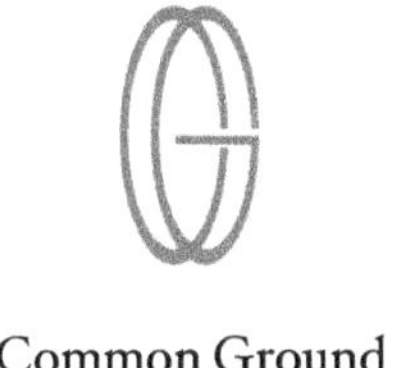

Common Ground

First published in Champaign, Illinois in 2012
by Common Ground Publishing LLC
as part of the On Museums series

Library of Congress Cataloging-in-Publication Data

Tranter, Deborah.
Museums and communities : changing dynamics / Deborah Tranter.
p. cm. -- (On museums series)
Includes bibliographical references.
ISBN 978-1-61229-067-6 (pbk : alk. paper) -- ISBN 978-1-61229-068-3 (ebook)
1. Cobb & Co. Museum--Management. 2. Cobb & Co. Museum--Public relations. 3. Carriages and carts--Museums--Australia--Toowoomba (Qld.) 4. Museums and community--Australia--Toowoomba (Qld.) 5. Museums--Public relations--Australia--Toowoomba (Qld.) 6. Museums-- Social aspects--Australia--Toowoomba (Qld.) I. Title.

TS2003.A82T667 2012
069.09943'3--dc23

2012008534

Cover Photo: Safeguarding heritage trades: Cobb+Co Museum – community partnership, by Tony Coonan

Series Editor: Amareswar Galla

Table of Contents

Part II : Part B

List of Tables

Foreword

The Inclusive Museum Book Series aims to publish significant research that brings together the academy and the heritage industry in understanding contemporary museum developments. It is an integral part of the Inclusive Museum Knowledge Community, which is one of the outcomes from the deliberations of the Cross Cultural Task Force of the International Council of Museums. The Community brings together an annual research conference, a scholarly journal, a book series and an online community of museum practitioners, researchers and thinkers.

Museums and Communities: Changing Dynamics by Dr. Deborah Tranter presents research that is based on what anthropologists call *emic* and *etic* perspectives. In many ways the corporate cultural transformation of the Cobb & Co Museum in Toowoomba, Queensland; and effective and evolving community engagement are studied through participant observation. It is a rare achievement in the field of museum studies anywhere in the world. She is at once an insider and an outsider in her research endeavour.

This book presents an important case study of a longer-term museum and museum policy development. It is of considerable value to other institutions, researchers and projects both nationally and internationally. Dr. Tranter recognises quite frankly the risk of subjectivity in her approach as she has been head of the museum studied in the book since its beginnings in 1987. She quotes key research on the risks involved and negotiates her way with exceptional professionalism and scholarship.

Her personal knowledge, presented dispassionately, adds considerable value to the study. It gives us a rare first-hand insight into many policy and development discussions and consultations. The book is a ground-breaking study within the frequently controversial attempt to apply cultural economic theories to the museum and heritage sector.

Overseeing Dr. Tranter's research was a great pleasure and honour for me. Many of us learnt travelling with her on this unique journey. We are also grateful to her for bringing Professor David Throsby into a deep engagement with the Queensland museum industry through lectures and master classes and most importantly to illustrate the Contingency Valuation Method that she chose to apply.

Common Ground and its President Professor Dr. Bill Cope are delighted to present the book to the readers. We are grateful to Jamie Burns, Managing Editor of Common Ground Publishing, for bringing out this quality case study research in a short time.

Professor Amareswar Galla, PhD
Editor, Inclusive Museum Series, Common Ground Publishing, Champaign, IL
Executive Director, International Institute for the Inclusive Museum, Copenhagen & Hyderabad

Preface

This book represents the culmination of twenty-four years of my professional experiences and research into museum management in a regional context in Australia. As the director of the Cobb+Co Museum in Toowoomba Queensland since its opening in 1987, I have both lead and benefited from changing dynamics between the museum and its community that have provided enormous benefits to both the institution and the community itself.

Research for this book was part of my PhD thesis that was awarded by the University of Queensland in November 2011.

As a result of my study program, I realised that the engagement process and subsequent outcomes between museums and their stakeholder communities are often neglected by both practitioners and academics. While much has been written and spoken about the need for museums to engage with and be responsive to their communities, many museums, in practice, still remain indifferent to their key stakeholders. Larger museums now generally at least claim to be 'audience focused', but, in reality, they are far from being responsive to the preferences of contemporary heterogenic communities. Audiences can be ambivalent about museum offerings, but there remain important and embedded symbiotic relationships between museums and their communities.

Of seminal importance is the fact that museums can play substantial leadership roles within communities. This occurs when the relationship between the museum and its community becomes entrenched with shared values. These values can facilitate social, cultural, and economic benefits for both museums and their communities. This book explores these values and how they can be expressed within a regional museum context.

The book is organised in two parts. Part A analyses the three transformations that have taken place at the Cobb+Co Museum, which is part of the Queensland Museum, between 1987 and 2010. This case study explores the effects that the changing dynamics between museums and their communities can have on both parties. It illustrates that while each of the Cobb+Co Museum's transformations represents a different, unique identity for the museum marked by a structural change, each change was integrated within the others. The three resulting diverse and hybrid identities evolved as the local community responded to specific national and international trends relating to museums and heritage. The transformations occurred through accumulative processes that represented both time and place specific adaptations to broader trends.

Part B of the book gives 'voice to values' by investigating how communities estimate and articulate the worth of their museums. Traditionally, politicians, policy makers, and other museum professionals have been recognised as the major stakeholders of museums, and the assessment frameworks adapted to value museums from their perspectives have been narrow. Recognition of the community as the primary stakeholder requires a very different methodology to effectively gauge a museum's worth. To assess the Cobb+Co Museum's value to its community, a 'Contingent Valuation Methodology' (CVM) study was devised to value the Queensland Museum, of which the Cobb+Co Museum is a part. This major study was undertaken in December 2008. Using a detailed survey instrument delivered online to nearly 1200 Queensland residents, both users and non-users of museums, the CVM study sought the participants' willingness to pay in dollar amounts for both existing products and services and for a raft of new developments proposed by the Queensland Museum. It also investigated a range of non-market values that were important to both users and non-users of the Queensland Museum.

The results obtained indicated that the people of Queensland placed a very high value on the Queensland Museum which was replicated by Toowoomba residents towards the Cobb+Co Museum. The true test of Toowoomba's community-museum relationship was manifested in the community's leadership of and support for the National Carriage Factory project, which opened in September 2010 as the Third Stage development of the Cobb+Co Museum.

Acknowledgments

I owe a special debt to Professors Amareswar Galla and Tom O'Regan from the University of Queensland for their support and guidance during my PhD program. Professor Galla provided me with a multiplicity of international frameworks on which to base my research, while Professor O'Regan helped me appreciate the potential of a new creative-cultural industry model embracing heritage and museums. Both encouraged me to believe that a museum in regional Queensland could have something significant to contribute to the wider museological sector.

I am also indebted to my employer, the Queensland Museum, and particularly to Chief Executive Officer, Doctor Ian Galloway, for his support with the Contingent Valuation Methodology Study – Valuing the Queensland Museum.

My commitment to changing the dynamics between the Cobb+Co Museum and its community was initially inspired by the former Chair of the Cobb+Co Advisory Committee, Mr Bill O'Brien, who taught me that communities matter and that the museum has a responsibility to play a leadership role in enhancing community development.

I also owe a debt of gratitude to the present and past members of the Cobb+Co Museum Advisory Committee who supported and challenged me throughout the transformational processes that the museum has undertaken since its inception in 1987. My special thanks to Doctor Dennis Campbell who chaired the committee during the museum's Third Stage Development and Doctor Mary Wagner and the members of the National Carriage Factory Committee who made this a reality on 4 September 2010, and to my staff who made it all work!

Finally, I want to thank my husband Mark, for his support, patience and hours spent proof-reading my work.

List of abbreviations

ABS	Australian Bureau of Statistics
CAA	Corporate Administration Agency
Cobb+Co	Cobb+Co Museum (formerly designated Cobb & Co. Museum)
CVM	Contingent Valuation Methodology
DCMS	Department of Culture, Media, and Sport (United Kingdom)
DEEDI	Department of Employment, Economic Development, and Innovation (Queensland State Government)
ICOM	International Committee of Museums
IRG	Industry Reference Group
KPI	Key Performance Indicator
MAGNT	Museum and Art Gallery of the Northern Territory
MOLI	Modes of Learning Inventory
MTQ	Museum of Tropical Queensland
NCF	National Carriage Factory
NOAA	National Oceanic and Atmospheric Administration
OECD	Organisation of Economic Cooperation and Development
PSVM	Public Service Value Model
QM	Queensland Museum
SQIT	Southern Queensland Institute of TAFE
TAFE	Technical and Further Education
TGWRTA	Toowoomba and Golden West Regional Tourism (formerly Toowoomba & Golden West Regional Tourist Association)
TQ	Tourism Queensland
TCC	Toowoomba City Council (amalgamated in 2008 into Toowoomba Regional Council)
TRC	Toowoomba Regional Council
TWRM	The Workshop Rail Museum
UNESCO	United Nations Economic, Social and Cultural Organisation
VFM	Value for Money
WTA	Willingness to accept
WTP	Willingness to pay

Chapter 1
Introduction

For a tree to grow well, the seed can be international,
but the soil must be local

Su Donghai
Professor of National Museum of China and
Project Leader of Ecomuseums in Guizhou Province, China

1.1 Overview

Museums and communities – what are the connections? Are they static or dynamic? Who leads and who follows? What are the outcomes? Who actually benefits? Is it really worth the cost in the long run? Museums in the twentieth-first century must find local answers to these questions which will underpin their successful operations.

The ongoing development of the Cobb+Co Museum in Toowoomba, Queensland is the focus of this book. It covers the period from its inception in 1987, when the Board of the Queensland Museum accepted a donation of a significant collection of horse-drawn vehicles that had been the property of a Toowoomba businessman, to the opening of the National Carriage Factory in 2010.

The Queensland Museum itself had been established in 1862, one of the very first public institutions founded in the new colony of Queensland which had only been separated from New South Wales three years earlier. During nearly 150 years of operations, the Queensland Museum experienced many ups and downs, but in the 1980s was determined to embrace opportunities presented by the Queensland Government to establish branch museums across the State. The Cobb+Co Museum became the third major branch of the Queensland Museum when it opened in the recycled floriculture pavilion on the site of the old Toowoomba Showgrounds.

Toowoomba, located on the Great Dividing Range in Southern Queensland, has been the major service centre and unofficial 'capital' of the fertile Darling Downs region since the 1840s, when the first European settlers arrived with their flocks of sheep and later farming equipment. In 1987 the Cobb+Co Museum's horse-drawn vehicle collection characterised the community's long held identity underpinned by traditional rural values.

The land on which the Cobb+Co Museum would operate was excised from the former Showground site that had been acquired by the Queensland Government for Technical and Further Education (TAFE) purposes. Covering 1600m², the Cobb+Co Museum consisted of one very large gallery in which was displayed its 39 horse-drawn vehicles, a reception area including workspace and small adjacent retail outlet. A theatrette, outdoor courtyard, blacksmiths shop and some storage space completed the complex.

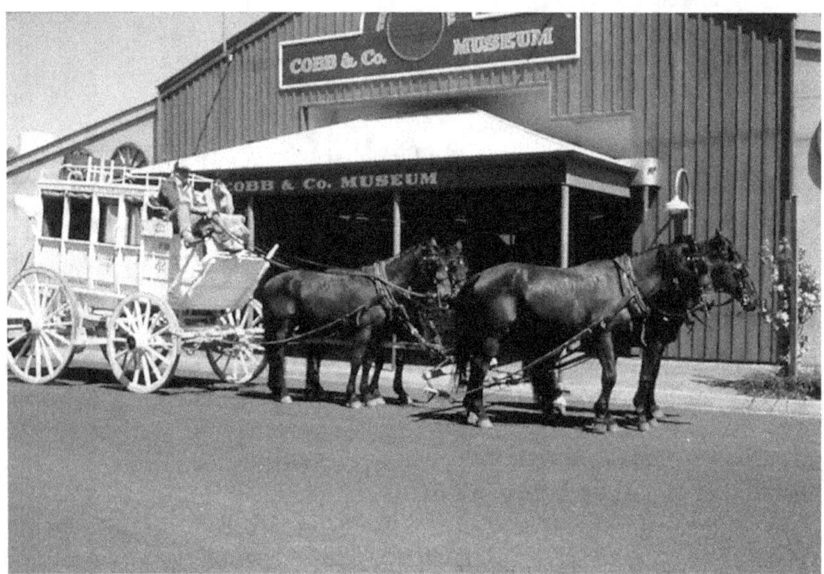

Cobb+Co Museum Stage 1 1987

The museum's name pays tribute to Australia's largest horse-drawn coaching company, Cobb & Co. Founded by four young Americans in the gold rush days of the 1850s, Cobb & Co. coaches ran in all mainland Australian states. Coaches bearing the name Cobb & Co. also operated in New Zealand, South Africa and Japan.

In many outback areas of Australia, especially in Queensland where Cobb & Co. had its most extensive operations, the company was responsible for providing reliable and efficient transport and communication systems before the railways and motor vehicles replaced the final coach in 1924. The Cobb+Co Museum positioned itself as the custodian of the Cobb & Co. legend, a story which still holds a prominent position in the nation's cultural identity.

In 1987 when the Cobb+Co Museum opened, two staff were appointed, both with curatorial responsibilities, in line with the Queensland Museum's traditional museological outlook at that time. However, from its inception, the Cobb+Co Museum also had a very strong focus on education and learning. Initially this was evidenced in the development by the Cobb+Co Museum of the first curriculum based learning programs for schools within museums in Queensland.

In its first full year of operations, 13,407 people visited the Cobb+Co Museum. Visitor numbers gradually increased during this stage to reach 18,486 in 2000-2001.

In the early 1990s, planning commenced to develop a new museum model requiring a significantly different approach to community engagement. This would involve partnerships with the Southern Queensland Institute of TAFE (SQIT), co-located on the old Showground site with the museum, and the Toowoomba City Council. In 2001, the museum doubled in size with the opening of Stage Two. New galleries were designed to tell a changing array of local stories and provide mixed-use spaces, which were available for both internal and community use. During its Stage 2 iteration, the museum also broadened its education focus from formal education programs for schools to free-choice lifelong learning. Programs were designed for the wellbeing of the community from very young children to senior citizens in nursing homes. Visitor numbers for Stage 2 plateaued at just under 40,000 per annum by 2008-9 (Cobb+Co Museum, 1988-2009).

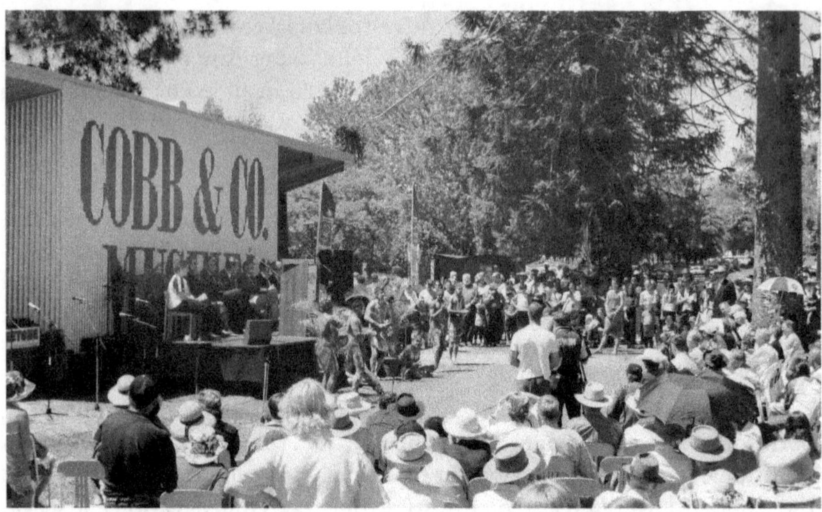

Cobb+Co Museum Stage 2 opening celebrations 2001

Planning for Stage 3 commenced in 2006, when a community partnership was formed to develop a facility that would enable the Cobb+Co Museum in conjunction with SQIT to become a centre for teaching heritage trades, thus expanding the museum's education and learning focus into vocational education. The National Carriage Factory (NCF) project which resulted had at its core a determination to safeguard traditional trades, crafts and skills. Although doubling the size of the museum yet again, the NCF aspired to be more than just expanded physical spaces for teaching and production of heritage trade related products. Through combining cultural heritage with entrepreneurship, the Cobb+Co Museum embraced a strategy that would forge a regional creative-cultural industry based around heritage trades, crafts, and skills. In September 2010, this $8 million development was achieved through the leadership of Toowoomba's business community.

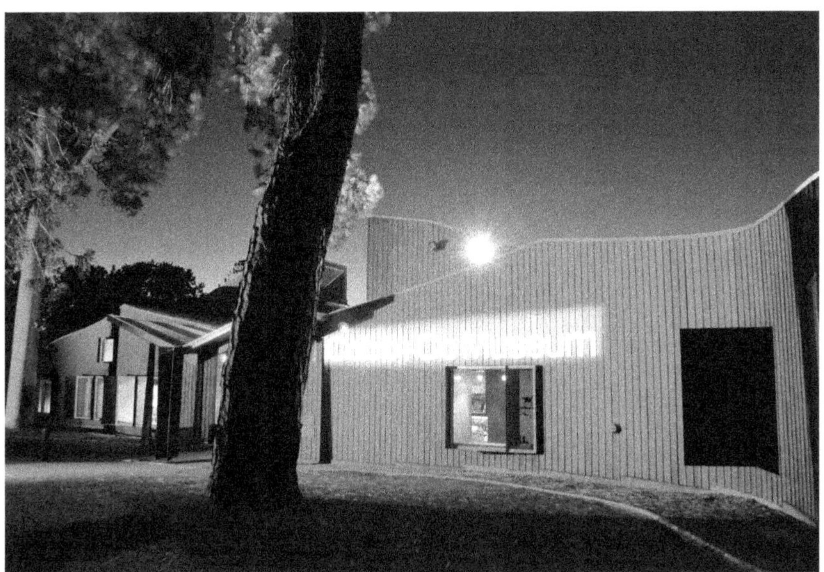

Light up Stage 3 2010

These ongoing developments are analysed in this book, as a case study of how changing community relationships can foster shared values and drive significant museological transformations which in turn can facilitate social, cultural, and economic benefits for both museums and their communities.

As Director of the Cobb+Co Museum since its inception in 1987, I was interested in assessing the degree to which this museum's evolution has reflected national and international museological discourses, and to what extent it has been a unique response to localised internal and external social, cultural, and political environments.

Hence this publication aims to apply practical experience to a theoretical framework in order to assess the usefulness, or otherwise, of the Cobb+Co Museum developmental model for application to other museums and their communities. Specifically, this study attempts to answer the following questions:

- Has the Cobb+Co Museum's transformation over the period of more than twenty years reflected general changes taking place in museums, or has it been time-and place-specific?
- To what extent are these transformations valued by the community?
- Can the processes enacted by the Cobb+Co Museum in developing and implementing its transformative models act as an exemplar for museums in other regions?

During the period from 1987 to 2010, the Cobb+Co Museum experienced three transformational stages, which are summarised in Table 1.1 below.

Table 1.1: Cobb+Co Museum's three-stage development, 1987–2010

Time frame	Transformational stage	Nature of transformation
1987 - 2001	Stage One	**Traditional museum model** of a predominately internal collection-focused institution, with a narrow research profile and a collection base limited to the horse-drawn vehicle collection
2001 - 2010	Stage Two	**Social enterprise model** of a community resource centre dedicated to lifelong learning and inclusivity. Includes broader exhibition themes and their associated public programs.
2010 -	Stage Three	**Creative-cultural industry model**, known as the National Carriage Factory, based on intangible heritage – specifically focusing on traditional trades, crafts, and skills.

Although each of these developments was marked by a building program with new exhibitions and public programs, it was more the community-related processes and functions that distinguished the Cobb+Co Museum's identity during each of the three stages.

Many of the developments discussed in this publication, are reviewed retrospectively through the lenses of both the academic literature of the time and as well as of today chronicling the changing practice of museology. This has enabled a thorough analysis of the impact of each major development on subsequent transformations at the Cobb+Co Museum against international developments. Some of the later Cobb+Co Museum enhancements have taken place concurrently with this study and have benefitted greatly from the clarity of vision and values formulated from an understanding of the literature and museological practices investigated. This has encouraged a much greater adherence to theorising the decision making processes in more recent years.

1.2 Rationale

This book attempts to mainstream museological developments in regional Queensland – an area that has not previously been identified as having anything significant to contribute to the broader study of museum practices. To date, there has been little attention focused on the development of the museum industry in Queensland as a whole, let alone regional Queensland. The only industry driven analysis – *Hidden Heritage: A Development Plan for Museums in Queensland 1995–2001* – is long overdue for revision (Lennon, 1995).

This longitudinal study of the Cobb+Co Museum through its three-stage formation between 1987 and 2010, fills a recognised void in studies investigating identity formation in museums – particularly regional entities in Australia.

Secondly, this publication contributes to understanding the dynamic processes that operate within communities and the leadership roles that cultural institutions, such as museums, can play to enhance the future of communities and museums themselves. It also investigates an innovative community engagement strategy that could have widespread applications for other cultural institutions in other communities.

Finally, the determination to give 'voice to values' through a major web-based study undertaken to measure the complexity and interrelationship of museum values from the community's perspective, has made a substantial contribution to the international pool of noteworthy valuation studies of arts and cultural institutions. The robust results achieved from the Contingent Valuation Methodology (CVM) study have delivered a new way of valuing the multifaceted Queensland Museum, of which the Cobb+Co Museum is a part. These results also provide a mechanism for demonstrating the museum's value in economic terms, which could have noteworthy applications for advocacy purposes.

The successful application of this methodology has great relevance for arts and cultural institutions in Queensland and, possibly, further afield. By inviting other major Queensland cultural institutions to participate in this study from its inception, and by sharing the study's results in an open manner, it is hoped that a common language may develop to express the value of arts and culture within Queensland.

1.3 Methodology

The range of methodologies employed in this study relates strongly to the professional involvement of the writer as a key actor in all the developments investigated.

This book is underpinned by an extensive multi-disciplinary literature review covering a wide range of international discourses relevant to the transformational stages of the Cobb+Co Museum. While it has been imperative to appreciate the international context of the transformations, it has been equally important to interpret these trends within the Australian, Queensland, and, particularly, the regional museum context.

This literature review has been supplemented by the author's practical museum experience that has accumulated during twenty-four years of managing the Cobb+Co Museum. In addition to this museum experience, the author has undertaken numerous site visits and work experience within many prominent cultural and heritage institutions in Australia, the United States of America, the United Kingdom, Vietnam, Scandinavian countries and in the Pacific. These field studies stimulated ideas and provided invaluable knowledge of more recent museological developments. As Director of the Queensland Museum's Regional Service program, the author has also spent many years working with local authorities and diverse communities across Queensland, acquiring knowledge of societal relations and political interplays, while also developing skills to positively influence the dynamics between museums and their communities.

One the major advantages of this analysis has been the author's ongoing leadership role in the development of the Cobb+Co Museum since its inception in 1987. However, this may also be viewed as a potential difficulty in the author being able to objectively assess the significance of the identity transformations undergone by the Cobb+Co Museum. This has been addressed through a conscious strategy of distancing the author from the events described by developing a retrospective understanding of cause and effect through situating the developments within multidisciplinary academic research and practical policy frameworks. All decisions taken in formulating and implementing the transformations undertaken at the Cobb+Co Museum have been rigorously reassessed retrospectively, or more recently concurrently as the case may be, in light of the diverse range of positions, ideas and examples provided by the extensive range of literature reviewed.

With these safeguards in place, any negative limitations caused by the author's personal involvement have been minimised and it is submitted are greatly outweighed by the author's insight, understanding and knowledge of the museum's transformation and how this was influenced by the community's personalities and relationships with the museum. The author's professional involvement as the main instigator of the museum's strategic and operational directions provided first-hand knowledge of the subject and the underlying motivations behind the developments that have taken place over two decades.

It is strongly argued that the author's 'practical knowledge' of all the issues, personalities, policy frameworks, museum theories and practices, and tourism and educational frameworks, as well as her ongoing involvement with local governments and major economic development, tourist, cultural, and educational regional organisations, has provided a unique practical perspective complementing and, many times, supplementing the academic literature surrounding this subject.

Bourdieu vigorously criticised researchers with 'phenomenological knowledge' that failed to 'reflect on itself' by rigorously 'questioning the conditions of its own possibility'. However, this situation does not apply in this case, as the museum's Advisory Committee has consistently subjected the management of the Cobb+Co Museum to critical analysis of the strengths, weaknesses, opportunities, and threats that underpinned the development of every strategic and operational plan (Bourdieu, 1977, p. 3). To further counteract any such criticism, all decision making processes that were responsible for the Cobb+Co Museum's transformations have been rigorously reviewed against the then existing, and more recent academic literature. Critical analysis of all decisions has been essential in a practical sense as well, as community opinion and involvement has varied greatly over the twenty-four year timeframe and, as a result of the changes the museum has undergone, the community's attitude to the Cobb+Co Museum has changed from lack of interest to ownership.

Likewise, the value of objectivity is not underestimated, with elements of both subjectivism and objectivism recognised as useful in understanding social phenomena. There is an imperative:

> ...to integrate the truth of practical experience and of the practical mode of knowledge which learned knowledge (objective analysis) had to be constructed against (Bourdieu, 1977, p. 4).

At the same time, the author recognises that both these positions have inconsistencies:

> Objectivism in its various forms fails because of a superimposition of a quasi-mechanistic set of rules upon a social situation which does not account for the origin or genesis of those rules, or for their immediate production. Equally, subjectivism fails because it takes for granted that which is subjectively produced without accounting for the objective system of production which is a condition for the production of any quasi-spontaneous action in a given social situation (Rasmussen, 1981, p. 275).

Consequently, there is a 'need to escape from the ritual either/or choice between subjectivism and objectivism in the social sciences' (Bourdieu, 1977, p. 4), and transcend the dichotomies which have shaped theoretical thinking about the social order for so long. As Bourdieu has argued:

> We [should] subordinate all operations of scientific practice to a theory of practice and of practical knowledge and inseparably from this, to a theory of the theoretical and social conditions of the possibility of objective apprehension – and thereby to a theory of the limits of this mode of knowledge (1977, p. 3).

Although the author has been a central player in the developments under discussion, there have been other major contributors. From 1988, the Cobb+Co Museum has been assisted by an Advisory Committee – a sub-committee of the Board of the Queensland Museum – that is comprised of representatives of community, business, and government bodies and that has overseen the transformations that have taken place at the Cobb+Co Museum. The pluralist model of regime theories suggest that the use of multiple stakeholders, as was evidenced in the ongoing role of the Advisory Committee, causes decision-making and resource distribution to be more equitable, and allows multiple groups, including minority and small, special-interest groups, to influence outcomes (Stroker, 'Regime Theory and Urban Politics' (1995) quoted in Evans, 2005). The ongoing reviews and assessments provided by the Cobb+Co Museum Advisory Committee have provided stakeholder direction to the ongoing transformational processes that occur at the museum. Discussions within the Advisory Committee have always being frank and honest, and author is committed to providing an equally frank and honest assessment in this publication.

The predicament of the researcher being a long-term participant in the subject of the research is not unique as demonstrated by Phillip Batty in his Doctorate (PhD) study of the development of Aboriginal Radio and Television in Central Australia. Batty played a prominent personal role in the organisation under consideration, but he was judged able to provide an 'objective' account of events in which he was 'subjectively' involved, particularly in the context of personal relationships (Batty, 2003). Batty acknowledged Bourdieu's position that the possibility of the researcher influencing his or her own research results is not only 'likely', but is an inevitable part of the research process (Bourdieu, 1990; Harker, Mahar, & Wilkes, 1990). Batty's 'mobile positioning' approach of a variety of 'speaking positions' and methods for presenting the research results has also been adopted in this publication (Batty, 2003).

1.4 Key Concepts

1.4.1 Community

Community is a particularly contested concept. Rarely would 'a community' be homogeneous, nor would any one person belong to a single community. 'Community' relates to:

> ...a population living in an area, conscious of the affinities and the differences which characterise its elements, as well as the conflicting relationships between these and their environment and to whom at least the future is common (Davis, 1999, p. 60).

Communities can be defined using a variety of determinants, such as shared historical or cultural experiences; specialist knowledge; demographic/socio-economic factors; identities (such as national, regional, or local identities relating to sexuality, disability, age, or gender); or visiting practices. Communities can also be identified by their exclusions from other communities (Mason, 2005, pp. 206-207).

The Cobb+Co Museum's community is defined using a propinquity criteria rather than the concept of group membership. It is identified primarily as Toowoomba residents and those living within the Toowoomba Regional Council area (Guetzhow, 2002). A community, in contrast to a neighbourhood, is distinguished not only by its defined specific territory or place, but also by its social organisations and institutions and by the prevalence of social interaction on matters concerning similar interest (Steffen, 2008, p. 14).

In acknowledging the diversity of the Toowoomba community, it is interesting to note that Aboriginal community elders, who one would generally not expect to have close links with a museum of European technology, approached the author in 2000 seeking a space in the Stage Two Cobb+Co Museum. This resulted in the development of the Binangar Centre and has led to ongoing exhibitions and public programs.

'Community engagement' refers to the connections between governments – including public service utilities (such as museums), citizens, and communities – that relate to policies, programs, and service delivery issues.

It incorporates a wide variety of interactions, ranging from information-sharing to community consultation and active participation in decision-making. A hallmark of community engagement is community 'in-reach' into public institutions, as opposed to organisational 'out-reach' into communities (Queensland Government, 2005 p. 5).

1.4.2 Contingent Valuation Methodology (CVM)

CVM is a survey-based stated preference methodology that provides respondents the opportunity to make economic decisions concerning a non-market good (Carson, Flores, & Meade, 2001, p. 198; Cowell, 2004, p. 32). A CVM study uses a carefully described hypothetical scenario that respondents (both users and non-users of the public good) understand and believe to be plausible. The survey participants are then asked to make a hypothetical monetary transaction to indicate the value they ascribe to the public good (Santagata & Signorello, 2000). Usually the question refers to a change in goods or services offered by an institution, such as when participants are asked to indicate a monetary value to a proposed redevelopment of spaces, or new exhibitions or programs.

In practice, respondents are asked to indicate their maximum willingness to pay (WTP) for an increase in the level of provision of a public good, or the minimum amount of compensation they would be willing to accept (WTA) as compensation for a reduction in the level of provision of a public good, given their current income,as well as current levels of market prices and other background conditions (Kling, Revier, & Sable, 2004). The author adapted this methodology to undertake a major study of the value of the Queensland Museum to its community, as is analysed in Chapter Six.

1.4.3 Creative industries

Creative Industries as a concept has only recently emerged to describe those industries underpinning the new or creative economy. These are industries that mobilise talent, creativity, and entrepreneurship to produce a range of creative goods and services underpinned by symbolic meaning (Bakhshi & Throsby, 2010, p. 10; Department for Culture Media and Sport, 1998). Exactly what constitutes a creative industry is open to debate, with many commentators continuing to argue that the creative industries are 'not yet conceived, explained, narrated or understood' (Holden, 2007, p. 4).

The term 'creative industries' is often confused with the earlier term 'cultural industries'. The term 'cultural industries' was popularised in the 1970s and 1980s when cultural sector products and services were grouped together to persuade local, state, and national governments to support specific arts and cultural activities in order to promote the economic benefits these activities delivered to regional communities (Hartley, 2005, pp. 5,13; David Throsby & Hollister, 2003, p. 11). There still seems to be two diametrically opposed groups referencing creative and cultural industries, with one group stressing industry groupings, and the other stressing individual creativity. Complaints are still voiced about the 'arbitrary exclusivity of the creative industries sector' (Stuart Cunningham, 2002, p. 54).

There is also no consistency regarding the inclusion, or otherwise, of heritage and museums within the industry sectors that produce the 'symbolic goods' – ideas, experiences, and images – that underpin the creative industries (Bilton & Leary, 2002, p. 50; David Throsby, 2008c). To overcome this dilemma, the term 'creative-cultural industries' is preferred. This more expansive definition combines the two individual terms – 'creative industries' and 'cultural industries' – and enables museums and heritage to be included as an essential part of any discussion about the industry sectors underpinning the new economy.

1.4.4 Culture

Culture plays an important role in defining and preserving cultural identity. Culture is viewed in this publication as a capital asset accumulated by an individual or a community whose members reference it to connote their identity (Santagata, 2002, p. 1; Stanley, 2005, pp. 22-24; Venturelli, 2002, p. 395). Culture can incorporate numerous attributes, including 'distinctive spiritual, material, intellectual and emotional features that characterize a society or group'. Although frequently linked to the arts, culture incorporates much wider attributes, including 'modes of life, the fundamental rights of the human beings, value systems, traditions and beliefs' (UNESCO, 1994, p. 2).

1.4.5 Cultural economics

Cultural economics is concerned with applying economic thinking to the production, distribution, and consumption of all cultural goods and services and it supersedes a discipline dealing with the 'economics of the arts' (Towse, 2003, p. 1). Cultural economics recognises the significance of both the economic and cultural (though not necessarily monetary) values of cultural assets and suggests a range of methodologies to measure both (Cameron, 2006, p. 72; de la Torre, 2002, p. 4; Poll & Payne, 2006, p. 2; Wavell, Baxter, Johnson & Williams for Robert Gordon University, 2002, p. 7).

The term 'cultural capital' is used to define the values associated with cultural heritage assets, including tangible formats, such as buildings and artefacts, and intangible or intellectual capital, such as the language, literature, music, ideas, traditions, beliefs, and customs shared by a group of people (David Throsby, 2002, p. 103).

Values flowing from cultural assets are complicated, multifaceted, and diverse. However, they have been usefully segregated into three components:

- Instrumental values – the utilitarian and instrumental benefits, or 'knock-on' effects, of culture that often accrue from social and economic benefits;
- Intrinsic values – these relate to the subjective experience of culture intellectually, emotionally, and spiritually and are often expressed as 'arts for art's sake'; and
- Institutional values or public goods – these are created by cultural organisations through the processes and actions that these organisations adopt when they interact with the public (Holden, 2005).

Individuals derive benefits from cultural assets through participation and the direct use of services, as well as through a range of non-use benefits. These non-use benefits include gaining satisfaction from the knowledge that these goods will be available for possible future use ('option benefits'); that these goods exist for others to enjoy ('existence benefits'); and that these goods will continue to exist for future generations to enjoy ('bequest benefits') (Whiting & Outspan Group, 1999).

1.4.6 Heritage

Heritage is that part of the past that we select for contemporary purposes – whether they be economic or cultural (including political and social factors) – and that we choose to bequeath to future generations (G. J. Ashworth & Graham, 2005, p. 7; Clark, 2006, p. 3; L. Smith, 2006, p. 52). Although it references the past, heritage is always a creation of the present. It ascribes present-day values to aspects of our inheritance from the past (Jowell, 2005, p. 12; McManus, 1997, p. 92).

Heritage encompasses the natural environment and biodiversity, as well as the cultural domain, through material assets, such as historic buildings and all types of artefacts. Collectively, this category is referred to as 'cultural heritage' and is valued not only for its aesthetic values or for its usefulness, but also as an expression of the cultural development of a society (Koboldt, 1997, p. 53).

Recently, intangible assets and experiences have been given more prominence in identifying heritage values. These intangible assets include cultural practices, knowledge, and living experiences. More specifically, they relate to things such as trades and craft, traditions, language, memory, scientific study, relations, actions, processes, social models, and forms of governance (Cogo, 2005, pp. 95-96).

Heritage can also encompass experiences that happen at sites or during the acting out of certain events. It is an ongoing process of remembering and memory-making; of mediating cultural and social change; and of negotiating and recreating values, meanings, understandings, and a sense of place and identity (Scheiner, 2005, p. 85; L. Smith, 2006, p. 307; L. Smith & Waterton, 2009, p. 291).

1.4.7 Heritage industry

Heritage industry as a concept came into academic and popular usage in the 1980s when it became synonymous with the manipulation (or even invention) and exploitation of the past for commercial purposes (Merriman, 1991, p. 8). In one sense, heritage is an industry as it is a modern activity based on using resources from natural and human history that are deliberately controlled and organised, with the aim of producing a marketable product that may be educational, recreational, or environmental, but, is primarily, financial (G. J. Ashworth & Larkham, 1994, p. 16; McManus, 1997, p. 92).

1.4.8 Heritage trades

Heritage trades include the traditional trades, crafts, and craftsmanship required to preserve heritage products and services. This term refers to the trades that embody the ongoing innovation and creativity that is reflected in many masterpieces from the past (UNESCO, 2003). At the Cobb+Co Museum, the term embraces both Indigenous and non-Indigenous (European) iterations.

1.4.9 Identity

Identity – a complex Western concept – is individually expressed within social processes and experienced by demonstrating loyalty to groups that share common characteristics, such as nationality, gender, socio-economic factors, sexual orientation, interests, family loyalties, religion, ethnicity, work, and culture. An essential element of identity is the idea of 'the other' (as opposed to the individual under consideration) (Woodward, K. quoted in, Batty, 2003, p. 17; Watson, 2007, p. 269)

People symbolise and express their identities with objects, both personal and public, whose importance remains integral to the way individuals and communities articulate their sense of themselves, even when the meanings of these objects change over time (Watson, 2007, p. 273).

1.4.10 Museum

Museum is identified today as an institution of memory: 'a place that stores memories and presents and organises meaning in some sensory form'. The museum is both the physical place, as well as the memories and stories told in exhibitions and public programs (Gurian, 1995, p. 37; 1999, p. 3).

Although slight variations are endorsed in different countries (American Association of Museums; Davies, 2005, p. 73; Museums Australia, 2002), a museum is generally defined functionally as:

> ...a non-profit making, permanent institution in the service of society and of its development, and open to the public, which acquires, conserves, researches, communicates and exhibits, for purposes of study, education and enjoyment, material evidence of people and their environment (International Council of Museums).

1.4.11 Museology

Museology is defined as a 'branch of knowledge concerned with the study of the purposes and organizations of museums' (George Henri Rivière, 1958, p. 34). As a multidisciplinary sphere of knowledge, it can be used to designate the theory, processes, and philosophy of museums; museum structure and development; the practices of museum work in dealing with collections; and the experiences of museum visitors.

The term 'new museology' was popularised by Peter Vergo in a publication of that same name in 1989. The concept illustrated the dissatisfaction felt about the traditional or 'old' museology that focused on collections, research, and professional curatorial methods at the expense of museum aims relating to audiences, community, and public education. New museology embraces the idea of minority voices being empowered in museums. It focuses on location, identity, and development, as well as commercial activity. Ecomuseums are frequently identified as the personification of new museology at work, because of their emphasis on community involvement (de Varine, 2005b; Hauenschild, 1998; Vergo, 1989, p. 3).

The concept of the post-museum is more readily embraced today as an ideal for contemporary museums that focus on a variety of societal perspectives and values. Perhaps, most importantly, the post-museum focuses on intangible heritage and the emotions of visitors, because it is directly linked to the concerns and ambitions of communities. The post-museum will hold and care for objects, but it will concentrate more on their use, rather than concentrating on the accumulation of further objects (E Hooper-Greenhill, 2000b, p. 152).

1.4.12 Public good

Public good is a good or service that generally does not exclude any individual's consumption and is non-rival in that it can be consumed by several individuals simultaneously, and the act of consumption by one individual does not reduce the possibility or the value of consumption by others (Hesmondhalgh, 2007).

'Public value' refers to what the public, itself, values and is prepared to pay for a public good or service. The concept of public value was formulated as part of a theory of public management that was developed by Harvard academic Mark Moore in 1995 (Moore, 1995). It underpins the premise that public sector management needs to recognise the public as the client, rather than the customer, for government-funded public services.

1.4.13 Social enterprises

Social enterprises are (usually non-profit) organisations that blend social and commercial methodologies to achieve their outcomes, which can include improving society through creating social change. Museums can be included in this category (Dees, Emerson, & Economy, 2001). The Cobb+Co Museum identified itself as a social entrepreneur during its Stage Two development, as the museum sought to fill the gap between the public and commercial sectors and to work with its community to facilitate social improvement (Ashoka, 2006).

1.5 Outline of the book

This book is in two parts. Part A includes Chapters Two to Four, which addresses the three-stage development of the Cobb+Co Museum. Each of these chapters uses a consistent methodology of an initial theorisation of significant international developments, concepts and models supplemented by analysis of applicable museological frameworks. These are then assessed against historical and contemporary events relating to the Cobb+Co Museum, to understand the drivers for each stage of development and the community-museum dynamics at play.

Chapter Two identifies the international and national contexts that enveloped and transformed understandings of heritage and museums up to the late 1980s. These contexts provided the museological framework that underpinned the formation of the Cobb+Co Museum in Toowoomba, Queensland, in 1987.

In 2001, Cobb+Co Museum opened its Second Stage development. Chapter Three investigates the museum's changing identity during the period from 2001 to 2010. During this stage, the Cobb+Co Museum was transformed from having a traditional collection focus, as a branch of the Queensland Museum, to being a regional museum and community resource centre.

Chapter Four explores the opportunities museums have to develop into creative-cultural industry hubs and, subsequently, play a significant role in the creative economy. In 2010, the Cobb+Co Museum's Stage Three transformation was instigated with the opening of the National Carriage Factory – a facility developed to safeguard heritage trades, crafts, and skills through embedding them within a regional economic, social, and cultural development framework.

Chapters Two to Four illustrate that each of the Cobb+Co Museum's transformations represent a different, unique identity for the museum. Each transformation was marked by a structural change, but each change was integrated within the others. These changes did not signify a specific shift in the museum or community's values, but represented ongoing adjustments to pre-existing practices and philosophies. They were a result of changing community dynamics and changing museum trends. The transformations occurred through accumulative processes that represented both time- and place-specific adaptations to broader trends.

Part B, consisting of Chapters Five and Six, gives 'voice to values' by analysing how museums are valued by their stakeholders. Chapter Five provides an understanding of the ways in which museums are valued by their stakeholders and how these concepts of value have changed over time. It focuses particularly on how to evaluate the relationships and values that exist within the Toowoomba community and the Cobb+Co Museum.

In working with the Toowoomba community, it became obvious that for locals 'one doesn't have to visit to value' the Cobb+Co Museum. This meant that many traditional methods of measuring support, such as the number of people entering the museum, became irrelevant. In order to ascertain a more reliable measure of the public value of the Cobb+Co Museum and the proposed development of the National Carriage Factory, alternative methodologies needed to be investigated. From this literature review, which includes fifteen CVM studies of cultural goods, the Contingent Valuation Methodology was adapted by the author to use in a major study that aimed to ascertain how Queenslanders value their state museum.

Chapter Six is devoted to the development, implementation, and assessment of the Contingent Valuation Methodology (CVM) study undertaken to value the Queensland Museum, of which the Cobb+Co Museum is a part. This significant study was conducted in December 2008, prior to funding being announced for the construction of the National Carriage Factory project.

The final chapter summarises the research findings and answers the three questions posed above arguing that in considering the future of museums in Australia, particularly in regional communities, there are specific and general lessons to be learned from the Cobb+Co Museum's transformational developments between 1987 and 2010.

Part I

Part A

Chapter 2
Heritage and Museums

The Museological Frameworks Underpinning the Identity of the Cobb+Co Museum, Stage One, 1987–2001

2.1 Introduction

This chapter, together with Chapters Three and Four, constitutes Part A of this book. This section concentrates on the evolving identity of the Cobb+Co Museum in Toowoomba, Queensland, during its three-stage transformation from 1987 until 2010. It is argued that each of these stages reflect and are moulded by the changing dynamics between the museum and its community. This chapter addresses the First Stage development of the Cobb+Co Museum, from its opening as a branch of the Queensland Museum in 1987, until 2001.

This chapter also analyses the museological framework and political parameters that surrounded the establishment of the Cobb+Co Museum as a specialist museum of transport heritage. As a new branch of the Queensland Museum, the Cobb+Co Museum inherited much from its parent body, which, like many other major state and national museums, had experienced a range of evolutionary developments during its long history. At the time, the opening of the Cobb+Co Museum was perceived by many as another opportunistic response by the Queensland Museum to expand across the state. This response was derived from the museum's decision, in the 1980s, to establish branches and campuses throughout regional Queensland.

The Cobb+Co Museum was also developed in response to the idea that museums were a subset of heritage that had significant tourism potential. It was hoped that establishing museums would contribute to the revitalisation of communities that had been heavily impacted by economic downturns in the 1970s and early 1980s. Queensland witnessed the community museum movement gathering momentum across the country during this period, often as a reaction to the decline in broad-acre farming and other traditional rural industries. As the Cobb+Co Museum gradually adopted a new approach to its community, it assumed a leadership role in the regional tourism industry and, by the mid-1990s, had developed a significant support role for other community museums across the state.

2.2 Chapter organisation

To understand the wider museological context and parameters within which the Cobb+Co Museum was conceived, an investigation of a number of the more significant international and national advances in the museum sector will be undertaken. Initially, this will concentrate on recognising the generic nature of museums that evolved within a British and, to a lesser extent, European context. The impact of other museum traditions – including those in the United States of America and the alternative museum models addressing new museological concerns that appeared in the second half of the twentieth century[1] – will also be addressed.

This chapter will also analyse the significant influence of the emergence of the heritage industry as an economic, as well as social and cultural, driver in many Organisation for Economic Cooperation and Development (OECD) countries. Large numbers of museums, of all persuasions, that were propagated during the second half of the twentieth century contributed to the proliferation of heritage products and the pervasiveness of the heritage industry.

From these discussions of the philosophy and frameworks underpinning the history of museum development and the emergence of the heritage industry, significant concepts will be identified that impacted on the establishment and early development of the Cobb+Co Museum in Toowoomba, from 1987 until 2001.

From these broader perspectives, this chapter will then address the nature of the Queensland Museum and its emerging branch structure from the mid-1980s. Despite the strong historical factors, the Cobb+Co Museum, even from its inception, presented some unique responses to its local environment that set it apart from the other branches of the Queensland

---

1. The then United Kingdom Minister for the Arts, Richard Luce, stated, in November 1986, that 'once in every fortnight somewhere in the United Kingdom a new museum unfolds its treasures to the public gaze' (Hewison, 1987, p. 84).

Museum and, to an extent, the other museums in Australia. An analysis of these responses will conclude this chapter of the First Stage development of the Cobb+Co Museum.

2.3 What is a museum?

Museums are one of the institutions created by communities, states, and nations to help conserve and interpret the identity of an area through the preservation of its cultural and natural heritage. Although no two museums are identical, there are a number of common functional characteristics. The International Council of Museums (ICOM) defined a museum as:

> ...a non-profit making, permanent institution in the service of society and of its development, and open to the public, which acquires, conserves, researches, communicates and exhibits, for purposes of study, education and enjoyment, material evidence of people and their environment (International Council of Museums, 2007).

Slight variations on this definition have been endorsed in different countries. In the United Kingdom and Australia the educational function of a museum is more prominent, while in the United States an additional clause relates to the employment of professional staff in order for a collecting organisation to be classified as a museum (American Association of Museums; Davies, 2005, p. 73; Museums Australia, 2002).

The absence of any reference to staff in the Australian definition has ensured that there are hundreds and hundreds of cultural and natural heritage collecting organisations across the continent that are designated as museums but are run by volunteers who have no professional training or understanding of museum practices.

Current museology tends to stress the significance of museums as places that store memories and that present and organise meaning in some sensory form. Museums in this context include 'both the physicality of a place and the memories and stories told within them' (Gurian, 1999, p. 3).

Museums, as a general concept, have a long history, dating back to the second millennium BC in Mesopotamia. However, the word 'museum' comes from the Greek word 'mouseion', which was the name of a temple dedicated to the Muses and was, hence, primarily a religious site (Alexander & Alexander, 2008, pp. 3-4; Boylan, 2004, p. 1; Pitman, 1999, p. 9). It is believed that it was probably not until the Renaissance that the classic denotation of museums as 'cabinets of curiosities' was propagated. The Ashmolean Museum, which was founded at Oxford University in 1683, is generally considered to be the first museum established by a public body for public benefit (Alexander & Alexander, 2008, p. 57).

2.4 British museums as public institutions

The most dramatic development for museums in Great Britain took place in 1753, with the passing of the British Museum Act. This legislation explicitly constituted the British Museum as a new national museum[2] to be 'not only for the inspection and entertainment of the learned and the curious, but for the general use and benefit of the public' (Merriman, 1991, p. 1). The British Museum provided the museological model for each Australian state, including Queensland, when they established their own museums in the middle of the nineteenth century.

The more common pattern for museum development in Great Britain involved learned societies[3] – literary, philosophical, natural history, or antiquarian – who established their own museums to promote their ideals, educational opportunities, public enlightenment, and 'a sense of civic identity' (Bennett, Trotter, & McAlear, 1996, p. 3).

In 1845, the British Parliament passed the first Museums Act which allowed local boroughs to levy rates in order to establish public museums. In 1870 the first Public Libraries Act was passed which extend the practice to public libraries. According to Bennett, viewing these development in hindsight, this legislative activity eventually resulted in the establishment of a network of public museums, which he suggested showed a commitment 'to the notion of purposeful educational activities' that could support the 'character reformation of the workingman', while solving major social problems as espoused by 'the Romantics' belief in the soothing effects of art and culture' (Bennett, et al., 1996, p. 5).

In 1851, the first free publicly-funded museum in Britain with unrestricted public access opened at South Kensington. This Museum of Science and Art was established to house much of the material from the Crystal Palace – the central display of the 'Great Exhibition of the Industry of all Nations' in London in 1851 – and combined art with design and cutting-edge industrial developments. It provided:

> ...a break point in both the narrative of museum history, and in the wider economics of material culture, presenting an opportunity for the new 'products of Industry' to merge with art and entertainment (and museum artefacts) in a previously unimaginable new leisure space (Cummings & Lewandowska, 2000, p. 54).

Towards the end of the nineteenth century, networks of large natural history and science museums emerged, concomitant with the acquisition of colonial empires by European powers. Tony Bennett categorises these institutions, symbolised by the French and British natural history museums, as 'evolutionary museums' and 'a new kind of memory machine':

---

2. The British Museum was established as a result of a unique opportunity. In his will of 1753, the former London physician and collector, Sir Hans Sloane, offered King George II a collection of eighty thousand objects for the nation, on the proviso that 'the collection be kept for the use and benefit of the publick, who may have free access to view and peruse the same' (quoted in Mather, 1986, p. 302).

3. An early example was the Natural History Society of Northumberland, Durham and Newcastle upon Tyne, which opened its museum one evening each month to the 'general public' of Newcastle in 1835 (Boylan, 2004, pp. 2-3; Darnell, Johnson, & Thomas, 1998, p. 78; Davis, 1999, p. 64).

> [By] basing their practices on the post-Darwinian synthesis of the historical sciences, [they] made a new set of interconnecting times publicly perceptible. The telling of each time in the form of a unilinear development sequence provided the conditions for their amalgamation in a totalizing narrative, in which the history of the earth supplied the master time, which calibrated the histories of life on each, and those of human civilization, cultures and technologies (2004, p. 24).

Symbolic of European empire building was the emerging interest in acquiring anthropology, archaeology, and ethnology collections. These were either more general in nature – such as the museums established in the British industrial centres of Glasgow, Manchester, and Liverpool – or primarily devoted to the anthropological field – such as the National Museum of Ethnology in Leiden.[4] However, these museums employed the same systematic linear projections as those used in the natural sciences, with colonised people 'being back-projected into the prehistoric past' (Bennett, 2004, p. 19). As Bernice Murphy states:

> Human history became incorporated within an exegetical system devised by natural science, one that shifted the interpretation of non-Western and Western societies as no longer coeval but located *sequentially* according to orchestrated characteristics of purported progress (Murphy, 2005, p. 71).

To some extent, the preoccupation with collection acquisition as a symbol of colonial power and prestige would diminish the original aims of the museum being for the 'general use and benefit of the public'. However, as seen in a letter to the *Glasgow Herald* on 31 August 1901, there remained a belief in the educational goals and social reform benefits derived from visiting a museum, such as the Kelvingrove Art Gallery and Museum: 'Let the classes and masses meet together at Kelvingrove and, believe me good will come of it' (M. Gray, 2006).

British museums merged private collections into public institutions and subsequently supported, in theory at least, the educational purpose of improving the quality of life of the working man. Yet, by the end of the nineteenth century, this public-learning mission was dissipating because of the rapid accumulation of large collections of art, natural history, and military history that sought only to reflect the wealth, power, and prestige of the British Empire and other major European Powers.

2.5 American museums compared to British traditions

The museum traditions that evolved in the United States of America (U.S.A.) were largely inherited from Great Britain. Historical societies, again, played an integral role in the formation of these museums. The first museum in the U.S.A. was established by the Charleston Library Society, which, in 1773, decided to collect specimens of animals, plants, and minerals that represented the natural history of South Carolina (Pitman, 1999, p. 9).

---

4. The Leiden Museum was founded, in 1837, with a collection of five thousand items gathered in the Far East (Alexander & Alexander, 2008, p. 72).

Public education was also a strong motivation for the formation of the early museums in the U.S.A. and accessibility for the working classes was considered pivotal. The Charles Wilson Peale's natural history museum in Philadelphia opened in the evenings, throughout the 1780s, specifically to enable the labourer and artisan to attend (Neil Kotler, Kotler, & Kotler, 2008, pp. 11-12). Even the larger art museums that were founded in the 1870s were motivated by principles of education, and sought to address: 'the practical needs of designers and retailers and set standards for American craft persons and manufacturers to aspire to' (DiMaggio, 1991, p. 45).

A number of museums in North America were also created as a result of donations of large private collections to state or public ownership. The Smithsonian Institution is one such example, which opened in Washington D.C. after the U.S.A. government accepted a major bequest from Englishman, James Smithson, in 1846. As the U.S.A.'s national iconic museum, the Smithsonian Institution espoused the ideal of increasing and diffusing knowledge (Pitman, 1999, p. 5) and was managed by 'the state for the benefit and education of the national citizenry' (Tony Bennett quoted in, Boswell & Evans, 1999, p. 238).

Despite the fact that most museum founders asserted that they sought to use their museums to promote education, most museums in Europe and the U.S.A. generally evolved into 'celebratory institutions' that had other civic functions. In Europe, it would appear that 'many museums were created as instruments of ruling classes and governments to celebrate and glorify the national culture and the state' (Neil Kotler, et al., 2008, p. 11; Watson, 2007, p. 270). These museums, through 'social objectification of the past and organized memory around diverse artefacts', were devoted to preserving the memory of the most powerful time in their nation's history (Misztal, 2003, p. 389). Museums proved that 'the past is the possession of those in power' (McBryde, 1985, p. 6).

> Public museums were from the beginning embroiled in the attempt to culture a public and encourage people to imagine and experience themselves as members of an ordered but nevertheless sentimentalised nation-state (S. Macdonald, 2003, p. 5).

Steven Weil identified three different types of European museums, all with a celebratory state function.[5] In contrast, in the U.S.A., museums were:

> ...created by individuals, families and communities to celebrate and commemorate local and regional traditions and practices (Neil Kotler, et al., 2008, p. 11).

Because museums were generally the property of large individual benefactors (art museums particularly), they effectively became 'privately owned "celebrations" of the community's first families – those successful in polit-

5. These included the European art museum, which celebrated acknowledged masterpieces; the natural history museum, which celebrated Western humankind's place in nature; and the history museum, in its European state-owned incarnation, which celebrated military victory (Weil, 2002, p. 198).

ics, professions or business' (Weil, 2002, p. 198). Although the museums were, in theory, not-for-profit organisations, many acted more like private museums in which the patron was supreme – and had an army of curators to serve him – and acquisition, conservation, and research were the key functions (DiMaggio, 1991, p. 45; Weil, 1983, p. 4).

More significantly, the museums' missions were also changing from public education to collections and research:

> With the acquisition of masterpieces, museums began to see their primary intellectual and cultural authority coming from their collections rather than their educational and community purpose. Museums shifted the direction of their energies from public education and inspiration toward self-generated, internal, professional and academic goals (Skramstad, 1999, p. 3).

2.6 Twentieth-century developments in museum practices

While, during the twentieth century, collections dominated most museums, there were also some new and different museum models developing. These included interpretation centres at historic sites, open-air museums, science and technology centres, and children's museums. These institutions had a vastly different collection focus (if they had collections at all), but shared a common mission of aspiring to be places not of academic scholarship, but of education and entertainment, wonder and discovery, and enjoyment and conversation (Skramstad, 1999, p. 2).

When Colonial Williamsburg opened in 1926, it was the first open-air museum in the U.S.A. Funded by John D. Rockefeller, this in-situ reincarnation of the first capital of Virginia became the personification of 'educational entrepreneurship' (Yetter, 1992, p. vii). The concept of 'educational entrepreneurship' was first popularised in the 1840s by P.T. Barnum, who created bold alternative museums that effectively 'submerged the scientist in the showman' and resulted in 'a curious mix of education and entertainment' (R. Flint quoted in Harrison, 2005, p. 43). In 1929, another entrepreneur, Henry Ford, created an open-air museum in Michigan, which consisted of relocated buildings.[6]

Ford, together with Julius Rosenwald, was also jointly responsible for the establishment of the country's first industrial or 'science technology' museums in the 1930s.[7] These museums had no collections – instead concentrating on new scientific and technological development – and developed a strong sense of social and educational purpose. Rosenwald stressed the entertainment value of displaying operating machinery and models that had 'mechanical processes of production and manufacture, which visitors could

---

6. The Henry Ford Museum and Greenfield Village Museum.

7. Both Rosenwald's Museum of Science and Industry in Chicago and Ford's Edison Institute in Dearborn, Michigan, emphasised the importance of entertainment and education.

manipulate themselves' (Rosenwald 1921 quote in Alexander & Alexander, 2008, p. 96). In many ways, these first industrial museums were the forerunners of contemporary science centres (Skramstad, 1999, p. 5).

The earliest example of a science centre devoted to explaining scientific principles through hands-on exhibits was the Exploratorium in San Francisco, which opened in 1969. Its founder, Frank Oppenheimer, aimed to provide enlightenment for the many people for whom 'science is incomprehensible and technology frightening' (S. Macdonald, 1998, p. 189). Science centres remain, until the present time, promoters of strong learning outcomes – hallmarks of museums' *raison d'être.*

The emergence of museums for children continued this focus on education and learning. The first such museum opened in Brooklyn in 1899, which was followed, in 1913, by the Boston Children's Museum, which displayed many collections catering to children's interests. In the United Kingdom, the relevance of museums for children's education was recognised, in 1902, with the passing of the Education Act in Britain. This act, which gave formal recognition to the time spent by children during a museum visit as equivalent to time spent in the classroom, encouraged school visits to museums during school lesson time, and, for the first time, classed children as 'citizens-in-waiting' (Bennett, et al., 1996, p. 6).

In the U.S.A., Samuel P. Langley, the Secretary of the Smithsonian Institution at the turn of the twentieth century, made himself honorary curator of a new Children's Room. In a letter addressed to himself, he spoke on behalf of children who up to then 'never had a fair chance in museums':

> We cannot see the things on the top shelves, which only grown-up people are tall enough to look into, and most of the things we can see and would like to know about have Latin words on them, which we cannot understand: some things we do not care for at all, and other things which look entertaining have nothing on them to tell us what they are about (Skramstad, 1999, p. 4).

Perhaps it was because of the interest shown by the Smithsonian Institution in children's learning that contributed to the phenomenal growth in children's museums across the U.S.A. This trend, however, was not replicated in the United Kingdom, and marked a significant difference between museological developments in both countries.

Throughout the twentieth century, many of these alternative museum models, with their strong adherence to educational goals through object and activity-based learning, were accepted, if not entrenched, within the museum sector.

2.6.1 Communities versus collections

Prior to World War One, there was some interest among traditional American museums in resurrecting the original concept of museums as community learning facilities. Both John Cotton Dana and George Brown Goode extensively advocated for museums to reconnect with their communities.

John Cotton Dana, a librarian and the founder and director of the Newark Museum, campaigned for a new style of museum – 'a definitely, useful, teaching type' of institution – dedicated to serving the population as a whole (Carol Duncan quoted in Halpin, 1997, pp. 49-50).[8] To Dana, 'the worth of the museum is in its use' (Peniston, 1999, pp. 76, The New Museum Series no. 74). He argued that 'the one and obvious task' for museums was to add:

> ...to the happiness, wisdom and comfort of members of the community. Learn what the community needs and fit the museum to those needs (Dana quoted in Weil, 2002, p. 111).

Dana was a vocal critic of what he saw as the elitist nature of most art museums, and he argued for the replacement of the patron's museum with a social museum to reflect the country's changing culture (Halpin, 1997, pp. 49-50). Dana reflected the ideals of the art and craft societies emerging in the 1920s that wanted to pay:

> ...less attention to fine art, and more to the decorative arts and design; more attention to local working-class publics and immigrant groups, less to patrons and collectors; more accessibility and less grandeur (DiMaggio, 1991, p. 47).

George Brown Goode, from the Smithsonian Institution, echoed Dana's position on the museum's community responsibilities. In an address in 1889, he stated:

> The museums of the future in this democratic land should be adapted to the needs of the mechanic, the factory operator, the day labourer, the salesman and the clerk, as much as those of the professional man and the man of leisure (Goode quoted in Grove, 1978, p. 38).

Despite the strong advocacy, in the early years of the twentieth century, for community-centred learning institutions, rather than collection-focused research museums, there was no general acceptance of Goode's philosophy.[9] In reality, many of these ideals remained generally unaccepted within mainstream museums for many decades.

It could be argued that for most of the twentieth century, educational outcomes were no longer the primary objectives of museums. In 1928, the Miers Report was blunt in its condemnation of the ineffectiveness of museums, caused by detachment from their communities:

> Most people in the country do not really care for museums or believe in them; they have not played a significantly important part in the life of the community to make ordinary folk realise what they can do (Davis, 1999, p. 65).

---

8. Dana and his brothers operated a small printing press, the Elm Tree Press, in their family's store in Woodstock, Vermont. His influence on museological thinking resulted from his essays, collectively called *The New Museum Series*. Three of these booklets – *The New Museum*, 1917; *The Gloom of the Museum*, 1917; and a *Plan for a New Museum*, 1920 – together with a number of his other writings, were republished by the Newark Museum in 1999 (Peniston, 1999).

9. The Cleveland Museum of Art, in 1913, was an exception when it proclaimed its intention to provide an industrial training school to enhance adult education (Neil Kotler, et al., 2008, pp. 11-12).

Museums had evolved into elitist establishments in which professional curators pursued their academic interests without public interference or accountability. In Miers' opinion, museums needed to cooperate more fully with the community by developing travelling exhibitions and educational services (Davis, 1999, p. 65).

By 1942, the publication of *The Museum as a Social Instrument* was still criticising museums' lack of commitment to public education and community service:

> Museums, in the drive to build and collect, became hypnotised by the charm of collecting and scholarship and forgot their responsibilities to the public. Museums soon became little more than isolated segments of European culture set in a hostile environment (Low quoted in R. R. Macdonald, 2006, p. 29).

This situation continued into the 1970s and 1980s. By this time, the explosion in museum development[10] had stretched patrons' resources so far that government intervention was needed. However, at the same time, there were increasing demands for museum programs and quality service delivery to satisfy social, education, and leisure markets (DiMaggio, 1991, p. 48). Not surprisingly, during this period of rapid museum development and expectations, new museological ideas that advocated alternative museum models and directions also emerged.

2.7 New museology defining change

The 1960s and 1970s witnessed significant political and cultural changes that strongly influenced the development of a new museology.[11] The impact of these revolutionary developments found gradual expression in new museums and led to extensive redevelopment of some established museums, particularly in former European colonies, and most particularly in South America. There was an emerging desire to represent the less vocal and politically-empowered sectors of society within museum offerings. Al-

---

10. Forty-seven percent of all U.S.A. history museums have opened since 1960 (Neil Kotler, et al., 2008, p. 13). While, in Australia, forty-six percent of museums were established in the 1980s (Bennett, et al., 1996, p. 11)

11. Hugues de Varine traced the origins and impetus of this new museology to a number of phenomena, including:
    - The recent independence of the majority of formerly-colonised countries, particularly in Africa;
    - In North America, equal rights movements among Afro-American, Latino, and American-Indian groups;
    - In Latin-America, revolutionary movements and the emergence of aboriginal and mestizo cultures;
    - The 1968 'students movement' in Europe;
    - The re-discovery of the cultural and social values of small local communities; and
    - The identification of traditional cultural institutions with elite and captive publics (leading to) the heritage site becoming essentially a leisure place for the rich and the educated, an educational aide for school parties, and a 'must' for wandering tourists (de Varine, 2005b, pp. 51-52).

though, in the past, there had been sporadic attempts in some museums to incorporate a wider range of people and stories, there had been no consistent action or belief in the need to do so.

The initial appearance of women as both subjects for displays and actors within museum institutions, for example, coincided with the emergence of the suffragette movement, and was marked by the opening in 1893 of the Women's Building in the World Columbian Exposition held in Chicago[12] – the first museum devoted to women. Although, by contemporary standards, these displays were limited in scope and devoted to presentations of the domestic arts, they were, nevertheless 'a major symbol of women's claims to be accorded equal representational status with men' (Bennett, et al., 1996, p. 6). Despite this initiative, women remained a minority group within the museum profession, and their stories were rarely explored in exhibitions until well into the 1970s and 1980s.

During the 1980s, there emerged a new museological approach to community, which included indigenous people and other minority groups and focused on improving their representation in museums. In 1985, the International Movement for New Museology (MINOM) – which was affiliated with the International Council of Museums (ICOM) – was formed in Lisbon, Portugal. It attracted museum workers who were dedicated to active and interactive museology, and particularly encouraged the participation of 'native and other underrepresented groups' (International Movement for a New Museology).

New museologists sought a change from the 'old' museology that was perceived as too much about 'museum *methods* and too little about the purpose of museums' (Vergo, 1989, p. 3). They sought to project museums as 'democratic, educational institutions and instruments for identity building and social development within the community', particularly at the local and regional level (Hauenschild, 1998, p. 6). Museums imbued with this new museological thought moved from being object-focused to people-focused, and became 'active' museums that involved communities in the processes of representation and interpretation (Walsh, 1992, p. 162). This form of public participation in museum work has been described as 'people's museography' – a process in which the community representative is no longer just 'a visitor; he becomes a decision-maker, an actor, a museographer and an agent of multiplication' (Hauenschild, 1998, p. 10).

12. Despite this, women were not readily accepted in the museum field. At the inaugural meeting of the American Association of Museums, in 1906, there were only two women among the seventy-one delegates present. It is not clear when the first woman managed to negotiate a 'toehold on the payroll of an Australian museum', but the Science Museum of Victoria employed two women in the 1880s to prepare models for the 'Colonial and Indian Exhibition' of 1886 (M. Anderson & Reeves, 1994, p. 108).

2.7.1 New museums – neighbourhood, eco, and integral museums

It has been argued that these new museologoical developments found unique expression in three parallel but independent social contexts: neighbourhood museums in the United States of America; integral museums in Latin America, particularly in Mexico; and ecomuseums in France and Quebec (Hauenschild, 1998, p. 6). Each of these three different concepts of new museums have much in common, though their specific origins are unique. Crucial to each museum is the active role that its community members theoretically played in shaping the museum concept and participating in its operations to facilitate socio-cultural and economic development of their region or territory.

The most specific of these new museum models – the 'neighbourhood museum' – was initiated in 1967, when the Smithsonian Institution established the Anacostia Neighbourhood Museum in the Anacostia section of Washington, D.C. – an area inhabited primarily by African-Americans. Originally planned as an outreach centre for the Smithsonian Institution's collection and services, this museum was intended 'to mediate between traditional, established Smithsonian museums and the African-American public they did not reach' (Anacostia Community Museum, 2011; Hauenschild, 1998, p. 56; James, 2005). In a similar manner, other neighbourhood museums, such as the Casa del Museo, which was developed in Mexico, were set up in marginalised local communities. These were initially organised by national institutions, but they soon formulated their own 'significant educational goals such as identity building, coping with everyday problems, improving living conditions and effecting societal development' (Hauenschild, 1998, p. 86)

The second museum model was the 'ecomuseum', whose forebears are found in the folk-museum movement that was initiated in Scandinavia with the opening of the Skansen Open-air Museum in 1891.The ecomuseum was first formerly identified in 1972 to be a museum that adopted a more vernacular, democratic, and inclusive museology than that practised by traditional museums. UNESCO endorsed the following definition in 1985.

> An ecomuseum is an instrument conceived, fashioned and operated jointly by a public authority and a local population. The public authority's involvement is through the experts, facilities and resources it provides; the local population's involvement depends on its aspirations, knowledge and individual approach (George Henri Rivière, 1985, p. 182).

Emerging mainly in depressed rural areas, the ecomuseum was seen as a new way of preserving community identity and conserving and celebrating community heritage values through shared 'cultural touchstones'. At the same time, the ecomuseum sought to address social and economic issues, particularly in regions in which 'desertification' was pronounced (Davis, 2005, p. 365; de Varine, 2005b, p. 54; Maggi, 2005, p. 63).

Ecomuseums are disparate and flexible institutions that reflect the diversity of territories and their inhabitants and that constantly evolve to represent community development and strive to encourage the participation of the population (Joubert, 2005, p. 92; Scheiner, 2005, p. 88). In 1978, Hugues da Vairne – one of the architects of ecomuseology – described the ecomuseum as: 'an instrument of popular participation in regional planning and community development' (quoted in Joubert, 2005, p. 92). A more deliberate definition that focuses on function and mission was endorsed at the workshop that is known as Long Networks – Ecomuseums and Europe, held in Trento in May 2004:

> An ecomuseum is a dynamic process by which communities preserve, interpret and value their heritage in relation to sustainable growth. Ecomuseums are based on community consensus (Cogo, 2005, p. 97).

Today, ecomuseums are located throughout the world, with more than four hundred registered on the international database. They are prominent throughout Scandinavia and are expanding in France; Italy; Canada; South America; and throughout Asia, particularly in China (Davis, 2007, p. 198). There are many different iterations of ecomuseums, including some organisations that prefer to describe themselves as 'living history museums'[13] or 'community museums'.

The third museum model – the 'integral museum' – incorporates many characteristics common to the other two new museum models. The term 'integral museum' – coined at the joint UNESCO and ICOM meeting held in Santiago, Chile, in 1972 – highlights the essential responsibility of a museum to serve all members of its community, including the marginalised people living in urban areas (International Movement for a New Museology). This new, comprehensive view of a museum as an institution that is dedicated to the 'conservation of cultural, natural and environmental heritage' also provided a link to the tourism sector and possible future economic development (Gomez de Blavia, 1998, p. 23).

In general, the ecomuseum was aimed towards conserving and celebrating the memory of its community, but the integral museum, like the neighbourhood museum, focused more on the community's social and political objectives (de Varine, 2005b, p. 53; Joubert, 2005, p. 91).

While conceived initially as a specific Latin American reaction, the integral museum concept could also be viewed as a legitimate response to the civil rights movement in the U.S.A. since the 1960s. This movement was responsible for bringing:

---

13. Melbourne's Living Museum of the West Inc. exemplifies this trend. It describes itself as a community museum with an ecomuseum focus. It operates in the western region of Melbourne in the state of Victoria, Australia. More commonly known as The Living Museum, it was developed in 1984 to support an area that was then heavily populated by migrants and was seen as disadvantaged. Although this museum displays a number of key ecomuseological concepts, it has little focus on promoting sustainable growth within the community (Melbourne's Living Museum of the West Inc, n.d.)

> ...issues of opportunity and equality to communities whose histories had largely been ignored by conventional museums – the middle and working classes, the poor, immigrants and non-white races (Davis, 1999, p. 66).

It would appear that the influence of these new museum models fluctuated over time, responding to leadership direction and community interest and involvement. After the death of its long-term director, John Kinard, in 1989, the Anacostia Neighbourhood Museum reverted to an outreach centre for the Smithsonian Institution, rather than remain embedded within the Anacostia community. Today, the Anacostia Community Museum's mission does not even mention its special relationship with Anacostia. Instead, it has absorbed the Smithsonian's agenda, stating that it:

> ...challenges perceptions, broaden perspectives, generate new knowledge, and deepen understanding about the ever-changing concepts and realities of 'community' (Anacostia Community Museum, 2011).

The importance of leadership in new museums is particularly significant as the conduit between the museum and the community. This became evident in the development of the Cobb+Co Museum.

2.7.2 Widening the focus of museum concerns

The social movements of the 1970s had a strong impact on mainstream museum culture and the formation of different types of museums. Bernice Murphy identified these changes as dealing with 'repressed otherness within', relating to things such as feminism, popular histories, ethnic diversity, and multiple forms of sub-cultural identity (Murphy, 2005, p. 72). Pressure was placed on museum professionals to expand their civic role, particularly by identifying the changing position and prominence of women and by actively involving minority groups, ethnic communities, and indigenous people. Rick West, the former director of the National Museum of the American Indian, refers to this process as 'in reach'. He states that if museums are to engage in real community building, it is 'not about how museums reach *out*; it is about how we allow the public to reach *into* our institutions' (Rick West quoted in Archibald, 2004, p. 209).

These major developments in museums during the 1970s have been responsible for diversifying the nature of museum collections and exhibitions and changing the relationships of museums and communities. They are accountable, to a degree, for the mass development of new museums in the 1980s, as well as the gradual emergence of a new museology in the final decades of the twentieth century.

The proliferation of new museums and the redevelopment of older institutions necessitated a shift in management focus to economic viability and a subsequent focus on commercial activities. This has become a characteristic of new museology. In many ways, Barnum's much earlier model of 'edutainment' as the core focus of museums was being replicated by major institutions. This trend was evidenced by a fixation on the economic potential of the 'blockbuster phenomena' that appeared towards the end of the twentieth century (Pitman, 1999, p. 10).

However, mainstream museum culture, for most of the twentieth century, continued to be internally-focused. The attention was not on visitors or the public good, but on 'the accumulation and management of museum collections and the professionalisation of museum workers and museum work' (Skramstad, 1999, p. 6). Nevertheless, it was obvious that the great collecting phase of nineteenth century European-model museums was over. The emphasis, even in traditional museums, by the end of the twentieth century, was on using (interpreting) the object, rather than on further unrestricted accumulation.

In contrast to the nineteenth century romantic notion of museums as instruments of national pride and identity, there has been a noticeable decline in the strength of any given national history, as displayed in national museums. The suggestion is that:

> ...centred, singular identity constructions are being superseded by identities predicated on cultural mixing and crossover, on intercultural traffic rather than boundary demarcation (S. Macdonald, 2003, p. 6).

Instead, a proliferation of alternative or vernacular histories has developed, including social, economic, populist, feminist, ethnic, industrial, and many other issues. By the last quarter of the twentieth century 'a pluralisation and indeed a contemporarisation of history' was occurring in at least some museum sectors (Urry, 1990, p. 227).

However, seventy years after Dana preached that the true work of the museum 'was in enriching the quality of its visitors' lives' (Peniston, 1999, p. 15), and sixty years after the publication of the Miers Report, the same sentiment of 'making museums matter' was being espoused by Stephen Weil in his many writings and presentations. For Weil, at the end of the twentieth century, there still needed to be a 'new museum model' – one in which public service was the overriding mission. For a museum to matter it must:

> ...use its very special competencies in dealing with objects to contribute positively to the quality of individual human lives and to enhance the well-being of human communities (Weil, 1999, p. 2).

The museum had to change from 'being about something to being for somebody' to be relevant to society in the final decades of the twentieth century. Weil continued to ask museums difficult questions that most museum professionals ignored. These questions included:

- Does the museum accomplish its mission effectively and efficiently, with better results at a lower cost than other organisations can accomplish?
- What does the museum offer that is distinctive and of special value to its community that other organisations do not offer (Weil, 1994, p. 347)?

Some museums, such as the neighbourhood, eco, and integral museums, were established with the particular purpose of integrating museology into society and could be seen as attempts to positively address Weil's concerns. However, there has been no consistent approach to museum philosophy or practice during the twentieth century. Museums continued to state a desire to serve a social purpose, but there remained numerous public restrictions on accessing this public good. However, museums have exhibited ongoing changes that:

> ...proceed on the basis of interrogating and renegotiating earlier practices and philosophies, many of which continue in one form or another to underpin the identity of museums today (E Hooper-Greenhill, 2007a, p. 368).

2.7.3 Impact of changing museologies on the Cobb+Co Museum, Stage One

When the Cobb+Co Museum opened in 1987, it was a product of many of the museological traditions interpreted by the Queensland Museum – Cobb+Co Museum's parent body. By the late 1980s, the Queensland Museum was still a traditional collection- and research-focused institution dominated by professional curators. However, it had recently undergone a major relocation from the iconic building it had long resided in, to a new cultural precinct in Brisbane, the capital of Queensland. This relocation had an accompanying expectation that the museum would provide engaging visitor experiences through new permanent and regularly-changing exhibitions. Very gradually, some aspects of new museological thought emerged, such as tentative attempts to represent women and Aboriginal and Torres Strait Islanders as actors and subjects. However, community engagement, as advocated by new museologists, was not apparent in the Queensland Museum until the late 1980s.

The relocation to the South Bank precinct did offer much greater prominence to the Queensland Museum's long-held interest in children's education and its relationships with the formal education sector. The Cobb+Co Museum inherited these concerns and, from its inception, identified and implemented opportunities to use the museum's resources to support formal education programs.

The Cobb+Co Museum's unique identity was formed through its relationship with its community, which was forged through its Advisory Committee's and Chairman's determination that the Cobb+Co Museum would play a leadership role in its community, as advocated by Dana, Goode, and Weil. This identity would undergo many transformations as the dynamics between the museum and its community evolved.

The establishment of the Cobb+Co Museum in the late 1980s was also impacted by other broader issues relating to the heritage industry, particularly as interpreted in regional contexts.

2.8 Heritage industry

During the 1980s, a proliferation of heritage preservation policies and development strategies engulfed many OECD countries. These were mainly directed towards the rejuvenation of former industrial sites that had high heritage and tourist value. Governments invested in these developments because they believed in their potential to assist recovery from the severe economic and social decline affecting many cities, ports, and regions in those countries at the time (Scheiner, 2005, p. 88).

This trend accelerated during the Thatcher Government in Great Britain in the 1980s, when authorities at all levels started to embrace the heritage-led revitalisation of former industrial sites and ports as a solution to the high unemployment caused by de-industrialisation in these areas.[14] It has been argued that the rate of such change was greater in Britain than elsewhere:

> [It] occurred at a time when many local authorities were developing more of a strategic role with regard to economic development and saw in tourism a way of generating jobs directly and through more general publicity about their area (Urry, 1990, p. 211).

A new phenomenon – a heritage industry – developed in these regions through 'producing something new albeit with recourse to the past' (Kirshenblatt-Gimblett, 1998, p. 151). There was an explosion of new heritage attractions, products, and services that were linked to recreational and tourist activities. Heritage became a value-added industry that gave a second life to a building or site.[15] The heritage industry also became a natural ally for tourism.

> Once a site, building, object or way of life can no longer sustain itself as it once did, it survives, which is to say, it is made economically viable, as an exhibition of itself, as a representation of itself. Heritage and tourism are thus collaborative industries, heritage converting locations into destinations and tourism making them economically viable as exhibits of themselves (Kirshenblatt-Gimblett, 1998).

Recycling heritage buildings and materials also had environmental benefits.[16] They also provided cost-effective employment opportunities for

---

14. This movement would lead to the furious heritage debates among academics and others over the true impact of an industry based on preserving and interpreting the past (see Section 3.5, below).

15. 'Something like one new museum or heritage site was opening in Britain every two weeks' (Richard Luce, Minister for the Arts 1986 quoted in Hewison, 1987, p. 84).

16. Research shows that older housing costs less to maintain and occupy, over the life of the building, than more contemporary housing. Pre-1940 buildings tended towards the optimal use of natural sources of light and ventilation, and were better suited to the local climate. The least environmentally-friendly buildings were constructed from 1940–1975 (Department of Sustainability and Environment, 2006, p. 44).

former industrial workers, who were transformed from intensive manual labourers into guides and re-enactors in the newly designated heritage tourism sites.[17] Heritage projects were promoted as:

> ...one of the very few forms of labour-intensive employment which is actually growing. Politically it rests on a broad base of do-it-yourself retrieval projects in which local initiatives serve, in some sort, as a surrogate for municipal enterprise or state intervention (Samuel, 1994, p. 294).

There was great support for redeveloping heritage attractions – an industry that exploited the twin themes of nostalgia and commercialism. Funding from central government, local authorities, public industry, and private business, together with money from Europe and the English Tourist Board (Catterall, 2005, pp. 104-106), enabled the development of many significant heritage-led revitalisation and tourism projects in decaying regional industrial areas and port districts across the United Kingdom.[18]

John Urry summarised the impact of the rapid de-industrialisation of Britain in the late 1970s and early 1980s:

> On the one hand, it created a profound sense of loss, both of certain kinds of technology (steam engines, blast furnaces, pit workings) and of the social life that had developed around such technologies (Urry, 1990, p. 211).

The catchcry of urban or rural regeneration was for revitalisation, not just of dilapidated buildings, but also of a deteriorated quality of life (Lorente, 1996, p. 2):

> Regeneration is not simply about bricks and mortar. It's about the physical, social and economic well being of an area; it's about the quality of life in our neighbourhood. In relation to the physical, this is as much about the quality of public realm as it is about the buildings themselves (Office of the Deputy Prime Minister, quoted in Evans, 2005, p. 966).

Regeneration projects need to be dynamic progresses that provide challenges and change. At times, this requires a completely new concept of a modern museum, such as the Guggenheim in Bilbao. This project demonstrated:

> ...the use of modern art museums in the transformation of cities from industrial to post-industrial era and urban regeneration using 'culture' as a focal point for cultural change in identity to transform a society (Baniotopoulou, 2000, p. 1).

---

17. It has been estimated that the cost of one new job in tourism is £4,000, compared with £32,000 in the manufacturing industry and £300,000 in mechanical engineering (Lumley, 1988, p. 22).

18. These include the World Heritage sites of Ironbridge Gorge in Shropshire, and New Lanark on the Clyde River, south of Glasgow. Other prominent attractions include the Big Pit and Rhondda Valley Coal Industry Interpretative Centre in Wales; Wigan Pier's 'The Way We Were' Heritage Centre; Albert Dock in Liverpool; and Lothian near Edinburgh, which transformed the Prestongrange and Lady Victoria mining collieries into the Scottish Mining Museum (Annabel Dicks, 1999; A. Dicks, 2003; Edwards, Llurdes i Coit, & Carles, 1996, p. 342; N. Johnson, 2009, pp. 48-49; Rojek, 1993, p. 204; B. West, 1988).

Although it was not completed until July 2006, the redevelopment of Kelvingrove Art Gallery and Museum in Glasgow is a good example of this strategy. This project has been described as involving:

> ...an ambitious sense of the potential of culture to replace shipbuilding and heavy industry as a driver of the local economy, for the city fathers made a conscious effort to create an art gallery explicitly to change [Glasgow's] image from decaying rust belt to cultural tourist destination (O'Neill, 2007, p. 380).

Davison expressed a less proactive view when he asserted that heritage was able to take hold over the United Kingdom because of 'a sense of disorientation, of decline and even of national immaturity or confusion' (Davison, 1991, p. 5). It has also been argued that the spectacular growth in heritage products, including museums, historic homes and gardens, and industrial sites in OECD countries, particularly Britain, simply represented the development of a post-industrial society in which:

> ...the ex-miner, now employed at the former coalmine to show tourists around, is a metonym for the structural change in the economy from one based on heavy industry to one based on service (Urry, 1990, p. 226).

Similar developments occurred across Australia in industrial cities, ports, and regions, and, more significantly for this discussion, in regional and rural areas. In the 1970s and 1980s, rural communities in Southern Queensland experienced fundamental structural changes as a result of a severe decline in the Australian pastoral and agricultural industries. These communities, like their counterparts elsewhere in the world, were drawn towards heritage-led revitalisation projects, linked to tourism, as one possible solution to their social and economic problems. Many examples of local history museums and historic precincts developed in 'stagnant and declining regions' in Southern Queensland (Davison, 1991, p. 5).

The formation of the Cobb+Co Museum in Toowoomba, the capital of the Darling Downs agricultural region, appeared to some in the community to fit this pattern of heritage-led revitalisation:

> To the locals [these attractions] provide tangible evidence of the community's better days; to the visitors they offer a pleasant respite from the visual monotony of Twentieth Century architecture (Davison, 1991, p. 5).

Also significant for the future developments at the Cobb+Co Museum was a revival of interest in the heritage trades and crafts that underpinned the industrial era and that, to some people, were the cultural expression of a 'pre-scientific' era (Hassard, 2009, p. 285).

Adopting a legal framework, international heritage lawyers, Lyndel Prott and Patrick O'Keefe, advocated that heritage trades and crafts should be represented within five categories of moveable/immoveable and tangible/

intangible heritage, which are expressions of culture or evidence of a way of life (Prott & O'Keefe, 1992, p. 307).[19]

This interest in traditional trades was the catalyst for the first real linkages between the Cobb+Co Museum and the state training organisation (SQIT) that was co-located on a site in Lindsay Street, Toowoomba. Interest in this heritage trade training ultimately provided the motivation, opportunities, and direction for future developments at the Cobb+Co Museum. By the time these developments were realised, the heritage trades, as an expression of intangible heritage would be adopted within a post museological concept identifying that heritage does not reside 'solely in the *materiality* of the past' (Hassard, 2009, pp. 284-285).

2.9 Queensland Museum – the parent body of the Cobb+Co Museum

Despite the importance of the many international museological and heritage industry influences mentioned above, the ultimate reason for the establishment of the Cobb+Co Museum was the development of the Queensland Museum's branch structure in the 1980s. The establishment, profile, and early development of the Cobb+Co Museum was influenced most directly by its parent body's (the Queensland Museum) traditions and practices, the Queensland Government's regional development agenda, and the development of the community museum movement across Queensland.

2.9.1 Early Australian state museums replicate British models

All early museum development within Australian was heavily influenced by British museum habitus[20], because the new colonies in New South Wales were part of the British Empire. According to the *Argus*, Melbourne's leading newspaper at the time, museums in the Australian colonies, like those in Britain, were essential so that 'the educated classes would not to fall behind in the march of civilization' (Goodman, 1999, p. 261).

---

19. These five categories include:
    - Monuments or sites, including gardens and parks;
    - Movable objects, including artworks; objects of historic, archaeological, or scientific importance; and objects of daily life;
    - Intangible concepts, such as ideas, patterns of behaviour, and traditional skills;
    - Rituals, ceremonies, oral history, and the performing arts; and
    - Preserved information relating to the other four categories (Prott & O'Keefe, 1992, pp. 307-309).

20. According to Bourdeau, habitus is a set of dispositions that generate practices and perceptions (Bourdieu, 1977, p. 82).

The first museum in Australia was the Sydney Colonial Museum, established in 1829.[21] Each of the other colonies developed museums of a similar style, although inter-colonial rivalry ensured that there was little or no interaction. Local support was not essential to establish these colonial museums, because they each developed strong links to overseas collecting institutions – most noticeably the British Museum, which, in 1859, celebrated its one-hundred-year anniversary (M. Anderson & Reeves, 1994, p. 91). The Carnegie Report in 1933 described this situation:

> During the whole of this period, from 1830 to 1900, and, indeed, for several years later, there was not only no co-operation among museums, but rather a state of complete and utter indifference between them, part of which was undoubtedly due to the local jealousies of the period (Markham & Richards, 1933, p. 7).

The early history of the Queensland Museum exemplifies this pattern of state museum development in Australia. It also demonstrates the general history of museums in Australia that, until the 1980s, was 'littered with tales of parsimony and neglect, interleaved with brief interludes of expansion' (M. Anderson, 1993, p. 4).

2.9.2 Queensland Museum history, 1862–1970

Following the British and American models, the Queensland Museum evolved from a learned society's desire to promote its ideals. In March 1859, the early founders of the Philosophical Society of Queensland, under the leadership of Charles Coxen, established a museum to house collections of the state's natural heritage. This was motivated by the belief that, in every highly civilized community, 'a public museum is a necessity' (George Brown Goode quoted in Mather, 1986, p. 305). Starting very humbly, the Philosophical Society received a small Queensland Government grant of one hundred pounds to open its museum within temporary rooms of the old Windmill building in Wickham Terrace, Brisbane. Towards the end of January 1862, the first displays were opened to the public, and the Queensland Museum was born.

In 1879, the state government gained responsibility for the Philosophical Society's growing collection of artefacts and specimens, and accelerated plans for a purpose-built building in William Street, Brisbane. Under the leadership of its curator, Charles De Vis, the collection expanded to include 'curios, machinery, weapons and furniture', as well as a number of anthropological collections from the South-West Pacific, in a manner reminiscent of the best European museums of that period (Mather, 1986, pp. 201, 222).

Within a very short period, the William Street premises proved to be inadequate, and public pressure led to lobbying for a new site. The government acquired and completed the National Agricultural and Industrial As-

21. Five years later, the museum's name was changed to the Australian Museum, as it is still called today.

sociation of Queensland Exhibition building on Gregory Terrace, and the Queensland Museum relocated to this new site at the end of 1899. This imposing structure would define the Queensland Museum for nearly a century, although the building was more impressive in appearance, than functional and practical for the purposes of a major museum (Markham & Richards, 1933, pp. 24, 27).

Throughout the twentieth century, the Queensland Museum experienced periods of growth and decline that reflected changing economic conditions and the state government's varying levels of interest (Markham & Richards, 1933, pp. 24, 27). In 1910, with the appointment of Ronald Hamlyn-Harris, there was a revival of collection activities and a new focus on learning, particularly for children, which was encouraged through a series of educational programs (Mather, 1986, pp. 108-109). In 1916, the museum reached an agreement with the Queensland Department of Public Instruction to offer a program of talks for organised school visits.[22]

Although the Queensland Museum, in a similar way to other Australian state museums, languished during World War One and for most of the interwar period, in 1938, there was a revived interest in education programs as a result of a grant of one thousand pounds from the Carnegie Foundation. The end of World War Two, in 1945, marked a period of renewed activity within its accommodation constraints, under the directorships of George Mack (1946–1963), Jack Woods (1963–1969), and Alan Bartholomai (1969–2000). Scientific research continued to be the major focus of staff endeavours, which resulted in the ongoing publication of the *Memoirs of the Queensland Museum* from 1891.[23]

In contrast to its scientific research, there was almost a total lack of interest in either collecting or exhibiting historical material. Unlike the situation in most European countries and the U.S.A., in which preservationist lobbies had prevailed and rudimentary forms of heritage legislation had been enacted by the late nineteenth century, Australia did not respond in a similar fashion until well into the second half of the twentieth century (Bennett, 1995a, p. 136).[24]

This situation gradually changed after 1970, when the Queensland Parliament enacted the *Queensland Museum Act 1970,* which mandated the collection of applied science, history, and technology materials by the Board of Trustees ("Queensland Museum Act 1970," s12(2)(a)). This act would prove

22. In 1918, these lectures to school groups attracted twenty-six classes from eighteen schools. The museum also offered classes for handicapped members of the community and the Director personally held classes for deaf children (Mather, 1986, pp. 108-109).

23. From 1891 until 1912 this publication was known as the *Annals of the Queensland Museum.*

24. The Australian Council of National Trusts was formed in 1965, in contrast to the much earlier formation of the National Trust in Great Britain, in 1895.

'a major turning point in the history of the institution', although the Board did not initially respond enthusiastically to this demand (Queensland Museum Board of Trustees, 1971 -1979, p. 1).

The Queensland Museum was not alone among Australian state and national museums in its failure to embrace social history collections and exhibitions. The Pigott Committee, commissioned by the Commonwealth Government in 1975 to investigate the state of museums in Australia, lamented the poor representation of heritage collections, and chastised the major museums for their continuing lack of interest in Australian history.[25] In contrast, the Committee somewhat over-enthusiastically commended the local museum movement, which they saw as filling a vacuum left by the state museums:

> In the last fifteen years, hundreds of small museums have been founded as a result of the quickening interest in Australian history. This has been primarily a grass-roots movement, one of the most unexpected and vigorous cultural movements in Australia this century (Pigott, 1975, p. 21).

There was only a very gradual move away from the traditional focus on technological collections towards encompassing a social history dimension, and Australian museums were still far from allocating historical significance to folk culture. It was not until the mid-1990s that the first attempt to investigate the significance of folklore and intangible heritage in a regional setting was documented in the Moe Folklife project.[26]

The other significant development that resulted from the *Queensland Museum Act 1970* was the Queensland Museum's new legislative ability to establish branch museums across the state.[27] By the late 1980s, the Board of the Queensland Museum had enthusiastically enacted this clause to establish branch museums in regional Queensland, which included the Cobb+Co Museum in Toowoomba.

2.9.3 Queensland Museum on the move

The decision to relocate the Queensland Museum to Brisbane's South Bank, in October 1986, represented a new beginning for the Queensland Museum by integrating it into the state's cultural life, along with the State

---

25. Only five institutions across the continent, including the Queensland Museum, had curators for whom the title of 'history' is appropriate (quoted in Bennett, 1995a, p. 143). The first curator for History and Technology at the Queensland Museum, Dr Dan Robinson, was appointed on 10 April 1972.

26. This study documented more than fifty different types of handcrafts and showed 'conclusively that an industrial town, economically one of the most depressed in Australia, has a rich culture of everyday life and a talented population' that can produce cultural and economic benefits to the region (Davey, 1996, p. 23).

27. The *Queensland Museum Act 1970* empowered the Board 'either alone or by agreement and in conjunction with any other person or body (to) establish, maintain and control branches of the Museum within Queensland' ("Queensland Museum Act 1970," s25(1)).

Library, the Queensland Art Gallery, and the Queensland Performing Art Centre. The Queensland Government was keen to develop a vibrant cultural space at South Bank. South Bank was promoted as:

> ...a series of exciting environments where the entire community can be involved in the celebration of a vast array of cultural events (quoted in Trotter, 1996, p. 19).

In determining the Queensland Museum's future direction, following its transfer to South Bank, its Board decided to include new museological concepts for its exhibitions, and, later, its public programs. They highlighted, in theory at least, front-of-house, rather than back-of-house, activities. This new direction aimed:

> To maintain and preserve its existing collections, to prepare regularly changing exhibitions for the public which are object based...supporting these with a temporary exhibition programme...and provide travelling exhibitions to other parts of the State, and to communicate knowledge to the public and integrate its educational activities with the requirements of the State Education Department (Annual Report Queensland Museum 1983, pp.4-5).

The new Queensland Museum facility was eighteen thousand square metres – three times as much display space as in the old building. This provided great opportunities to integrate displays in individual display pods, which, it was declared, would be replaced on a regular basis. The inclusion of a Reference Centre and community access gallery spaces for temporary displays heralded the Board's desire to make the Queensland Museum more accessible to the community. Travelling exhibitions were planned as a way of enabling regional communities' access to the Queensland Museum's collections. The continuation of an active program of fieldwork ensured curators and other specialists were active across the state.

In keeping with emerging overseas trends, both formal and informal learning opportunities were enhanced and new programs developed. From the mid-1960s, Queensland Museum had an active program in which specifically-acquired educational artefacts were loaned to teachers in Brisbane and its surrounding areas. After the move to South Bank, a more formally organised Loans Service was also developed, although this occurred more as a result of morphing existing staff interests, rather than a concerted action by Queensland Museum. The Loans Service remained a tangential program that was delivered mainly by volunteers.[28] To complement the Loans Service, the museum introduced an education program to take objects and programs directly to schools in distant and disadvantaged areas. From as early as 1979, the Department of Education seconded a teacher to the museum to become the outreach officer.

However, despite the new facility and the greater emphasis on outreach services and education programs, many of the traditional practices and much of the traditional structure of the Queensland Museum remained in-

28. With the support of an army of volunteers, the reach of the Loans Service expanded greatly because of an agreement with the Department of Education to use the Department's regional offices as distribution centres.

tact. The majority of the museum staff were in curatorial areas, particularly within the biodiversity section. All of the Directors (now 'Chief Executive Officers') of the Queensland Museum had been curators within the biodiversity or geosciences programs. Even the Curator of History and Technology had a scientific, rather than historical, background. The Queensland Museum was still very much a natural history museum following its relocation to South Bank. The task of preserving Queensland's moveable cultural heritage remained the responsibility of the community museums springing up across the state and nation.

2.10 The community museum movement in Queensland

In Queensland, as occurred in the other Australian states, a number of community museums were created as a result of the economic and social changes taking place in regional communities in the 1970s. These changes were due to the effects of globalisation; falling commodity prices; and changes in farming techniques, such as increased mechanisation, which resulted in decreased labour demand (Witcomb, 2003, p. 149).

At this time, there was a growing concern by communities that the region's heritage was being irretrievably lost. Often, community museums were established to save the contents of farm sheds and other objects that were left behind by retiring property owners. The museums were, in fact, reserving specific places for these objects, and they considered that the more objects that could be saved, the better.[29] At this time, there was also a focus on preserving buildings, which often involved relocating them to a new museum complex or heritage village. The buildings were treated as artefacts, but they had the added advantage of being able to house even more objects – even if they did so very inadequately. As early as 1974, the Hope Committee of Inquiry into the National Estate criticised the development of large numbers of 'pioneer settlements and country museums', which needed 'much better co-ordination and much more professional skill' (Committee of Inquiry into the National Estate, 1974, pp. 192, 195). The 'storehouse' approach of the community museum movement in regional Queensland was significantly different from the new museum models discussed in Section 2.7.1, above.

Within community museums, there was little consideration of the object's condition or completeness and little time to record histories or stories about the vast number of objects being donated or loaned. Museums weren't necessarily concerned about an object's origin or relationship to the

29. Proud community museum volunteers constantly reminded the author in the 1980s and 90s about their collections of 'forty-five mother pots irons' and 'thirty-three Singer sewing machines', not to mention their collections of hundreds – if not thousands – of bottles and shells.

local community. The author often described museums in regional Queensland in the 1980sand 90s as 'the last stop before the dump' for people cleaning out their sheds (Tranter, 2006b).

Despite the museological inadequacies of the community museums developed in regional Queensland at this time, more and more communities supported their establishment. They believed that their heritage was important and needed to be saved, because it contributed to a sense of civic pride and confidence, helped develop shared values, and brought people together to strengthen communities at a time when these communities were under threat (Jowell, 2005, p. 16).[30]

The community museum movement was an attempt to recreate the social cohesion within the communities that were being destroyed through the break-up of many long-established family farms. Research indicates that the ongoing activity generated by the community museums created opportunities for socialisation – which fostered social cohesion and individual and group identity – when other traditional opportunities for this were being destroyed (Stanley, 2006, p. 2). Ironically, while group belonging is a critical component of citizenship capacity, it is also suggested that it can be threatening to other (outside) communities (p. 3). This could also account for the inability of many community museums to embrace new and/or younger community members.

By the end of the twentieth century, after thirty years or so of, at times, frantic collecting, many community museums were no longer able to adequately house the artefacts they aimed to save. Too many museums were characterised by sheds and surrounding yards full of rusting iron work and machinery (Winkworth, 2005). Pressure on space became so great that many museums were forced to virtually cease collecting, which had left their community's heritage collections 'stuck' in a time warp predating the 1960s.

In this fledgling stage of community museum development, the Queensland Museum played no real role, even though, as early as 1974, the Hope Committee of Inquiry into the National Estate in Australia recommended including moveable property of great importance within the National Estate.[31]

The Board of the Queensland Museum instigated a more proactive approach in 1982, when it convinced the state government to introduce a grant scheme to assist community museums.[32] As local museums were multiplying

---

30. These community heritage values were developed by standing citizen's juries across the United Kingdom, which were established by the Heritage Lottery Fund. The author's own professional experience in regional Queensland also resonates strongly with these findings.

31. This report referenced the significance of the Ilfracombe Museum's collection of horse- and bullock-drawn vehicles near Longreach in Queensland (Committee of Inquiry into the National Estate, 1974, pp. 192, 195).

32. The individual grants that were available under the *Grant Towards Local Museum Activities Scheme* were limited to a maximum of three thousand dollars and did not include support for capital works.

at the rate of nearly one a month in the early 1990s (Bartholomai, 1991, p. 370), the $190,000 available for community museum grants quickly became inadequate.[33] Because the scheme was so popular in regional communities, the Queensland Museum was able to exert some limited professional influence over the standard of museum practices. However, by 1995, these grants were described as 'band-aids used to patch up local problems and keep the life blood of community museums flowing' (Lennon, 1995, p. i).

There were two Queensland Government funded reviews of the community museum sector and its relationship to the Queensland Museum during the 1990s.[34] These reviews informed the major study of the sector published as: *Hidden Heritage: A Development Plan for Museums in Queensland 1995-2000* (Lennon, 1995). It was this report that recommended the establishment of the Museum Resource Centre Network (MRCN), which employs Museum Development Officers (MDOs). These Queensland Museum staff live and work in regional Queensland, which overcomes the problems associated with using external consultants who do not have any ongoing commitment to these regional communities (Witcomb, 2003, p. 151).[35]

The public image and perceived value of the community museum movement, often expressed as 'the last stop before the dump', would have negative impacts on the Cobb+Co Museum during its early days. Dispelling this image and playing a leadership role in supporting community museums[36] would become a significant concern for the Cobb+Co Museum. This role would increase dramatically when the management for the Museum Resource Centre Network across Queensland was assumed by the Director of the Cobb+Co Museum in 2003.

2.11 Distributed Queensland Museum

The Queensland Museum had a further impact in regional Queensland after 1984 when it opened its first regional branch in Gympie, following the state government's earlier decision, that all proposals for departmental museums be considered by the Queensland Museum. This created the opportunity for a statewide network of branch museums. Originally, the Board proposed a 'hit list' of preferred locations, including Rockhampton, Townsville, and Cairns, which were significant sites on the road and rail transport links across the state (Bartholomai, 1991, pp. 356-357). However, external events

---

33. In 1995, there were approximately one hundred and seventy-five small grants distributed by the Queensland Museum.

34. *Review of the Arts in Queensland*, 1990, and a *Policy Review of the Queensland Museum*, 1992.

35. By 2009, there were six MDOs based in regional centres who provided professional museum services to hundreds of small collecting organisations across the state.

36. The author, as Director of the Cobb+Co Museum, Chaired the Industry Reference Group for the *Hidden Heritage Development Plan*.

provided opportunities for branch development outside these guidelines, with the Board prepared to 'seize any opportunity' to establish branches (Mather, 1986, p. 297).

Eventually, there were nine separate branch museums operating across Queensland. Each was a result of different individual local contexts and relationships, which resulted from a mixture of internal and external advocacy and opportunities. By 2010, the branch structure had stabilised at four major museums and one minor display centre.

2.11.1 WoodWorks, Gympie

The first branch, WoodWorks, located just north of Gympie, opened in March, 1984, after the then Forestry Department proposed a joint permanent display of forestry activities, relating to the local timber industry, in an attempt to preserve the remains of this declining regional industry as a heritage tourism attraction (Bartholomai, 1991, p. 257).[37] WoodWorks was never really recognised internally as a major Queensland Museum branch museum, because there were no curatorial staff and no research component, nor were any Queensland Museum staff based in Gympie.

Over a twenty-year period, the number and expertise of the former Forestry Department demonstrators declined and there was no capital investment in either the displays or public programs. When the Department announced it was withdrawing from the Gympie Conference site, which included the museum, WoodWorks was forced to close. The operation closed to the public, as a branch of the Queensland Museum, on 30 June 2008, after twenty-four years of operation.[38]

2.11.2 Glenlyon Dam, Stanthorpe

Although always referred to as a branch of the Queensland Museum, the Glenlyon Dam Display Centre, which opened in 1986, was a very small facility with an unmanned fauna display that interpreted local natural heritage. It was located in the popular camping grounds of the Glenlyon Dam area outside Stanthorpe. This static display was given little attention or improvement over the years and an agreement was signed in 2005, with the then Stanthorpe Shire Council, to take over the facility and displays that were donated by the Queensland Museum.

---

37. Staff employed at this site would be local forestry workers and volunteers – former employees who would operate the working displays as a visitor attraction. Open days, which included the operation of the steam-driven sawmill, were very popular in the early days, attracting up to eight thousand visitors.

38. Because of community pressure, the Queensland Government donated the WoodWorks facility to the newly amalgamated Gympie Regional Council. The Queensland Museum, in turn, donated the collections and displays that could allow Woodworks to reopen as a council-run museum.

2.11.3 Museum of Tropical Queensland (MTQ), Townsville

In Townsville, the North Queensland branch of the Queensland Museum (renamed the Museum of Tropical Queensland (MTQ)) opened in June 1987. This occurred as a result of an approach from the Great Barrier Reef Wonderland Association Inc. to the Queensland Museum to become a partner in a major tourist development on the Townsville Harbour (Bartholomai, 1991, p. 358).

The original 880m^2 building had only a modest display space, with more than half the building devoted to collections, storage, and staff facilities. The limited exhibitions were 'a mixture of traditional systematic zoological, geological, anthropological and applied arts' (Bartholomai, 1991, p. 358). The museum's collection and curatorial expertise was originally associated with the flora and fauna of Tropical Queensland, particularly relating to corals. The curator-manager was transferred from Brisbane to Townsville to lead this branch development.

Because the museum was located fourteen hundred kilometres from South Bank, Brisbane, MTQ developed a parochial attitude, as was prevalent in the local community. Local businesses raised considerable funds to retrieve artefacts from the *Pandora* shipwreck – an enterprise that would become the focus for the museum's Stage Two development. This display was opened on 3 June 2000, and the Queensland Museum's maritime archaeology section transferred to MTQ to work on this project. Gradually, a more generalist approach to exhibitions and public programs has evolved, particularly with the introduction of a free community pass for local residents.

2.11.4 Museum of Mapping and Surveying, Woolloongabba

The Museum of Mapping and Surveying opened in Woolloongabba, Brisbane, in 1988. This occurred after the Department of Lands, Mapping, and Surveying formed a partnership with the Queensland Museum to accession its large collection of historical items associated with the exploration and mapping of the state into the Queensland Museum's collection. This branch has always had a strong research profile, even though the only staff member was an employee of the Department of Lands, Mapping, and Surveying. This small branch is still maintained by its two partners, but does so without any additional display space or program development.

2.11.5 History and Technology Branch, Coomera

A storage facility for the proposed History and Technology branch at Coomera was completed and handed over to the Queensland Museum on 26 June 1989. Despite the museum's intention to establish a Technology

Centre there, it remained a storage facility until the property was sold in 2001. Following this, the collection was relocated to an alternative storage facility at Hendra in Brisbane. The concept of a technology museum was then abandoned.

2.11.6 Sciencentre, Brisbane

The Sciencentre represented a different approach to branch development for the Queensland Museum. Responding to increased pressure by the education sector for an interactive science centre, the Queensland Museum Board agreed to establish a branch in a restored building in William Street, in inner city Brisbane, in October 1989 (Bartholomai, 1991, p. 361).

In contrast to its other branches, the Sciencentre would not hold any collections or employ any curatorial staff; its emphasis was on interactive science education. A partnership was formed with the Department of Education, which provided a senior science teacher on secondment to develop the curriculum-based exhibits and public programs.

Following a positive response from schools, the Sciencentre relocated into much larger premises, in the Old Printery Building in George Street, Brisbane, in September 1992. In an effort to address the original concerns of the Institution of Engineers, a travelling Sciencentre Roadshow[39], took the Sciencentre to schools across the state. In January 2003, the Sciencentre closed and again relocated – this time across the Brisbane River into the Queensland Museum South Bank facility. It was eventually reopened there in September 2004.

2.11.7 Museum of North Western Queensland, Mount Isa

The Museum of North Western Queensland was opened in Mount Isa in 1995, because the Queensland Museum hoped to acquire and display a world-class mineral collection in two of Mount Isa's facilities – the Frank Aston Underground Museum and the John Middleton Mining Display and Visitor Centre. One of the Queensland Museum's Brisbane-based curators was appointed in the managerial position.

This branch did not attain its potential as either a collection and research centre, or as a significant tourist attraction. Responding to local council interest, the Queensland Museum closed this branch in May 2002 and transferred its assets to the Mount Isa City Council to form part of an integrated tourist attraction: Outback@Isa.

---

39. The Roadshow consisted of a prime mover and trailer loaded with exhibits and manned by four science communicators.

2.11.8 The Workshops Rail Museum (TWRM), Ipswich

In 1991, an agreement signed between the Queensland Museum and the Commissioner for Railway enabled a Queensland Railways Historical Museum in Ipswich to be established as a Branch of the Queensland Museum (1990-91 Annual Report Queensland Museum Board of Trustees, 1980 to 2007-8, p. 7). However, it was not until August 2002 that this branch of the Queensland Museum opened at The Workshops Rail Museum (TWRM) in North Ipswich. Working in partnership with Queensland Rail, the state government requested that the Queensland Museum take over the management of the new twenty-million-dollar facility at the heritage-listed Ipswich Railway Workshops. TWRM has subsequently created a unique niche visitor experience aimed at those with an interest in steam train trips, including young children with a fascination of 'Thomas the Tank Engine'. TWRM holds extensive collections and archives and has a very focused curatorial and collection management program. Its local community links continue to be centred on former Queensland Rail employees – who hold reunions on the site once a year – and a small number of volunteers who work on site.

2.11.9 Branch development summary

Since 1984, the Queensland Museum has operated as a distributed museum with up to nine separate branches or campuses at any one time. There has been some debate – depending on government requirements and local conditions – between a more decentralised 'house of brands' model, in which the individual branches assume a position of local autonomy, and the 'One QM' centralist model. Although the Queensland Museum Board initially sought to be proactive in its branch development, since 2002 it has consolidated its position as a response to dwindling resources and changing state and local government interests. In 2009, the Queensland Museum had adopted a 'One QM' approach to its delivery of museum services to Queenslanders, regardless of where they lived in the state. These services were delivered from the four main museum campuses: the Queensland Museum in South Bank, TWRM in Ipswich, Cobb+Co Museum in Toowoomba, and MTQ in Townsville.

In more recent years, the Board of the Queensland Museum has shown its desire to cooperate with local government in handing over displays in Stanthorpe, Gympie, and Mount Isa, and has developed partnerships with the Toowoomba and Townsville Regional Councils that enable free access to the Cobb+Co and MTQ, respectively, for all residents living in those council areas. There has also been an ongoing desire to cooperate with Cairns Regional Council in the development of a regional museum in Far North Queensland, though this project is still in its developmental stages in 2010.

The Queensland Museum continues to place a strong emphasis on regional services based on research programs in biodiversity, geosciences, culture, and history, including Aboriginal and Torres Strait Islander Cultures. A separate Regional Services Program, initiated in 2003, operates from the Cobb+Co Museum in Toowoomba, and augments the delivery of museum services across Queensland.

Table 2.1 below illustrates the complicated story of the Queensland Museum's branch development between 1984 and 2010.

Table 2.1: Queensland Museum branch development 1984–2010

Branch	Initial Partners	Date opened	Date closed	Collection focus	Public Programs	Staffing[40]
Woodworks GYMPIE	Department of Forestry	1984	2008 – given to local council	Historic forestry tools	Demonstrations and open days	Dept staff
Glenlyon Dam Display Centre TEXAS	State Water Commission	1986	2005 – given to local council	Fauna of the region	Nil	Unmanned
Museum of Tropical Qld (MTQ) TOWNSVILLE	Great Barrier Reef Wonderland	1987 – Stage 1 2000 – Stage 2		Maritime archaeology, Great Barrier Reef corals	Travelling displays and children's programs	QM curators and FOH staff
Cobb+Co Museum TOOWOOMBA	Nil	1987 – Stage 1 2001 – Stage 2 2010 – Stage 3		National collection of horse drawn vehicles	Education and children's programs; heritage training; travelling and temp displays	QM curators and FOH staff
Museum of Mapping and Surveying BRISBANE	Department of Lands, Mapping, and Surveying	1988		Historic mapping and exploration equipment	Outreach lectures	Dept staff
History & Technology Branch COOMERA	Nil	1989	2001	Large technology storage facility	Nil	Unmanned

40. QM staff include back-of-house (BOH) staff – curators, collection managers and conservators, and business managers – and front-of-house (FOH) staff – education officers, visitor service officers, display and information technology staff, and retail and coffee shop staff.

Sciencentre BRISBANE	Education Queensland	1989 – Stage 1 1992 – Stage 2 2003 – Stage 3 at South Bank		No collections	Education programs; Roadshows	Education Qld staff and QM FOH staff
Museum of North-Western Qld MT ISA	Nil	1995	2002 – given to local council	Minerals	Nil	QM staff manager
The Workshops Rail Museum (TWRM) IPSWICH	Department of Railways (QRail)	2002		Historic rail	Children's programs and steam train rides	QM curators and FOH staff

2.12 Cobb+Co Museum, Toowoomba

Toowoomba was not originally identified as a desirable location for a Queensland Museum branch, because it was considered to be too close to Brisbane. However, when a significant collection of horse-drawn vehicles was offered by the family of a former Toowoomba businessman, the Queensland Museum Board, following a well-established process used by many international museums, decided to accept the collection and subsequently opened a new museum to house it. Although the reason for the formation of this third significant branch of the Queensland Museum was different to other branches, the Cobb+Co Museum was still conceived within the prevailing philosophy and policy direction of all the other branches.

In 1982, after protracted negotiations[41], the Queensland Museum Board accepted the donation of the W.R.F.(Bill) Bolton Collection of horse-drawn vehicles, which formed the basis of its new branch. Bill Bolton had displayed this collection in his private Cobb & Co. Museum of Australiana in Toowoomba from 1956 until his death in 1974. In 1980, the original museum site caught on fire, and locals rescued the vehicles from the flames. This generated a deal of concern in the community about the future of the collection. This initiated the local community's ongoing involvement with the collection and, subsequently, with the Cobb+Co Museum. The Toowoomba City Council temporarily stored the fire- ravaged collection, until 4 December 1987, when the Cobb+Co Museum finally opened as a branch of the Queensland Museum.

This was the first Queensland Museum branch founded specifically to house a new collection that was donated to the Queensland Museum on the premise that the vehicles would remain in the region. The Cobb+Co branch was modelled on both WoodWorks, with its focus on a single theme of heritage technology, and the Townsville branch, with its traditional museum concern regarding collection management and research. Later in the museum's development, there would be comparisons between the Cobb+Co Museum and TWRM as specialist transport museums.

2.12.1 Founding philosophy

In these early days, the Queensland Museum did not have a well-developed strategic plan or direction for its branch museums. All its branch museums were placed under the management of the Curator of History and Technology, and the Bolton horse-drawn vehicles were accessioned into the Queensland Museum's History and Technology collection. Cobb+Co Museum was, in many ways, seen simply as another research facility and exhib-

41. These negotiations, which occurred between the Chairman of the Board, Mr Connal Gill, and Mrs Marion Bolton, commenced in 1976 (Bartholomai, 2005).

ition space to house the twenty-eight horse-drawn vehicles that had been donated, along with eleven other horse-drawn vehicles from the state collection that augmented the Cobb+Co collection. These vehicles were displayed in the 1600m^2 recycled floriculture building that was part of the old Toowoomba Showgrounds. This building, with a small amount of surrounding land, was excised from its original block when the land was acquired by TAFE Queensland for its new Toowoomba College.

The Cobb+Co Museum opened with only minimum interpretation of the horse-drawn vehicles as examples of transport technology.[42] With only one wooden horse in the collection, there was limited opportunity to display the vehicles effectively within a social history framework to a generation of visitors who had no experience of this mode of transport. The visitor experience was limited to viewing the carriages, reading the associated display labels, and perhaps watching a blacksmith demonstration replicated on the Woodworks model[43], or viewing a recycled WoodWorks video in the theatrette. There was an assumption that the museum's clientele would be elderly (as at WoodWorks) and would have some previous knowledge of the vehicles in the collection. An additional problem was a distinct lack of space for visitors, owing to the large number of vehicles displayed in the facility.

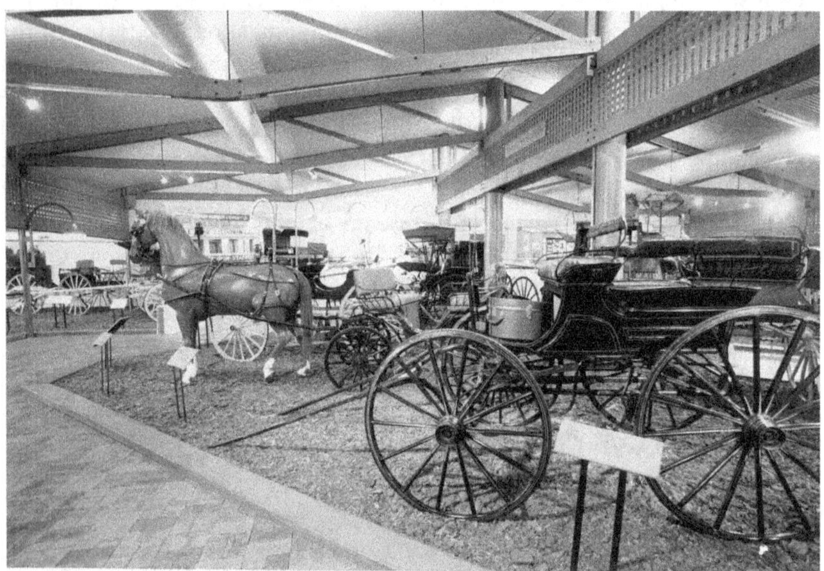

Vehicle Gallery 1987

The Queensland Museum's traditional museological approach was dominated by its concern for collections and research, and a focus on employing professional curators to undertake these roles. The development of the

---

42. There was one diorama of a bogged dray, but no other interpretative features.

43. A new blacksmith shop was incorporated into the complex, but was not originally developed as a working concern.

Cobb+Co Museum mirrored this approach, with the appointment of only two staff, both of whom had research roles, with one also fulfilling the role of Curator/Manager.[44] It was to this latter position that the author was appointed in October 1987. However, the author's appointment to this position was unusual for the Queensland Museum at that stage in its history. As a historian, rather than a research scientist, and as an experienced secondary school teacher with expertise in curriculum development and innovative learning programs, the author was unlike other Queensland Museum curators. Also, in contrast to other Queensland Museum branch appointments, in which staff were transferred to regional areas from Brisbane, the author had lived and worked in the Toowoomba region for the previous fifteen years; had a strong family connection to the heritage of the region; and had extensive community networks, particularly within the important education sector in Toowoomba. Not surprisingly, research and education were to be the dual focuses for the Cobb+Co Museum during its first phase development.

If the Queensland Museum showed little interest in relating to its regional museum communities, the residents of Toowoomba were equally indifferent to the new Cobb+Co. Museum. By 1987, the best part of a decade had passed since the fire had threatened to destroy the horse-drawn vehicle collection, and the community had been stirred into action. There had been a Cobb & Co. Museum in Toowoomba since the mid-1960s and, to many locals, the new museum was simply the old museum relocated. Heritage was not a high priority in the local community, and the author was subjected to a wave of consternation, particularly from teaching colleagues, relating to their perceived value of the museum. The feeling that the community viewed museums as 'the last stop before the dump' was all too frequently demonstrated in these early days, when cars, trucks, utes, and trailers that were loaded with waste disposal items would detour past the museum to offer their contents on their way to the tip. The author was determined that the Cobb+Co Museum would work to dispel this entrenched image of heritage and museums, which reflected the manner in which many people of the Toowoomba region perceived community museums.

2.12.2 Operating culture – challenging the prevailing museology

The local community's emotional attachment to and interest in the Bolton vehicle collection had certainly waned by the end of 1987. At the time, this was not a particular concern for the Cobb+Co Museum, as its main interest, in these early days, related to collection management and research activities.

---

44. This was modelled on the Townsville branch, which opened a few months prior to Cobb+Co. MTQ had a Curator/Manager and Curatorial Officer, but also an Administration Assistant and three part-time Museum Attendants.

One of the significant features of the Bolton donation was the inclusion of an extensive research collection, including written interviews with old Cobb & Co. drivers and grooms, original company records, various artefacts, and large numbers of original photographs (*W.R.F. Bolton Collection*). This offered valuable primary source material for future research projects. By the early 1990s, the staff of the museum had completed a number of publications providing historical accounts of the Cobb & Co. coaching company (Tranter, 1990, 1992; Tranter & Powell, 1992).[45]

This traditional museum concern with research was augmented from the museum's beginning by the rapid development of curriculum-based learning programs for primary and secondary classes, teacher in-service and pre-service, and the publication of object-based learning resources that were linked to school curricula and were made freely available to every state school in the region (Tranter, 1988a, 1988b; Tranter & Douglas, 1995, 1997). Although the Queensland Museum had provided some learning programs for school group visits for a number of years, the importance of curriculum-based learning was not yet realised. At this stage, the one Education Officer employed by the Queensland Museum was not a practising teacher with the necessary knowledge, skills, and experience to implement such programs. In contrast to the traditional museum attempts to attract individual school groups to visit museums for a one-off class visit, the Cobb+Co Museum forged an ongoing mutually beneficial relationship with the Toowoomba education sector. By 1990, a part-time Education Officer, who was a practising teacher, had been appointed to the Cobb+Co Museum in response to demand from schools. At this time, one hundred and twenty classes from schools were visiting the museum – a total of 3,356 students in that year.[46] Within a very short period, a formal learning environment had been established at the Cobb+Co Museum, which contrasted with the belief that museums are more effective informal or free-choice learning facilities for social or family group engagements (Falk & Dierking, 2002).

While realising the significance of the collection of horse-drawn vehicles[47], the Cobb+Co Museum also used its education focus to expand its range of exhibition themes. By converting a section of the gallery into a temporary display space, the museum provided a program of regularly-changing temporary displays, as well as children's activity programs during school holidays (Cobb+Co Museum, 1988-2009). Although programs such as this are now an expected museum function, in 1988, formal and informal educa-

45. In 1997, there was a further publication about Cobb & Co. activities in Japan (Tranter, 1997).

46. These two-hour curriculum-based learning programs involved photographic interpretation and object-based learning strategies to assist teachers to develop historical enquiry skills in their students (Cobb+Co Museum, 1988-2009).

47. It was quickly realised that the Cobb+Co Museum's carriage collection was, arguably, the finest collection of horse-drawn vehicles in Australia, and the collection was subsequently promoted as such.

tional programs that were conducted by qualified and experienced teachers in a museum setting provided a unique experience for Toowoomba families. Similar family learning initiatives were not replicated anywhere else within the Queensland Museum at this time, and would not be established until many years later.

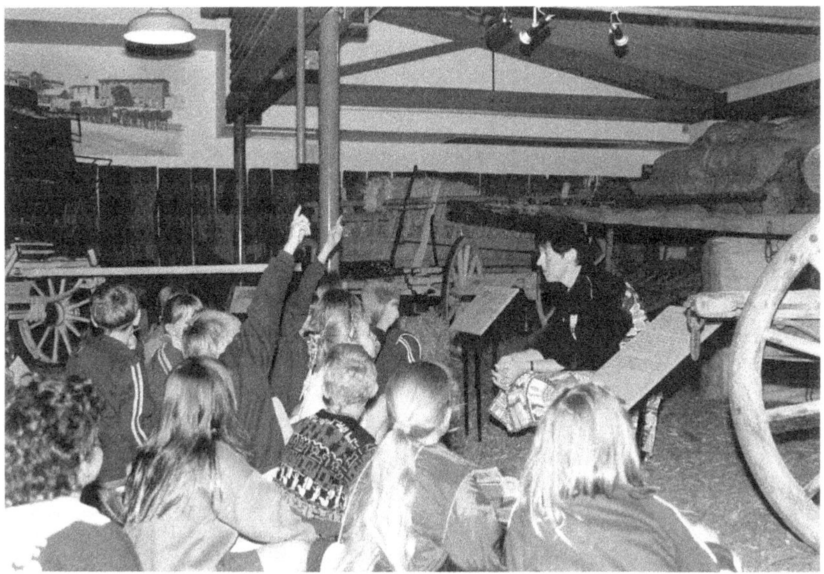

The director working with students on curriculum learning programs 1988

Structurally, the branch was located within the History and Technology section of the Queensland Museum, but the Cobb+Co Museum soon experienced multiple dichotomies. In the early days, the Cobb+Co brand was dominant in order to encourage parochial support; there was little local reference to it being a branch of the Queensland Museum. There were other tensions within the museum relating to determining whether the museum should focus on: traditional technology versus social history; research and collection management, as opposed to visitor experiences; education versus entertainment; and the development of the museum as a local community resource centre and/or a tourist attraction. These tensions would be addressed by the Advisory Committee, which enabled the local community a strong voice in the museum's development.

2.12.3 Advisory Committee links Cobb+Co Museum to its community

One of the most significant policy directions regarding branch development that was initiated by the Queensland Museum was the Board's decision to establish:

> ...a Management Committee, to represent the Museum and the local community and delegate to it responsibility for day to day operations of the Branch (Bartholomai, 1991, p. 360).

In reality, the Management Committee was established as an Advisory Committee – originally without any terms of reference – that met quarterly. Although it did not fulfil its original role as a Management Committee, the Cobb+Co Museum Advisory Committee, which was formed in 1988, provided a vital link with the local community, and instigated a pragmatic approach to working within this community.[48]

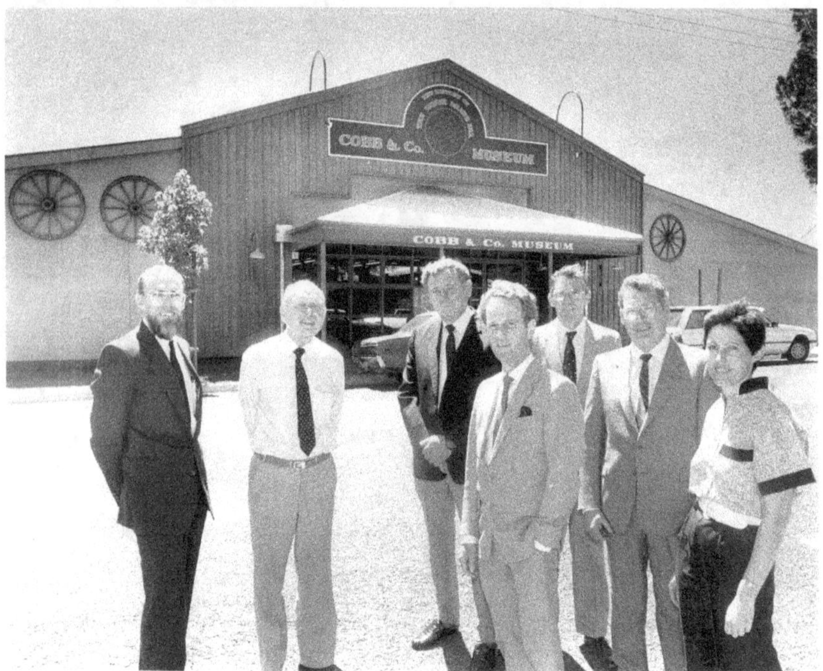

members of the first Advisory Committee 1988. Long term chairman Bill O'Brien second from left

Two main initiatives were instigated by the Advisory Committee under its second Chair, Mister Bill O'Brien[49], in the early 1990s, which contributed to the unique strategic direction developed by the Cobb+Co Museum to address the apparently 'diametrically opposed discourses' that the Cobb+Co Museum was subjected to in its early days (Trotter, 1996, p. 263). These projects included the development of an ongoing relationship with the

48. The Committee comprised six members, including the Chair, who was then also the Chair of the locally-significant Heritage Building Society; representatives from TAFE; the Bolton family; one of the city's leading business families; the local state member of Parliament; and a local councillor, who was also manager of the regional tourist association.

49. Bill O'Brien was Chair for fifteen years, which contributed to a consistent developmental approach to the Cobb+Co Museum and its identity within the community.

Southern Queensland Institute of Technical and Further Education (SQIT), which was co-located on Lindsay Street with the museum. This relationship would eventually lead to SQIT transferring sufficient land to the museum for its future expansion, as well as leading to the introduction of training programs in heritage trades.

A proactive engagement with the regional tourism industry was the second long-term approach instigated by the Advisory Committee. This was a remarkable initiative because, at the time, museum professionals negatively viewed tourism as the domain of 'the white shoe brigade' that marketed an image of 'sun, sand, surf', and the Gold Coast's artificiality. It seemed impossible to develop an alliance between the tourism industry and museums that were focused on collection management, research, and education. Despite this prevailing attitude, the Cobb+Co Museum became the first museum in Queensland to embrace the tourism industry as a partner.[50] It would be a long time before the museum sector in Queensland acknowledged the vital role that museums can play in the tourism industry 'as gatekeepers, key-holders and as iconic representations of authentic heritage and culture' (Walker, 2005, p. 4).

Through the encouragement of the Advisory Committee Chair, the author assumed a range of community leadership positions, as the Cobb+Co Museum focused on making itself 'really useful' to its community in the manner advocated by Goode, Dana, Weil, and Archibald (Archibald, 2004; Dana, 1917; Grove, 1978; Peniston, 1999; Weil, 2002).

Robert Archibald, the President and Chief Executive Officer of the Missouri Historical Society in Saint Louis, advocates that cultural institutions should play crucial leadership roles in their communities. The author's own experiences in the Toowoomba community resonate strongly with Archibald's sentiments when he writes:

> ...our work is not about history and markers [exhibitions]. It is about sustaining community... [and] sharing the story with the whole community. Museums are means, not ends... and urban museums are special because they are precisely positioned in those places where we make the future (Archibald, 2006, p. 14).

During the 1990s – a time of economic downturn and high unemployment in the region – the Cobb+Co Museum was actively involved in its community through the author's leadership roles in many community, industry,

---

50. As Chair of the Toowoomba & Golden West Regional Tourist Association, the Cobb+Co Museum's Director coordinated the Joint Tourism Regional Strategy for the Toowoomba & Golden West and Southern Downs Regions which incorporated twenty-seven local government areas (Taylor Byrne, 1996). Based on the success of that strategy, the Director was invited to chair the Reference Group, which developed the first cultural tourism strategy for Queensland (Arts Queensland, 1997). It was not until TWRM opened in 2002 that any other section of the Queensland Museum seriously engaged with the tourism sector.

training, and professional organisations.[51] The concept of the Cobb+Co Museum as a public good did not enter the vernacular at this stage, though, in reality, it was starting to perceive itself as a resource to be used for the betterment of its community. The Advisory Committee Chair's determination that the museum and its Director should play a leadership role in the community was of paramount importance for the transformations of the Cobb+Co Museum during the early years of the twenty-first century.

2.12.4 A bigger picture

While an interest in using the resources of the Cobb+Co Museum for formal educational purposes had been articulated by the author prior to the branch opening, there was no thought that visitors would be interested in learning about the trades associated with the vehicle collection, especially blacksmithing, wheelwrighting, and saddlery. Despite this, the museum began investigating the possibilities of preserving these specific heritage trades. In conjunction with SQIT[52], a national survey was undertaken to ascertain the number and condition of horse-drawn vehicles in private and public collections in Australia.[53] The further aim of the survey undertaken in 1992 was:

> To discover the extent of interest in trade courses associated with the production and restoration of the vehicles, and the demand for vehicle restoration and vehicle purchase (Fraser, 1992, pp. 4-5).

---

51. The author held the following positions:
- President of the Toowoomba and Golden West Regional Tourist Association;
- Board member of *Growzone* – a Southern Inland Queensland Regional Economic Development Organisation;
- Board member of the Southern Inland Queensland Area Consultative Committee to Commonwealth Department of Education, Employment Training, and Youth Affairs;
- Member of the Heritage Collections Council, which represented regional, specialist, and local museums in Queensland;
- Toowoomba and South West Representative of Arts Training Queensland;
- Vice-Chair of the Toowoomba and Region Employment and Training Network;
- Council Member of the Southern Queensland Institute of TAFE and Toowoomba College Councils;
- Executive Member of the Toowoomba Historical Society;
- Member of the Toowoomba Regional Arts Development Fund Committee;
- Life Member of the Toowoomba Events and Tourism Corporation, and Treasurer from 1992–1995; and
- Member of the Tourism Training Queensland Toowoomba and Darling Downs Regional Committee (Cobb+Co Museum, 1988-2009).

52. Previously, the two institutions had collaborated on the development of computer-generated construction drawings of a Cobb & Co. Coach, which were produced as part of the publication *Cobb & Co.: Coaching in Queensland* (Tranter, 1990).

53. The survey was sent to three hundred and twelve organisations with an interest in historic horse-drawn vehicles, as well as seventy-five carriage and harness clubs throughout Australia.

Further national and international research was conducted into formal and informal heritage trade training and production facilities associated with horse-drawn vehicles in the U.S.A., Great Britain, and Europe, between 1993 and 1996 (Powell, 1997; Tranter, 1993). Based on these reports, a feasibility study for a heritage trade training facility at the Cobb+Co Museum was commissioned in 1996 (Coopers & Lybrand Consultants, 1996). Funding for a facility was acquired from the Commonwealth Government as part of the Centenary of Federation celebrations in 2001, but it was insufficient to complete the carriage factory project. Consequently, in a very short timeframe, a new concept for a Stage Two of the Cobb+Co Museum was developed. Rather than attempting to tackle the heritage trade program with inadequate resources, the Cobb+Co Museum decided, instead, to focus on transforming itself into a social enterprise, with an aim to create a lifelong learning resource centre for its community and to develop as a significant part of the region's tourism industry. However, the concept for a heritage trades training facility was not abandoned, and would later be achieved when the community took the lead in lobbying for its Stage Three development – the National Carriage Factory project.

2.13 Conclusion

The Cobb+Co Museum began in Toowoomba in 1987 as a branch of the Queensland Museum. At the time of its creation, it was a product of both the prevailing museum philosophies and the expansionist activities of the heritage industry. In many respects, the establishment of the Cobb+Co Museum was part of the Queensland Museum Board's aim to establish branch museums across the state wherever opportunities arose. However, the museum's development between 1987 and 2001 was more a response to its unique collection and specific location, its personnel and their educational expertise, and its Advisory Committee's commitment to community 'usefulness'. From its inception, when the Queensland Museum's butterfly logo was symbolically removed from the front entry door, the Cobb+Co Museum displayed a parochial outlook, strongly acknowledging its local connections to Toowoomba to the detriment of the Queensland Museum brand.

There was, at the same time, some evidence of the filtering through of international museum traditions to the Queensland Museum and, subsequently, to its branches. These included a strong emphasis on curatorship, collection management, and back-of-house activities, at the initial expense of visitor services. However, the Queensland Museum had also, at times, recognised the importance of an educative role, by supporting an out-reach Loans Service and the secondment of teachers from Education Queensland. Cobb+Co Museum expanded this commitment to education with the appointment of an experienced teacher as its curator/manager, who was determined to use the museum as a facility to engage the educational community through object-based learning that was linked to the Queensland schools' curricula.

Community expectations for the Cobb+Co Museum were also reflective of an emerging heritage industry, with its fledgling hopes for a heritage-led economic revival in regional Queensland, as a result of new tourism products and marketing campaigns. The first appearance of heritage tourism in the Toowoomba region, in the early 1990s, was achieved through the leadership role of the Cobb+Co Museum within the regional tourism association and other local economic development organisations.

In summary, the Cobb+Co Museum was founded as a traditional collection-focused branch of the Queensland Museum after the Board accepted a donation of a significant collection of horse-drawn vehicles, which had been collected by a Toowoomba businessman in the 1950s and 1960s. When a fire threatened the collection in 1981, locals rescued the vehicles and initiated what would become an important and unique link between the collection and the community. However, by 1987, when the Cobb+Co Museum opened, the community's interest had waned. Over the years, this relationship between the museum and the community would be reinvigorated.

Over time, many of the international museological ideas, practices, and heritage tourism directions, which were discussed in this chapter, were invoked. Even during the early days of Stage One, the Cobb+Co Museum had been undergoing an identity transformation, as it moved its focus from a traditional collection-based institution towards a more client and community responsive institution, and became a facility that was dedicated to preserving its community's tangible and intangible heritage. These transformations could only occur because of changing museum and community dynamics. The nature of these changing dynamics and the community engagement strategies employed by the Cobb+Co Museum will be explored further in Chapter Three, which analyses the museum's Stage Two transformation, which commenced in 2001.

Chapter 3

Museums as Social Enterprises Engaging their Community

Cobb+Co Museum, Stage Two, 2001–2010

3.1 Introduction

Within five years of the Cobb+Co Museum opening, planning had commenced to develop a new museum model. This would involve national and international research; partnerships with SQIT, the Toowoomba City Council, and the regional tourist association; and a significantly different approach to community engagement. In 2001, when Stage Two of the Cobb+Co Museum opened, it embraced new museological approaches to its community, rather than continuing as a more traditional collection-focused institution.

During Stage Two, the Cobb+Co Museum developed characteristics of both a community-centred and client-centred museum, nurturing both bonding and bridging functions that would contribute to the community's store of social capital (Landry, 2009). Its commitment to community engagement underpinned its belief that increases in social capital can only occur from interactions between a reasonably broad spread of people that develop trust through positive, rather than negative, experiences. These interactions depend on the availability of 'space, time, opportunities, precedent and the valuing of process' (Cox, 1995, p. 20).

The museum consequently developed mixed-use spaces, which were available for both internal and community use. It concentrated on service delivery for the wellbeing of its community through its involvement in a range of programs, as well as formulating initial plans for the safeguarding of local traditions, such as heritage crafts and trades. In contrast, its role as a client-centred museum focused on audience involvement, rather than content delivery, with the staff seeing themselves primarily as educators interested in promoting free-choice learning among their targeted audiences (Gurian, 2006, p. 48). Collection management and curatorial activities no longer dominated the museum. These activities were now at the service of public programs, which had the important role of 'validating both the unique stories of diverse cultures and the shared story that unites all the members of a society' (American Association of Museums, 2002, p. 28).

The Second Stage development of the Cobb+Co Museum would see the museum identify itself within the new museological framework as an educational institution directed towards making the community aware of its identity, strengthening the community identity, and instilling confidence in the community about its potential for development (Hauenschild, 1998, p. 8).

3.2 Chapter outline

The main focus of this chapter is the analysis of the Second Stage transformation of the Cobb+Co Museum, which involved developing the museum's identity as a regional museum and community resource centre, based on the concept of a not-for-profit social enterprise operating within the wider social economy. This analysis will involve mapping the organisational features and activities undertaken by the Cobb+Co Museum onto this social enterprise model.

Underlying the new museology that was embraced by the Cobb+Co Museum was the belief – that was consistently reiterated by the Advisory Committee – that the museum needed to derive its direction and sense of worth from its community or client stakeholders, rather than from the collection it preserves (Dees, et al., 2001; Dees, Emerson, & Economy, 2002; Gillespie, Meehan, Nickson, & Winchester, 2002). Robert Janes summarised these sentiments:

> Museums exist in, of, by and for society and are obligated to continually ponder their work in an effort to be worthwhile and make a difference (Janes, 2007a, p. 234).

As part of this process, a three-tier model of stakeholder involvement was identified. The museum needed to project a multifaceted profile to its audiences by becoming a 'hybrid place, combining recreation and learning' (Neil Kotler, 2001, p. 423). The Stage Two Cobb+Co Museum developed multi-personalities, as a:

- Recreation centre;
- Place to learn;
- Research laboratory;
- Craftsperson's Mecca;
- Tourist attraction;
- Cultural industry incubator; and
- Community hub – 'a great good place' (Oldenburg, 1997).

This meant changing staff from being object-focused instructors to client-centred 'includers', working in a social enterprise environment (Gurian, 2006, p. pxi).

There is a focus on understanding how cultural institutions, such as museums, can play leadership roles within community development agendas, with reference to the specific applications developed by the Cobb+Co Museum in response to its own community. These all contributed to making the Stage Two Cobb+Co Museum a community resource centre dedicated to supporting lifelong learning opportunities for community members, particularly for those groups not traditionally supported by museums. These groups included the very young, teenagers, older senior citizens, and Indigenous members of the community. The special role of community volunteers will also be assessed within this chapter.

The community engagement models developed during Stage Two will be scrutinised in this chapter, and their applicability to other cultural organisations and communities will be explored. The success of these strategies was ultimately responsible for the Stage Three transformation of the Cobb+Co Museum, which culminated in the completion of the National Carriage Factory project in 2010.

3.3 Formation of Cobb+Co Museum, Stage Two

Within five years of opening, the Cobb+Co Museum was seeking new directions for its future development in conjunction with its community. In the 1992 to 1993 Cobb+Co Museum Annual Report, it was recognised that the museum:

> ...has now reached a watershed in its development. It has outgrown its present site and there are severe pressures on staff facilities including research and library space, storage and workshop areas, and especially adequate temporary display space (Annual Report 1992-3 Cobb+Co Museum, 1988-2009, p. 10).

The crux of any expansion project by the Cobb+Co Museum would be the availability of land. The original Toowoomba Showground site was acquired by the Queensland Government in 1987 for the Toowoomba TAFE College, except for one former pavilion and a small amount of surrounding land, which was excised from the original block for the Cobb+Co Museum. For the museum to expand on this site would require TAFE to donate land to the Board of the Queensland Museum.[54] Because the land was designated for educational purposes, for any further Cobb+Co Museum development to occur on that site, a strong argument had to be developed around the vocational learning outcomes associated with the heritage trades. After prolonged negotiations, 'a negotiated understanding with SQIT over land use' was achieved in 1998[55], which permitted the expansion of the museum (Annual Report 1997-8 Cobb+Co Museum, 1988-2009, p. 2).

After undertaking extensive national and international research[56], a feasibility study for a heritage trade training facility at the Cobb+Co Museum was commissioned in 1996. Funding for this study was acquired through a complicated process, which indicates the way the Cobb+Co Museum was becoming integrated into the region's economic development planning processes. A grant for fifty thousand dollars was awarded to the Toowoomba Employment and Training Network (TRETN) from the Federal Government's Office of Labour Market Adjustment (OLMA) to undertake a market assessment and feasibility study of the proposed Cobb+Co Museum and SQIT joint venture – the Carriage Building Factory and Heritage Trade Training Facility. This major study was project-managed by the author, as Director of the Cobb+Co Museum (Coopers & Lybrand Consultants, 1996).[57]

As a result of the outcomes of this feasibility study, a Value Management Project for the expansion of the Cobb+Co Museum was undertaken by the Department of Works' Project Services section on behalf of the Queensland Museum. Their final report 'supported by an extensive group of local and regional community, business and government organisations' formed

---

54. Original negotiations with the Toowoomba College of TAFE over the land use were disrupted when local TAFE colleges across Southern Inland Queensland were amalgamated into the regional Southern Queensland Institute of TAFE (SQIT).

55. The land transfer agreement was signed in 2000 – by the then Minister for Employment, Training, and the Arts, the Honourable Paul Braddy – however, the transfer was not finalised until 2009, even though the Stage Two Cobb+Co Museum opened in 2001.

56. In 1993, the author undertook a Churchill Fellowship to the U.S.A., which entailed: working at Colonial Williamsburg, the Museums of Stony Brook on Long Island, The National Museum of American History at the Smithsonian, and Concord Historical Society Museum in New Hampshire; visits to old Sturbridge Farm, Vermont Museum, Wells Fargo Museum in San Francisco, and the Gene Autry Museum in Los Angeles; and attending the American Carriage Championship in Santa Ynez, California.
The Cobb+Co Museum's Assistant Curator won the Queensland Museum Stan Colliver Scholarship in 1996. He spent nine weeks travelling through Europe, the United Kingdom, and Canada visiting museums, workshops, and factories associated with horse-drawn vehicles and trade colleges in order to research production, conservation, preservation, and display techniques for horse-drawn vehicles and heritage trades.

57. The author was also a member of TRETN and was appointed Director of the Cobb+Co Museum in 1995.

the basis of the subsequent funding applications to the state and commonwealth governments (Annual Report 1997-8 Cobb+Co Museum, 1988-2009, p. 2).

The Cobb+Co Museum was successful in acquiring funding from the Commonwealth Government as part of the Queensland Heritage Trails Network (QHTN) – a major state-wide project to mark the Centenary of Federation of the Commonwealth of Australia, in 2001. This hundred million dollar investment into the future of regional Queensland was designed to enable communities 'to work with their heritage places, collections and stories to stimulate economic activity and increase employment in regional and rural areas of the State' (Queensland Government, 1999). QHTN, modelled on the traditional 1980s heritage-led regional revitalisation schemes, attempted to converge place-marketing and its associated heritage industry programs with local economic development, through increased tourism activity in regional Queensland. It could be argued that it represented 'a sort of first-generation attempt to manipulate symbolic asset (in this case heritage sites) in pursuit of local economic growth' (Allen J. Scott, 2004, p. 464).

Cobb+Co Museum, as one of the designated QHTN projects, was under the assumption that it was being funded to fully develop the Carriage Building Factory and Heritage Trade Training Facilities, as per the original application that included the architect's detailed drawings. However, this was not to be the case. Only two million dollars – a third of the funding requested – was allocated to the Cobb+Co Museum. Because this was insufficient funding to complete the Carriage Factory project, an alternative approach had to be formulated in a very short timeframe.

The new concept for Stage Two of the Cobb+Co Museum would see the museum transform into a social enterprise and learning resource centre for its community. The original concept for a unique heritage trade training facility would, eventually, be achieved in 2010, following a community-led initiative. The museum's strategy that underpinned the achievement of the National Carriage Factory project will be examined at the end of this chapter.

3.4 Social enterprises model

In 2001, Cobb+Co Museum Stage Two opened with a philosophy that museums are more-than-profit organisations with a social objective to make a difference in society and in the life of individuals by creating social change through heritage values while blending social and commercial methodologies to achieve their outcomes (Dees, et al., 2001, p. 9; Drucker, 1990, p. 45). As such, museums can be classed as social enterprises, because they can mobilise and reproduce social capital (Laville & Nyssens, p. 637).

The term 'social enterprise' has many definitions and interpretations. The term can be 'highly inclusive, embracing all organisations and their activities that are not defined as either public or private'. Alternatively, it can adopt a more restrictive classification that takes into account the 'appropriateness of an organisation's social mission, governance structures and creation and distribution of profit (or surplus)' (D. Jones & Keogh, 2006, p. 14). The Cobb+Co Museum's adherence to principles of social entrepreneurship meant that it was focused on creating social capital through enriching and enlivening the cultural, social, and intellectual life of all Queenslanders (Queensland Museum, 2005).

The museum believed that through the networks, norms, trusts, and shared values that make up social capital, communities are linked together, as well as being 'instrumental in facilitating an understanding of the interconnectedness of society and the interests within it' (Janes, 2009, p. 102). Social entrepreneurs have been described as acting as the change agents for society – seizing opportunities that others miss, improving systems, investing new approaches, developing new solutions to social problems, and implementing these new solutions on a large scale to change society for the better (Ashoka, 2006). The 'bottom line' of the not-for-profit organisation is its positive social outcomes, impacts, and results (Sheppard, 2000, p. 67).

As a more-than–profit organisation, the museum pursues social outcomes, or public good, through forging high levels of community trust alongside an emphasis on more business orientated practices (Dees, et al., 2001, 2002; Drucker, 1990; Laville & Nyssens; Weisbrod, 2000). This business objective is often difficult to achieve because non-profit firms, such as museums, have very high fixed costs, particularly wages, relative to their variable costs. They also tend to produce at 'a lower price and higher output level than for-profit firms that are monopolies' (Throsby and Withers quoted in, Netzer, 2003, p. 333).

However, any museum seeking to be recognised as a social enterprise needs to operate as:

> ...a business with primarily social objectives whose surpluses are principally reinvested for that purpose in the business or the community, rather than being driven by the need to maximise profit for share holders... Social enterprises create new goods and services and develop opportunities for markets where mainstream business cannot or will not go (D. Jones & Keogh, 2006, p. 11).

Although viewing itself as a social enterprise institution, the Cobb+Co Museum did not match any of the seventeen different types of social enterprises outlined in Smallbone's *Researching Social Enterprise* Report (Dees, et al., 2001, pp. 4-9; Smallbone, Evans, Ekanem, & Butters, 2001, pp. 13-17). As a campus of the Queensland Museum, with a central budget and need to adhere to state public service administrative policies, practices, and procedures, it would be difficult to align Cobb+Co Museum with more traditional social enterprises. In addition, the museum had a number of core corporate facilities, such as conservation, exhibition design, library, and photography services, that could only be accessed from the Queensland Museum's headquarters in Brisbane, which could potentially make it extremely difficult for the Cobb+Co Museum to respond to its local community's needs. However, despite these restrictions on its independence, the Cobb+Co Museum maintained its local autonomy, particularly in its public programming, which was designed to meet the needs of its primary stakeholders – the Toowoomba community. In doing this, the museum exemplified the principle that Grossman and Rangan described theoretically as 'the greater the degree of program customization, the greater the force for autonomy' (2001, p. 330).

To some extent, this was not surprising, given the museum's commitment to local face-to-face customised delivery, local fund raising, the introduction of a local volunteer program, and strong local leadership delivered through its Advisory Committee – a focus that, according to David Fleming, is a crucial element in the creation of the 'Museum of Social Enterprise model' (Fleming, 2006, p. 3).

3.4.1 Cobb+Co Museum – mission-driven

By 2001, the Cobb+Co Museum had realised that it had to reinvent itself as a non-profit organisation that serviced its community in order to prosper (G. Anderson, 2000, p. v). However, before it could be of real civic use, the Cobb+Co Museum had to rebrand itself to help identify the museum as being part 'of' the local culture, as well as being 'about' it (Gurian quoted in, Linett, 2006).

The Cobb+Co Museum preferred to adopt the descriptor 'more-than-profit', rather than 'not-for-profit' or 'non-profit,' in relation to its Stage Two iteration, as it is a more positive term that 'invites exploration of the organisation's core values, mission and outcomes which put people first' (D. Jones & Keogh, 2006, pp. 19-20).

A number of key characteristics of social enterprises were replicated within the Cobb+Co Museum's Stage Two operations, including its:

- Not-for-profit status;
- Desire to meet social objectives through engaging in economic activities;
- Use of voluntary labour;
- Financial situation that is not wholly dependent on the state, but has to generate funding from a variety of sources, including one-off grants and commercial activities;
- Governance structure that it is not owned by individuals – the managers of the organisation do not 'own' the enterprise or have an economic interest that can be sold to other firms or individuals; and
- Use of any surplus of revenue over expenditure, which cannot be appropriated by the managers of the organisation, but must be reinvested in ways that further the stated purposes of the organisation (Netzer, 2003, p. 331).

To achieve its goal of making a difference in its community, Cobb+Co Museum Stage Two developed two principal strategies for civic engagement: program-based relationships and audience development (H. Hirzy quoted in, American Association of Museums, 2002, p. 15). It also formulated a number of core tenets around establishing the 'relationships, networks and local partnerships' that unpinned its mission (Jeannotte, 2005, p. 125). These included the belief that the museum is:

- Fundamentally educational in purpose, but still offers unique, compelling, and cross-generational forms of entertainment and social engagement;
- A place for ideas and dialogue that uses its collections to inspire people, develop identity, and safeguard memories;
- A democratic institution that believes in the concept of social justice – the museum is funded by the whole of the public and, in return, it strives to provide an excellent service to the whole of the public; and
- Empowered to help promote good and active citizenship, and to act as an agent of social and cultural change.[58]

This belief in the capacity of the Cobb+Co Museum to assume a crucial support role within its community reflected many of the ideas espoused by proponents of a new museology. These ideas banished any thoughts of isolating the museum from its community in any self-sufficient manner. Rather, the Cobb+Co Museum wanted 'to open itself outwardly to its community, in order to be of service to society' (Hauenschild, 1998, p. 9). The museum defined for itself a more sustainable role in its community by undertaking more practical, socially responsible work that went far beyond education and entertainment (Janes, 2007b, p. 143). However, it was also aware that, as a social enterprise, it was not its role to solve social inequality issues on its own, but to work alongside many other institutions and individual agents:

> [Museums] must consider their impact on society and seek to shape that impact through practice that is based on contemporary values and a commitment to social equality (Sandell, 2002, p. 110).

An example of Cobb+Co Museum's commitment to bettering its community is the role the museum played when it supported the Toowoomba and Region Employment and Training Network (the Director was the Vice Chair) in its application for extensive job creation funding for the region. As part of the funding, Cobb+Co Museum delivered a heritage collection accessioning project that provided training and employment for twelve long-

58. These values were not generally articulated in print in 2001, but they nevertheless permeated the thinking of the Director and Advisory Committee members as they planned and implemented the Stage Two transformation of the Cobb+Co Museum. These core values are now seen replicated in many larger museums' strategic planning documents, such as at the National Museum Liverpool, as well as underpinning many ecomuseum developments.

term job seekers, while developing a comprehensive accessioning tool and training manual to facilitate the on-going documentation of community museum collections across Queensland.

Since the economic downturn in the 1980s, there have been increasing demands from public service management for greater accountability of public funds, as governments at all levels direct their attention to policies and practices delivering 'economies, efficiencies and effectiveness' (C. Scott, 2007a, pp. 33-41). This frequently causes difficulties for a social enterprise operating within the social economy, such as a museum, because its performance needs to be realistically assessed against its mission, not its financial returns (Collins, 2005, p. 5).

Social enterprises, particularly those in the cultural domain, have also been subjected to other changes in government policies. These have included a concerted effort by many central governments to distance themselves from the delivery of various public services, including the transfer of institutions, such as national museums, to independent boards outside direct government control. At the same time, cultural institutions are having their discretionary government funding reduced while being subjected to increasing demands for more and more public outcomes (Boylan, 2006, p. 9).

This operating environment has necessitated major changes in the business practices of cultural institutions, including significant engagement in commercial activities in order to increase earned income, and major fundraising activities (G. Anderson, 2004; Falk & Sheppard, 2006; Neil Kotler & Kotler, 2000). However, there were many in the wider museum fraternity who questioned this change in focus:

> Are museums compromising their educational purposes, losing their primacy as centres of research and learning by becoming emporia – 'businesses' almost as well-known for their gift shops and restaurants as for their galleries and special exhibits (Skramstad, 1999, p. 3)?

While governments emphasised the need to reform internal practices and business operations, social enterprises simultaneously needed to ensure that they had not lost sight of their mission to deliver social outcomes. Richard Gillespie and his partners stress that:

> Government agencies and non-profit organisations are increasingly being asked to assess their value not just in terms of programs, but rather in terms of social outcomes. In this social enterprise model, the emphasis will be on the effectiveness of the organisation in delivering measurable social outcomes (Gillespie, et al., 2002, p. 2).

Emphasising social outcomes and impacts begs the question – 'for whom?' This, in turn, puts pressure on social enterprises to identify and address stakeholders' needs.

3.4.2 Realisation of stakeholders

The realisation of the different stakeholders to whom the Cobb+Co Museum was accountable represented a major change in the museum's operational environment after 2001. Up to that stage, the museum had not been consciously accountable to any external clients; it felt solely answerable to the Board of the Queensland Museum.

The identification of social enterprise stakeholders is not a simple task because there are multiple constituencies that these organisations must account to for their performance. The Cobb+Co Museum identified and explored a three-tier model of stakeholder interests. The primary stakeholders or customers are clearly recognised as the first voices in the museum. They are the local residents who are directly associated with the museum, such as staff; committee members; and volunteers; as well as local community members, both users and non-users of museum services. By 2001, there were still too many local residents who were uninterested in the Cobb+Co Museum, and did not visit the museum – not necessarily because they were against visiting museums, in general, but because they had no relationship with the Cobb+Co Museum (Gurt & Torres, 2007, p. 522). A focus of Stage Two was to identify the community as the museum's primary stakeholders and to attempt to address their specific needs in partnership with other community organisations. The museum needed to develop its core ideology to correlate with the desires of its community (Falk & Sheppard, 2006, p. 166).

The secondary stakeholder group that was identified included businesses and local and state governments that might benefit or be affected by the museum's operations. Partnerships with these secondary stakeholders would be new for the Cobb+Co Museum during its Stage Two development, but would also prove to be crucial for any further development.

The tertiary stakeholders were the tourists or non-local visitors who might visit or consume Cobb+Co Museum products or services (Whiting & Outspan Group, 1999). In planning heritage tourism facilities, such as QHTN, tourists are usually the only stakeholders considered. This inevitably results in the facilities failing to attract permanent support from the primary and secondary stakeholder groups – groups that can offer substantially more support.

When the Cobb+Co Museum opened in 1987, there was no expectation that the museum would engage with its community in any particular way, except for the underlying assumption that community members would visit the facility. Concern about museums and their intersections with communities is only a recent phenomenon, which often gets 'bogged down' in terminology, because 'community' is a particularly contested concept.

Communities are rarely homogeneous or exclusive, because a person can belong to a number of different communities, depending on how the concept is defined (Guetzhow, 2002, p. 14).

With regard to the Cobb+Co Museum, its community was identified as Toowoomba residents and those living within the Toowoomba Regional Council area. While acknowledging the diversity within the Cobb+Co Museum's community, it is interesting to note that the Toowoomba Aboriginal community also identifies with the Cobb+Co Museum's collection, despite the fact that the vehicles were originally interpreted only as examples of European technology. Today, the museum includes stories of Aboriginal ownership of the Cobb & Co Coach No. 100 and the Four-in-Hand Buggy, known as the 'Jimbour Coach'.[59]

The museum's focus on the community as its primary stakeholders was instigated as a result of a specific project that the museum undertook in 1998. A historic wooden horse from Toowoomba, known as *Harkaway*, was 'threatened' by possible overseas sale.[60] In an attempt to raise money to purchase the horse, the museum appealed to the public through the local media. During 1998 and 1999, more than three hundred and fifty local residents and businesses contributed to the 'Save *Harkaway* Fund'. Television, newspapers, and radio responded enthusiastically to the museum's plea for support, and the media continued to report on the project after the horse was acquired and was undergoing conservation treatment in Brisbane (Year in Review 1998-99, Cobb+Co Museum, 1988-2009, pp. 4,6).

---

59. Without realising their connection to the vehicle collection, local Aboriginal elders approached the Cobb+Co Museum in 2000 to ask for space for a language centre in the expanded museum. This resulted in the development of the Binangar Centre and its ongoing learning programs, exhibitions, and activities. An Aboriginal Language Access Officer was appointed in early 2001 (Year in Review 2000-2001, Cobb+Co Museum, 1988-2009, p. 4).

60. *Harkaway* had stood outside the local coachbuilder's, Col Ferguson's, factory in Russell Street, Toowoomba, for many decades prior to Ferguson's death in the early 1970s. Following this, the horse had been sold and removed from Toowoomba. The current owners of the horse offered it for sale to the Cobb+Co Museum in 1998.

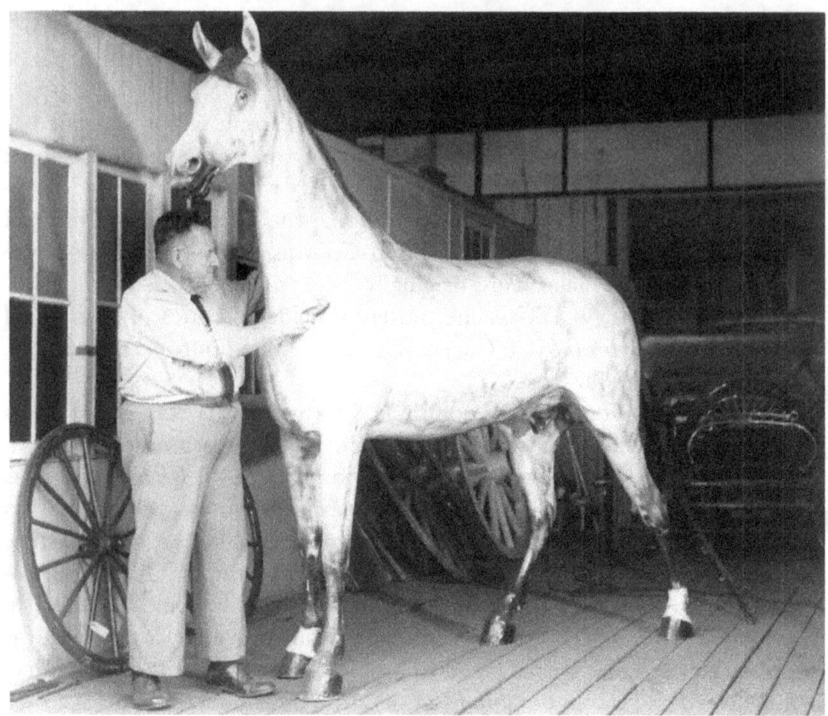

Toowoomba coachbuilder Col Ferguson with his prized wooden horse *Harkaway* @1960

This was the first time the museum had made a direct appeal to its community and engaged them in a heritage project as primary customers. This progress highlighted what Bella Dicks describes as the need for heritage to be marketed to local residents (A. Dicks, 2003, p. 34). Laurajane Smith's analysis of heritage as a relational idea was also exemplified in the *Harkaway* project. This horse had played a major role in local community celebrations for over forty years. It was often 'ridden' by young children who accompanied their parents each week to the building society located adjacent to Ferguson's Coachworks. The *Harkaway* project awakened many individual and community memories – stories that were recorded by the museum. Heritage was identified by the Cobb+Co Museum as a significant community cultural process:

> ...it is about how individuals and groups actively take up positions in relation to sites, buildings, events, histories. It becomes a 'way of knowing and seeing'. In engaging with heritage, people are constructing a sense of their own identities (L. Smith, 2006, pp. 52-53)

The *Harkaway* project proved to be of catalytic importance in transforming the Cobb+Co Museum into a new model of a community resource centre, because this project showed how to successfully engage the community as the primary customers in the heritage process. This exercise also demonstrated the chasm then existing between the Queensland Museum's overall prevailing priorities for academic historical research and its general lack of interest in recording community heritage.

3.5 History, heritage, and community identity

The term 'heritage' is, itself, a contested concept that has only recently emerged in a more positive light after years of being grounded in heritage debates occurring in academic circles, particularly in the United Kingdom. These debates resulted from disquiet about the widespread development of an industry based on heritage products. The protaganists focused on the apparent dichotomy between formal history in the academic and museum worlds, and heritage as understood in a community sense. The proliferation of heritage sites, products, and services, dating from the 1980s, led one historian to declare:

> ...once it is appreciated how many things there are to which the word 'heritage' is attached, from national institutions to garage doors, the word becomes absurd (Hewison, 1987, p. 11).

Despite some obvious economic benefits created by the new heritage developments, there has been severe criticism that the heritage industry's products were based on nostalgia and selling an experience of the past that was too sanitised, sentimental, uncritical, and patronisingly appealing to a mass audience, rather than reflecting reality (Davison, 1991; A. Dicks, 2003; Hewison, 1987; Lowenthal, 1985; Merriman, 1991; Samuel, 1994; Wright, 1985)

To some critics, the heritage industry is centred on the exploitation and distortion of the past for commercial ends and is a result of the failure of modern society to face the future after the decline of industrialisation.

The essence of the debate seemed to be the fact that heritage has been applied in two very different ways with two very different aims. One aim was positive, with a focus on community care and concern for the culture and knowledge that will be passed on to future generations 'to serve people's need for a sense of identity and belonging' (Merriman, 1991, p. 8). The other was a negative commercially-driven aim, linked to the term 'heritage industry', which had become synonymous with the manipulation (or even invention) and exploitation of the past for commercial ends (p. 8).

Historians continued to worry about the history displayed and interpreted in museums being converted or subverted into a less positive heritage fixation. According to Lowenthal, a wide chasm separated the two concepts – one desirable, one not so positive:

> History is all about truth, the study of the past in its own terms and for its own sake. It aspires to be objective, precise, accurate, universal and detached....Its collective nature set it apart from memory (Lowenthal, 1985, p. 213).

> [In contrast] heritage falsifies the True Past. It is unabashedly partisan, shallow, chauvinist and mendacious. It bends and re-shapes the past to a present purpose. It sentimentalises, fabricates and distorts (Lowenthal, 1996, p. 104).

The debates drove 'a cleavage between professionals' and the public's perceptions' of the past. Chasms were created between 'majority and minority, elite and folk, rulers and ruled, trained and amateur' over how to 'identify, safeguard and interpret the past' (Gathercole & Lowenthal, 1990, p. 303). The division and confusion between history and heritage for the layperson often resulted from the dominance of written primary source documentation in academic circles, in which the value of oral evidence and personal memory was not recognised.[61] This perpetuated the divide between objective history and subjective heritage. Ironically, the upsurge of public interest in heritage coincided with a rapid decline in the study and teaching of history, both in schools and universities.[62] Although this situation was of great concern to the professional historian, it was occurring at the same time that general public interest in local and family history was rapidly increasing. In fact, it could be argued that:

> ...if history was thought of as an activity rather than a profession, then the number of practitioners would be legionary (Samuel, 1994, p. 17).

Although heritage debates are currently less prevalent, there still seems to be an ever-growing body of scholarly work attempting to give meaning to the terms 'history'; 'heritage', including the subsets 'national heritage' and 'cultural heritage'; 'the past', including 'the National Past'; 'memory', singular and plural and the use of 'collective memory'; 'myths'; and 'identity'. In contrast to the history domain frequented by academics and museum curators, individuals and communities regularly use the terms 'history', 'heritage', and 'the past', as transposable concepts. For them, the dissection is more along the lines of a personal sense of the past – nostalgia created by memories, family histories, personal objects, and photographs – and an impersonal sense of the past, which is often reinforced by state and national museums' traditional thematic displays (Crook quoted in Merriman, 1991, p. 5). Today, heritage has a much more positive image as playing a central role in personal and community identity-making:

---

61. During the 1950s to 1970s there were, of course, some academics in both the U.S.A. and Great Britain who saw the value in oral history (Kavanagh, 2000, p. 54).

62. Majors in history in U.S.A. universities declined during the 1960s and 1970s from ten percent to barely two percent of university graduates (Lowenthal, 1985, p. 377). In Queensland, history, as a stand-alone subject, was not taught in primary schools for over thirty years. However, in 2012 with the introduction of a National Curriculum in Australia, history will be one of the four compulsory curricula areas for all students from prep to grade ten.

> Heritage is a cultural and social process; it is the experiences that may happen at sites or during the acting out of certain events; it is a process of remembering and memory making – of mediating cultural and social change, of negotiating and creating and recreating values, meanings, understandings and identity. Above all, heritage is an active, vibrant cultural process of creating bonds through shared experiences and acts of creation (L. Smith, 2006, p. 307).

Through recognising the importance of personal stories in the *Harkaway* project, the Cobb+Co Museum gradually blended history and heritage together. It realised that it was the community that was the museum's primary stakeholder and learned that heritage 'is not a matter for the experts but for the people.... [it is] about a people's sense of belonging' (Davison, 1998, p. 8).

People investigating their family histories were responsible for helping to transform 'genealogy from an elite pursuit into a popular preoccupation' – a pursuit that was boosted by advances in affordable technology (Lowenthal, 1985, p. 367). Ordinary people could now 'voice' their own stories and bypass professional historians and curators. A 'dynamic, potent and alternative process of social memorising' was created, which contested 'the position of formal history in providing the pre-eminent narrative of human society' (Murphy, 2005, p. 73).

This upsurge of public interest in local and personal heritage was reflected by the growth of the conservation movement[63] and other large-scale 'plebeian' interest groups associated with heritage, including steam engines – from stationary engines to trains, from motorised farm machinery to early motor vehicles, and even including windmills (Urry, 1990, p. 213; Wright, 1982, p. 122).[64] Individuals and communities discovered heritage as an industry and personal leisure occupation and began perceiving museums as tangible expressions of community concern for the preservation of its heritage and identity (see Section 2.10 for an analysis of the Community Museum Movement in Queensland).

63. By the end of the 1980s, the National Trust – a grassroots action group – was the largest mass organisation in Britain, with 1.5 million members (Urry, 1990, p. 213).

64. The site shared by the Cobb+Co Museum and SQIT has a public art installation of historic windmills that attracts enormous interest from residents, visitors, and windmill 'fanatics' from all over the country.

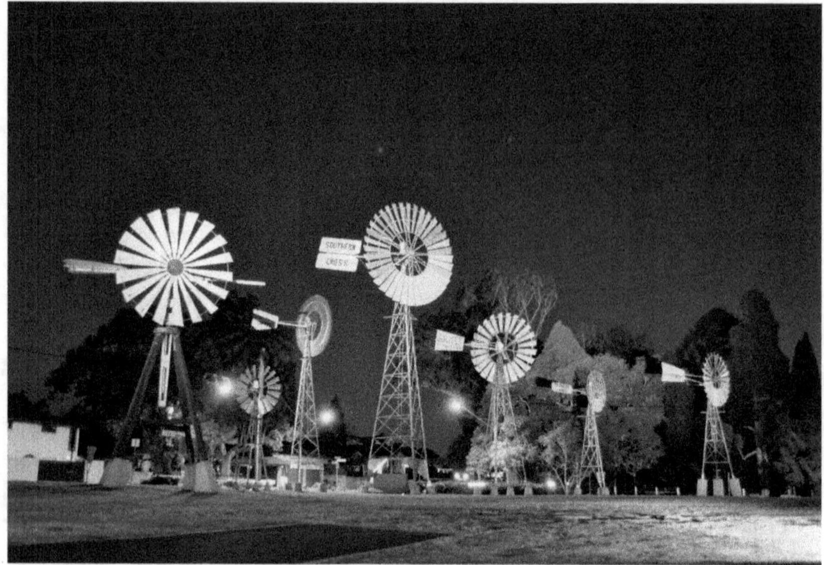

Public art installation *Windmills on Show* adjacent to the Cobb+Co Museum 2010

New museology also embraced the social history movement, gradually penetrating traditional state and national museums as a few innovative curators started to transform the way in which collections were interpreted. In 2010, David Fleming, the Director of National Museums Liverpool, reflected that:

> The growth of the discipline of social history in museums has been the single most important factor in the democratisation of museums and the opening up of access and social inclusion policies (Steel, 2010, p. 25).

However, this movement to voice the 'hidden heritage' of the working classes in museum exhibitions – rather than only displaying the traditional histories of the ruling class – initially made little impression on the Queensland Museum as a whole. The Queensland Museum's philosophy only began to change when the Cobb+Co Museum began gradually applying a social history perspective to what was previously considered a technological collection of horse-drawn vehicles.

This new social history dimension, which provided a small voice to minority groups and other traditionally disenfranchised sectors, necessitated a whole new collaborative approach between museum professionals and communities. Successful examples of these collaborations began to emerge during this period, as did new models of museums, including ecomuseums and integral museums (see Section 2.7.1 for an analysis of eco and integral museums).

3.5.1 Heritage stimulating cultural changes

The ability of heritage to stimulate significant cultural and social change in the community was evidenced during the early days of the Stage Two transformation of the Cobb+Co Museum. The first temporary exhibition held in the new facility was *Federation: Queensland's Story*, which opened on Australia Day – 26 January 2001.[65] This exhibition told distinctive Queensland stories about the process that led to the Federation of the Australian states, and focused particularly on William Henry Groom. Groom was Toowoomba's first Mayor, in 1860. He was a long serving member of the Queensland Parliament and the only former convict ever elected to the Commonwealth Parliament. Despite playing a crucial role in the development of the local and regional community, by 2001, William Henry Groom's story had been 'lost to his community'. The museum felt that Groom – a teenage convict transported to New South Wales, who 'made good' through his many occupations and public services – could become an important role model for local teenagers, particularly those who encountered adversity in their early years. A lifelike model of Groom was produced by the Queensland Museum's preparatory section to literally bring 'him to life'.[66]

65. The temporary exhibition space, known as the Groom Gallery, was completed well ahead of the remainder of the building, which was not officially opened until 5 October 2001.

66. William Henry Groom was responsible for establishing many of the iconic features of Toowoomba, such as Queens Park, Picnic Point, the *Chronicle* newspaper, the first Building Society (now *Heritage Building Society*), and the Royal Agricultural Society and Show Grounds. He supported small farmers, or 'selectors', and townsfolk against the entrenched interests of the 'squatters' and large pastoralists. His story and experiences were told to one hundred and ten separate class groups who visited the museum's exhibition in the first six months of 2001 (Year in Review 2000-1 Cobb+Co Museum, 1988-2009, pp. 2-3).

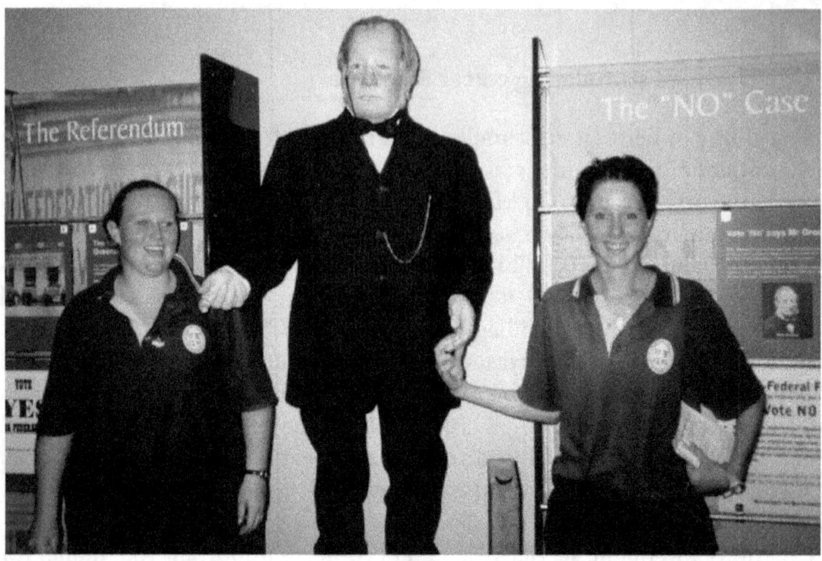

William Henry Groom created for the Federation exhibition 2001

Today, William Henry Groom has been embraced by the Toowoomba community as its most significant historical figure. The renovated City Hall has a William Henry Groom Room reserved for community use and the local council has introduced the William Henry Groom Scholarship, which is awarded each Australia Day to a young resident engaged in community activities. All school students in the region now have the opportunity to learn about William Henry Groom, because his story continues to be told in the Cobb+Co Museum and is incorporated in many museum learning resources, as well as those developed by the Toowoomba Library (Tranter & Douglas, 1997, pp. 20, unit 21 activity at the Toowoomba Historical Society).[67]

The Groom story reflected the Cobb+Co Museum's emerging realisation that it could play a significant role within its community by becoming an effective 'institution of memory', responsible for caring for the memories of the past and making them available for present and future use (Gurian, 2006, pp. 2, 89).

The community-wide effectiveness of this approach was exemplified in 2005, when the Toowoomba City Council undertook a program of extensive community consultation to develop the 'Our Toowoomba towards 2050

67. In 2004, to commemorate the Centenary of Toowoomba as a city, Cobb+Co Museum developed the exhibition – *Toowoomba: from Swamp to Garden City* – and a year-long series of public programs and changing mini displays that were developed by primary and secondary school groups, including a pre-school group of three and four year olds. William Henry Groom, as the City's first Mayor, was again the focus for this celebration (Year in Review 2003-4 Cobb+Co Museum, 1988-2009, p. 2).

Community Plan'. In answer to queries about 'what the community values', the majority of residents identified the city's heritage and history as highly valued attributes (Toowoomba City Council, 2008, p. 16). This was a remarkable change in community attitude from the prevailing negative view in 1987, which was discussed in Section 2.12.1 above. The community's new appreciation of its heritage values would motivate strong individual and collective support for the National Carriage Factory project when initiated in 2006.

3.6 Cobb+Co Stage Two – safeguarding community heritage

During the period 1987 to 2001, the Cobb+Co Museum had been heavily involved in a range of community economic, social, and cultural organisations, as described in the previous chapter. To quote Elaine Heumann Guian:

> Museums are social-service providers...because they are spaces belonging to the citizenry at large, expounding on ideas that inform and stir the population to contemplate and occasionally to act (Gurian, 1999, p. 18).

Gradually, the museum recognised that its concerns and objectives were identical to those of the people it served and that it had the ability to positively influence its regional community. Robert Archibald, from the Missouri Historical Society, describes this as becoming a community activist:

> Those of us who work in cultural institutions must be involved in communities so that we can translate issues and concerns into our internal agendas. But in addition, we must be involved beyond our walls in meaningful ways if we are to bring anything important to the civic table. We must accept our responsibilities as citizens with special expertise if our institutions are to be relevant to our communities, however we define those communities. In one sense we must become a part of our audience, more community-minded in defining our ends, [and] much more capable of evaluating the efficacy of our efforts (Archibald, 2004, p. 203).

Using a similar premise to that espoused by Archibald, the Second Stage transformation of the Cobb+Co Museum demonstrated the museum's commitment to be useful to its community. This underlying belief embodied the concept that the value of museums 'is in direct proportion to the service they render the emotional and intellectual life of the people' (Kinsey, 2002, p. 1 quotes the American Association of Museums). In addition, when the Cobb+Co Museum transformed into a community resource centre, it understood that the museum, itself, is important as a place in which visitors can 'actively engaged with its social and physical context to make personal meaning' – a function that is as critically important as the resources and services within the museum (Falk, 2006, p. 162; Fulton & Jackson, 1999, p. 46).

In particular, the Cobb+Co Museum set out to 'deconstruct many of the existing boundaries' that had isolated museums from their community (W. R. West, 2000, p. 107). It encouraged the community's gradual appreciation of its own heritage and sense of identity by: providing formal and informal learning programs targeted to school curricula, providing opportunities for intergenerational learning, initiating and trialling heritage trade training programs, establishing models for community museums and cultural heritage collecting organisations, and becoming a distinctive place-marker and community hub.

Distinctive features for Stage Two, which opened on 5 October 2001, were the creation of a community 'third place' in which visitors would be welcomed with country hospitality in the new *Cobbs* Coffee Shop. Also significant would be the partnership with Toowoomba City Council that enabled free access for local residents to the museum, the decision to use the museum's exhibitions and public programs to strengthen community identity through exposure to its heritage, and the provision of learning opportunities for everyone from the very young to the city's most senior citizens.

3.6.1 Creating a community hub

The symbolic heart of Cobb+Co Museum Stage Two was not a major new exhibition, but the opening of *Cobbs* Coffee Shop as a central feature of the museum, with a separate entry for locals to use. This informal community meeting place overlooked the children's innovative activity space, the *Coach Stop*, as well as the National Carriage Collection Exhibition. Usually, at this time, museum coffee shops were relegated to the back of the facility as something of an afterthought. These facilities were generally leased out to commercial operators. Their functions were to provide refreshments for visitors in the hope that the visitors might then spend more time looking at the displays and, most importantly, to generate revenue through the negotiated lease arrangements. In fact, the inclusion of a coffee shop in the museum's Stage Two development was not permitted by the QHTN initially, and the original plans 'hid' the coffee shop kitchen within a Visitor Service Centre hybrid space. Once Cobb+Co Stage Two opened and its coffee shop had established a reputation as 'a good community place', coffee shops were then encouraged in other QHTN facilities.

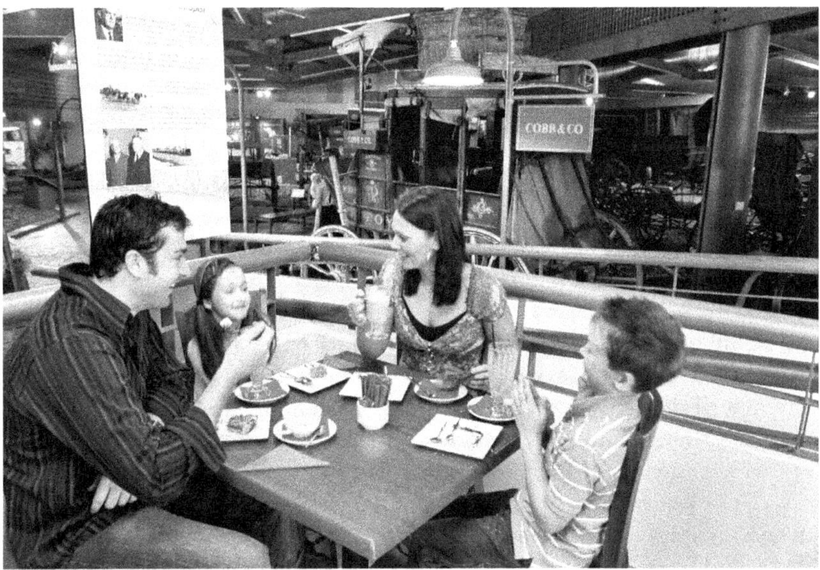

Cobbs Coffee Shop overlooking the vehicle gallery 2001

More recent research indicates that an ideal shop mission should be 'to enhance the visitor experience by making an integrated experiential feature of the shops as an added cultural/artistic activity' (McIntyre, 2010, pp. 183,185,190-181):

> The provision, positioning and marketing of a good museum shop, along with a cafe, child activity spaces and changing exhibitions and events (assumed to have linked shop content) were amongst the most mentioned responses for the enhancement of the visit experience and encouraging re-visits (p. 191).

Without the benefit of this research, the Cobb+Co Museum, nevertheless, adopted a very similar approach. The museum ran both its coffee and retail shops in-house, and employed and trained its own staff as its core front line operators. The atmosphere of country hospitality and the culinary quality of the coffee shop were closely linked to the museum's collection, and the retail shop offered 'items which help the visitor to retain the memory of the visit, and to communicate the event to others' (Hutter, 1998, p. 101).

Cobbs Coffee Shop was developed as a civic space where strangers could safely associate together and visitors and locals intermingle. Staff and volunteers were readily available to answer questions, provide information, and generally converse with the public. For locals, particularly those with small children, the adjacent *Coach Stop* activity centre, which could be supervised from the coffee shop, became a favourite destination. The positioning of the coffee shop, literally, at the front and centre of all museum activities, effectively created a safe and less intimidating 'congregant space' into which visitors were welcomed (Gurian, 2006, p. 93).

The social enterprise model of developing a commercial operation to fund a core mission outcome, such as collections management or research, was taken a step further at Cobb+Co. Here, the coffee shop was run on sound business principles with the aim of producing the 'best coffee in town', while delivering on the museum's core mission of community enhancement.

Cobb+Co Museum Stage Two, with its prominent coffee shop, was modelled on Ray Oldenburg's informal public gathering places designated as 'great good places' or 'third places'.[68] These places serve the community well, because they are inclusive[69] and local and they bring people of all ages together in a place in which they are all recognised and called by name. There is a sense of 'membership' in a third place (Oldenburg, 1997, pp. xvii-xviii, xxiii). *Cobbs* Coffee Shop brings youths and adults together in a relaxed environment. It is identified as a place for retired people, as well as children, and a place for SQIT staff and other community members to meet informally, as well as a place to conduct business. Oldenburg, together with Jane Jacobs and Robert Putman, are convinced that many problems in contemporary society, including alienation in the workplace and soaring divorce rates, directly link to the disappearance of third places and the subsequent decline in social capital (Jacobs, 1965; Putnam, 2000). The Cobb+Co Museum, in its second phase transformation, consciously set out to fill this void by becoming a community third place (Falk & Sheppard, 2006, pp. 66-67; Gurian, 2001, p. 98).

3.6.2 Removing barriers to community access – Toowoomba City Council partnership

To become an effective community resource that could be used and owned by the residents of Toowoomba, the Cobb+Co Museum had to become more accessible to its community. One of the major barriers to this accessibility was the entry fee that the state government had insisted be charged on all Queensland Museum regional branch museums (R. G. W. Anderson, 1998, p. 184; Bailey & Falconer, 1998, p. 171).[70] This was in contrast to free

---

68. One's home and office are designated a person's first and second places.

69. The Cobb+Co Museum was determined to include opportunities for Aboriginal and culturally diverse communities to participate in the development of exhibitions and public programs. In April 2001, a training workshop, entitled *A Keeping Place or Other Options for Preservation and Protection of our Cultural Heritage*, was attended by thirty-five Aboriginal people from throughout the region in preparation for the development of the Binangar Language Centre at the museum. An Indigenous Language Access Officer was based in the centre in a partnership between the Cobb+Co Museum and the Kombumerri Aboriginal Corporation for Culture (Year in Review 2000-2001, Cobb+Co Museum, 1988-2009, p. 4).
Each year, the museum works with a different culturally diverse community group to develop a display and series of public programs to celebrate Harmony Day, on 21 March. This has included celebrating Papua New Guinea's thirtieth Anniversary of Independence with the exhibition *Having the Neighbours Over: Papuan New Guineans in Toowoomba*. With the Pureland Learning College in Toowoomba, a display titled *Cultivating Wisdom, Harvesting Peace* was developed and another with recently arrived Sudanese refugees titled *Our Journey* (Cobb+Co Museum, 1988-2009).

entry at the major Queensland Museum facility in South Bank, Brisbane. To regional communities, particularly local authorities, this was an injustice. While Brisbane residents were able to enjoy the numerous exhibitions at the large and diverse Queensland Museum facility at South Bank free of charge, Toowoomba residents were forced to pay to see the National Carriage Collection, which they had rescued from fire, at the Cobb+Co Museum. Consequently, underpinning the Stage Two development was the critical need to remove the entry charge for local residents. Elaine Hermann Gurian echoed the same point when she declared:

> The major and undeniable problem with charging is that it is a means test. In the current situation only those who can afford the cost, and think the experience is valuable enough to pay for, can have access to the patrimony that belongs to us all (Gurian, 2006, p. 133).

Negotiating a partnership with Toowoomba City Council became the lynch pin for the successful transformation of the Cobb+Co Museum when Stage Two opened in October 2001 (Minutes of Meetings on 23 February and 25 May 2001, Cobb+Co Museum, 1988-2010). Fortunately, there had been some spasmodic community lobbying of local councillors for a local history museum in the lead up to the Centenary of Federation in 2001. This had been met with little interest, but it presented an opportunity for the Cobb+Co Museum to position itself as the regional museum for Toowoomba. Working in partnership with the then Deputy Mayor, Peter Wood, a proposal was submitted to Toowoomba City Council to provide free access to local residents to visit Cobb+Co Museum in exchange for an annual fifty thousand dollar contribution from the council. In addition, the council would provide the museum with access to the council's staff, as well as other support, to develop exhibitions relating to the local natural and cultural (including Indigenous) heritage that were to be displayed in the new Toowoomba Gallery at the museum. The initial agreement, for the years 2001–2004, included funding for an Aboriginal trainee to be employed in the Museum's Binangar Centre while undertaking a Certificate in Museum Practice (Cobb+Co Museum, 2001).[71]

In 2004, the partnership was renegotiated, but received opposition from council staff who interpreted support for the museum as diverting revenue from the council's own cultural service delivery. Personal relationships between the Director and Chair of the Advisory Committee and individual councillors eventually prevailed, and the free entry for locals was extended until 2007, but without any increase in the council's contribution to the museum. In 2007, a major upheaval occurred in local government in

---

70. It has been argued that an entrance fee is only a small proportion of the total effective price faced by a visitor to a museum. Other elements include the cost of travel to the attraction, subsistence expenditure, and the entrance fee (Darnell, 1998, p. 189).

71. This accredited program had been negotiated through the Director's chairmanship of the Museum Industry Subcommittee of Arts Training Queensland.

Queensland, which forced council amalgamations.[72] The new Toowoomba Regional Council commenced operating on 15 March 2008, servicing a population of one hundred and fifty-five thousand residents, living in an area of nearly thirteen thousand square kilometres. This amalgamation caused severe community consternation and enormous upheavals in the provision of local government services in the region. When it was time to renegotiate the free entry agreement, there was a completely new council, with only one former Toowoomba councillor still in office.[73]

The new council was struggling to bring any sense of common purpose or unified identity to the now much-expanded local authority area. The museum proposed to use its exhibitions and public programs to emphasise the shared natural and cultural heritage of the broader region and subsequently present a cohesive Toowoomba regional identity to support the council's position. All residents in the Toowoomba regional council area would now be able to access the Cobb+Co Museum free of charge, in return for the council's increase financial contribution of sixty-five thousand dollars.[74] This partnership was renegotiated when Stage Three opened. One of the strong motivating forces for councillors in supporting the partnership with the Queensland Museum was their belief in the Cobb+Co Museum's ability to 'teach children about their history' (Tranter, 2007).

3.7 Lifelong learning and museums

The delivery of formal education programs was always a primary focus for the Cobb+Co Museum, but this concern with learning outcomes became much more pronounced in Stage Two. The delivery of lifelong learning opportunities, with their capacity to enhance community social and cultural capital, became the museum's mantra. This position was reinforced by major research in the 1990s that reaffirmed that many museum practitioners and visitors consider museums to be primarily educational organisations, with capacity to generate effective learning through the provision of enjoyable and entertaining visitor experiences (Falk, 1999, 2000; G. Hein, 1998, p. 153; Moussouri, 2002, p. 20).

There is also a long-running debate over whether museum visits, which are part of people's leisure activities, should be recognised as having more to do with relaxation than education pursuits. A major study in 1973 of 7,230

---

72. Toowoomba City Council was merged with seven surrounding, but much smaller, shire councils – Cambooya, Clifton, Crows Nest, Jondaryan, Millmerran, Pittsworth, and Rosalie – to form the Toowoomba Regional Council.

73. The community had voted in the former Mayors/Deputy Mayors from the seven surrounding shires, rather than sitting Toowoomba City Councillors.

74. This model of a local government partnership with the Queensland Museum was then replicated in Townsville, with a free community pass for all residents to the Museum of Tropical Queensland.

Canadians' leisure-time activities and attitudes towards visiting museums undertaken by Dixon, Courtenay and Bailey found that respondents expected museums to perform an educative role.

> People feel museums are important to them; they are not going as frequently as they might because (an) educative involvement is lacking (Dixon, Courtenay, & Bailey, 1974, p. 245).

However, more recent research by Zahara Doering on European museum audiences indicated that 'diversion, curiosity and spontaneity' were more likely characteristic of visitor intentions than structured learning (Doering, 1999, p. 4). Marilyn Hood concurred, finding that while frequent museum participants might stress educational opportunities, less frequent visitors are more likely to indicate that the museum is a place for 'exploring and discovering, for enjoying a relaxed family outing and for having a good time with other people' (Hood, 1983, p. 56; 1995).

More recently, understanding personal motivation for museum visits and learning outcomes has become a major preoccupation of museum studies programs and professional research in museums.[75] Doering identified four types of museum-going experiences. These included:

> ...social experiences; cognitive experiences (information-gathering, meaning-making); object experiences (viewing beautiful, rare or valuable things); and introspective experiences, in which objects and settings trigger memories and associations, feelings of spiritual connections, and a sense of connectedness to a culture and community (Doering, 1999, p. 10).

Understanding and serving visitor needs has become both a necessity and, to some extent, the hallmark of a successful museum in the twentieth-first century.

3.7.1 Learning for personal identity

Few academics today express any doubt regarding the importance of museums' roles in identity making or identity reinforcement (S. Jones, 2000, p. 4). To Hooper-Greenhill, learning is now 'conceptualised as interpretive, open-ended and identity-focussed'. She reminds museum practicians that 'learning in museums is never just about learning about the collections, it is also about the shaping of views about the self' (E Hooper-Greenhill, 2007a, pp. 372,375). Falk and Dierking agree and insist that:

> ...at its most basic level, all learning is about affirming *self.* In particular, free-choice learning is the way we find out more about who we are and how we fit into our physical, social, and cultural world (Falk & Dierking, 2002, p. 16)

Visitors are attracted to museums for many different reasons, but these reasons appear to be underpinned by a general desire to affirm one's own 'self-image of intelligence, cultural awareness and curiosity' (Spock, 2006, p.

75. In her PhD research project, Lynda Kelly, using her work at the Australian Museum in Sydney, developed a 5P model of museum learning – person, people, process, purpose, and place (Kelly, 2006).

179). These museum visitors seek to build identity in some way – to explore, to seek certain experiences, to recharge, or for some other reason (Falk, 2009, p. 31).

Further research has indicated that each museum visitor has a unique entrance identity that can vary from visit to visit, depending on the individual and the group context in which the visit is being conducted. These museumgoers are seeking to have their 'entrance personal identity resonate through their museum experience' (Rounds, 2006, p. 144). There is an assumption that 'individual visitors bring their own narrative to the museum'. Their individual interests and desires lead them to seek various points of entry into specific relationships with museum institutions (Mastai, 2007, p. 175). It has been argued that:

> An individual's identity-related needs motivate him or her to visit a museum and provide an overarching framework for that visit experience. But the museum itself is not passive. The realities of the museum also play a role in bending and shaping the individual's museum visit experience (Falk, 2009, p. 10).

After a lifetime investigating the motivations of museum visitors, John Falk espoused a new 'predictive model' of the museum visitor experience, in which visitors are actively engaged in using the social and physical context of the museum to make personal meaning (Falk, 2006, p. 162):

> The essence of the model is that each museum visit experience is the synthesis of the individual's identity-related needs and interests and the views of the individual and society of how the museum can satisfy those needs and interests (Falk, 2009, p. 36).

Exactly how learning occurs during and after a museum visit and what museum's can do to affect better learning outcomes is still debatable (Bickford, 2010, pp. 250-251). Gaynor Kavanagh described a three phase process of visitor engagement with museums. While the first level results in learning outcomes, the other two result in alternative personal impacts that may or may not involve learning in any formal sense:

- The cognitive level underpins lifelong learning, which is achieved through knowledge gained or through the achievement of some form of insight and additional understanding from the exhibitions presented;
- The pragmatic or social level takes place in personal time and aims to achieve some form of social union through shared experiences with others. The subject of the exhibition is of only secondary importance; and the more contentious
- The 'Dream Space' deals in sub-rational image formation that can 'energize both imaginations and memories while illuminating feelings which can be anarchic and unpredictable, leading to all sorts of possible outcomes (including negative outcomes) from the museum visit' (Kavanagh, 2000, p. 3).

Rounds identified two types of personal learning that can typically occur in museums. 'Extrinsically motivated learning' is characterised by acquiring knowledge that is 'deep, systematic and consistent' and for which there is a specific purpose that is usually limited to curriculum-based learning programs. In contrast, 'intrinsically motivated learning' is driven by curiosity and enhances the mind's capacity for creative thinking. It does not usually have a specific known use at the time and it is systematic of the informal or free-choice learning associated with museum visitations (Rounds, 2004, pp. 393-394).

Also debatable is the precise nature of the impact that museums can have on their community, and what lifelong learning engagement strategies are suitable for museums. The Cobb+Co Museum initially operated in isolation from its community during its First Stage development. However, this attitude changed in its Second Stage development, when the museum recognised that the pivotal role for any social enterprise is to provide a public good, and, in the case of the museum, this would be delivered through achieving learning outcomes for its community.

3.7.2 Queensland Museum's lifelong learning agenda

In 2003, the Queensland Museum, as an organisation, identified the need to become more proactive in fostering lifelong learning, both internally and within the wider community. The potential for learning in museums was now being recognised for its 'experiential and holistic nature involving knowledge together with emotions, feelings, skills and actions' (E Hooper Greenhill, 2004, p. 168).

In response to this belief, the author argued for a new Strategic Learning program to embed a culture of lifelong learning within the Queensland Museum. This was incorporated into its Regional Services program. This program, with its headquarters in Toowoomba under the leadership of the Director of the Cobb+Co Museum, was charged with 'ensuring that all Queenslanders have access to the services of the Queensland Museum irrespective of where they live in Queensland' (Annual Report 2003-4, Queensland Museum Board of Trustees, 1980 to 2007-8, p. 11).

A key function of the Lifelong Learning Strategy was to provide opportunities for professional development for all Queensland Museum staff and volunteers. Not only was it essential for the institution to embed lifelong learning within its staff for their own personal benefits, it was also important that staff and volunteers play a much more proactive role in providing positive visitor experiences as a prerequisite for visitor personal identity reinforcement and learning. It was well recognised that 'one of the most critical elements in influencing the museum experience is the attitude of the museum worker' (Eilean Hooper-Greenhill, 1988, p. 223).

As Director of Regional Services[76], as well as Director of Cobb+Co Museum, the author was determined to implement the Queensland Museum's lifelong learning agenda with its underlying principle that museums should be places where visitors of all ages can engage in free-choice learning (D. Anderson, 1999; Milne, 2006). This form of learning is more often experienced as a pleasure, in contrast to formal learning, which can often be seen as a chore (Packer, 2006, p. 330). Cobb+Co Museum Stage Two would provide learning experiences that were:

> ...self-directed, voluntary, and guided by individual needs and interests – learning that we will engage in throughout our lives. Since it is the learning that we do when we want to, by definition it involves a strong measure of choice – choice over what, why, where, when and how we will learn (Falk & Dierking, 2002, p. 16).

While there has been a noticeable increase in awareness of the importance of museums as centres of learning in the past few years, most museums by the end of the twentieth century regarded education in the 'second order of their priorities, after collection management and display' and only 'few included education in their mission statement' (D. Anderson, 1999, p. 3).

3.7.3 Cobb+Co Stage Two learning agenda

During Stage Two, the Cobb+Co Museum was characterised by new free-choice inter-generational learning opportunities, as well as retaining its traditional curriculum-based programs for school groups. In a United Kingdom study that investigated the value of education in museums, eighty-four percent of the teachers surveyed agreed that their museum visits were curriculum driven (E Hooper-Greenhill, 2007b, p. 21). This trend was also reflected in teachers' comments after visits to the Cobb+Co Museum. Teachers sought curriculum-linked programs for their students, particularly in areas that they found more difficult to teach in the classroom due to a lack of relevant learning resources or training. Programs in Aboriginal studies and local history are frequently requested, as are developmental programs to enhance historical and scientific enquiry skills.

The education staff working at the Cobb+Co Museum realise the inherent power of object-based learning in a non-formal learning environment, such as a museum. Specific learning programs have been developed around each of the Cobb+Co Museum exhibitions, supported by hands-on

---

76. Besides its responsibility for Strategic Learning, Regional Services also included:
- The Museum Resource Centre Network that supports regional museums (see Section 2.10 above);
- The Loans Service that provided public access to the Queensland Museum's education collections from thirty distribution depots across the state;
- Travelling Queensland Museum exhibitions; and
- The Sciencentre road show and BioBus travelling biotechnology display centre.

additional artefacts and photographs that are used to develop interpretative processes and enquiry skills (Tranter, 1988a, 1988b). The museum is also fully aware that learning 'does not occur in a vacuum' and has ensured from its inception that it remained part of the wider formal and non-formal educational infrastructure in the Toowoomba region.[77]

The Cobb+Co Museum's ability to provide self-directed free-choice learning opportunities for its community relies on the combination of its exhibitions, its public programs, and its unique facilities (D. Anderson, 1999, p. 3). As Eilean Hooper-Greenhill has indicated:

> Learning in cultural organisations has enormous potential; it is experiential and holistic, involving knowledge together with emotions, feelings, skills and actions. Learning in archives, libraries and museums is rich and multi-dimensional; people make their own meaning of their experiences, and the outcomes of their learning contribute to building individual and collective identities (E Hooper-Greenhill, 2004, p. 168).

To be effective, the museum's public programs had to become more proactive and provide direction for the future, rather than being only a selective interpretation of past events and activities (Edson & Dean, 1994, p. 9).

3.7.4 Learning for the very young at Cobb+Co Museum

This belief in the value of learning in museums is not limited by age; it should start with programs for children younger than school age. The Cobb+Co Museum also acknowledged that providing 'cultural vaccination' through exposing young children to enjoyable experiences in museums at a very young age was probably the best guarantee that they would continue to visit museums throughout their lives (Falk, 1998, p. 41; C. Gray, 1998, p. 95).

Following this philosophy, the Cobb+Co Museum developed its *Little Cobbers* program. Centred on a large box, in which a different museum artefact is hidden each session, the program includes rhymes and story-telling, craft activities, museum tours to discover treasures, and a play in the Coach Stop Activity Centre. Most families also included a visit to the coffee shop during each visit.

---

77. The museum was frequently recognised for its innovative curriculum-based learning programs. It was awarded the Queensland National Trust's John Herbert Award and the Queensland Galleries and Museums Achievement Award (GAMAA). The Australian Teachers Association Darling Downs Chapter also recognised the quality of the Cobb+Co Museum's educational programs on a number of occasions.

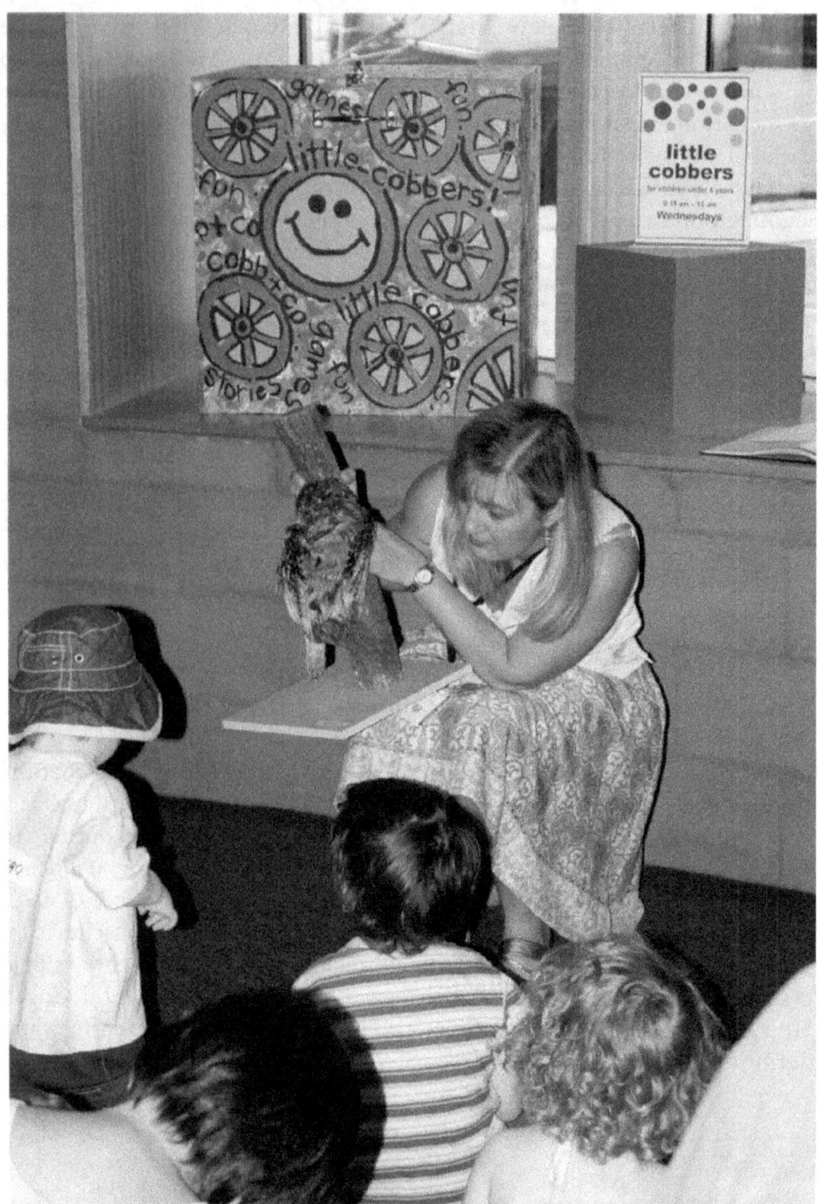

Little Cobbers program for very young children 2007

While having been developed independently, it could be argued that the underlying purpose of *Little Cobbers* parallels the early childhood learning philosophy advocated by the Association of Children's Museums (ACM). This sees children and families coming together in a new kind of 'town square' in which play inspires lifelong learning (Nguyen & Falls, 2004, p. 61). Cobb+Co Museum realised that the real audience for this program were families, not just children, and that museums need to focus on the creation of extraordinary family learning experiences, which result from social interaction between family members. This can be a difficult undertaking and Cobb+Co Museum employed two education officers to ensure that family learning was incorporated:

> ...[in] an integral way within all aspects of the design and development of each exhibition – especially the creation of a visitor experience that fully and completely supported family collaboration and conversation, as well as appealing to both children and adults (Falk & Sheppard, 2006, p. 84).

The Cobb+Co Museum also took its learning programs for very young children and their parents and grandparents to a much wider audience when it developed a large travelling exhibition – *Kids Time: A Century of Learning through Play*. This hands-on approach to an exhibition was conceived around five 'cubby houses' full of toys and activities that related to different eras of the twentieth century.[78] The popularity of this exhibition arose from the intergenerational social and cultural learning that was fostered by the interactive exhibits, which afforded:

> ...opportunities to promote talking, communication, and doing things together; to receive personal feedback; to engage in 'learning by doing'; and to apply content knowledge to everyday life (Falk, Scott, Dierking, Rennie, & Cohen Johes, 2004, p. 187).

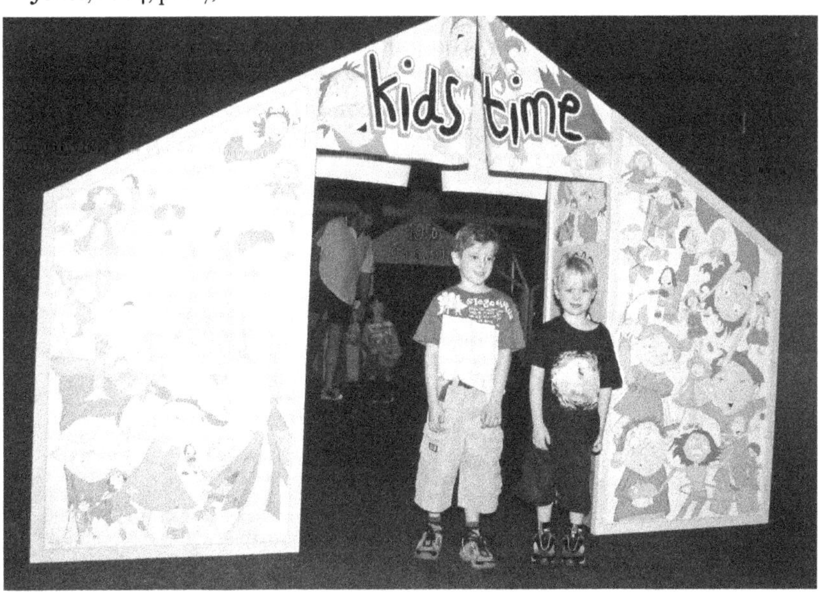

Kids Time: A Century of Learning through Play travelling exhibition entry 2004

78.One of the cubby houses related to the present, a second related to the 1970s (when parents of the young visitors were children), a third related to the 1950s (the childhood time of their grandparents), the fourth related to the 1930s, and the fifth to the 1910s. This award-winning popular exhibition travelled across the Eastern states of Australia for three years.

3.7.5 Programs for teenagers

The museum also experimented with public programs that aimed at developing specific exhibitions to encourage 'other voices' than the curators to be heard. For the opening of Stage Two, a sixteen-week Sport and Options program for high school students, entitled *We're History*,was undertaken. Twelve fifteen-year-old students from grade ten at Toowoomba State High School accepted the museum's invitation to forego their weekly sports' afternoon and instead co-curate the exhibition, *Toowoomba Teens 2001,* for the new Introductory Gallery. During this time, the students and their teacher worked with museum staff to plan, design, and install the display, as well as preparing and conducting the opening function and promoting the exhibition.

Toowoomba Teens 2001 provided a snapshot of teenage life in Toowoomba at the beginning of the twentieth-first century. As the years passed, this exhibition continued to play a significant role in documenting the rapid changes in technology that have affected many aspects of teenage life since the beginning of this century. This very successful program identified the often-neglected museum audience of fifteen-year-olds, and attracted attention within in the local media, who followed the students' weekly progress. A DVD of the making of this exhibition was produced by the local television station, WIN TV, which was incorporated into the display. This project also attracted interest from the wider museum fraternity (Insley, 2002; Tranter, 2002).

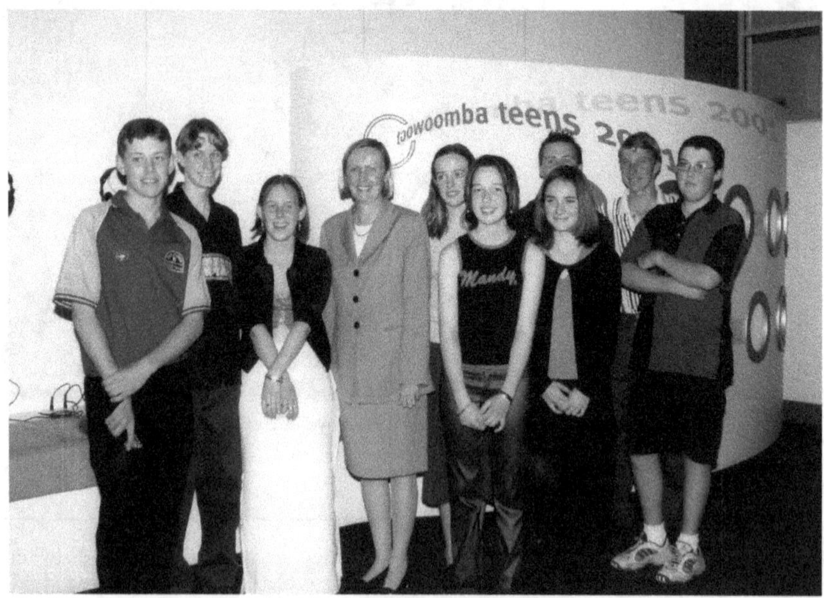

Toowoomba Teens 2001 student curators

There was a strong correlation between the *We're History* project learning outcomes and the findings of a United Kingdom study on the value of museum learning. This report identified that:

> Experimental projects working with school-aged children and young people outside the school context have found participants, especially older boys, to be very highly motivated and here there is great potential for development (E Hooper-Greenhill, 2007b, p. 44).

3.7.6 Outreach to senior citizens

To the Cobb+Co Museum, it is obvious that the museum is 'part of a sociocultural system that creates and disseminates value' and that it contributes to every stage of educational development, for the very young through to those in the 'third age' (D. Anderson, 1999, p. 4; H. Hein, S., 2000, p. 35). The 'third age' category encompasses a rapidly expanding cohort that includes early retirees, who are still very active, to very senior citizens, who are afflicted with different levels of impairment. In developing its *Reminiscence* project for nursing home residents in 2009, the Cobb+Co Museum was addressing the needs of the residents with serious impediments. This project was developed through working with a group of specially-trained museum staff – including early-retiree volunteers and the nursing homes' diversional therapists – who co-curated themed loan kits of artefacts and programs to encourage the residents to reminiscence and subsequently establish or re-establish their unique identities (Cobb+Co Museum, 2010). The *Reminiscence* project was, in reality, part of the Cobb+Co Museum's 'paradigm shift from textual to a visual literacy' in all its public programs – less lecturing to visitors and more conversations with them (Pitman, 1999, p. 11).

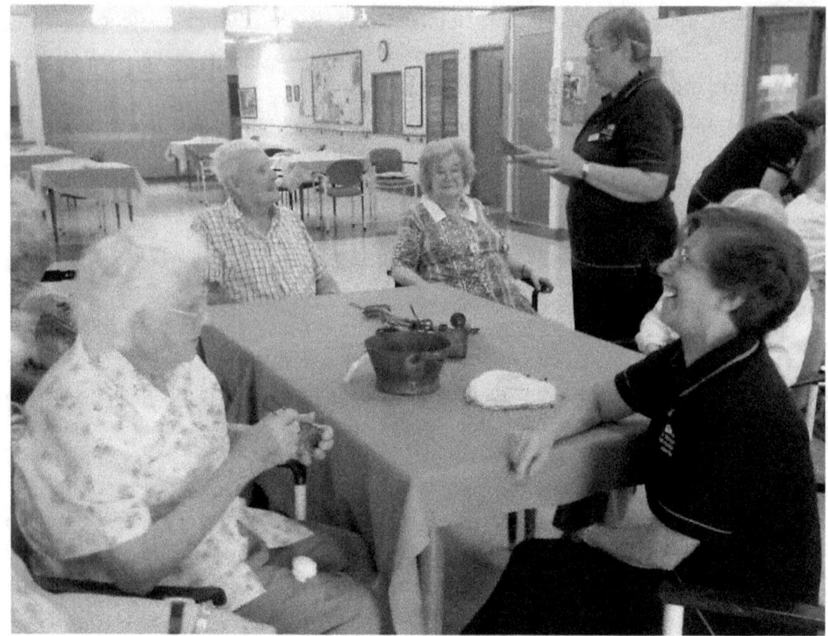

Cobb+Co volunteers taking reminiscence kits to nursing home residents 2010

These public programs, which were directed to the most neglected community sectors in terms of general museum focus – the very young, teenagers, and the very elderly – demonstrated the Cobb+Co Museum's determination to make its Stage Two facility a place that was 'really useful to its community'.

In developing a new model for the Cobb+Co Museum, it was recognised that the most important focuses of a museum should be a combination of the narratives presented and the messages conveyed by the museum's story tellers, staff, and volunteers, and the ability of social groups to experience these together (Gurian, 1999, p. 17).

There were many other exhibitions and programs which served unique purposes developed by the museum. These include:

- The Aboriginal Cultural program for international students that was developed and delivered in partnership with local Indigenous elders; and
- The involvement of university pre-service teachers in the delivery of the museum's holiday programs to enable university students to develop skills in working with parents and grandparents in inter-generational learning programs.

However, it could be argued that the museum's volunteer program best demonstrates its community focus.

3.7.7 Volunteerism

Volunteerism can assist a museum in a many ways in helping it achieve its community-focused agenda, while providing the community members, who elect to become volunteers, with a more intense lifelong learning experience (Cobb+Co Museum, 1988-2009).

At one level, these volunteers are seeking personal learning opportunities, while developing a sense of doing work that connects them to something beyond themselves. It responds to Archibald's call to create a sense of belonging in people:

> Places are produced in that wonderful interaction of people, places, narrative and time (Archibald, 1999, p. 150).

In her research on community relationships, which was developed by the Arizona Museum of Natural History in Mesa, Colp-Hansbury highlighted the role of positive volunteerism in not only supporting the museum's functions, but also being critical in the museum's capacity to engage its community. She relates how:

> ...volunteers who have invested in the museum as a place will be more willing to engage in the type of talk that will get others committed (Colp-Hansbury, 2009, p. 196).

The formation of the Cobb+Co Museum's volunteers program in 2001 was a response to this belief in the critical role that volunteerism plays in creating ongoing community engagement opportunities. Many volunteers are highly stimulated and intrinsically motivated, in contrast to paid staff who are often extrinsically motivated (Frey, 1998, pp. 123-124). Cobb+Co Museum volunteers, by participating in the delivery of learning programs to other members of the community, have engaged in their own learning as well as creating a positive self-image and enhancing identity reinforcement. They have promoted the museum in the media, to the community, and to visitors, and advocated on the museum's behalf to government at all levels.

Volunteers operate on a number of levels within the Cobb+Co Museum, including membership of its Advisory Committee. This committee has guided the museum's development since its inception in 1988, but its leadership role in developing and implementing the National Carriage Factory community engagement model was of paramount importance. It was this engagement philosophy and the community's responses to it that would determine the Stage Three development of the Cobb+Co Museum.

3.8 Stage Two – community engagement model

Despite its commitment to a social enterprise model in Stage Two, within four years, a new concept for the Cobb+Co Museum was being developed. In 2005, the Board of the Queensland Museum endorsed the Cobb+Co Museum's Advisory Committee's recommended strategy of community, business, and government engagement to develop a new museum model for Stage Three – the National Carriage Factory project. To forge authentic and sustainable community partnerships, the Cobb+Co Museum had to be completely committed – an aim that would require a focused and unwavering vision, extensive management and engagement skills from staff and volunteers, strong personal relationships, and perseverance. The desire to be civically engaged had to become embedded into the museum's DNA (Diane Frankel of Irvine Foundation quoted in Conwill & Roosa, 2003, p. 45). Engagement in this project moved the Toowoomba community well beyond information and consultation and into active participation within the Cobb+Co Museum (Queensland Government, 2005 pp. 5-7). This was to be a two-way process in which:

> The aspirations, concerns, needs and values of citizens and communities are incorporated at all levels and in all sectors in policy development, planning, decision-making, service delivery and assessment and involve citizens, clients, communities and other stakeholders in these processes (Brisbane Declaration 2005).

Such an engagement campaign had not previously been undertaken by the Queensland Museum. It was a campaign of broad-based advocacy defined as being 'all about promoting your organisation to a wide range of people, whether they are politicians, potential funders or the public' (Heal & et.al., 2010, p. 39).

The project was, in many ways, an example of a true private-public partnership. The campaign for private support was officially launched in September 2006 with the formation of the National Carriage Factory Appeal Committee. Once sufficient support was secured from community and business, the Appeal Committee then focused on convincing the state government to provide the remaining funding required. When state government funding was announced in late 2008, in quick succession, the final building plans were endorsed; tenders were called; and, in July 2009, construction of the National Carriage Factory commenced. New exhibitions were planned, designed, and installed, and the building opened in September 2010.

This successful process was only possible because of the Cobb+Co Museum's unique underlying characteristics. These included:

- The long involvement and commitment of the community representatives on the Museum's Advisory Committee;
- The location of a TAFE College adjacent to the Cobb+Co Museum, with some vacant land not required for TAFE's own needs;
- Extensive research that identified national and international models that could be replicated or modified for use in the Toowoomba community;
- An established national reputation for museum innovation in a regional setting;
- A demonstrated audience for uptake of heritage trade trading programs;

- An independent economic impact analysis on which a sound business case could be developed;
- Production of high-quality consistently branded visual promotional materials;
- Community respect for the museum, developed over a lengthy period of program delivery and partnerships;
- Extensive staff-community personal relationships;
- Ongoing media support; and
- A community committed to preserving its unique heritage values.

3.8.1 The concept

The National Carriage Factory project commenced with a simple, but unique, concept of developing a teaching space for heritage trades within a museum setting. This narrow focus for the expansion of the Cobb+Co Museum was essential to align to TAFE's vocational training agenda, because SQIT was being asked to transfer the land on which the National Carriage Factory would be built. This proposition was successful in achieving the transfer of the required land from the Department of Training to the Board of the Queensland Museum.[79]

However, there were many other stakeholders who needed to be persuaded to support the National Carriage Factory if the project was to be realised. The community would not financially support an extension of what could be seen as a TAFE training project that was the responsibility of the state government. Consequently, the National Carriage Factory project had to articulate multidimensional concepts with specific emotional hooks to appeal to different sectors of the community, politicians, and businesses from the region and further afield.

The project's underlying notion of a heritage trade training facility was expanded using economic, social, and cultural frameworks. Different groups of potential supporters were identified and analysed according to how they would or wouldn't value the National Carriage Factory project. Consideration was given to the economic impact of the project, in terms of both potential use and non-use values (see Section 5.4 for an analysis of economic values of cultural organisations).

A social framework was easy to identify for the project, because the Cobb+Co Museum could demonstrate its effect on its community as a learning centre and civic space. The National Carriage Factory project would enable

79. Although the then Minister agreed to the land transfer in 2000, and Cobb+Co Museum Stage Two had been built on part of the land in 2001, there was still a number of negotiations before the final land transfer was effected in 2009 – three years after the National Carriage Factory Appeal had commenced.

the museum to play a much-enhanced social role within the wider regional community.[80] However, the emotional appeal to key stakeholders would be most effective on a cultural level. The project's various manifestations would be linked together in an economic and social web conveyed in the slogan: 'History is in Our Hands'. This concept not only symbolised heritage trades and their associated hand-made products and skills, but also promoted an invitation to become involved in a unique history-making project with a high measure of aesthetic, spiritual, historical, symbolic, and authenticity value.

3.8.2 The methodology

In 2005, when the Board agreed to implement the National Carriage Factory project, it was on the assumption that the community would contribute towards the eight million dollars required, with the remainder forthcoming from the state and commonwealth governments. This was a significant target for the Queensland Museum whose annual operating budget for 2005-6 was $25.725 million and the Cobb+Co Museum only generated $325,000 from its own operations in the same financial year (Queensland Museum Board of Trustees, 1980 to 2007-8, p. 65).[81] In addition, the state government would need to increase the Queensland Museum annual financial allocation to cover the additional operational expenses of the National Carriage Factory project.[82]

Based on this belief, the Board agreed, in 2005, that the Queensland Museum Foundation would work with the Cobb+Co Museum Advisory Committee to develop a community engagement and fundraising methodology for this project (Minutes of Meeting 26 August 2005 Cobb+Co Museum, 1988-2010).

Initially, a National Carriage Factory Appeal Planning Committee – a sub-committee of the Cobb+Co Museum Advisory Committee, which included the Head of the Foundation – was established to prepare the Cam-

---

80. This argument was given greater momentum once the Toowoomba Regional Council was formed in 2008 from the amalgamation of eight smaller local authorities, creating an expansive regional community within the new council borders.

81. By 2009-10 the QM operating budget had grown to $29.567 million, of which QM generated $8.7 million, the remainder was government grants. In the same financial year Cobb+Co Museum received $1.066 million for its total operations (Board of the Queensland Museum, 2010, pp. 48,77).

82. Until the development of Stage Two of the Cobb+Co Museum, Queensland Museum's capital projects were funded by the Queensland Government, with an additional operational budget also provided by the government. However, Cobb+Co Museum Stage Two, funded instead from the Commonwealth Government through the Queensland Heritage Trails Network, did not attract any additional operational funding from the state government. The Board of the Queensland Museum had to absorb the additional ongoing expenses into the overall Queensland Museum budget.

paign Plan (Queensland Museum Foundation, 2005). This plan provided a professional methodology and structure to the campaign and established performance targets that had to be met at each stage before the process would proceed. This allowed a way out for the committee members who had limited previous experience in working on a professional fund-raising project. The Toowoomba community also had a poor philanthropic record, particularly in the cultural domain. Committee members were conscious of the community's initial backlash against an earlier cultural project – an enterprise that was associated with the Empire Theatre capital redevelopment plan – and were fearful for their reputations if the project did not receive sufficient community and government support in order to proceed as planned (see Section 4.3.1).

The Minutes of the First Appeal Planning Committee, on 13 September 2005, provided the framework for its operations:

- The Appeal Planning Committee falls under the aegis of the Queensland Museum Board, Queensland Museum Foundation, and the Cobb+Co Museum Advisory Committee, and will be supported by these groups at all times; and
- The Appeal Chair will be researched and identified by the Appeal Planning Committee and recruited with the support of key Queensland Museum and Queensland Museum Foundation executives, if required. He/she will act as the figurehead of the Appeal.

The Appeal Planning Committee would identify and help recruit the Appeal Chair, as well as develop the business case and be involved in the preparation of the marketing plan and development of promotional collateral (Cobb+Co Museum, 2005-2006, 2006). Using the slogan, 'History is in Our Hands – Rebuilding the Legend', the campaign focused on hands and tools, and hand-made products and skills. All support documentation was designed to a very high quality with great visual appeal to dispel the idea that heritage and history were concepts only to be associated with the past, not the present and the future (Cobb+Co Museum, 2006).

It was recognised that the National Carriage Factory concept would need to be presented by a single spokesperson, such as the museum's Director, who would ensure a consistent message was delivered with passion and great understanding, and who would also provide a strong personal identity to the project. One of the great strengths of the National Carriage Factory project was the reputation of the Cobb+Co Museum for consistent and reliable service to its community. Jim Collins insists that brand reputation 'built up on tangible results and emotional share of heart' is the 'link factor in social sector activity' because:

> ...potential supporters [must] believe not only in your mission, but in your capacity to deliver on that mission (Collins, 2005, p. 25).

Another essential communication tool was the effective presentation of high-quality, high-impact action photographs of heritage artisans at work. These photographs helped convey clear economic, social, and cultural messages. The Appeal Planning Committee could relate to Julie Nightingale's insistence that there is only limited benefit in museums advocating their projects simply in terms of public worth. Rather, she argues, museums should advocate an inspiring project that is elucidated by curators or others who are passionate about telling the story. Such personalities should also spearhead the campaign, rather than museums relying on marketers who only provide a packaged product (Heal & et.al., 2010, p. 46).

To complement the public campaign, a display of the National Carriage Factory project was developed and installed in the museum's Introductory Gallery.[83] Besides profiling the museum's project to visitors, this gallery provided an ideal venue for discussions between the Foundation and Committee members and prospective supporters of the project (Minutes of Meeting 27 May 2005 Cobb+Co Museum, 1988-2010).

Another task for the Appeal Planning Committee was to develop the 'sales pitch' and identify what would be the 'ask' and who would do the asking. It was agreed that the Head of the Foundation would be the sales person, but that she would always be accompanied by the most appropriate member/s of the Appeal Committee, because the 'ask' would vary among potential sponsors.[84]

Potential sponsors and key personnel to spearhead the project were also identified at this stage. These included national companies and trusts; local and regional businesses; community members; media supporters; and government personnel at the local, state, and national levels. To encourage community optimism in the project, funding was sought and acquired from a national organisation prior to the public launch of the campaign.[85]

3.8.3 Formation of the National Carriage Factory Committee (NCFC)

The Appeal Planning Committee recognised that it had to attract the right people to the project and that the appointment of the Chair for the National Carriage Factory Committee (NCHC) was the most significant position that had to be filled. This was set as the first key indicator to be achieved for the project to proceed. It was recognised that:

> The right people can often attract money, but money *by itself* can never attract the right people. Money is a commodity; talent is not. Time and talent can often compensate for lack of money, but money cannot ever compensate for lack of the right people (Collins, 2005, p. 17).

---

83. The display included a 3D model of the National Carriage Factory building, and case studies of three heritage trades to be taught in the factory.

84. A deal of research would go into identifying potential sponsors and linkages between their interests and the National Carriage Factory project.

85. The five hundred thousand dollars received before the public launch helped to convince some of the NCFC members of the national significance of the project and of its widespread appeal.

The position of Chair was critical and had to be a person within the community from whom 'everyone would take a phone call' and who would be able to mobilise community support for the National Carriage Factory Appeal. It was decided that Doctor Mary Wagner[86] would be the ideal Chair for the project. It was also identified that the Chair of the Queensland Museum Foundation Trustees – a highly respected former Governor of Queensland, Major General Peter Arnison AV, CVO (Retd) – would be asked to make the approach to Doctor Wagner.

Once Doctor Wagner had agreed to accept the position of Chair of the NCFC, a series of intimate presentations were made to a small number of selected community and business leaders who had been identified as possible NCFC members. Personal invitations from the Chair assured attendances at these functions and individual approaches by the Chair to join the NCFC were successful.[87] Each of the original NCFC members remained committed throughout the project. The strength of the Committee was based on the members' pre-existing personal relationships, and these were further developed between the Chair and Committee members as the project proceeded. Although nearly all Committee members became donors themselves, as Julie Nightingale stresses, the aim was not to persuade them 'to open their own chequebooks but rather to open their address books' (Heal & et.al., 2010, p. 54).

The tone of the NCFC meetings was always one of good fellowship – they were strategic, but they were first and foremost social occasions, full of laughter and fun. This ensured they were consistently well-attended. The Committee always celebrated milestones achieved and the Cobb+Co Museum and Queensland Museum Foundation were at pains to show personal appreciation and public acknowledgement for the roles played by the NCFC Chair and Committee members.

All NCFC members became advocates for the Cobb+Co Museum with a kind of evangelism that might normally be expected from the Director and staff, but not others. The Committee consistently advocated the National Carriage Factory project as a cause, a principle, and an opportunity, as well as a public good. There was always belief among the Committee members that the project would succeed, because the Cobb+Co Museum was 'in sync

---

86. Mary Wagner is the matriarch of the local Wagners family business, which, in 2009, was acknowledged as the most significant regional business in Queensland's one hundred and fifty years of statehood. She continues to be heavily committed to many community and business groups and philanthropic activities across the community. Her work was acknowledged by the University of Southern Queensland when she was awarded an honorary doctorate for her services to the community.

87. The final NCFC consisted of the Chair, two members of Cobb+Co Advisory Committee (the Chair of this Committee was the deputy Chair of the NCFC), eight community/business leaders, the Head of the Queensland Museum Foundation, and the Director of the Cobb+Co Museum.

with its constituency', and the core ideology of the National Carriage Factory project was consistent with the desires of the consumers in the Toowoomba region (Falk & Sheppard, 2006, p. 166).

One of the first approaches to the community was to the local media, in order to canvass support. The Cobb+Co Museum had developed a long history of media support, but it had not previously attempted anything of this scale. A detailed media campaign was prepared and eventually implemented with the support of all local media outlets.

The National Carriage Factory project was launched on 5 September 2006 – by Major General Peter Arnison, Chairman of the Queensland Museum Foundation Trustees, and Doctor Mary Wagner, Chair NCFC – at a dinner and presentation to one hundred and thirty selected guests (Year in Review 2006-7, Cobb+Co Museum, 1988-2010, p. 14). This was followed by a series of corporate presentations, including one at Government House in Brisbane, which was hosted by the then Governor of Queensland (now Governor-General of Australia), Quentin Bryce, as Patron of the Queensland Museum Foundation. At the same time, a strategy to involve the state government was developed, and support was sought from the then Premier, Peter Beattie, as part of a Community Cabinet consultation, in Toowoomba in 2006. The NCFC members used their contacts within the Premier's Department; with ministerial staff; and with the local member for Toowoomba North, who was the State Attorney General at the time. Once the NCFC appeal started to attract considerable local support, this community backing was used by the NCFC and the Queensland Museum Board to further help leverage state government support.

3.8.4 Success, but not exactly as planned

As with all projects of this nature, many things do not go according to plan, and a degree of flexibility is required when executing the strategic plan. Although the local federal government member had been approached early in the planning process – with an application for one million dollars for a 'shovel ready' project – the application was not assessed until after the election, in 2007. This election resulted in a change of government, with the Australian Labor Party elected as the new federal government. This led to a change in the criteria for federal funding for regional projects, which eliminated the National Carriage Factory project's eligibility for any funding from this source.

In 2009, the international economic climate deteriorated with the onset of the Global Financial Crisis. Although Australia did not officially go into recession, a number of national companies that had originally expressed interest in supporting the National Carriage Factory project were, by 2009, no longer in a position to commit financial support. With the extended timetable for the project, the original budget of eight million dollars for the

NCF building alone was escalating at a rate of thirty-five thousand dollars per month – an increase that was making the complete project nearly impossible to achieve.

The two-year timeframe to nurture a major sponsor also proved too long to maintain the original staff at the Queensland Museum Foundation[88], though staff at the Cobb+Co Museum and the long term residents recruited for membership of the NCFC remained committed over the life of the project. Despite this change in the Foundation staff, this did not affect the project, and private fundraising proceeded as a result of the persistent individual approaches by the Chair and members of the NCFC.

In December 2008, when the state government finally announced that it would support the National Carriage Factory project with a four million dollar grant, there was concern that the budget increases might result in a need to re-scope the project. Modifications to the original plan were subsequently prepared. Tenders for the complete construction of the National Carriage Factory project, as well as a modified version, were finally completed in May 2009. Fortunately, the quotes from the local builders were very competitive and the total project was able to proceed.

3.8.5 Application to other community projects

The National Carriage Factory community engagement strategy and fundraising methodology is generally applicable to other large-scale community projects. The Foundation's fundraising principles and approaches provide a solid structure for implementation by any well-organised group. A major key to success was the ability of the Cobb+Co Museum to leverage off its many years of successful community engagement and service delivery. The museum's brand reputation was enviable. Built upon years of tangible results and emotional 'share of heart' by the community, potential supporters not only believed in the National Carriage Factory project as part of the museum's mission, but also in the museum's capacity to deliver on that mission (Collins, 2005, p. 25).

The many significant leadership roles that the museum played in the community over many years enabled it to establish strong personal relationships with many key community, political, and business leaders. The museum was able to demonstrate that successful advocacy needs to be structured and based on long term thinking. Through its history of success, it was able to attract the key people who prefer to be associated with success stories, not failures (Heal & et.al., 2010, p. 42).

There were, however, some specific characteristics that may not necessarily be transferable to other situations. The Cobb+Co Museum had a range of internal capacities generated by its long term staff performances and by the Director's personal connections within the Toowoomba com-

---

88.Two Foundation Heads and three other Foundation staff changed during the five-year process.

munity. The dearth of local leadership in museums is not often recognised as a one of the key challenges facing twenty-first century museums that are grappling with community engagement strategies. Local leaders provide:

> ...a deep understanding of the locality in which they had been born and subsequently lived and worked and had links to many communities within it. Their expertise and knowledge [should be] widely respected by their peers inside and outside the museum walls and by the communities they served (Watson, 2007, p. 482).

Janes stresses the importance for museum leaders to think of themselves as members of their communities if they are to effect meaningful changes. He regrets that this rarely happens, because the people in charge of many cultural institutions are frequently 'itinerant, in fact or spirit, as their careers require them to be':

> These various public servants all have tended to impose on the local place and the local people programs, purposes, procedures, technologies, and values that originate elsewhere (W.Berry quoted in Janes, 2009, p. 170).

Other unique characteristics of the Cobb+Co Museum's situation included its access to Queensland Museum in-house expertise – particularly the Queensland Museum's graphics skills, which were capable of producing high-quality documentation at an affordable price. This would prove crucial at the beginning of the NCF's major advocacy campaign. The same argument can apply to the detailed planning of the building. Cobb+Co Museum staff had a clear vision for the total project, as well as the details of each section, and worked closely with architects from the Queensland Government's Project Services, which helped save time and money.[89] These considerable expenses were underwritten by the Board of the Queensland Museum. The development of complete plans very early in the process are essential for planning budgets for funding proposals and producing visuals as part of the 'sales pitch'.

Cobb+Co Museum used its strengths in planning, community engagement, long term media relations, organisational stability, and respected personnel to implement a multifaceted advocacy process to raise the support and financial backing required to achieve its objectives. Other organisations that have an inspiring vision and possess comparable characteristics, determination, and a flexible approach to changing economic and political landscapes could successfully replicate the process used to develop the National Carriage Factory for their own significant projects. In Toowoomba, the Empire Theatre Stage Three development is being closely modelled on the National Carriage Factory community engagement strategy. Two members of the NCFC are involved in the Empire Theatre Planning Committee and are using their prior experience with the Cobb+Co Museum to ensure the success of this additional major cultural infrastructure project in Toowoomba.

---

89. Cobb+Co Museum used the same architect, Don Watson, for its Stage Two development, so there was an established working relationship between the parties.

3.9 Conclusion

Stage Two of the Cobb+Co Museum, which operated from 2001 until the opening of the National Carriage Factory in September 2010, exhibited many features of a social enterprise or more-than-profit organisation dedicated to social outcomes that would make a difference in its community. A mission emphasising community engagement, social capital, and the delivery of public good for its community stakeholders became central operational focuses, as did working in a more efficient business-like manner. During this stage, the Cobb+Co Museum was transformed from a fairly traditional collection-focused branch of the Queensland Museum (though with a concentrated agenda on formal curriculum-based learning outcomes) into a regional museum and community engaged resource centre based on social enterprise modelling.

During Stage Two, the Cobb+Co Museum developed characteristics of both a community-centred museum that was primarily concerned with the wellbeing of its communities and the preservation of heritage traditions, and a client-centred institution in which the staff saw themselves primarily as educators interested in promoting free-choice learning among their targeted audience. This audience included many groups that were often not recognised as stakeholders by museums at that time, including the very young; teenagers; the very elderly; and Aboriginal people – traditional owners and historic families and residents from culturally diverse backgrounds.

The museum developed mixed-use spaces that were available for both internal and community use. Its new features were all community-focused, including new galleries to tell local stories, a central coffee shop that operated as a community meeting place, and public programs geared towards lifelong learning for the very young to senior citizens. A new relationship with the community flourished when the Toowoomba City Council agreed to support free entry for all local residents to the museum.

The museum expanded its collection and narratives, as well as concentrating on service delivery for the wellbeing of its community, through its involvement in a range of programs and through formulating its initial plans for the safeguarding of traditional crafts and trades. Stage Two witnessed the museum's emerging ideological commitment to having audience involvement, rather than content delivery, as its priority – from back-of-house to front-of-house activities. It positioned itself within the new museological framework as an educational institution that was proactive in strengthening community identity.

The concept of a not-for-profit or more-than-profit social enterprise operating within the wider social economy was the framework on which the Stage Two transformation was developed. Realisation of the museum's community stakeholders and its desire and ability to be 'useful' to its community underpinned this transformation. The museum's Stage Two identity was essentially that of a 'hybrid place, combining recreation and learning' (Neil Kotler, 2001, p. 423).

A three-tier model of stakeholder interests and interactions with the Cobb+Co Museum was espoused. In response to its primary stakeholder interest, the Cobb+Co Museum embraced multifaceted roles within its community. Cultural engagement was the catchcry, and this became hard to distinguish from community development and the growth of citizenship (Andrew, Gattinger, Jeannotte, & Straw, 2005, p. x).

In many ways, the Cobb+Co Museum had embraced all the significant features of a 'responsive museum'. It had become:

- More audience-centred across the whole organisation;
- Engaged in an ongoing dialogue with its audiences and potential audiences;
- Appreciative of the fact that local residents 'did not have to visit to value' the museum;
- More accessible in all aspects of its operations;
- Focused on inviting community representatives to participate in internal decision-making;
- An important leader in the wider community;
- Learning-focused – a notion that pervaded all operations and was championed by senior management;
- Supportive of innovative exhibition programs, design, and interpretation;
- Focused on developing programming to target priority audiences;
- Funded through sustained and varied sources; and
- Focused on promoting professionalism (Lang, Reeve, & Woollard, 2006, pp. 227-228).

Underpinning the success of Stage Two was the involvement of community volunteers – particularly the Advisory Committee members. The development of the National Carriage Factory project through its structured community engagement process is tangible evidence of the success of the Cobb+Co Museum Stage Two social enterprise model. Its success was also reflected in the changed language used by the community when referring to the museum. No longer was it designated as 'the museum' or the 'Cobb+Co Museum', but rather 'Cobb and Co' – a title that referred to the museum as being the community's own place, rather than an external institution. The museum had made itself a vital part of community life, and an instrument in fostering its community's sense of identity and solidarity (Neil Kotler & Kotler, 2000, p. 178).

At the same time, the community engagement strategy was also the catalyst for the Museum's Stage Three development – the National Carriage Factory, which opened in September 2010 as a hub for a regional creative industry based on heritage trades.

Chapter 4

Museums as Creative-Cultural Industry Hubs

The Formulation and Development of the National Carriage Factory from 2010

4.1 Introduction

The Third Stage transformation of the Cobb+Co Museum commenced with the opening of the National Carriage Factory in September 2010. In many ways, this could be viewed as a natural evolution from the museum's Stage Two iteration of a social enterprise model based on interdependent relationships with its community (Janes, 2009, p. 25). The community's decision to strongly support the National Carriage Factory was ultimately responsible for the realisation of this project and the Third Stage transformation of the Cobb+Co Museum.

The National Carriage Factory also represented a natural progression from the Cobb+Co Museum's original status as a traditional collection and research facility that focused on the national carriage collection of horse-drawn vehicles, and the international custodianship of the Cobb & Co. coaching legend. The National Carriage Factory was, in essence, an idiosyncratic concept based on the catalytic value of the museum's horse-drawn vehicle collection and its embedded trades, combined with its ability to weave this heritage into the community. It set out to forge museum traditions with unique community characteristics and to safeguard heritage trades, crafts, and skills.

On one level, the National Carriage Factory project can be seen as an ongoing attempt to implement a variety of new museological tenets, because it was community-focused with an emphasis on community needs. As in Stage Two, the Cobb+Co Museum reflected the concerns of the society in which it was located. Its relationship with the communities it served was renegotiated and reinvented as its purposes developed and changed (Watson, 2007, p. 13).

However, most significantly, Stage Three represents an attachment to the new museological ideas advocated by post-modern museum affiliates, particularly in its determination to ensure that:

> ...intangible heritage complements...tangible objects. memories, songs, cultural traditions and (heritage trades) ... now seen as embodying culture's past and future (E Hooper-Greenhill, 2000a, p. 81)

The National Carriage Factory project aspired to be more than just an expanded physical space. Through combining cultural heritage with entrepreneurship, the Cobb+Co Museum embraced 'a blue ocean strategy' that forged a creative-cultural industry based around heritage trades, crafts, and skills (Kim & Mauborgne, 2004, p. 81). As a hub for *Hand Made in Country,* the National Carriage Factory could be seen as a facility and community driver that addressed the convergence of culture, commerce, education, and entertainment (Landry, 2003, p. 16).

It was nevertheless realised that the potential of the National Carriage Factory would be limited unless a broad regional approach to the development of a creative-cultural industry hub, based on the heritage trades, was adopted and implemented. The only regional organisation with the potential to facilitate the required level of regional support for the concept was the Toowoomba & Golden West Regional Tourist Association (TGWRTA). Working with TGWRTA and Tourism Queensland (TQ), *Hand Made in Country* was scoped and identified as a catalytic regional tourism project for the Toowoomba Regional Council area – the major population area covered by TGWRTA.

The Third Stage of the Cobb+Co Museum transformation involved innovative strategies that would shift the operational focus of the museum from 'the product – or service-space to the experience-space' meshed around safeguarding heritage trade skills (Bakhshi & Throsby, 2010, p. 17). It was also conceived as a project of both national and international significance that 'will preserve forever the traditional heritage trades that created the legend of Cobb & Co.' (Cobb+Co Museum, 2006, p. 3).

The local community's social, cultural and economic circumstances were changing in the first decade of the twenty-first century, and this provided opportunities for the Cobb+Co Museum that were not available a decade earlier when the Stage Two development opened. As a new museum concept, the National Carriage Factory would provide a chance to expand the Cobb+Co Museum's community involvement and audience reach; to develop new art forms associated with personalising the museum visit; to create new sources of economic and cultural value; and to spur new business models, including those incorporated in the *Hand Made in Country* concept (Bakhshi & Throsby, 2010, p. 13).

4.2 Chapter outline

This chapter commences by identifying the changing social, cultural, and economic dimensions that were confronting the Toowoomba region at the end of the first decade of the twenty-first century that provided the platform on which the Third Stage transformation of the Cobb+Co Museum was realised. Even if the community was ready to support change, the concept for further development at the Cobb+Co Museum had to be inspirational and require significant innovation and creativity. Innovation is, today, an essential element of the future economic prosperity and quality of life of a community, so it needed to be firmly embedded in all aspects of the museum's operations in its Third Stage transformation, including its:

> ...products, services, business processes and models, marketing and enabling technologies (Department of Innovation, Universities and Skills (DIUS) 2008 quoted in Bakhshi & Throsby, 2010, p. 12).

There were five major concepts that provided the innovation and creativity that informed the National Carriage Factory project. These will be analysed in turn throughout this chapter.

Initially, an investigation of the applicability of creative-cultural industry models to heritage and museum settings and their effect on the development of the National Carriage Factory project will be undertaken. The complexity of the creative industries will be explored to position museums within this framework.

The second item that will be analysed is the International Convention on Intangible Heritage – with its emphasis on safeguarding heritage trades, crafts, and skills – and how it was adapted as the major reference point for the Stage Three development. From this Convention, the Cobb+Co Museum adopted a position of championing heritage trade training as a means of bringing these trades, crafts, and skills out of a time warp embedded in pre-industrial attitudes, products, and processes for the ultimate social, cultural, and economic benefit of the community.

From these broader enmeshing concepts, specific new museological developments will be explored, including ecomuseology and the more recent economuseum model. Finally, the regional economic development concept, *HandMade in America* – which espouses the heritage and economic value of crafts and cultural products in western North Carolina, U.S.A. – will be scrutinised for its contribution to the formulation of the Cobb+Co Museum's own *Hand Made in Country* concept.Its conception underpins the operations of the National Carriage Factory and attempts to firmly embed it within the economic, social, and cultural development of its regional community.

The implementation of the National Carriage Factory project is an ongoing exercise that only commenced with the opening of Cobb+Co Museum Stage Three, in September 2010. Its future is yet to be realised, so this chapter can only identify the strands that will initially be pursued by the existing Cobb+Co Museum management. As evidenced throughout the history of the museum, the future of the museum will never be certain, particularly if it continues to respond to its community as its primary stakeholders.

4.3 Toowoomba: the home of the Cobb+Co Museum

To position the Stage Three development of the Cobb+Co Museum within its regional context, some analysis is necessary of the changes emerging in the economic, social, and cultural landscape in the first decade of the twenty-first century, and the manifestation of these changes in regional Queensland, particularly in the Toowoomba area. There will be no attempt to understand the underlying forces caused by the Global Financial Crisis, nor the subsequent economic situation in regional Queensland, but, rather, an identification of the opportunities these situations created and the actions undertaken by the Cobb+Co Museum in response to its understanding of the changing economic climate. This new fiscal landscape encouraged the Cobb+Co Museum to investigate the possibility of merging the growing public interest in intangible heritage – expressed through the safeguarding of heritage trades, crafts, and skills – with creative-cultural industry cluster modelling.

One of the emerging characteristics of the creative-cultural economy seems to be 'a tight interweaving of place and production system' into a 'symbiotic convergence of built form, economy and culture'. These characteristics can be generated in a specific location that is frequently, but not always, a large urban area in a major city (Allen J. Scott, 2004, pp. 468, 479). If this is the emerging pattern, it is essential to consider the unique characteristics of Toowoomba as the location base for the Cobb+Co Museum and its creative-cultural industry model, *Hand Made in Country*.

Toowoomba has a long history as the undeclared capital of the Darling Downs – a conservative rural farming area in Southern Queensland. In many ways, the region 'attracted and mobilised the agreeable and conscientious personality types' who reflected 'the status quo orientation and don't-rock-the-boat values' of a rural industry–dominated economy (Florida, 2008, p. 202). In the past, this characteristic proved a hindrance to large scale creativity and innovation in the region and encouraging an outmigration of 'the open types who tend to be the source of new creative energy and innovation' (p. 202).

In the first decade of the twenty-first century, the region was caught up in the mining boom, which caused heated and prolonged conflict over the conversion of large tracts of arable farming land into extensive open cut coal mining sites or drilling areas for oil and gas production. There is currently emerging an unlikely new coalition of farming and environmental leaders who are coordinating widespread community action to try to stop the mining activity on productive farms.

The region, particularly Toowoomba, has a strong educational focus, with an over-representation of large private secondary-level education colleges – many of which are also boarding schools for rural students. This, together with a significant university – The University of Southern Queensland – and a series of technical and further education training colleges – which had been amalgamated into the Southern Queensland Institute of TAFE – provide for the community's lifelong learning needs.

4.3.1 The impact of mainstreaming heritage values

For the successful implementation of the Cobb+Co Museum's Stage Three development, the most significant change in community attitudes was the mainstreaming of heritage values. This was not unique to Toowoomba, but reflected a much wider societal outlook that was evidenced in:

- The rapidly rising valuation of older homes, particularly those preserving heritage architectural features;
- Community interest in restoring former public buildings, particularly old court houses, railway stations, and post offices, and giving them a 'new lease on life' as prominent community markers;
- The popularity of heritage machinery clubs, vintage and veteran car clubs, steam train societies, vintage aircrafts, and air shows;
- The variety and membership base of historic re-enactment groups;
- Heritage-based tourism products, and marketing campaigns featuring heritage products, services, and values;
- Genealogical society membership and research activities;
- Publications of family, local, community and business histories;
- Government-funded community celebrations of historic milestones;
- Annual festivals and events incorporating historic themes;
- Prime-time television programs devoted to antiques, archaeology, museum conservation, and tracing family histories; and
- The implementation of a new Australian national school curriculum that, for the first time, includes history as a compulsory core subject for all primary and secondary students (Tranter, 2010a, p. 93).

Specifically, the Cobb+Co Museum identified a significant change in the local community's responses to innovative cultural heritage developments, as reflected in the re-commissioning of the Empire Theatre in Toowoomba

– the largest regional theatre in Australia, and an architectural showpiece. The Empire Theatre originally opened in June 1911, operating as a flourishing silent movie house until February 1933, when fire broke out and it was almost completely destroyed. In November 1933, the theatre reopened with an art deco architectural style, in keeping with the fashion of the 1930s.

It was abandoned in the early 1970s and used as a storage facility for TAFE for many years prior to the Toowoomba City Council's decision to redevelop it as a performing arts centre. Vociferous community reaction to this proposal saw the defeat of the then Mayor and Empire champion, Ross Miller, in the local government elections in 1996. However, the theatre eventually opened in mid-1997, and the community has gradually embraced it. It has a significant community membership program with two hundred and seventy active volunteers carrying out a range of both front-of-house and back-of-house activities, while raising over four hundred and fifty thousand dollars for the institution. A church theatre was added to the complex during its Second Stage development, and a Third Stage is planned for construction in 2012 (Empire Theatres Pty. Ltd., 2010, p. 11).

Evidence of this supportive attitude to the development of significant cultural products and services was interpreted by the Cobb+Co Museum as reflecting some real diversification of the psychological makeup of the people of Toowoomba. According to Jason Rentfrow:

> ...it is as likely that the 'psycho-social environment' will be as important in the successful development of creative industries, or more so than the region's business climate and economic structure (Jason Rentfrow quoted in Florida, 2008, p. 202).

4.3.2 The impact of broadening community leadership

Another characteristic of the changing community profile has been a noticeable broadening of the community's leadership base. This has justified the confidence in the capacity of the community to embrace the innovative creative-cultural industry model that was proposed for the National Carriage Factory. It was essential that the members of the National Carriage Factory Committee emerged as cultural visionary leaders able to inspire the community to generate support for the Cobb+Co Museum. According to John Landy, potential leaders for the National Carriage Factory Project would need:

> ...to reveal the social and economic dynamics that affect us, explain where museums fit in, and show us where we have come from and where we might be going. The combination of skills called for is a mix of moral and emotional leadership, and the managerial leadership needed to rebuild confidence in our institutions (Landry, p. 19).

A study of eight small regional towns in Queensland found that the distinctive characteristic of the more innovative communities was the availability of broad based leadership. The study concluded that:

> The more innovative towns could be differentiated by the proportion of their people who were regarded as having expertise, relative to the proportion who were regarded as leaders. A large critical mass of experts provided the 'leadership' that was widely distributed throughout the more innovative towns, rather than being solely vested in a recognised few (Plowman, Ashkanasy, Gardner, & Letts, 2003, p. 59).

It was well recognised that to achieve the objective of Stage Three – the construction of the National Carriage Factory – a focused and targeted political campaign would be required. The NCF was always conceived as having to be a citizen's movement in parallel with a political process that addressed community needs or latent desires. It required leadership with inspirational thinking to create and articulate a unique vision that the community would embrace (Gorbey, 2002, p. 5).

4.3.3 NCF a place-marker for community development

When the National Carriage Factory project was launched in 2006, it was embraced by the Toowoomba community. It became obvious that there were many diverse reasons behind this support – some to do with tourism and place marketing, others to do with current use or the 'existence', 'option', 'future', or 'bequest' values associated with the Cobb+Co Museum.[90] As the campaign progressed, the potential of heritage trades and artisans' products – including training programs as export commodities delivering social, cultural, and economic benefits to the region – was embraced. The Cobb+Co Museum was viewed as the logical hub for the agglomeration of a new creative-cultural industry model based on the latent opportunities existing around the heritage trades that could be used to exploit the 'local cultural symbologies' through imbedding them into unique products with authentic character (Power & Scott, 2004, p. 7; Allen J. Scott, 2004, p. 468).

Although not a great world city or even a major suburban area, Toowoomba could nevertheless be seen as possessing opportunities for interweaving place and production systems that were identified as essential features of the new cultural economy. It was recognised that:

> ...outputs that are rich in information, sign value and social meaning such as that of cultural industries are particularly sensitive to the influence of geographic context and creative milieu (Mizzau & Montanari, 2008, pp. 653-654)

The National Carriage Factory was conceived and born in this environment.

---

90. See Section 5.4 for an analysis of the broader non-use benefits derived from museums.

Physically, the National Carriage Factory project doubled the size of the Cobb+Co Museum. The architecture of the completed building was, itself, to become a symbol of the community's heritage aspirations, establishing a connection to both the past and the future. This provides a clear example of how places are 'constructed within a collective consciousness, building on both past and present cultural associations and memories' (M. Smith, 2007, p. 94).

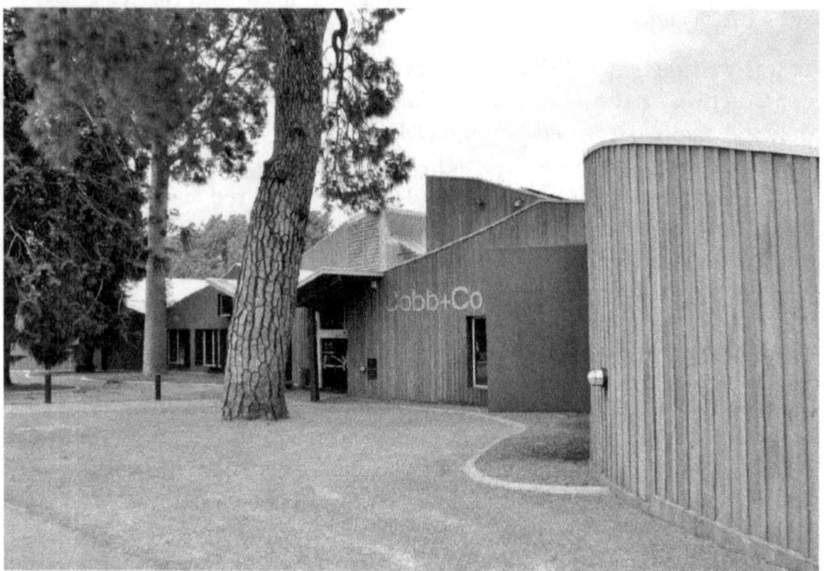

NCF front of building

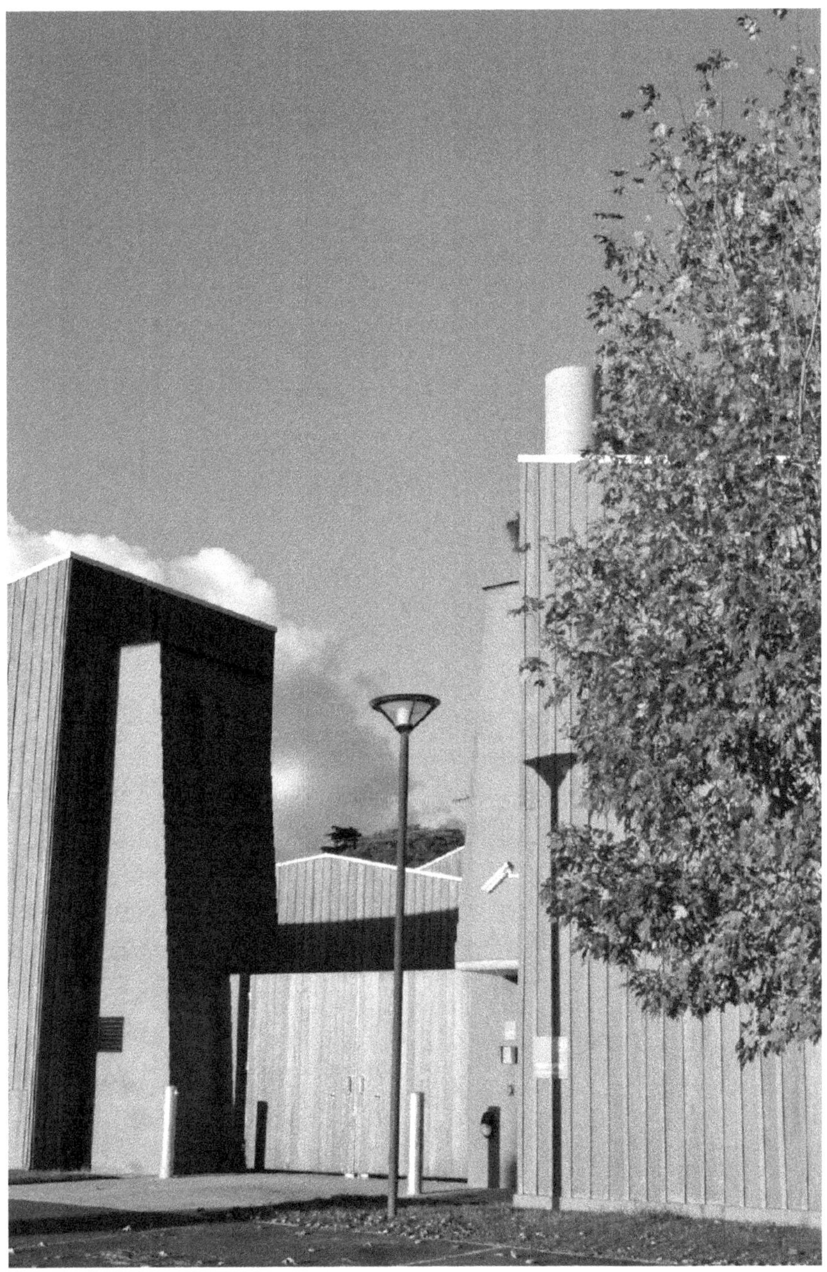

NCF back view

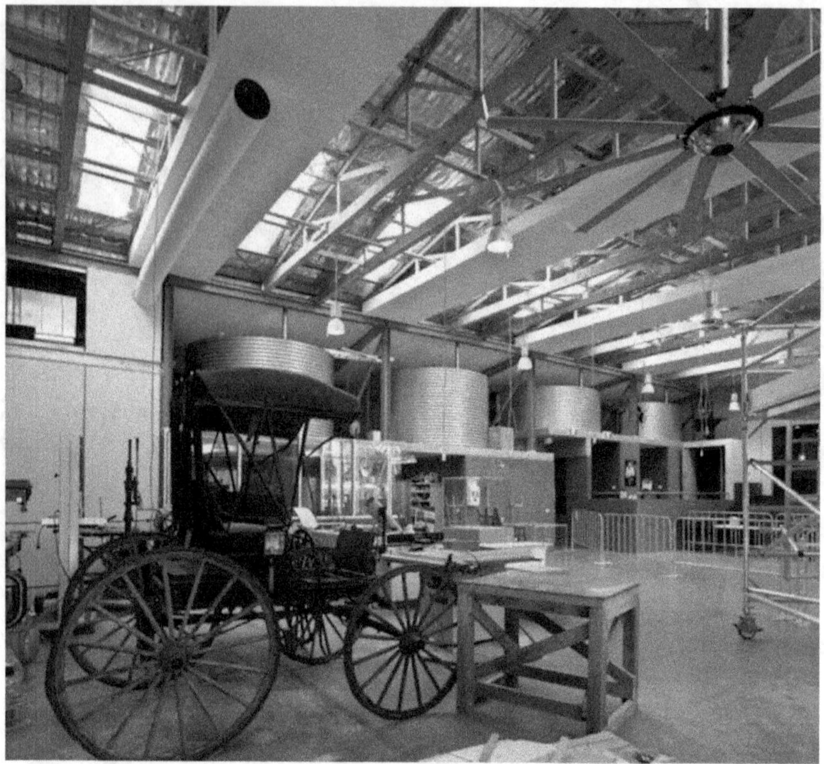

Environmental sustainable features of the Factory space

The museum building incorporates environmentally sustainable design features and improvements to provide a richness of visit experiences through interesting spatial encounters, while reflecting on quality workmanship that uses a variety of natural materials and finishes. The museum now aspires to be the living heart of the city, if not the region, through creating value in a way that the public can participate in, enjoy, and react to.

In 2011, the Cobb+Co Museum was awarded the Regional Australian Institute of Architects' William Hodgen's Award for the Building of the Year.[91] Part of the citation for this award acknowledged that:

> The Cobb+Co Museum is the culmination of over 20 years of partnership by the facility director and designer. While the site has had a long period of development the final result presents a considered, convincing place (Gleeson, 2011, p. 16).

Overall, the actual building was designed 'to add to the public domain and reinforce what people find delightful about living and working in [a place]' (Kemper, 2007, p. 60).

The dominant features of the new structure are the Factory and Blacksmith Shop – spaces in which the heritage trades are safeguarded and transferred to the next generation and in which the adaptive potential of traditional techniques are simultaneously explored for profitable outcomes for the artisans; the community; and, ultimately, the museum.

Complementing the Factory are the redeveloped and expanded National Carriage Galleries. These interpret the horse-drawn vehicle collection through story-telling and memory-making that enable the object – the carriages and their imbedded heritage trades – to become the inspiration for new products. From the time when the community rescued the vehicles from fire in the early 1980s, the carriage collection has always been the catalyst for community interest in the museum. The success of the museum was a result of its ability to use the carriage collection as a primary mechanism to connect the community to its heritage.

---

91. The author's Architect's Brief for the Cobb+Co Museum included the following requirements:
- The building had to be a place-marker for the Toowoomba community;
- The building had to mesh seamlessly into the existing structure;
- The building had to reflect the strong heritage values that underpin both the museum and the community's cultural identity;
- The museum's mission of safeguarding heritage trades had to be imbued in the building's design, the materials used, and the finish, in order to demonstrate a commitment to master craftsmanship throughout;
- The building had to symbolise the museum's obligation to develop a creative-cultural industry based on the heritage trades for the social, cultural, and economic wellbeing of the community;
- The project was focused towards the future, so the building had to reflect a modern prosperous future that the community would be proud to be associated with;
- The building had to be a welcoming 'third place' for locals and visitors alike – a place where the community would meet in a safe environment and where the community would welcome visitors with a sense of country hospitality; and
- The building had to interpret the museum's position within the Old Toowoomba Showground site (Tranter, 2006a).

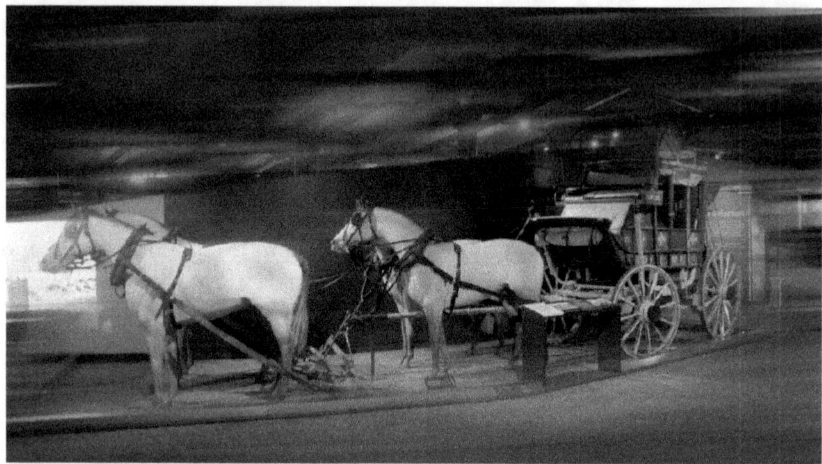

Cobb & Co. Coach 100 and five-horse team in the new vehicle gallery 2010

Visitors to the redeveloped Cobb+Co Museum are struck by the new expansive entry, which includes a welcoming much larger coffee shop with an innovative children's play-pit that, since opening, has been adopted by the community as their special place. This area also includes the retail shop, which specialises in hand-made products from the artisans who practise their trades in the Factory and Blacksmiths Shop and who are engaged as tutors and volunteers at the museum.

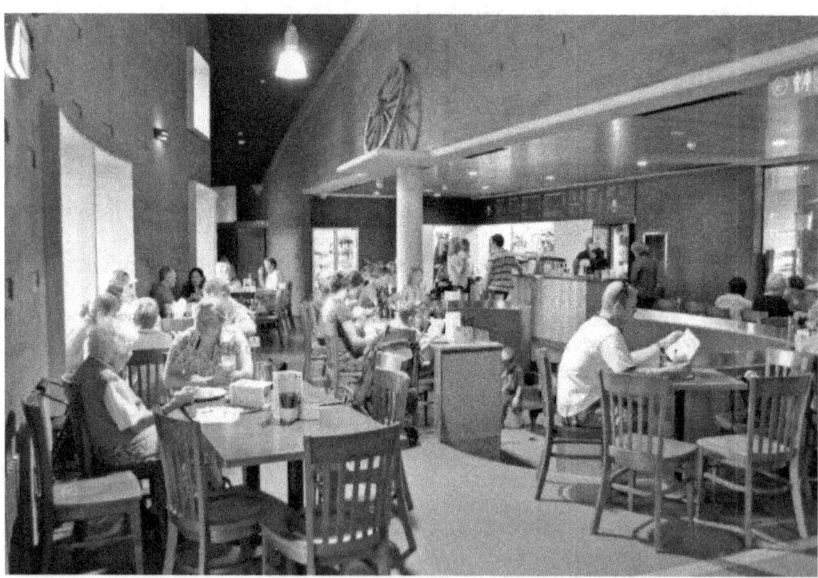

New coffee shop with children's play-pit

The other features of the new museum replicate and enhance the Stage Two focus of a social enterprise. The museum has become a community resource centre that enables the community to tell their stories and share their memories, while creating new ones within a lifelong learning environment. These components include new permanent and temporary gallery spaces, including an expanded Binangar Aboriginal Centre, community meeting spaces, and an enclosed outdoor courtyard for public programs.

4.4 Creative-cultural industries model underpinning the NCF

By the beginning of the twenty-first century, there was evidence that the old economy that existed in many OECD countries, which was based on traditional models of capitalism and industrialisation, was being transformed by the emergence of new industries developing creative products and services. These industries were characterised by knowledge generation and the mobilisation of innovation, talent, creativity, entrepreneurship, and new ideas (McRobbie, 2002, p. 385; 2004, p. 133). Referred to as the 'creative economy'[92], this movement supports the idea that 'information is the key to the future and the concept of creativity is being co-opted as the driving force' (David Throsby & Hollister, 2003, p. 11).

A number of contemporary commentators suggest that the critical element underpinning the creative industries in this new economy is creativity. Peter Drucker, stated that 'every organisation needs one core competence: *innovation*'. It has even been suggested that Walt Disney considered creativity to be so important that he paid his creative staff more than he paid himself (Barrett, 1998, p. 47). Other significant characteristics can include: individuals (or independents) or small to medium enterprises with unique production systems[93], high risk production, research

---

92.The term 'creative economy' is used in this paper to encompass a range of alternative descriptors used by various commentators, such as 'new economy', 'knowledge economy', and even 'cultural economy'.

93.Andy Pratt identified four to six cultural productions systems applicable to the creative industries. These include:

1. *Content origination*, which involves the generation of new ideas – usually by authors, designers, or composers – and the value derived from intellectual property right;
2. *Manufacturing inputs*, which describes ideas that must be turned into products and protypes using tools and materials – for example, the initial recording of a song or the manuscript of a book;
3. *Reproduction*, which refers to the need that most cultural industry products have to be mass produced. Examples include printing, music, broadcasting, and the mass production of original designs;
4. *Exchange* involves the relationship to the audience or market place. This takes place through physical and virtual retail via wholesalers and distributors, as well as theatres, museums, libraries, galleries, historic buildings, sports facilities, and other venues and locations;
5. *Education and critique* covers both training and the discourse in critical ideas; and
6. *Archiving* refers to libraries and the 'memory' of cultural forms (Pratt, 2004, pp. 22-23).

and development, investment in information and communications technologies (ICTs), and education and training (Caves, 2000; Flew, 2005; Florida, 2003; Greffe, 2008a; Howkins, 2001, 2002; Leadbeater, 1999; Leadbeater & Oakley, 1999; Oakley, 2004; Allen J. Scott, 2004).

The number of opportunities to emerge remains somewhat hypothetical at the moment, though many commentators hold high hopes for the impacts of creative-cultural industries, even though these are difficult to measure. Allen Scott insists that industries based on creativity constitute an important and growing element of contemporary economic systems, particularly in large metropolitan areas, and even in some modest-size towns in which they make a 'sizable contribution to absolute employment and income' (Allen J. Scott, 2004, p. 465). Bakhshi and Throsby have similarly assessed the creative economy as contributing significantly to growth in value-added employment and exports (Bakhshi & Throsby, 2010, p. 10).

The creative economy is evidenced in many different formats. One of the more politically fashionable outcomes appears to be in the rebranding of a district, town, or region as 'creative' in an attempt to harness economic impact. An often-cited example is the Guggenheim Museum in Bilbao, which transformed the city's international reputation by using culture to brand itself to 'attract students, inward investment and tourists' (Leadbeater & Oakley, 1999, p. 304).

Singapore's marketing strategy to rebrand itself as the 'global city of the arts', and New Zealand's 'Creative New Zealand' advertising slogan, are other schemes that propagate the 'creative element across all industries', rather than highlighting specific creative industries. 'Creative New Zealand' developed a 'two prong approach':

> It invests in its traditionally defined 'creative industries' following on the success of Peter Jackson's 2002–4 *Lord of the Rings* film trilogy and (attempts) to identify and support 'creativity' across the economy as a whole including design and packaging as a key competitive factor in New Zealand's manufacturing economy (Bilton, 2007, p. 163).

Most commentators agree that the basis of the creative economy are the creative industries. Stuart Cunningham suggests the term creative industries was first identified as 'a way of integrating sectors of the British economy in which creative inputs add significant economic and social value' (S. Cunningham & Hearn, 2003, p. 6). The unique characteristics of the creative industries have been identified by the United Kingdom professional interest group, Focus on Creative Industries:

> [Creative Industries] deal in value and values, signs and symbols; they are multi-skilled and fluid; they move between niches and create hybrids; they are multi-national and they thrive on the margins of economic activity; they mix up making money and making meaning (Stuart Cunningham, 2006, p. 35).

However, a universal definition of the creative industry proves elusive. John Hartley argues that this has to do with historical, rather than categorical ideas, and insists that creative industry concepts vary geographically, depending on local heritage and circumstances:

> Most notably in the USA, creativity is consumer – and market-driven whereas in Europe it is caught up in traditions of national culture and cultural citizenship (Hartley, 2005, p. 5).

The Creative Industries Task Force in the United Kingdom (1998) described the creative industries as a collection of:

> ...activities which have their origin in individual creativity, skill and talent and which have the potential for wealth and job creation through the generation and exploitation of intellectual property (Stuart Cunningham, 2006, p. 5).

Other definitions highlight the often non-pecuniary dimension of the creative production of symbolic goods (ideas, experiences, and images) created from aesthetic and semiotic content. Here, the value created is primarily dependent upon the play of symbolic meanings and how these are interpreted and decoded by the end users (viewer, audience, reader, or consumer) to find value within these meanings (Bilton & Leary, 2002, p. 50). Allen Scott prefers to describe the basis of the creative economy as cultural-products industries that deliver:

> ...goods and services whose subjective meaning, or, more narrowly, sign-value to the consumer, is high in comparison with their utilitarian purpose (Allen J. Scott, 2004, p. 462).

To Scott, the cultural-products industries are characterised by independents or 'swarms of small producers complemented by many fewer numbers of larger establishments' who practise 'flexible specialisation and are in a more or less equivalent phrase, to neo-artisanal forms of production' (Allen J. Scott, 2004, pp. 465-467). Scott also provides a framework for functional characteristics of the cultural-products industries, which include limited outputs that, nevertheless, have high symbolic value. These are created by relatively large inputs of capital and/or labour, with some degree of 'locational agglomeration' (Allen J. Scott, 2004, p. 468). Places for agglomeration become the 'essential hubs or platforms from which cultural producers pursue strategies of wider contestation of global markets' (Lorenze, Scott, & Vang, 2008, p. 590)

John Howkins insists that the term 'creative industries' should include those industry sectors that rely on 'brain power' to deliver the intellectual property outcomes that become the '*currency* of the creative economy' (Howkins, 2002, pp. 19, 23). Taking this approach allows him to define a very broad range of industries and sectors that are based on copyright laws, but would also include all those industries and sectors that deal in patents, such as science and electronics, within a creative industries framework. This has led to what Hesmondhalgh condemns as meaningless and 'impossibly nebulous categories of trademark and design industries' purporting to be part of the creative industries (2007, p. 146).

Other commentators attempt to document the actual industry sectors that should be considered integral components of the creative industries. Stuart Cunningham has identified thirteen such industry sectors, including advertising, architecture, arts and antique markets, crafts, design, designer fashion, film, interactive leisure software, music, television and radio, performing arts, publishing, and software. He recognised that each of these industry sectors has the potential for wealth and job creation through the exploitation of intellectual property (Stuart Cunningham, 2006, p. 13).

All these industries are distinguished by their outputs of cultural products and services and cultural experiences. Rifkin argues that the underlying commonality of these industries is that they 'commodify, package, and market experiences as opposed to physical products and services'. Their stock and trade is selling short-term access to simulated worlds and altered states of consciousness (Rifkin, 2000, p. 365). This view is supported by Bakhsi and Throsby who insist that the primary function of the creative industries is 'the creation of cultural value' (Bakhshi & Throsby, 2010, p. 19).

4.4.1 Is there a significant demarcation between 'creative' and 'cultural' industries?

The term 'creative industries' has a very recent origin and usage in the public domain and has, in some ways, absorbed the slightly older term, 'cultural industries'. The latter concept was popularised in the 1970s and 1980s by arts professionals who were attempting to persuade local, state, and federal governments to provide ongoing funding for arts and culture. Instead of pressing the intrinsic value of the arts in a climate of fiscal restraint, they focused on their inherent instrumental values in growing a broad-based assortment of cultural industries for the economic benefits they delivered to regional communities (Hartley, 2005, pp. 5,13). These cultural industries could then embrace the commercial industry sector – principally focusing on film, broadcasting, advertising, publishing, and music – that also delivered popular culture to a national population (Stuart. Cunningham, 2005, p. 284). Chris Bilton prefers to concentrate on the essence of the creativity that underpins both concepts. For him:

> 'Cultural industries' indicates that creativity grows out of a specific cultural context and emphasises the cultural content of ideas, values and traditions [while] 'creative industries' emphasises the novelty of ideas and products and places creativity in a context of individual talent, innovation and productivity (Bilton, 2007, p. 164).

The shift from 'cultural' to 'creative' has been described as a sensible move from a term with elitist connotations in the United Kingdom to one that 'annexed a whole literature of new management-speak as well as the dynamism of the young'. The new term became closely linked to Tony Blair's 'Third Way' and to a 'discourse of entrepreneurship' (O'Connor, 2004, p. 39).

Hartley suggests that the new term 'creative industries' combines 'but then radically transforms' the two older terms of 'creative arts' and the 'cultural industries' (Hartley, 2005, p. 6). He hypothesises that the creative industries are an amalgam of the arts as 'incubators of creativity' and the cultural industries (David Throsby & Hollister, 2003, p. 11). Bakhshi and Throsby insist that:

> ...the arts play a central role in the creative industries, a role that complements their essential artistic and cultural functions (Bakhshi & Throsby, 2010, p. 10).

If arts are a significant component of the cultural industries and if there is a strong relationship between the cultural and creative industries, what is the role of culture, and where do heritage and museums fit in?

4.4.2 Culture in the cultural industries

There is much discussion around the definition of culture, which was once described as 'one of the three most difficult concepts in the English language' (R. Williams 1976 quoted in Stanley, 2005, p. 22). A tripartite categorisation of the components of culture has been proposed as a useful framework.[94] These components include: artefacts, such as matters of livelihood and the entire technology of supplying goods and services; sociofacts, which cover aspects of kinship, family relationships, and social organisations; and mentifacts, which refers to cerebral, psychological, or attitudinal characteristics, including religion, magic, language, and basic values systems (Edwards, et al., 1996, p. 353).

The significance of culture is that it, alone, can give people the means to better understand and engage with life, and it can, as such, play a key role in reducing inequality of opportunity, which, in turn, can help 'slay the sixth giant of modern times – poverty of aspiration' (Jowell, 2004, pp. 17-18).

According to Shalini Venturelli, three traditions have dominated our thinking about culture:

- The aesthetic tradition, and its association with excellence in the fine arts;
- The anthropological tradition, and its understanding of culture as a received and shared symbolic system of a 'whole way of life' of a society; and
- The industrial or commercial tradition, which understands cultural products as industrial commodities sold to consumers (Venturelli, 2002, p. 392).

---

94. An alternative tripartite organisation was proposed by Jon Hawkes. These aspects included:
    - 'Mind-set' – our values, aspirations, identity, and/or history (content);
    - 'Mediums' – the processes and mediums through which we develop, receive, and transmit these values and aspirations (practices); and
    - 'Artefacts' – the tangible and intangible manifestations of these values and aspirations in the real world (results) (Hawkes, 2001, p. 4).

The third tradition, which recognises the new role of culture as a source of value-adding, will hold prominence in the creative economy. This requires:

> ...a shift in policy thinking away from questions of how to preserve cultural forms, practices and institutions of the past – the 'museum paradigm' of cultural policy – towards developing the environment that is most conductive to creativity and the generation of new cultural forms (Venturelli, 2002, p. 395).

The essence of these new cultural forms is their core of creativity, which, it is argued, is 'produced, deployed, consumed and enjoyed quite differently in post-industrial societies from the way it used to be' (Hartley, 2005, p. 18). Creativity, in all its formats, must play a significant role in the post-museum if these institutions are to remain relevant to post-industrial societies.

Dick Stanley has dissected 'culture' into three component parts. His designation of culture (C) refers to the artistic and creative activities that underpin such concepts as cultural industries, cultural institutions, and cultural activity (Stanley, 2005, pp. 22-24). Culture, in this sense, rather than any anthropological definition[95], underpins the National Carriage Factory post-museum philosophy.

In summary, there seems to be recognition that culture and its interpretation and preservation within the arts is one of the fundamental components of the cultural industries. These components can be merged with other symbolic-making industry sectors to make up the creative industries. These industries, in turn, underpin the creative economy, as well as becoming 'a valuable engine of civic renewal' (Saguaro Seminar Report, 2000, p. 1). For this publication, the concept of creative-cultural industries will be applied as an amalgam backdrop to investigate the potential for heritage and museums to function within the creative economy.

4.4.3 Is heritage part of the cultural industries?

The Queensland Government defines the creative industries in Queensland as consisting of six industry groupings[96], which it estimates are collectively worth nearly three and a half billion dollars annually, and which generate over one billion dollars in annual exports for Queensland. The industry groups include:

---

95. Culture is a capital asset accumulated by a community whose members refer to it to connote their identity (Santagata, 2002, p. 1). Culture is used to describe particular ways of life for a group of people or a period of time. A way of life can be known as a 'culture' if there are collectively understood representations of customs, traditions, beliefs, or values shared by a group or that prevail during a period of time (Introduction to the Information Development Plan for the Arts and Cultural Heritage, Australian Bureau of Statistics, 2008, p. 3).

96. These groupings replicate most of Cunningham's creative industry list of thirteen separate industry sectors (2006, p. 13).

- Music composition and production;
- Visual arts, design, and architecture (including fashion, jewellery, photography, and furniture design);
- Film, television, and entertainment software (animation and computer games);
- Writing, publishing, and print media;
- Advertising, graphic design, and marketing; and
- Performing arts (Queensland Government, 2010).

Unfortunately, this list does not include heritage or museums and, officially, these are not identified as creative industries and are not considered potentially able to contribute to Queensland's creative economy.

However, in a 2002 cultural policy document, entitled *Creative Queensland,* the state government proposed an expanded interpretation of cultural industries. In this official document, museums, archives, and libraries are sub-grouped with the arts, which – together with the media, entertainment industries, sport and recreation, urban planning, and architecture – are defined as making up the cultural industries (Arts Queensland, 2002, p. 24; 2007, 2009; Higgs & Cunningham, 2007, p. 27; Queensland Government, 2005).

Two diametrically-opposed camps that reference creative and cultural industries have emerged. One of these stresses industry groupings, and the other focuses on individual creativity. Meanwhile, many commentators continue to argue that 'the creative industries are still, in spite of all the attention they have received, not yet conceived, explained, narrated or understood' (Holden, 2007, p. 4).

Stuart Cunningham points out the 'arbitrary exclusivity of the creative industries sector' (Stuart Cunningham, 2002, p. 54). It is not surprising, though it is frustrating, that there are no universal definitions of creative or cultural industries and that there is no consistency regarding the inclusion, or otherwise, of heritage and museums. Cunningham references the United Kingdom Creative Industries Task Force Mapping Document 2001, in which the heritage sector is omitted, even though the arts are included. This occurs despite heritage's 'economic, creative and cultural characteristics being at least if not more robust than some of the sectors included' (Stuart Cunningham, 2002, p. 54).

It is interesting to note that in David Throsby's recent analysis of the six current models of the creative-cultural industries, only two – including the *Concentric Circles* model depicted below – mention museums specifically.[97]

---

97. The second model is known as *the Americans for the Arts* model. A third, the *US Trade-related* model, includes heritage in its core cultural goods and services (David Throsby, 2007).

Table 4.1: The Concentric Circles Model of the cultural industries

The Concentric Circles Model of the cultural industries

Core creative arts
Performing arts
Visual arts
Literature

Other core creative industries
Museums, libraries
Photographic services
Film production
Services to the arts

Core Creative Arts
Other Core Creative Industries
Wider Cultural Industries
Related Industries

Related industries
Advertising
Architecture
Clothing/fashion/design

Wider cultural industries
Printing/publishing
Radio/TV
Motion picture exhibition
Sound recording

No 10

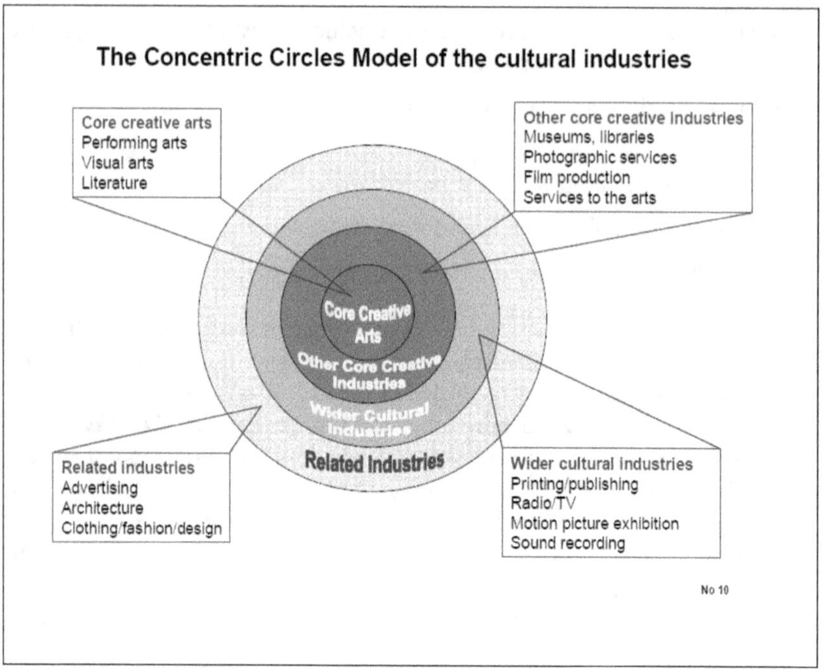

Museums are included in the second inner circle in this model, designated 'Other core creative industries' (David Throsby, 2008c, p. slide 10).

Frequently, academics and policy makers incorporate a wide spectrum of activities within their creative industries models, incorporating the information technology sector and even tourism and sport, while, at the same time, heritage may be excluded and some core museum activities, such as science research in natural history museums, will rarely be included in any creative industry definition.

As defined by the ABS in 2001[98], the arts, including museums and heritage, are a major component of the cultural industries[99], which 'collectively are activities which have their origin in individual creativity, skill and talent and which have the potential for wealth and job creation through the generation and exploitation of intellectual property' (L. Johnson, 2006, p. 297). As such, they form the basis of the creative industries and underpin the creative economy.

The central role of museums to the arts is evidenced in the government organisational structure in Australia. Museums are included within the arts portfolio of the commonwealth and all state and territory governments. However, the situation is not so straightforward for the heritage sector, as a whole, because, while 'moveable heritage' is incorporated within the Arts Ministry, 'built heritage' is usually located within agencies dealing with the environment. Only since the election of the national Labor Government in late 2007 have all aspects of heritage been combined within the one government department. In Queensland, departmental responsibility for heritage remains complicated. Museum funding is administered through Arts Queensland, while heritage site legislation is managed by the Department of Environment and Resource Management. Policies and funding specifically directed towards Indigenous art and cultural pursuits emulate from Arts Queensland, while Aboriginal and Torres Strait Islander cultural sites are managed by the Department of Environment and Resource Management.

For the discussion in this paper, the arts, including museums, are viewed as significant components of the cultural industries, and Myerscough's formulation of the arts is sufficient:

> The arts encompass a broad perspective which is not restricted to the public sector but includes independent provision alongside grant-aided activities and it covers the museums and galleries, theatres and concerts, creative arts, com-

---

98. In 2001, the Australian Bureau of Statistics (ABS) defined the cultural industries as comprising:
    - Printing and publishing (including newspapers, books, and periodicals);
    - Film, video, radio, and television;
    - Libraries and museums (including zoos, parks, and gardens);
    - Music and theatre production; and
    - Retail and support services to these activities (such as recording studios, book and magazine wholesaling, recorded music retailing, video hire outlets, and photographic studios).

    For the 'creative industries', all of the above were included, plus fashion, advertising, and interactive leisure software (quoted in L. Johnson, 2006, p. 297).

99. In Australia, there is even a general belief that the arts should include a 'much broader range of creative things' than those usually associated with the arts. An Australia Council's study completed in 2000 found that three-quarters of all people surveyed supported this view. However, they were vague about which specific activities should be included, and tended to refer to the 'Big A's' (high-end arts activities), while, at the same time, indicating their desire to expand the categories into the 'little-a Arts', such as craft activities (Saatchi & Saatchi, 2000, p. 81).

> munity arts, the crafts, the screen industries, broadcasting, the art trade, publishing and the music industries (Myerscough, 1988, p. 5).

If museums are part of the arts, then, as David Throsby argues, they will support a 'flourishing arts sector', which is one of 'the most enduring foundations upon which the cultural industries can be built' (David Throsby, 2006a, p. 39). The arts, including museums, also have a large role to play in contributing to the development of a culture of innovation in schools and other educational settlings (Australia Council for the Arts, 2005, p. 3). Proactive cultural institutions, such as museums, are starting to see a new role for themselves:

> As ... cities have shifted from industrial to post-industrial to knowledge-based economies, museums have begun serving as economic catalysts in their own right, versus just as jewels in a city's crown (Gail Lord quoted in Seligson, 2009, p. 47).

Furthermore, Throsby maintains that the cultural industries incorporating museums are 'placed in many respects at the leading edge of development into the twenty-first century' (David Throsby, 2001, p. 134).[100]

In conclusion, the National Carriage Factory was conceived as a hub for a regional creative-cultural industry, based on the heritage trades, crafts and skills, to deliver economic, social, and cultural benefits for its community. This was despite the fact that heritage and museums are not always identified as core components of the creative industries, particularly in Queensland. However, there was firm belief within the Cobb+Co Museum and its Advisory Committee that the National Carriage Factory project would flourish as a facilitator of the 'emerging creative renaissance'. Cobb+Co Museum Stage Three could serve as a 'validator of new artists and new art forms', as well as becoming an 'incubator and repository of creative expression' through its knowledge of traditional crafts and trades, skills development, and sources of inspiration for new designs and processes through its collections, exhibitions, and public programs (Chung, Wilkening, & Johnstone, 2008, p. 17).

However, the creative-cultural industry model has not been the sole tenet on which the National Carriage Factory was developed. Equally important was the museum's post-museological concern to safeguard the heritage

---

100. In discussing London as a creative city, Charles Landry espouses the broad-ranging impact that can flow from cultural activities. Cultural activities can:
- Help engender the development of social and human capital;
- Transform the organisational capacity to handle and respond to change;
- Strengthen social cohesion;
- Assist in personal development;
- Increase personal confidence and improve life skills;
- Create common ground between people of different ages;
- Improve people's mental and physical wellbeing;
- Strengthen people's ability to act as democratic citizens; and
- Develop new training and employment routes (Landry, 2001, p. 241).

trades as the essential innovative components of the creative-cultural industry model that would become *Hand Made in Country*.

4.5 The post-museum – more than physical collections

By the beginning of the twenty-first century, new museological ideas were being merged into post-modern concerns. However, this was not a straightforward set of museological ideas or a well-defined theory. Hooper-Greenhill has identified a large group of 'disparate theorists' now devoted to analysing post-modernity:

> ...understood as an emerging form of society – either 'after' implying the dissolution of modernity or seen as the latest stage of modernity (E Hooper-Greenhill, 2007a, p. 367).

The concept of a post-museum is not straightforward or static. It refers to a contemporary museum that is fundamentally different from the traditional museum and that is intended to embrace a variety of societal perspectives and values, with the traditional museum perspective being only one voice among many. The post-modern museum is not curtailed by its architecture. It focuses more on processes and experiences, and it reaches 'into the spaces, the concerns, and the ambitions of communities':

> The development of the post-museum will represent a feminisation of the museum. Rather than upholding the values of objectivity, rationality, order, and distance, the post-museum will negotiate responsiveness, encourage mutually nurturing partnerships, and celebrate diversity (E Hooper-Greenhill, 2000a, p. 82).

The post-museum will hold and care for objects, but will concentrate more on their use, rather than on further accumulation (E Hooper-Greenhill, 2000b, p. 152). It will concentrate on information as its primary commodity and will aim public programs and community events – that will project a 'cacophony of voices', diverse perspectives and 'conjoint dynamic processes' around the development of exhibitions (Burton & Scott, 2003, p. 58; E Hooper-Greenhill, 2000a, p. 81).[101]

In his article, 'Interpreting the New Museology', Max Ross identified a climate of 'increasing reflexivity' in the museums he investigated in the West Midlands in the United Kingdom. In these museums, he concluded that the museum professional's identity has shifted from 'legislator' to 'interpreter' of the widespread social range of material culture now displayed in these museums. This, in part, has aided the transformation of contemporary museums from 'exclusive to socially divisive institutions' (Ross, 2004, p. 84).

---

101. Examples include contemporary exhibitions based on oral history and intangible heritage at the New Jersey Historical Society in Newark, New Jersey (Yerkovich, 2006).

Museums are now acknowledging the importance of memories, songs, cultural traditions, and oral histories as embodiments of a culture's past and future (E Hooper-Greenhill, 2000a, p. 81). The post-museum, which is something more than a passive repository site, is now emerging as a place in which intangible heritage complements or even replaces lost tangible objects.

As objects become secondary to the discourse that is created within the museum, social memorising and the opportunities for learning and connection that can come out of these dialogues are accentuated, as is the multiplicity of contending voices and the histories projected. These voices now more frequently include migrants and refugees, Indigenous peoples, and colonised populations. This infuses the post-museum with a post-colonial view that rejects the portrayal of the people of the past as 'exotic other', without connecting them to the present world. The emphasis is on engagement between visitors and the exhibition, as opposed to objectification. However, this can be a difficult task for museum professionals who must ensure they have an inclusive world view (Colp-Hansbury, 2009, pp. 6-8).

The rise of museums and sites of collective trauma, such as those relating to the Holocaust, are challenging witnesses to the emergence of divergent voices espousing these contested histories. Bernice Murphy describes this development as:

> ...a conscious discourse of 'liberation' of a host of new gendered, ethnic and sub-cultural identities with the rise of identity-discourses since the 1970s ... the museum as a singular institutional form and totalised mode of discourse has mutated into a pluralisation of museums employing a range of discursive practices (2005, pp. 74, 76).

The availability of new technology and social media exacerbates the pluralistic nature of museums today by making the virtual museum both a reality and a necessity in any visitor-focus environment.

At the beginning of the twenty-first century, the pendulum seems to have swung too far for some museum professionals. Ironically, there is now serious debate about redefining the central role of collections in major museums, and a number of writers have lamented the 'fading' of collections at the expense of experiences. Stephen Weil states emphatically:

> An art museum without a collection is only a gallery. A children's museum or a science museum without a collection is only a discovery centre. A historical society without a collection is only an affinity group. A historic site without a collection is only a local attraction...and a museum without a collection is not a museum (Weil quoted in Alexander & Alexander, 2008, pp. 15-16).

Perhaps most importantly for its interpretation by the Cobb+Co Museum, the post-museum is concerned with intangible heritage, along with the emotions of visitors, because it is directly linked to the concerns and ambitions of communities. In essence, it attempts to make the museum part of the living culture of its time (E Hooper-Greenhill, 2000a, p. 81; Hudson, 1998, p. 49).

4.5.1 Traditional trades as intangible heritage

The underlying basis of the National Carriage Factory project was the principle of safeguarding the traditional trades, crafts, and skills that were embedded in the national carriage collection at the Cobb+Co Museum and implanting them into 'the living culture of the community'. The carriage collection always acted as the catalyst that brought heritage and community together – beginning when the community rescued the vehicles from fire in 1981.

Considering traditional craftsmanship as an intangible may be seen as a paradox because the outcomes are tangible objects. However, traditional craftsmanship is not simply about the products. It also involves the skills, knowledge, creativity, and innovation essential for the continued production of artefacts in an environment that encourages the transfer of skills and expertise onto new artisans to ensure the 'life' of the craft. Inspiration for the National Carriage Factory concept was found in the UNESCO Convention for Safeguarding Intangible Heritage (International Council of Museums, 2002; L. Smith & Akagawa, 2009; UNESCO, 2001, 2003). The Convention stresses that:

> ...our efforts to safeguard traditional craftsmanship must focus not on preserving craft objects – no matter how beautiful, precious, rare or important they might be – but on creating conditions that will encourage artisans to continue to produce crafts of all kinds, and to transmit their skills and knowledge to others, especially younger members of their own communities (UNESCO, 2003).

The Convention acknowledges the range and variety of heritage trades and crafts and the ongoing dynamic nature of heritage that can accommodate transformations, such as that from carriage-makers of the past to motor vehicle-makers of the present – who, in turn, will create the heritage 'masterpieces' of tomorrow (Cobb+Co Museum & Southern Queensland Institute of TAFE, 2008, p. 11).

To ensure the successful safeguarding of traditional trades and crafts, as expressed in the Convention for the Safeguarding of Intangible Heritage, two parallel processes are required. The first is to formulate and implement innovative formal and informal training programs which, while acknowledging both the 'traditional artisanry' underpinning the heritage trades and their inherent dynamic and innovative nature, enable skills and procedures to be transmitted from current practitioners to younger members of the community. The second equally significant requirement is to ensure that the safeguarding of traditional trades and craft is integral to the economic, social, and cultural wellbeing of the community. The Convention acknowledges that it would be a futile exercise to preserve the traditional crafts if done without embedding the craftsmanship into 'practices within communities, providing livelihoods to their makers and reflecting creativity and adaptation' (Article 2 (3), UNESCO, 2003).

The heritage trades embody a dynamic process of continuity and change and are best understood as a fusing of tangible heritage with intangible heritage. To make a living from the heritage trades requires 'talent, patience and a good head for business' (Svensson, 2008, pp. 123-124).

4.5.2 Releasing heritage trades from their time warp

Currently in Australia, as in other OECD countries, heritage trades and crafts are caught in a time warp of tradition and convention that is associated with pre and early Western industrialisation. The medieval trade guilds enshrined the traditional apprenticeship system into centuries of practice, until the advent of industrialisation. This system opened the gate to journeymen, encouraging them to increase their skills through a broad range of work experiences, often in different counties or even countries. Such a journey could culminate, in time, in peer recognition as a master tradesman or craftsman through presenting a masterpiece to the Trade Guild, and having them accept it (Cobb+Co Museum & Southern Queensland Institute of TAFE, 2008, p. 14). Quality workmanship, innovation, and creativity were the hallmarks of skilled tradesmen and master craftsmen in the pre-industrial era (Ford, 2009, p. 56).

However, the advent of industrialisation heralded the demise of this system. Industrialisation led to a general movement from tradesman, to overseer, to factory foreman, and resulted in these master craftsmen supervising less qualified workers who were only required to complete a limited number of tasks. The former master was transformed into a factory owner, and had to relocate from the workshop floor to the office, and from hands-on operations overseeing his apprentices to accounting and marketing concerns (Kinnery, 2009, p. 71).

There has been little interest in OECD countries, over the past century, in maintaining the traditional apprenticeship system for trades that were surpassed by new products and services. There were, of course, pockets of time-honoured heritage trade activity across these countries, particularly in regional areas. In Toowoomba, Col Ferguson's small carriage workshop, with the wooden horse *Harkaway* overseeing activities, continued to operate until the early 1970s, undertaking repairs to museum collections of horse-drawn vehicles and supplementing income by building 'original' Cobb & Co. coaches for collectors and tourist attractions. Innovation and creativity became the hallmark of this carriage work – a focus necessitated by the dwindling supplies of original horse-drawn vehicle components.

4.5.3 Attempts at revival of heritage trades

Today there are a few isolated attempts to revive and preserve traditional trades and crafts that are associated with 're-invented and revitalised' heritage sites. Stemming from the economic decline of the 1980s, there have been some concerted efforts, notably in Great Britain, to rejuvenate former industrial sites as 'living' heritage precincts. These include the Ironbridge Gorge in Shropshire, the Rhondda Valley Coal Industry Interpretative Centre in Wales, and Wigan Pier's 'The Way We Were' Heritage Centre. Not only were the buildings on these sites given a new lease on life, but the former employees of the sites were also provided with opportunities to maintain their trade and craft skills. Some critics make the distinction between 'crafts' and 'trades'[102], defining the former as 'part of the constructed heritage industry, even to the extent that the craftspeople become part of the exhibit' (Urry, 1990, p. 214). Chris Rojek takes this argument further by concluding:

> The action of modernity...destroys traditional crafts only to restage them as objects of display in the heritage industry (1993, p. 194).

In contrast to crafts, trades such as harness-makers and wheelwrights are frequently more valued, because they are seen as 'genuine historical reconstructions of authentic methods and techniques' (Urry, 1990, p. 214).

More recently, again in rural England, research by the Museum of English Rural Life has attempted to 'preserve' through documentation some rural trades and crafts as practiced by individuals who appear to be motivated by lifestyle choices (Museum of English Rural Life, 2008). Interestingly, the trend here, in contrast to the situation in the former industrial sites, is for such individuals to have little or no cultural or social connection to the source of the craftsmanship being revived (L. Smith & Waterton, 2009, p. 21). In either case, there is no specific formal training system involved in maintaining and improving the heritage crafts and trades skills (English Heritage, 2005, p. 8). A few ecomuseums (as discussed below in Section 4.6) also provide some contemporary models for safeguarding traditional customs, including crafts and trades.

4.5.4 Cobb+Co Museum heritage trade training concept

In contrast to the approaches mentioned above, the Cobb+Co Museum's position is to ensure that a regional creative-cultural industry will be forged around the heritage trades, with a formal mechanism by which these trades, crafts, and skills can be transferred to the next generation. It has

102. The simple definition that trades are based in industry and that crafts are based in cottages and homes has not applied in the NCF project because the term 'craftsman' is often recognised as a 'skilled' tradesman. The Cobb+Co Museum has adopted the stance that 'heritage trades' refers to concepts of both trades and crafts and that 'master craftsman' is a term valued by many of the museum's practising artisans, regardless of whether they are traditionally classified as a 'tradesman' or 'craftsperson'.

been argued that one should not underestimate the importance of reproducing, both formally and informally, professional skills and competencies in the local area because:

> ...social interaction and learning foster the acquisition of skills and progressive learning stimulates new interests and abilities (A.J. Scott & Garofoli, 2007, p. 10).

To achieve this aim, a unique partnership has developed between the Cobb+Co Museum and SQIT.[103] In 2008, the partners completed a major research project on the scope and availability of heritage trade training, both in Australia and overseas. The subsequent report, entitled *Heritage is in Our Hands: a Review of Heritage Trade Training*, developed options for new heritage trade training delivery methodologies for the National Carriage Factory project. It articulated 'a new approach, based on teaching and learning flexibility that recognises the value of different learning pathways'. For this project to flourish, flexible learning approaches that deliver diverse training pathways will 'hold the key to success'. To demonstrate the process, five case studies were presented in the Report, which covered areas of master craftsmanship in heritage building, traditional craft paper, Indigenous cultural heritage, heritage clothing and jewellery, and vintage vehicles. It is envisaged that any specific discipline could be accommodated within the proposed learning pathways to gain accreditation in Heritage Craftsmanship (Cobb+Co Museum & Southern Queensland Institute of TAFE, 2008, pp. 35-40).

As mentioned previously, the National Carriage Factory concept was motivated by a revived community interest in heritage. These trends are not limited to Toowoomba, or even Queensland. There is a worldwide increase in public interest in retaining the built and movable heritage icons that proclaim so much of our cultural heritage. As stated in the foreword to the Report, of primary importance is that:

> ...the skills necessary to conserve and maintain these valued cultural heritage icons both tangible and intangible are at risk of being permanently lost. We are also cognisant that there might be a very limited time-window available for action before many of these skills will be lost forever (Cobb+Co Museum & Southern Queensland Institute of TAFE, 2008, p. 3).

For many years, the Cobb+Co Museum has been delivering workshops in a number of heritage trades and crafts. Initially, these were limited to trades associated with horse-drawn vehicles and other equine trades. However, since 2006, there has been a diversification in the workshops to include such fields as lead lighting and copper foiling, bookbinding, silversmithing

103. The Cobb+Co Museum built the National Carriage Factory on land supplied by SQIT. This Factory will become the focal point for heritage trade training in the country.

and silver casting, traditional sign writing, leather work (besides plaiting and harness making), and felting and millinery. In 2009, the museum offered thirty different workshops, including the first series of heritage trade workshops for people aged twelve to sixteen years. The annual *Have a Go Festival* that is undertaken each February enables potential students to attempt various heritage trades and crafts, which helps keep alive these aspects of our intangible heritage.

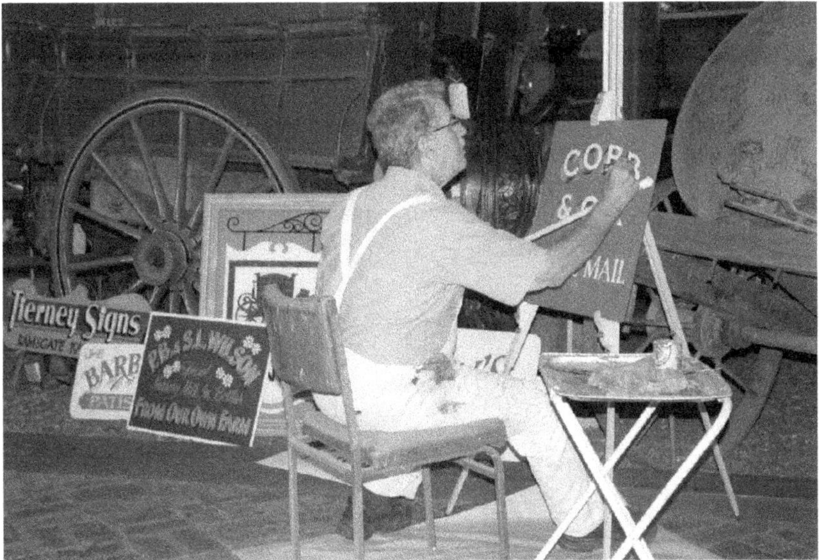

Traditional signwriter Peter Tierney

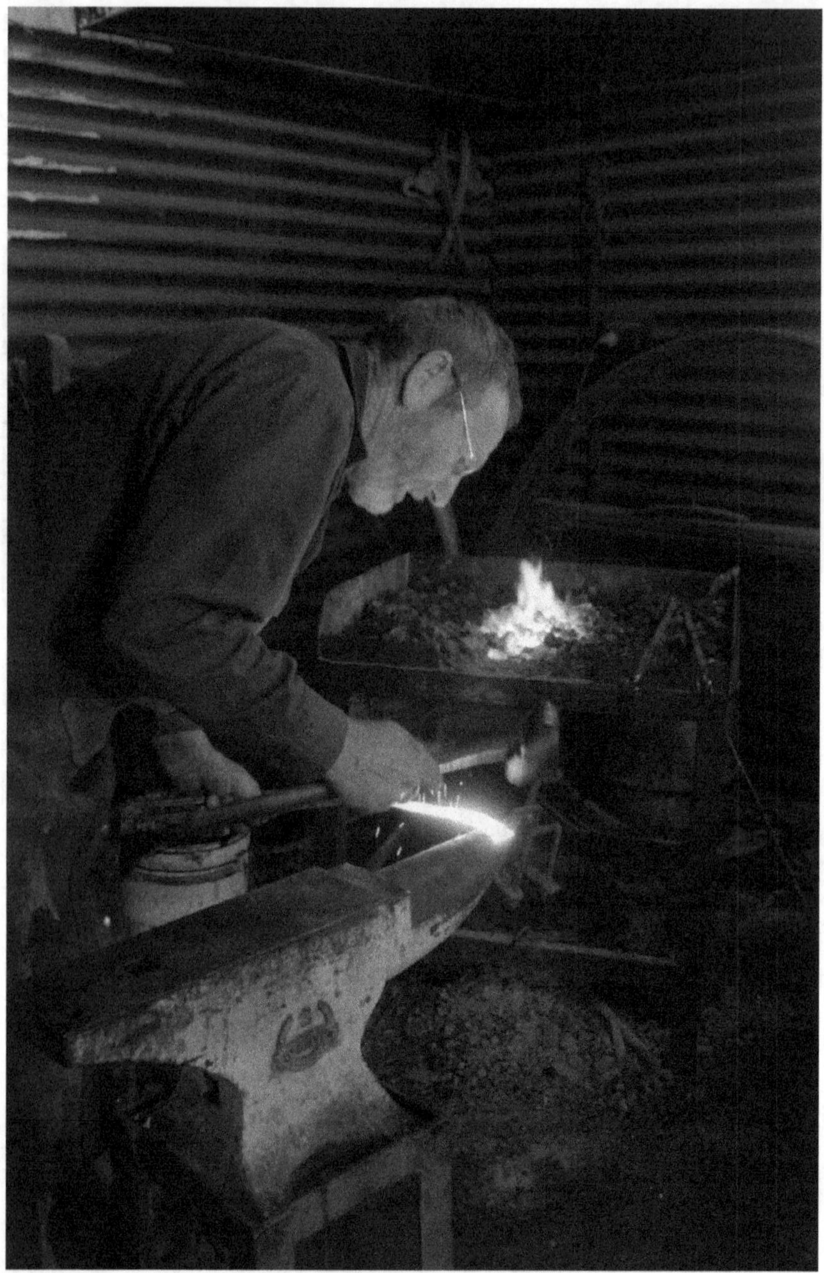

Master blacksmith Terry Drennan

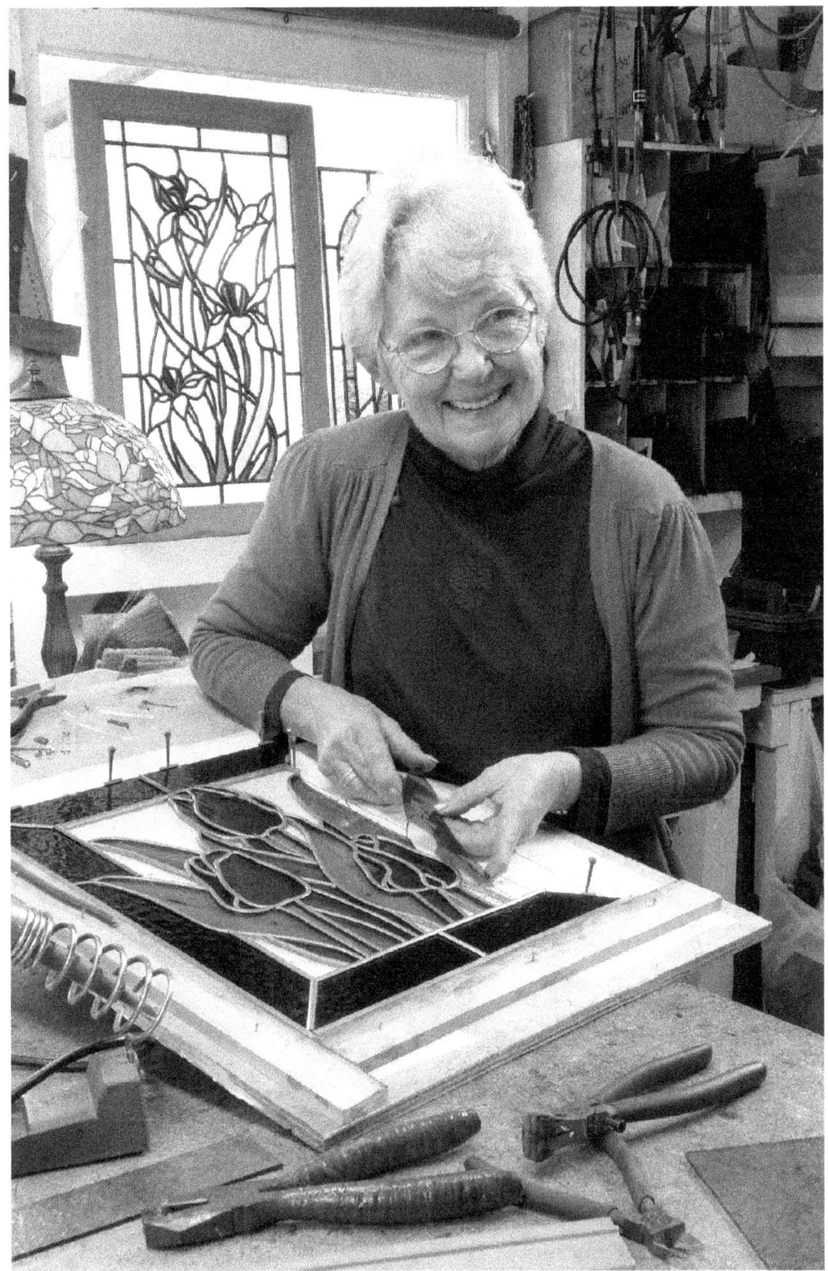

Lyn Swann glass artisan

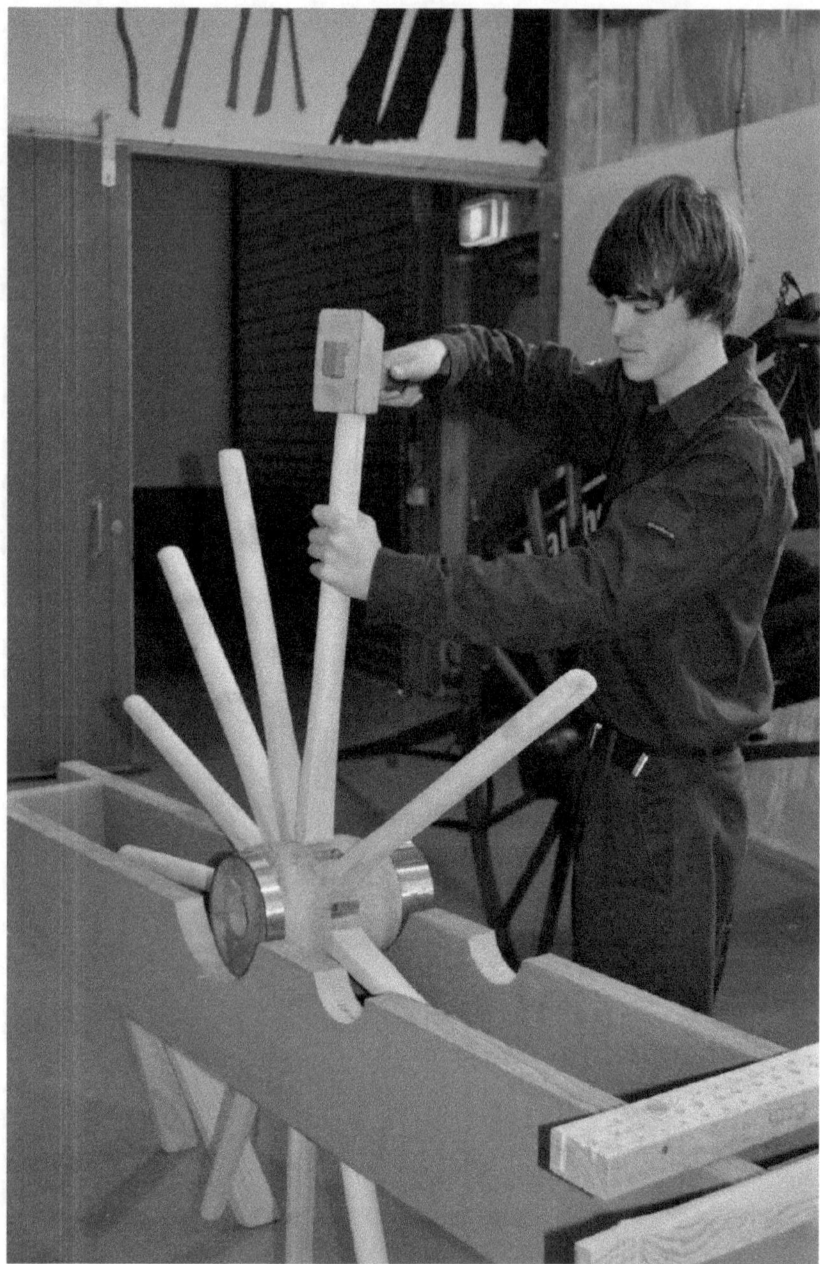

Cobb+Co's first heritage trade school-based apprentice Thomas Weir

Today, these traditions, skills, trades, and crafts are under threat. Changing technology and lifestyles now impose different priorities and demands on the ways these skills are passed on (Cobb+Co Museum & Southern Queensland Institute of TAFE, 2008, p. 3). However, there is no intention of preserving these traditional trades within a pre-industrial society 'time warp', because this would be of little benefit to contemporary society. Rather, the intention is to safeguard these trades by focusing on their inherent creativity and innovation and to encourage their adaptation with contemporary materials and techniques to produce new products that will resonate with present-day consumers.

4.5.5 Preserving Indigenous and non-Indigenous trades, crafts, and skills

The pioneering spirit and skills of Australians – the preserve of both our Indigenous and non-Indigenous people – are part of Australia's intangible and often hidden heritage. Through their innovation and passion, our forebears, both Indigenous and non-Indigenous, built and cared for Australia's historic landscapes and buildings and formed the legends that underpin the Australian ethos.

Although the development of Australia's pastoral industry is, today, mainly identified with non-Indigenous Australians, a number of older Aboriginal people and their families take great pride in the roles they also played. As a result of their involvement, many traditional European heritage trades were and still are practised.

At the Cobb+Co Museum, the story of an all-Aboriginal droving team is not unique, nor is the story of a skilled Aboriginal saddler working in Toowoomba in the second half of the twentieth century. There are now moves by some traditional Aboriginal communities to incorporate a museum component into their new cultural centres to enable the communities to preserve their stories as domestics and pastoral workers alongside their dreamtime cultural traditions. A typical story is that of Kev Carmody, one of Australia's best-known Aboriginal songwriters[104], who grew up on a pastoral property west of Toowoomba. Carmody spent his early working life as a wool presser, until the demise of the smaller pastoral properties in the early 1970s. His songs embody the rich rural oral traditions of both his Irish father and Murri mother and, through them, he recalls the harmonic rhythm of life he felt during his pastoral days – a rhythm that was destroyed when he moved to the city (Carmody).

104. Kev Carmody is best known for his collaboration with Paul Kelly on the song *From little things, Big things grow* – a song about the Aboriginal land rights movement in the Northern Territory.

This source of Aboriginal pride and achievement is often overlooked today because Aboriginal cultural heritage is largely identified with traditional 'dreamtime' cultures. These 'dreamtime' cultures, with their unique practices and skills, also contribute significantly to Australia's cultural identity. In partnership with the traditional owners of the land and the historic Aboriginal and Torres Strait Islander families who live in Toowoomba, the Cobb+Co Museum, through its Binangar Centre, has provisions in its training plans for the many varied and evolving formats of Indigenous cultural heritage. As part of the museum's program to help identify and meld Indigenous and non-Indigenous aspects of our national traditions, a demonstration project was developed. This involved an Aboriginal artist working with a local blacksmith and harness-maker to create a showpiece work of art that drew together European and dreamtime intangible heritage traditions. This project demonstrated that:

> ...traditional knowledge and techniques be they Indigenous or of the dominant society in origin, are harbingers of long-term sustainability as the wisdom of past adaptation is rediscovered (Janes, 2009, p. 134).

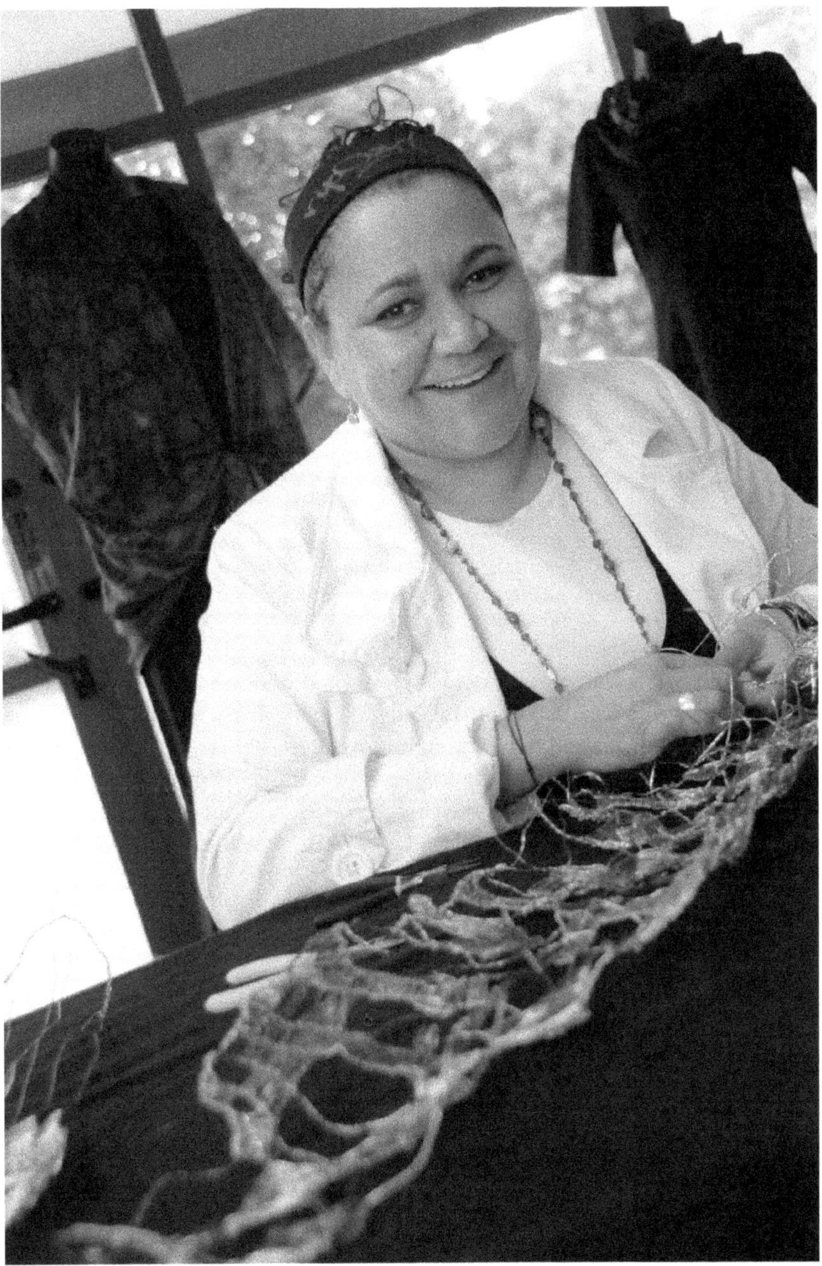

Aboriginal artisan Kim Walmsley creating a copper wire representation of a traditional collamon

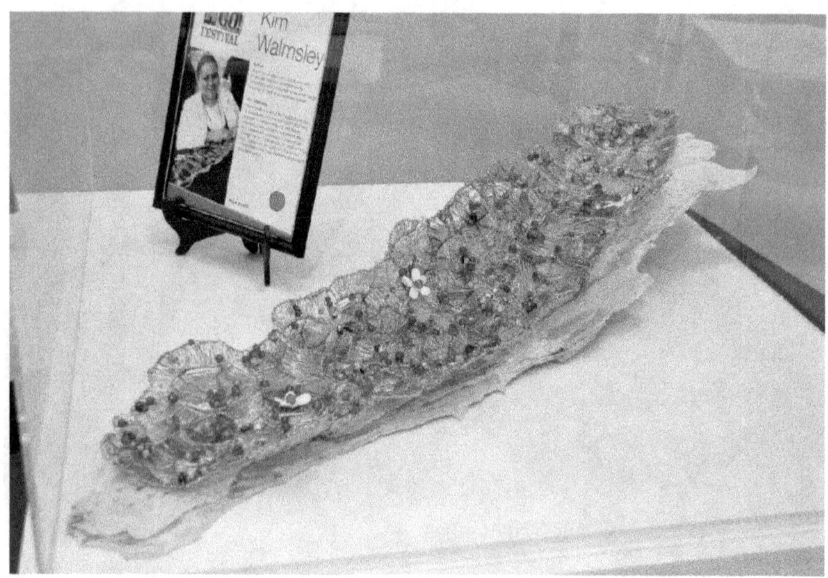

The completed artefact acquired by the Queensland Museum

The Cobb+Co Museum worked with Indigenous artisans who used traditional techniques and natural ochres from the Gummingurri stone arrangement site at Meringandan near the Bunya Mountains west of Toowoomba. Through these programs, the museum illustrated that strong 'chains of connection' still exist across time and place in Australia (Mulvaney, 1976, p. 72).

Highlighting Indigenous craftsmanship also demonstrates the strong connection between the underlying tenets of the National Carriage Factory project and new iterations of ecomuseology. This also inspired the Cobb+Co Museum to develop its model of a creative-cultural industry hub based on heritage trades, crafts, and skills.

4.6 Impact of the ecomuseum's community approach on the NCF

In developing the National Carriage Factory concept, the Cobb+Co Museum looked to international museum models that challenged the traditional concept of museums. The ecomuseum was identified as a useful example. Instead of isolating the museum from its community, the ecomuseum attempts to reach into communities by producing an endogenous product that is an integral component of daily life (de Varine, 2005a, p. 61).

The ecomuseum's forebears can be found in the folk-museum movement that was initiated in Scandinavia with the opening of Arthur Hazelius' Skansen Open-air Museum, in 1891. This museum was dedicated to preserving the buildings, rituals, and customs of fast-disappearing rural lifestyles across Sweden, including the skills of craftsmen who produced traditional products by hand (Alexander & Alexander, 2008, pp. 121-122; Bergdahl, 2005, p. 104; Crang, 1999, p. 8).

While Skansen initiated an early tradition of living history museums, the ecomuseum model – made popular in France in the 1970s by George Riviere – has had a more profound effect on museums and their community engagement models. In contrast to the local museum – which is often found in removed buildings 'replete with decontextualised objects, and lacking a consideration of both contexts and historical processes' – the ecomuseum, in theory at least, involves local people at the 'level of designing and developing the museum, as well as at the level of exhibit interaction' (Walsh, 1992, p. 163). In these institutions, the emphasis is equally on traditional architecture, craftsmanship, and the maintenance of 'historic processes rather than the equipment used to achieve them [so as] to ensure a continuity of skills associated with them' (Boylan, 2004, p. 5).

In much the same way that the local museum movement developed in regional Queensland, the ecomuseum was designed originally as a response to declining rural industries and the loss of old traditions and local identity. However, ecomuseums have an inbuilt flexibility to respond to local communities not replicated in community museums in regional Queensland. A number of Swedish communities, through working with their local authorities, have also created ecomuseums to respond specifically to the loss of industrial heritage associated with old mining and metal production (Bergdahl, 2005, p. 104). This response was different to that in the United Kingdom, where authorities invested heavily in heritage and cultural tourism facilities to revive former industrial sites and ports, often without local community input and support (A. Dicks, 2003, p. 34).

The ecomuseum concept was identified as part of the new museology at the International Council of Museums (ICOM) Conference in Quebec in 1992. These museums are distinguished by their original structures in situ at the regional level, as well as their political, social, and economic agendas. They have in common:

> ...a clearly political determination to meet the need for a heightened awareness of local heritage, and to assume joint responsibility for this heritage, considered as the cultural breeding ground of development (de Varine, 2008, p. 5).

A number of attempts have been made to underscore the distinguishing characteristics of an ecomuseum. In China, the nine 'Liuzhi Principles' were adopted.[105] These principles reiterate the need to be flexible in structure, governance, and activities so an ecomuseum can respond to its own community. They also emphasise the primary goal of social development and community wellbeing, without compromising traditional values, as a 'prerequisite for establishing ecomuseums in living societies' (Donghai, 2005, p. 3).

Ecomuseum projects must primarily aid sustainable development on a regional level by fostering a strong relationship between nature and culture; maintaining a total environment, including social, economic, and cultural; and safeguarding natural resources (Davis, 2007, p. 199). Today, as the movement to recognise the legitimacy of intangible heritage acquires momentum, the ecomuseum concept is gaining prominence.

Ecomuseology takes, as its starting points, the individual and collective needs of the community in which the museum is situated (Worts, 2006b, p. 128). The stated purpose of the ecomuseum is to provide

> ...a mirror in which a population could seek to recognise itself and explore its relationship to the physical environment as well as to previous generations, [while also] offering visitors an image to promote a sympathetic understanding of the work, customs and peculiarities of a population (Poulot, 1994, p. 66).

Ecomuseums develop holistic descriptions of places and communities, invest historical significance in the everyday economic and cultural activities of ordinary people, and tell family and local histories through the 'first voice'[106] and via historical re-enactments, while encouraging visitor parti-

---

105. The 'Liuzhi Principles' for the development of ecomuseums in China are:

1. The people of the villages are the true owners of their culture. They have the right to interpret and validate it themselves;
2. The meaning of culture and its values can be defined only by human perception and interpretation based on knowledge. Cultural competence must be enhanced;
3. Public participation is essential to the ecomuseums. Culture is a common and democratic asset, and must be democratically managed;
4. When there is a conflict between tourism and preservation of culture, the latter must be given priority. Genuine heritage should not be sold out, but production of quality souvenirs based on traditional crafts should be encouraged;
5. Long term and holistic planning is of utmost importance. Short term economic profits that destroy culture in the long term must be avoided;
6. Cultural heritage protection must be integrated in a total environmental approach. Traditional techniques and materials are essential in this respect;
7. Visitors have a moral obligation to behave respectfully. They must be given a code of conduct;
8. There is no bible for ecomuseums. They will all be different according to the specific culture and situation of the society they present; and
9. Social development is a prerequisite for establishing ecomuseums in living societies. The wellbeing of the inhabitants must be enhanced in a way that does not compromise the traditional values (Donghai, 2005, pp. 2-3).

106. 'First voice' is defined as 'both literal and metaphorical, of the actual carriers and custodians of cultures and their related heritage resources' (Galla, 2008, p. 11).

cipation in traditional activities (Maggi, 2005, p. 63). The more sustainable ecomuseum models, such as Halong Bay in Vietnam, embrace business development; tourism; training in safeguarding significant environmental or historic landscapes and buildings; and, occasionally, the safeguarding of traditional customs, including crafts and trades (Galla, 2002, p. 64).

The importance of local leadership in ecomuseology is uncontested. However, the emergence and regular turnover of local leaders will not occur unless community members are convinced that they are part of the heritage that is being encapsulated in the ecomuseum (Scheiner, 2005, pp. 86-87). It is important to highlight the roles of education and learning in ecomuseology, and the role of the museum specialist, particularly regarding the specialists' relationships with community volunteers. Maggi stresses the primacy of the locals, warning that the professionals 'cannot assume the voice of the communities and must never stand for their leaders'. They must, however – despite the difficulties of cost and personnel – develop diverse leadership skills in the local population by using a net-like paradigm of 'many teachers, many pupils', rather than the current educational model with a pyramidal paradigm of 'one teacher, many pupils' (Maggi, 2005, pp. 65-66). This scenario helps avoid conflicts between professional employees acting as consultants and imposing their ideas on the community, and volunteers who can feel sidelined if their local knowledge is ignored or undervalued (Joubert, 2005, p. 94).

To promote successful and sustainable development, it is important for museums to distinguish between external professionals and local community members, and to recognise the need for both groups to share leadership duties. In general, this has been the pattern to date. However, the unique combination of professional museum skills within local community leadership, as demonstrated by the Director of the Cobb+Co Museum, provided an alternative model that proved to be the key to the initial success of the National Carriage Factory project.

In summarising the outcomes of the 2005 *Communication and Exploration Conference* on ecomuseums in Guizhou, China, Su Donghai stressed the essential changing nature of ecomuseums, which must be able to adapt to changing community needs:

> The theory of ecomuseums and also the intention of the concept are in the process of a constant development, constant evolution (Donghai, 2005, p. 198).

The National Carriage Factory project adopted a number of ecomuseum principles. These included:

- The need for dynamic processes of innovation and experimentation;
- The ability to harness the resources of the community;
- The expertise to mediate between the present and tradition; and
- The desire to become:
    - A strategic instrument for the promotion of local culture and society;

- A centre for the creation of innovative ideas for the territory and its social and economic development, as well as for the implementation of the resulting projects; and
- A place of dynamic consensus (Cogo, 2005, p. 101).

While ecomuseology played a significant role in the development and implementation of the Third Stage transformation of the Cobb+Co Museum, it was not the only model referenced. Despite the diversity and flexibility offered by ecomuseums, the need to provide a range of sustainable income streams outside the main sources of public funding necessitated a broader vision for the National Carriage Factory than that offered by the ecomuseums.

4.7 The economuseum business approach incorporated into the NCF

The more recent innovation of the 'economuseum' provided insightful parallels to the National Carriage Factory project, with its combined focus on economic sustainability and conservation of heritage trades and crafts. Originating in Canada, the economuseum is a relatively new concept that adapts ecomuseology into small craft shops, with museums attached. The economuseum movement aims to combine culture and economics – specifically by promoting economic development, preserving local heritage, revitalising traditional crafts, and adapting craft products for contemporary use, while contributing to regional tourism (Simard, 1991, p. 231). The participant and primary beneficiary of the economuseum is the individual artisan – not necessarily the community. However, the wider community would benefit from the economic development generated through enhanced regional tourism activity.

The first economuseum was established in 1992 in Quebec, Canada. Under the direction of Cyril Simard, the Saint-Gilles Paper Mill revived a traditional French craft as the economic generator for sustainable business development ("Papeterie-Saint-Gilles,"). To some commentators, such as Robert Janes, the economuseum should represent an inspiration for museums searching for relevance in the twenty-first century, because this is a 'decidedly new take on the meaning of museums, heritage and the marketplace' (Janes, 2009, p. 134). According to Simard, an economuseum has three primary aims:

- To self-finance all operations;
- To create a new range of products, with the main concern being to conserve what is best in the tradition; and
- To contribute to the development of cultural and scientific tourism in the region by selling the product in a suitable museological setting (Simard, 1991, p. 232).

By 2009, the economuseum movement had grown to encompass fifty-five handicraft and agri-food trade businesses in fourteen regions in Quebec and four provinces in Atlantic Canada and Northern Europe. This innovative new cultural tourism model is based, in part, on 'second-generation' heritage activities that are showcasing and transmitting traditional trades and knowledge. The Economuseum Network promotes its craft or agri-foods business members as producing products that are:

> ...the fruit of an authentic technique or know-how. The business showcases artisans and craft trades by offering an area for interpreting its production and by opening its doors to the public. [They] are self-financed through the sale of their products, and make an innovative contribution to the cultural tourism sector (Economuseum Network).

With its regional organisational focus and promotion of heritage trades and their associated products, the economuseum concept offers a number of parallels to the National Carriage Factory (see Table 4.2). Both concepts identify the importance of education and training in producing business outcomes using cultural products, such as the heritage trades and its associated natural and cultural heritage traditions. According to its charter, the economuseum network aims to 'promote cultural diversity, a living heritage and sustainable development':

> ...by combining **culture** through the dissemination of traditional trades, **education** through the spread of knowledge and the **economy** through the support of craft businesses (Economuseum Network, 2010).

The economuseum members are, in essence, established small businesses 'concerned with integrity, knowledge and intelligent consumption' that co-operate through a regional tourism network. But they also recognise, like museums, the need to document and archive traditional production processes and interpret objects from the past. Unlike many museums, however, they also require their member artisans to interpret their contemporary production processes for visitors and to provide opportunities for visitors to purchase their unique products, thereby helping safeguard their trades, crafts, and skills (Economuseum Network; Janes, 2009, p. 136).

Colonial Williamsburg in Virginia, U.S.A., represents something of a hybrid economuseum. It is firmly entrenched in the tourism industry, offering a range of accommodation and hospitality services. Within its traditional workshops, which employ tradesman trained onsite, traditional trades and crafts are demonstrated to visitors and a range of merchandise is produced for sale. All activities are based on rigorous research that aims to replicate the life of Colonial Williamsburg when it was the capital of Virginia.

Not all museologists find the economuseum concept appealing or relevant. Some consider it to be nothing more than the whim of some commercially-minded people who have usurped the ecomuseum mantle and replace it with 'nothing more than a tourist-trap which makes and sells objects produced in the traditional way in front of the public' (de Varine, 2005b, p. 55).

However, the economuseum model, while still emerging, does represent a new opportunity for a group of cultural industry practitioners and institutions to succeed within the creative economy in ways neither envisaged nor thought applicable to ecomuseums in their current evolutionary formats. The strong links between the creative economy, heritage trades, training, and regional tourism espoused by the economuseum resonate strongly with the underlying tenets developed for the National Carriage Factory project. They also invite comparisons with *HandMade in America* – the regional development organisation established in western North Carolina, U.S.A., to promote economic development through the preservation of crafts and heritage skills.

4.8 HandMade in America's regional development approach adopted by the NCF

The Cobb+Co Museum established a working relationship with *HandMade in America*[107] – an economic development organisation based in Asheville, North Carolina, which adopts a broad regional approach to enhance sustainable progress in the many small communities scattered across the northern part of the state. Asheville was an appropriate model for Toowoomba, because both have a population of around one hundred thousand and both have similar mixes of commercial, educational, health, and service industries for their broader regions. Located in a gap in the Appalachian Range Mountains, Asheville also attracts large numbers of 'relocators' who use the region as their summer retreat, in a similar way that Toowoomba, on the Great Dividing Range, was once viewed by Brisbane residents.[108]

All the programs delivered by *Handmade in America* are aimed at teaching people in communities the skills to take control of their future through growing handmade economies based on craft[109], cultural heritage, and community assets (Garfield, 1997, p. 17; HandMade in America, 2010). The organisational focus is on the artisans who create handmade objects enmeshed in the cultural heritage and traditions of the region that preserve and enrich community life. One of its strength is its inclusivity – all communities and artisans are welcome to participate. It also extends its innovative role from

---

107. The author was invited to participate in a workshop with the staff and board members of *HandMade in America* in February 2010. Following this, the *HandMade in America* board member and furniture maker, John Gernandt, delivered a series of workshops with artisans and the new board members of *Hand Made in Country* in Toowoomba in November 2010.

108. The Information Centre in Asheville has as many brochures on relocating to the region as it has on visitor attractions.

109. These crafts include the beading and textile traditions of the local Native American people; the more recognisable European craftsmanship of furniture making and jewellery using semi-precious stones; as well as work in black and white metals, glass, ceramics, and textiles.

supporting the artisans, techniques, and products to finding creative and workable solutions to promote community engagement and economic development linked to tourism.[110]

The region surrounding Asheville is dotted with small towns in a predominately agricultural landscape, which, again, parallels with the Darling Downs region to the west of Toowoomba. *HandMade in America* has embraced its region by linking it together through a series of touring trails that connect and celebrate the region's assets and promote the region's creative economy. The tourism industry promotes the demand for craft work and labour-intensive products, and brings the 'market' to the artisan, thereby allowing artisans more time for creative expression and the production of unique objects (Greffe, 1994; HandMade Institute, n.d., p. 25).

Through these trails[111], *HandMade in America* created authentic and enriched experiences for visitors travelling along 'heritage corridors', where they can learn the story of the people behind communities 'whose lives are coloured by their art and whose art colours the lives of anyone who comes to know their work' (Fields, 2003, p. 6; HandMade Institute, n.d.; Silberberg, 1995, p. 364). By 2002, the approach was expanded to incorporate the agricultural products of the region. The *Farms, Gardens and Countryside Trails* added:

> ...a cultural component to traditional agritourism to showcase the special relationship between people and place, and expand the opportunity to attract high-end customers (HandMade Institute, 2005a, p. 3).

These cultural tourism activities, in which the 'landscape becomes a lever of economic development through tourism', are not unique to Asheville (Greffe, 2008b, p. 3). There are many examples of regions and towns that use heritage festivals, trails, regeneration projects based on industrial sites or rural lifestyles, and new museum development as defining characteristics in place-marketing that aims to encourage economic development through tourism. *HandMade in America* has supplemented these traditional activities by 'second-generation' activities. These activities range from immobile products, which have to be consumed on site, to mobile products, which are directed more to 'the physical export of local cultural products to markets all over the world' (Allen J. Scott, 2004, pp. 465, 470-471).

To demonstrate the effectiveness of these activities, *HandMade in America* has invested in a number of major research projects to attract support from and develop partnerships with all levels of government, philanthropic

---

110. To demonstrate the possible economic impact that can result from heritage and crafts in these often-forgotten and by-passed townships, a study of community development in six small towns with populations of 175 to 1,764 over the period 1996 to 2003 was published (HandMade Institute, 2005b).

111. *The Craft Heritage Trails of Western North Carolina*, first published in 1996, illustrated seven driving trails that linked four hundred heritage assets.

organisations, businesses, artisans, and communities[112]. One study used Richard Florida's 'super creative core' business classification as the basis of its survey of businesses residing in the heart of downtown Asheville. Through this, it was able to estimate that the total real estate value associated with the creative industries was $US61.7million (Florida, 2003; HandMade Institute, 2005c, p. 9).

HandMade in America's core values and principles highlight many post-museum aspirations, and resonate throughout the Cobb+Co Museum's Stage Three development. These values include:

- Building upon the heritage, resources, desires, hopes, and aspirations of the community;
- Involving the whole community;
- Focusing on authenticity and quality;
- Sharing stories with integrity;
- Providing local benefit; and
- Creating new and enduring partnerships (HandMade Institute, n.d.).

The economic development focus of *HandMade in America,* which was based on heritage and crafts to stimulate community development, was used extensively in formulating *Hand Made in Country* – the regional creative-cultural industry hub model that underpinned the National Carriage Factory project (Gernandt, 2010; Tranter, 2010b).

4.9 Hand Made in Country unpinning the NCF's regional significance

Based on the experience of *HandMade in America,* it was obvious that the National Carriage Factory's potential to become an effective hub for a creative-cultural industry centered on the heritage trades would be limited, unless a regional approach was adopted and implemented. Consequently, *Hand Made in Country* was conceived to position Toowoomba and the surrounding Darling Downs as the leading region in Australia recognised for its high quality handmade goods and services. It was defined as a:

> ...fresh and innovative approach to economic, education and community development [that] will help preserve the heritage trades for future generations and deliver valuable entrepreneurial skills for local artisans and the wider community (Hauritz, 2010, p. 4).

---

112. A comprehensive study in 2008 indicated the economic potential of the craft industries in Western North Carolina. This economic potential consisted of 2,200–4,000 full-time makers who contributed two hundred and six million U.S. dollars in total annual impact. This can be subdivided into:
    - $US86 million – craft artists;
    - $US31 million – craft consumers;
    - $US58 million – galleries/shops;
    - $US16 million – craft schools and non-profit organisations; and
    - $US15 million – craft suppliers and publishers (Gernandt, 2010).

Research had also shown that investment in heritage would be more sustainable if it was made in an area in which heritage did not already play a key role and in which there was a high level of economic integration (Greffe, 2004, p. 309). However, the greatest economic returns for a region were provided as a result of the linkage between safeguarding heritage trades and tourism through attracting high-yield and high-quality visitors – not necessarily large numbers of tourists – and providing them with people-to-people contact, as well as through matching locally-supported products to appropriate visitor groups (Jamieson, 2006, p. 13; Reisinger, 1994, p. 24).

NCF the hub of Hand Made firms

One of the basic tenets of *Hand Made in Country* was the realisation that to fulfil its potential as a social, cultural, and economic driver for the region it had to develop a national and international perspective. A number of creative-cultural industry models were investigated, including: the Los Angeles motion picture complex; Central Paris, with its 'traditional artisanal and fashion-orientated industries'; Manchester's Northern Quarter; Birmingham's Jewellery Quarter; Malaysia's Multimedia Super Corridor project; PiemonteGroove – Turin's electronic music scene; and the pottery district of Caltagirone in Italy. These models made it apparent that cultural-products firms agglomerate together in specialised clusters to provide a 'creative ecology of mutually supportive interactions' that maintain sustainable and endogenous growth by providing 'mutual support psychologically, financially and technically' (Mizzau & Montanari, 2008, p. 652; Pollard, 2004; Santagata, 2002, pp. 10-11; Allen J. Scott, 2004, pp. 479-480; Shorthose, 2004, pp. 153-154). By investigating Brisbane's tier two music scene, it was discovered that:

> Respondents who were clustered together in close geographical proximity to each other cited benefits of co-location as sharing of information and experience; learning new information or knowledge; sharing of skills; learning new skills, and sharing of personnel (Hearn, Ninan, Rogers, Cunningham, & Luckman, 2004, p. 104).

In addition, clustering creates centres of excellence that uphold and distribute best practices, while stimulating competition by bringing buyers and sellers together (Howkins, 2001, p. 141; Porter, 2000, p. 259; Queensland Government: State Development and Innovation, 2005, p. 47; Santagata, 2002, p. 2; Allen J. Scott, 2004, pp. 479-480). Howkins explores this symbiotic relationship within industry clusters further by suggesting that:

> They also offer high 'multiplier' effects. Any inputs from outside the cluster are quickly disseminated and internal knowledge and skills do not leak out. Clusters can lead to a high rate of synergy, the positive interchange of complementary resources that create a result that is more than the sum of its parts (Howkins, 2001, p. 141).

PiemonteGroove attempted to transform Turin into a 'city-laboratory' for electronic music that represented a sort of re-interpretation of the historical role of *avantgarde* that Turin (and Piedmont) used to play in the history of Italy. Mizzau and Montanari investigated this attempt, and their findings resonated strongly with the philosophy underpinning *Hand Made in Country* (2008, p. 668). They suggested a number of reasons to explain why proactive government intervention that supports the formation of cultural districts will encourage the aggregation of cultural industries to form 'agglomeration economies' that can enhance the longer term financial viability of small creative enterprises and independents:

> Transportation and information costs are reduced by the spatial proximity of actors. Members can use coordinating mechanisms typical of network form of governance; members allowed frequent formal and informal encounters [that] favour the emergence of social context that is characterised by a high level of embeddedness not only with each other but also add in third parties, restriction of access to the network, formation of a professional 'macroculture' (a system of widely shared assumptions and values), collective sanctions to members who do not behave appropriately, negotiating and contractual costs are reduced; formation of trust capital and sharing and cooperation which positively affect learning, creativity, innovation and knowledge creation and exchange (Mizzau & Montanari, 2008, p. 653).

Industry clusters can agglomerate into different types of cultural districts. These have been identified as:

- The 'industrial cultural district' (mainly based on positive externalities, localised culture, traditions in 'arts and crafts', and consumers' 'cultural lock-in');
- The 'institutional cultural district' (mainly based on property rights assignment and symbolic values);
- The 'museum cultural district' (mainly based on network externalities and the search for optimal size); and
- The 'metropolitan cultural district' (mainly based on communication technology, performing arts, leisure industries, and e-commerce) (Santagata, 2002, p. 2).

The Toowoomba regional characteristics mesh with the two models identified as the 'industrial' and the 'museum cultural' districts, particularly with the emerging pattern in a number of more successful regions in which individual smaller specialised, but complementary, firms cluster around a larger establishment that acts as a hub for wider production networks (Allen J. Scott, 2004, p. 462). The Cobb+Co Museum Stage Three development was identified as having the potential to play this role of a central hub in the same way as other learning institutions have in other districts. Michael Porter, from the Harvard Business School, suggests that:

> Clusters survive because of their proximity to sophisticated users and customers, their ability to draw employment from highly skilled pools of local talent, and their access to supportive regional institutions such as universities and vocational training institutions (quoted in Florida, 2008, p. 113).

4.9.1 Hand Made in Country planned as a catalytic regional tourism project

Despite the regional perspective of the Cobb+Co Museum Stage Three transformation, it was realised that a more broadly-based inclusive organisation, such as the Toowoomba & Golden West Regional Tourist Association (TGWRTA), was needed to initially host *Hand Made in Country* in order to maximise regional support. Working with TGWRTA and Tourism Queensland (TQ), *Hand Made in Country* was scoped and identified as a catalytic regional tourism project for the Toowoomba Regional Council area, which is the major population area covered by TGWRTA. As a result of this recognition, funding was provided by TQ to undertake an initial feasibility study to gauge support for the *Hand Made in Country* concept, and, more importantly, to identify artisans and assess their technical, production, and marketing skill levels, and their determination to grow their 'hobby' into a livelihood. This collaborative project would also assess the potential to take an ad hoc, loose cluster of producers, artists, manufacturers, and tourism and hospitality outlets and develop it into a professional, self-sustaining industry.

The study was carried out by Krista Hauritz – former manager of TGWRTA and member of the Cobb+Co Museum Advisory Committee. An innovative aspect of this study was a series of 'long lunches' – information sessions attended by ninety artisans that were held in five centres across the region. At these functions, questionnaires were distributed to identify support and genuine buy-in for the project. This survey had a greater than ninety percent response rate, with one hundred percent of respondents registering interest in the project, and ninety-eight percent considering paying commissions on their products and/or membership, where appropriate (Hauritz, 2010, p. 5).

The Feasibility Study was accepted by TGWRTA, and a Planning Subcommittee was charged with the task of implementing the report's three-year Industry Formation Strategy and Implementation Plan. This plan will direct regional efforts to develop and formalise the industry; improve communication networks; build industry capacity through training and workforce development; create new and innovative distribution channels; and focus on branding, packaging, further marketing, and market development. The plan will be outcomes-focused and will include developing entrepreneurial opportunities for the industry network to be self-sustaining, following the conclusion of the seed funding used to implement the strategy. Self-sustainability needs to occur through the development of industry-funded communication networks, industry memberships, pay-for-use training, and sales commission structures that lead to increased yield and productivity, which encourages new business and job creation.

Hand Made in Country will involve the direct linking with over three hundred stakeholders, including peak industry groups, associations, producers, artisans, and businesses throughout the region. Its success will depend upon:

- The number of artisans, businesses, and industry bodies in the network;
- Participants in training;
- Improved industry skills;
- Sales of products;
- Use of brand;
- Visitor numbers and yield per visitor; and
- The collective economic outcomes for industry and the number of jobs created.

These performance indicators will be constantly monitored to indicate the success of the project (Toowoomba & Golden West Regional Tourist Association, 2010).

The project was launched at the Regional Tourism Conference held in Toowoomba in November 2010. Leading furniture maker and *HandMade in America* Board member, John Gernandt, was invited as a guest speaker at the conference and was asked to run a series of workshops for artisans and potential *Hand Made in Country* Board members. The Cobb+Co Museum will be represented on the Board by the Museum's Operations and Visitor Experience Manager, who will be the inaugural Chair of *Hand Made in Country* in her position as an executive member of the TGWRTA Board.

The evolution of *Hand Made in Country* will be directed by its new Board and will reflect the skills of its members and the aspirations of the community. It will need to formulate policies and galvanise support to ensure that the basic components of the specific creative-cultural industry model, based on the heritage trades envisaged, are achieved. These include:

- A local community that is cohesive in its cultural traditions and in its accumulation of technical knowledge and social capital;
- A low level of product standardisation;
- Accumulation of savings and the presence of strongly entrepreneurial cooperative local banking (The Heritage Building Society – a major partner of the National Carriage Factory project – has established community banking enterprises across the region);
- An inclination towards open international markets (based on the agriculture, viniculture, and flora-culture models that exist in the region);
- Public financial support along the entire chain of the creation of value (from inception, to production, to marketing and sales);
- A high rate of creation of new firms as a result of 'social capability' and 'interactive learning' (through initial partnership with the Department

of Employment, Economic Development, and Innovation (DEEDI) and Department of Education and Training (DET)); and

- The ability to be district-minded, to become a local system, and to produce positive externalities in the field of design, technological innovation, managerial organisation, the creation of new products, labor market flexibility, and commercial distribution (Santagata, 2002, p. 4).

The initial success of *Hand Made in Country*, as demonstrated by its first *Studio Safari* in March 2011, has been recognised by a further Tourism Queensland grant to gauge the feasibility of extending the concept into the neighbouring regions of the South Burnett, to the north of Toowoomba, and the Southern Downs, to the south. Both sub-regions were identified as part of the original concept, but it was decided to limit the first phase iteration to the focus region surrounding Toowoomba.

The key roles of the Cobb+Co Museum will be to provide innovative formal and informal training in an effective interactive learning environment for the artisans. Opportunities for artisans to be recognised for their prior experience and practical learning will be implemented by the museum and SQIT. The museum appointed its first school-based apprentice in Heritage Trades in 2011 – again in partnership with SQIT.

As an emerging post-modern museum, the Cobb+Co Museum also aims to become the key place-marker for the project, with its impressive building, interpretative galleries, public programs, and product development facilities, as well as a sales and marketing centre for *Hand Made in Country*.

4.9.2 Embedding heritage trades into community development

The ultimate aim of *Hand Made in Country* is to foster a culture of creativity and innovation that will lead to economic, social, and cultural development in the region. Using the region's strengths in education and training, and capitalising on the quality and quantity of its natural, cultural, and intangible heritage products and services, the cultural-products industries being developed will aim to become environmentally-friendly and employ high-skill, high-wage creative workers (A. J. Scott, 2007, p. 1478). In this case, highly skilled heritage artisans will earn their income from delivering education and training, producing and promoting quality hand-made merchandise, and participating in the tourism trails and significant events. Other outcomes will include improved quality of life in the places in which the artisans congregate, and an enhanced image and prestige of the local region. Although it is only in its infancy, Galla has referred to this project as:

> One of the most impressive demonstration projects, bringing tangible and intangible heritage together through the First Voice, that I have come across in recent years (Galla, 2008, p. 17).

Galla's reference to the 'First Voice' is another distinctive component of the National Carriage Factory project. Usually used in reference to Indigenous peoples, the First Voice in this project has always been the local community – the primary stakeholders of the Cobb+Co Museum – who have taken the National Carriage Factory project to heart. Members of the business community have spearheaded the NCF Committee, which raised thirty percent of the project cost. The Committee also planned and implemented the public relations campaign that galvanised community awareness and support and was successful in acquiring state government funding that enabled the project to proceed in a time of financial downturn.

The National Carriage Factory project involved many community partnerships between the Cobb+Co Museum and education and training providers, tourism organisations and operators, retail outlets, and many other local and regional businesses. The business community supports the National Carriage Factory project because many see it as capable of strengthening the regional economy through enhanced experience-based tourism ventures that will attract a diverse range of visitors to events and activities, as well as high-yield participants involved in training, education, and learning programs.

Support has grown as the community has come to appreciate that this project has the potential to create a vibrant culture based on the region's natural, cultural, and intangible heritage – a culture that will become a capital asset by providing important patterns and symbols to promote a distinctive community identity. Already it is obvious that community enjoyment and wellbeing is derived from participation in cultural heritage traditions and the sharing of knowledge, skills, ideas, beliefs, values, spirituality, standards, and responses (Toowoomba City Council, 2008). This reflects a more widely accepted belief that:

> ...craft is chic and items that show the care, passion – gentle quirkiness – of the handmade variety are now must-have products, and more than a few people are making a living from crafty skills (Tait, 2010, p. 40).

The concept of using heritage trades and crafts to provide economic outcomes is not new. Examples include the Smithsonian Folklife Festival, in which 'thousands of craftspeople have walked away with millions of dollars in sales of their textile weavings and basketry, their pottery and paintings, their woodcarvings, metalsmithing and jewellery' (Kurin, 2004, pp. 8-9; 2007, p. 17); ecomuseums such as those in Halong Bay in Vietnam; economuseums in Quebec; and North Carolina's *HandMade in America* – a project in which a whole region is marketed for its craftsmanship (HandMade in America, 2010). *Hand Made in Country* is visioned to replicate, within the Toowoomba region, the outcomes delivered by these international models.

4.10 Conclusion

The Cobb+Co Museum's National Carriage Factory Stage Three development was devised as an amalgamation of ideas, values, and principles extracted from international models of creative-cultural industries, as well as the Convention for Safeguarding Intangible Heritage – particularly its focus on craftsmanship. Also strongly referenced were the emerging concepts of ecomuseology and economuseology. The regional community development approach from North Carolina, *HandMade in America*,was instrumental in providing the starting point and governance model for *Hand Made in Country.* The main characteristics of these and how they have been incorporated into the National Carriage Factory project itself – *Hand Made in Country*, specifically –are summarised in Table 4.2, below.

Table 4.2: Comparison Ecomuseum, Economuseum, Creative-cultural industry Model, HandMade in America and National Carriage Factory

Function/purpose	**1. Ecomuseum**	**2. Economuseum**	**3. Creative-cultural industry**	**4. *HandMade in America***	**5. National Carriage Factory**
Basic purpose	Conservation focussed on local identity	Conservation to bring out potential of object and craft	Conservation as pool of ideas	Conservation to bring out potential of craft	Combination of all four
Focus	The collective memory	The product and craft	The aesthetic qualities of the object	The product and the craft	The craft, the product, and collection of original objects
Attitude to the object	The object as evidence	The object as inspiration for new products	The object as personal fulfilment	The object as regional identity	The object as inspiration for new products, personal fulfilment, and regional identity
Attitude to production techniques	Ability to produce with traditional technology	Adaptive potential of traditional techniques	Profitability of the technique	Profitability of the technique	Adaptive potential of traditional techniques and profitability
Attitude to site and building	The global environment factor of identity	The building crystallises the specific character of the milieu	The building as a centre of life and creativity	The building as centre for community development	The building as a centre of community life and creativity
Main basis of activity	Life and experience of a community	Technologies of an active workshop	Creativity as an independent creator	Community development through craft activities	Combination of all four
Aims of training schemes	For understanding of local way of life	For production of quality objects and updating of techniques	For creation and production of quality objects	For production, marketing, and sales of quality objects	2, 3, and 4
Types of instruction provided	Cultural activity by local specialists and volunteers	By craftsmen	At further training level	At further training level	2, 3, and 4
Training and further training of staff	Self-instruction	Apprenticeship and specialist studies	Apprenticeship and specialist studies	Specialist studies	Apprenticeship and specialist studies

(This table is based on a model developed by Cyril Simard) (1991, p. 231).

The National Carriage Factory has been positioned within the creative industries model. It aims to nurture the creativity and skills that are inherent in the heritage trades as the basis for social, cultural, and economic development of the region. Its strength lies in its ability to fuse cultural and natural heritage, regional identity, commerce, education, and tourism.

The National Carriage Factory was also envisaged as a channel through which the Cobb+Co Museum could respond to the challenge of the post-museum philosophy that museums should facilitate activities aimed at bringing together heritage resources, volunteerism, and community participation, and aimed at engaging young people and their elders in a trans-generational communication process of constructive social, cultural, and economic development. In the case of the National Carriage Factory, these activities would be based on the innovative and creative possibilities embodied in heritage trades, crafts, and skills (Asia Pacific Regional Assembly of ICOM in Shanghai in October 2002 quoted in Galla, 2004).

In September 2010, the Third Stage transformation of the Cobb+Co Museum commenced, with the completion of the National Carriage Factory project. This resulted from a successful community engagement process that was implemented from 2006, which provides tangible evidence of the emerging relationships and new leadership roles between the Cobb+Co Museum and its community. The significance and future direction of the museum will depend on its community's needs and aspirations, the Queensland Museum's strategic objectives, and the ability of future Cobb+Co Museum management to work closely with the community.

The three transformations of the Cobb+Co Museum reflect, above all else, the changing dynamics between the museum and its community over the past two decades. During this period, the community has moved from being an indifferent bystander to being a full partner with the Cobb+Co Museum. During the National Carriage Factory Appeal, the community gave 'voice to its values', both qualitatively and quantitatively. How this was achieved will now be examined in more detail in Part B.

Part II

Part B

Chapter 5

What Value do Museums have and how can this be Measured?

5.1 Introduction

The previous three chapters formed Part A of this study, which investigated the three-stage transformations of the Cobb+Co Museum as an example of the positive effects that the changing dynamics between museums and their communities can initiate, particularly in regional areas. The research illustrated that each transformative stage of the Cobb+Co Museum responded to specific national and international developments that affected museums and heritage. These responses were also identified as singular reactions to the museum's location within the Toowoomba community in regional Queensland.

At its optimum, multi-intersections between a museum and its community, as demonstrated by the Cobb+Co Museum, can result in relationships that are highly valued and supported by the community. Part B, consisting of Chapters Five and Six, investigates how communities value museums and how this value can be measured.

Chapter Five explores the changing concepts of value that communities associate with museums. It concentrates on understanding the reasons various stakeholders value their museums. While politicians, policy makers, and other museum professionals have been recognised as the major stakeholders of museums, the frameworks adopted for assessing the value of museums have been narrow. Recognition of the community as the primary stakeholder necessitates a different methodology in order to effectively measure a museum's worth.

After analysing various methodologies for measuring the multifaceted nature of value derived from arts and cultural industries, the most useful model to emerge was the Contingent Valuation Methodology (CVM). This methodology was subsequently applied to a major study to measure the public value of the Queensland Museum, of which the Cobb+Co Museum is a part. This study, which was devised and developed in 2008, is analysed in detail in Chapter Six.

5.2 Chapter outline

This chapter will address the problem of measuring value in museums by evaluating the ongoing debates surrounding the measurement of the economic, social, cultural, and intrinsic benefits of museums as part of the arts and cultural industries. Museums, together with other arts and cultural industries – particularly in the United Kingdom, Canada, the United States of America, and Australia – have been subjected to increasing demands by funding bodies for more reliable outcome measurements. How and why museums have responded to these demands will form the first section of this chapter.

Eight different museum stakeholder frameworks will be identified in an attempt to understand who museums should be accountable to for their delivery of public goods and services, because these stakeholders will be the ones who assess the museum's value to themselves, both individually and collectively.

After an analysis of the benefits of using a cultural economic framework, the third section incorporates a review of the strengths and weaknesses of the various methodologies used to gauge the value of cultural goods that could be used to help quantify the public value of the Cobb+Co Museum. This literature review included fifteen CVM case studies, which were analysed in detail for inherent methodological weaknesses and attempts to negate them. The Contingent Valuation Methodology (CVM) was assessed as being capable of providing 'valid and reliable' measurements of the value of the Queensland Museum, as well as offering a consistent tactic for other arts and cultural industries to consider.

5.3 What value do museums have?

One of the more interesting and prolonged debates within the arts and cultural industries, since the 1980s, has been the question of the value of museums to the economic, social, and cultural life of individuals and communities, and this value's effect on regional regeneration and national development. This debate has affected national and local arts establishments, alike, because changes in government policies have had major effects on funding and accountability requirements.

Over this period, the arts and culture industries, including museums, have been valued by different stakeholders for their potential to deliver different outcomes at different times. According to the United Kingdom's then Arts Minister, Estelle Morris:

> Museums are as important to our quality of life as any of the public services, and their purpose and progress deserve more public debate than they have sometimes received. [They] are real links with their local communities within which they play an economic, educational and social role (Department for Culture Media and Sport, 2005, p. 4)

The National Museum Directors in the United Kingdom issued a joint vision and mission for the arts and cultural industries in 2006, in which they sought a commitment from the government that:

> ...it values the contribution culture makes to learning and education, creativity and economic vitality, social regeneration, health and community cohesion and that it will place the cultural sector closer to the heart of public policy making (National Museum Directors' Conference, 2006, p. 1).

Today, museums are more likely to be viewed within a topology of economic, social, cultural, and intrinsic values (C. Scott, 2003, 2006, 2007a, 2007b, 2007c), but this was not always the case.

5.3.1 From intrinsic to economic value

Prior to the 1980s, there was a simplistic value-assessment of museums as being part of the arts and cultural industries – summed up in the phrase 'arts for art's sake'[113] (M. Blaug, 2003, p. 476). Governments funded museums for their intrinsic worth as one of the essential components of any civilized society (McCarthy, Ondaatje, Zakaras, & Brooks, 2004, p. 1).

The 1980s represented something of a watershed for the arts and cultural industries that were caught in the wake of economic rationalism. These industries were not immune to the government's 'new public management' system and 'value for money' auditing, and this proved to be quite a challenge for the sector (Sara Selwood, 2004, p. 19). The long-held presumption of the intrinsic and social benefits of the arts for individual and community development was questioned, because this argument could not be supported with any reliable data. Anecdotal 'evidence' was no longer appropriate in the new era of accountability and impact measurement that was demanded by the arts funding bodies (Reeves, 2001, p. 7).

From the 1980s, the Thatcher Conservative Government in the United Kingdom looked to the arts and cultural industries as economic drivers in a struggling economy and they invested heavily in new 'flagship' cultural cap-

---

113. Though it has been argued that there is no absolute value in the arts (Carey, 2006, p. 249).

ital infrastructure projects – projects that were associated with major urban regeneration schemes. These were located in a number of areas that were then struggling former industrial cities, such as Glasgow, Manchester, and Liverpool (Lorente, 1996; Savitch & Kantor, 2002).

Some in the arts sector saw the potential to embrace the economic argument for its activities and for their alleged financial contribution to the nation (Belfiore, 2002; Belfiore & Bennett, 2007; Reeves, 2001; Sara Selwood, 2004).[114] Sara Selwood identified this as the time when the cultural sector reinvented itself as a 'wealth creator', particularly when lobbying for greater cultural participation in community development projects (Sara Selwood, 2004, p. 19).

It was not surprising that, in 1988, *The Economic Importance of the Arts in Britain* was published and that it became a powerful justification for continued public funding for the arts as economic drivers (Reeves, 2001, p. 8).According to its author, the arts needed to find alternative arguments to justify continued government funding at a time 'when central government funding on the arts was leveling off'. He reiterated that:

> ...arguments based on intrinsic merits and educational value were losing their potency and freshness, and the economic dimension seemed to provide fresh justification for public spending on the arts (Myerscough, 1988, p. 2).

Based on his research, Myerscough concluded that the economic potential of the arts to Britain was massive, because of the industry's major export earnings, its spin-off to other industries, its stimuli to tourism, its catalysts of urban renewal, and the improved images of regions that it created, which made them better places in which to live and work (Myerscough, 1988, pp. 148-150).[115] This seemed to provide the impetus for the government's development of systematic evidence-based management of the arts and cultural activity, and the demand that the arts justify their subsidies in economic terms (Sara Selwood, 2004, p. 19).

However, Myerscough's conclusions have not been without their critics. Some argued that problems with methodology made it impossible in many cases (or at least 'uneconomic') to undertake research 'to assess the precise benefits' of the economic impact of museums (Allison & Coalter, 2001, p. 40).

Myerscough also made some salient points about the intrinsic value of the arts and the needs of artists and cultural organisations for experimentation and innovation as the basic of economic modernisation in Britain (1988,

---

114. The Arts Council was particularly proactive, 'mounting a more positive argument for the expansion of public expenditure on culture on the grounds of its economic returns' (Belfiore, 2002, p. 95).

115. Based on a study of three separate communities – the Merseyside area of Liverpool, Greater Glasgow, and the smaller region of Suffolk around the town of Ipswich – he calculated that the arts generated an annual turnover of ten billion pounds – subsequently providing cost-effective jobs for 2.1% of the total employed population (Myerscough, 1988, pp. 148-150).

p. 8). Although these sentiments regarding the intrinsic value of the arts were downplayed at the time, they became popular around fifteen years later.

5.3.2 A broader cultural agenda: from economic to social values

Within a decade of the release of Myerscough's seminal work, the British Government's interest in the arts and culture began to broaden. With the election of the Blair Labour Government, a new social reform agenda became a high priority. In 1998, the Department for Culture, Media, and Sport (DCMS) was established and it announced massive increases in funding from the National Lottery Fund for the arts and museums, in order to deliver the government's social agenda of 'access, excellence and innovation, education and the creative industries' (Department for Culture Media and Sport, 1988, p. 1). Specific outcomes to be delivered included:

> ...enhancing social cohesion, improving local image, reducing offending behaviour, promoting interest in the local environment, developing self-confidence, building private and public sector partnerships, exploring identities, enhancing organizational capacity, supporting independence and exploring visions of the future (Reeves, 2001, p. 15).

But there were strings attached. The theme of 'public money being used appropriately to meet public objectives' would become the Department's mantra (Department for Culture Media and Sport, 1988). The government's modernising agenda required the cultural sector to justify its funding by demonstrating the social impact it was making, particularly in the area of social inclusion (Sara Selwood, 2002, p. 5). To do this, it created a structural framework that fostered a much closer alignment between service delivery, funding, performance information, and policy objectives (C. Scott, 2007a, p. 46).

As would be expected, competition for these funds also intensified. This, together with the government's demand for concrete evidence of 'value for money' assessed in relation to its three indicators – 'efficiency, effectiveness, and economy' – proved a real challenge to the arts and cultural industries and led to many years of concentration on data gathering simply to provide the evidence needed to justify funding (Sara Selwood, 2004, p. 20).

There were enormous government demands being placed on cultural institutions to 'value add' to the creative and leisure industries, while also providing 'knock-on benefits' for other industries involved in economic regeneration projects relating to cultural institutions and broadening their educational, outreach, and civil society activities, particularly in the regions (Travers & Glaister, 2004, p. 4). There was a general belief that the arts can somehow (not always identified) be a powerful medium in addressing wider social and economic needs, precisely because they build capacity for and experience of life (Bunting, 2007, p. 15).

It is not surprising then that, in 1997, this new convergence of interest in social issues witnessed the publication of Matarasso's research, *Use or Ornament?* Advocating the broader social benefits of the arts, which can occur from 'insignificant financial risk to public services', he insisted that the social and economic impacts produced are 'out of all proportion to their costs' (Matarasso, 1997, p. 81). He stated emphatically that:

> ...the real purpose of the arts is not to create wealth but to contribute to a stable, confident and creative society (Matarasso, 1997, p. v).

Despite the influence of Matarasso's work, which included a 'workable methodological framework for social-impact assessment' (Reeves, 2001, p. 16), it also attracted criticism for the methodology used (Merli, 2002, pp. 108-112) and for its basic premise that the arts are an 'intervening variable that can change the world' (Jensen, 2002, pp. 8-9). In many ways, the appearance of *Use or Ornament?* fuelled the debate, rather than quelling it.

Even so, by 2004, the Museums, Libraries, and Archives Council in the United Kingdom argued that it had 'clear evidence' to show the extensive impacts – social, economic, and intrinsic – that can be derived from museums, libraries, and archives. These included:

> ...support[ing] learning, skills and scholarship, crime reduction, rural development, economic and cultural regeneration, the knowledge economy, social exclusion, cultural diversity, creativity, re-skilling, e-government, homework support, community, citizenship and cultural identity and much more (Museums Libraries and Archives Council, 2004, p. 9).

At the same time in the United States, Peggy Wireman identified a range of economic contributions made by museums, such as providing jobs; supporting local businesses; attracting tourists; investing in local infrastructure and goods and services; and generating positive social impacts, including enhancing the quality of life, increasing community pride, and furthering public education (Wireman, 1997, pp. 22-29).

However, Stephen Weil warned against overstating the case for museums' potential impact, which is always very difficult to measure, because it is 'subtle, indirect and frequently cumulative over time' (Weil, 1999, p. 19). He argues that:

> Museums can wonderfully enhance and enrich individual lives, even change them, and make communities better places in which to live, but often only in synergy with other institutions (Weil, 1999, p. 12).

5.3.3 Arts for Art's Sake! Museums for their intrinsic value

This ongoing dispute over the value of the arts and cultural industries came to a head in 2003. In June that year, DEMOS – the Independent Think Tank for Everyday Democracy – organised a conference, called *Valuing Culture*, in response to overriding concerns that 'British policy with respect to the arts has become lopsided'. Specifically:

> ...the very strong emphasis in current policy on the actual and potential contribution of arts organisations to wider social and economic goals leaves under-articulated and ... undervalued the intrinsic worth of these organisations and their activities (Ellis et al., 2003, p. 3).

This sentiment was reiterated by the former Minister of the Department of Culture, Media, and Sport, Chris Smith, but only after he relinquished this ministerial position. He introduced the DEMOS Conference with a statement that was 'easier to say outside Government than it is inside':

> The arts and cultural activity, endeavour and engagement, require no justification other than their innate ability to move us, to excite us, and to enhance our lives (Ellis, et al., 2003, p. 1).

There has often being a simplistic equation that exposure to the arts will generate personal intrinsic benefits, which are dependent upon the intensity and frequency of this exposure. To maximise impact, however, participants required 'sustained involvement and full engagement – emotionally, mentally and sometimes socially' (McCarthy, et al., 2004, p. xvii).

Besides personal benefits, it is now recognised that the arts can provide general public good. The Rand Report identified this along a continuum of benefits that has private benefits at one end, moves through to situations involving private benefits with public spill over, and, at the other end of the scale, has public benefits that accrue to society as a whole (McCarthy, et al., 2004, p. xiii).[116] However, it is also acknowledged that a thorough understanding of the arts' inherent or intrinsic benefits will always be difficult, because these are often intangible and difficult to define and 'lie beyond the traditional qualitative tools of the social sciences and often beyond the language of common experience' (McCarthy, et al., 2004, pp. 37-38).

This renewed interest in the intrinsic benefits of the arts in recent times brings us back full circle fifty years – from an emphasis on intrinsic worth pre-1970s, to the concentration of economic instrumental values in the 1980s, followed by a focus on the potential for broader social outcomes, through to a renewed understanding of the intrinsic worth of the arts and cultural industries in the twenty-first century.

Although different economic, social, and intrinsic values associated with the arts and cultural industries were used by governments and arts and cultural institutions for their own purposes at different times, it is difficult to consider any value in isolation. The apparent dichotomy between the instrumental and intrinsic values of the arts, as articulated by Ellis and others, was discounted by Jamie Cowling. He emphasised the symbiotic relationship between instrumental and intrinsic values:

---

116. These benefits were summarised as:
- Private – captivation and pleasure;
- Middle – expanded capacity for empathy and cognitive growth;
- Public – creation of social bonds and expression of communal meanings (McCarthy, et al., 2004, pp. xv-xvi).

> The [arts] have a unique role to play in helping us meet wider social objectives, based not on an instrumental subordination of culture to wider goals but a recognition that it is the intrinsic nature of cultural and arts activity that provides its wider power (Cowling, 2004, p. preface).

The interrelationship between instrumental and intrinsic values also underpins UNESCO's Creative Cities Network Concept. When announcing Glasgow's appointment as the latest World Centre for Music in 2008, Director-General Koochiro Matsuura stated:

> We at UNESCO believe that culture not only makes an economic contribution, it provides meaning, and a sense of identity and continuity that is integral to the life of all societies (Brown, 2008, p. 2).

It is obvious that there is an interrelationship between intrinsic, economic, and social values. In order to measure and evaluate the impact of the arts and cultural industries, it is essential to develop integrated criteria and a responsive methodology to assess the multiplicity of values involved.

5.3.4 John Holden's solution to valuing culture

By 2005, research into economic, social, and cultural values in Britain, the U.S.A., and Canada was offering a broader picture of possible outcomes and opportunities for promoting the arts and cultural industries. John Holden spearheaded this research by identifying the significance of instrumental, institutional, and intrinsic value for the arts and cultural industries, including museums (Holden, 2005; Sara Selwood, 2005).

To Holden, instrumental values are still widely viewed by governments as of paramount importance because they collectively relate to the economic and broad range of social benefits that are the 'knock-on' effects of culture (Holden, 2005, p. 8). Some of the economic benefits, but not all, have market values, and these are often measured in dollar terms by economic impact assessments, particularly for major infrastructure projects. Social benefits, however, have value, but no market price and cannot be easily measured in dollar terms. Various 'outcome' studies have been devised to try to document social outcomes from investments in cultural programs. But, despite a preoccupation with data gathering for a considerable period of time, Selwood was still condemning the arts and cultural sector as late as 2004 for producing studies that lacked credibility and were mainly 'spurious' – providing limited evidence that could be used constructively (Sara Selwood, 2004, p. 72).

The second category, institutional values, relates closely to how the museum operates as a public institution. This includes the processes, actions, and attitudes that cultural institutions adopt when they interact with the public (Holden, p. 9). Institutional values are associated with generating social capital through creating public trust in public institutions. These values include honesty, objectivity, meaning, trusted expertise, modelling democracy, civil behaviour, representing stability and permanence, fostering relationships, upholding public standards, and sociability among citizens (C.

Scott, 2007a, pp. 186-190). To ascertain a sense of institutional values, qualitative data is often collected from public feedback and other stakeholders who work closely with the organisations in question.

The third category of cultural values relate to the arts' intrinsic benefits, which are often summarised in the phrases: they 'enrich people's lives' and are important 'in and of themselves'. These values refer to the subjective or intellectual, emotional, and spiritual experience of culture and are captured in personal testimony, qualitative assessments, anecdotes, case studies, and critical reviews (Holden, 2005, pp. 8-9).

A practical application of Demos' 'Public Value Triangle' was realised in heritage projects in the East Midlands and South Wales. In these projects, two citizens' juries were established to find out about the intrinsic values (why heritage matters); the institutional values (the ethos and behaviour of heritage organisations); and the instrumental values (the benefits of heritage projects) of each project supported by the Heritage Lottery Fund (Mattinson, 2006, p. 86). Defining intrinsic value[117], proved to be the most complicated, because it was made up of 'soft' benefits that are inherent in people's experience of heritage, and would incorporate elements such as aesthetic quality and historical and cultural significance (Accenture, 2006, p. 19).

Holden and Hewison, in their research for the Heritage Lottery Fund, evaluated a number of frameworks that can be used to articulate value, including the language of economics, anthropology, environmentalism, intangible valuation, public value and heritage practices. They identified no shortage of evaluation methodologies and Key Performance Indicators (KPIs) being cited, but, inevitably, these KPIs are heavily concentrated at the production end of the spectrum (the number of displays developed, the number of visitors attending a venue, and so on), rather than at the vital outcome consumption stage (the measured impact of public programs on participants) (Holden & Hewison, 2004).

Recognising the complexity of cultural values is one thing, identifying the benefit to recipients is another. Holden's response was his concept of 'cultural players', with the public identified as the primary stakeholders. Although not a homogenous group, the public's concern is primarily with what

---

117. Intrinsic values identified included:
- 'Knowledge values', which place heritage as central to learning about ourselves and society and understanding our cultural identities at both personal and community levels;
- 'Identity values', which deliver a sense of identity on a personal, community, regional, and national level;
- 'Bequest values', which reinforce the belief that we have a responsibility to care for heritage in order to pass on things that are valuable for future generations; and
- 'Distinctiveness values', which relate to the characteristics that make somewhere special. This was identified as a key spontaneous value for heritage and was viewed as extremely important because it is closely linked to personal and cultural identity (Mattinson, 2006, p. 89).

is characterised as intrinsic values. But the public, collectively, are also interested in how they are treated, and are acute judges of institutional value (Hewison & Holden, 2006, p. 16).

The other cultural players include politicians and policy makers and the professionals working within cultural institutions. These groups are considered secondary players (Holden, 2006, p. 21) and these players reference mainly instrumental outcomes. The Cultural Ministers' Council in Australia identified the concerns of its politicians and government officials:

> Policy makers are interested in social impact which they see in terms of individual well-being, especially self-esteem, skills and feelings of personal well-being. They are also interested in the development of social capital as seen in the level of community trust, the development of social networks, the evolution of different groups and the extension of social relationships and community (Australian Expert Group in Industries Studies & Cultural Ministers Council Statistics Working Group, 2004, p. 41).

The following Value Matrix in Table 5.1 illustrates Holden's hypothesis. Only politicians and policy makers are fixated on instrumental values; the public and professionals are more concerned with intrinsic values and, to a lesser extent, institutional values:

> The public do not relate the arts to the things that politicians worry about – economic regeneration, social inclusion, healthy communities and the rest... The public cares most about intrinsic value and to a degree about institutional value because these two things construct and reflect their sense of who they are (Holden, 2006, p. 24).

Table 5.1: Value Matrix illustrating John Holden's concept of 'cultural players' and their value frameworks

	Values	Values	Values
Cultural players	Intrinsic	Instrumental	Institutional
Public	x		x
Professionals	x		x
Politicians/ policy makers		x	

While the public, 'the authorising environment', 'value their cultural life and cultural facilities more than politicians and [even professionals] think they do' (Holden, 2006, p. 39), intrinsic values are still not adequately articulated:

> ...the ideas don't resonate with most legislators and policymakers. The concept of 'arts for art's sake' seems to have insulated the arts from demands that it be useful and contributed to it being viewed as 'remote, esoteric and removed from life' (McCarthy, et al., 2004, pp. 37-38).

While a typology of values relating to the arts and cultural industries, including museums, was being identified, the researchers agreed that there was also a need for 'a new language' capable of reflecting, recognising, and capturing the full range of values that can be derived from the arts and cultural industries (Holden, 2004, p. 2). While the *Valuing Culture* Conference did address the demand on cultural organisations to use instrumental arguments to justify their public funding, there was no attempt to provide reliable methodologies to measure the various hypotheses presented.

5.3.5 Arts and culture as public goods

Holden's conclusion, regarding the significance of institutional values to the individual, reflects Mark Moore's earlier work relating to the concepts of public good and public value. Moore argued for a renewed emphasis on the overall mission and purpose of an organisation; its organisational processes; and its operational outcomes, including the important role 'public managers can play in maintaining an organisation's legitimacy in the eyes of the public' (R. Blaug, Horner, & Lekhi, 2006b, p. 6; Moore, 1995).

In the United Kingdom, public value became a popular concept, with two different interpretations embedded in the government's 'new public management' system. The first defined public value as 'a process, a way of doing public management'. The emphasis was on public sector managers who were to improve public services and maximise public value. The latter 'presents public value as a guide to performance measurement' by adapting private sector business-management thinking to public sector organisations (Clark, 2006, p. 2; Keaney, 2006, p. 9).

The Right Honorable Tessa Jowell, the then United Kingdom Secretary for State for Culture, Media, and Sport, expressed the concept of public value as essentially 'what the public values'. Although simplified to the extreme, this emphasised that it is the public that must 'authorise' the value that should be pursued (R. Blaug, Horner, & Lekhi, 2006a, p. 24; Jowell, 2005).

In their analysis of state arts agencies in the U.S.A., Moore and Williams Moore also advocated embracing the arguments for public value of the arts, including the many different instrumental, institutional, and intrinsic benefits. They argued that:

> Art is good for its own sake; that artists are particularly deserving of public support; that individuals spend time and money on the arts because they value them. That the arts produce economic benefits for individuals and communities that support them; that the arts help make better neighbours, better citizens, and a stronger civic and democratic culture; and that human beings have an inalienable right to express themselves through the arts and to be challenged by others' artistic expressions (Moore & Williams Moore, 2005, p. 31).

However, public value is not static; it oscillates constantly in a state of 'valorisation'. There can be no equilibrium, because values vary as they are influenced by a number of things, including what aspects the media focuses on, changing education systems, changing government policies, and changing modes of financing (government subsidies versus market pricing) (Klamer, 2004, p. 4).

To Arjo Klamer, the arts are best identified as a 'common' good, rather than a public good. This is because the arts are not completely public, because non-members can be excluded from the group in a number of ways.[118] The arts are not truly private either, in the sense that individual ownership makes no sense where values are socially constructed (Klamer, 2004). Museums are commonly cited as mixed goods, because they benefit their community at large, as well as their users (D. Noonan, 2002, p. 2).

The concept of the arts, including museums and heritage, as public or common goods will continue to evolve as more reliable methodologies are devised to measure their impacts on individuals and communities. Some of the more concerted efforts have emerged from Canadian studies, specifically relating to the outcome of ongoing exposure to heritage products and services.

5.3.6 Valuing heritage – Canadian contributions to the debate

The Canadian Government was interested in the interrelationship of the social effects of culture and the public benefits that are derived through prolonged and sustained participation in arts and heritage projects. Building on some of the concepts in the Rand Report, Dick Stanley, in 2004, was commissioned to lead an Initiative to Study the Social Effects of Culture (ISSEC).[119] This research identified the significance of different types of involvement and the potential outcomes for participants:

> Direct involvement in the arts is more intense than audience participation, whereas audience participation is more widespread than direct participation. The more widespread and intense the participation of community members the greater the impact will have on cultural and social factors (Guetzhow, 2002, p. 4).

It was also postulated that regular exposure to community arts projects and heritage experiences as participants, not just one-off visits to heritage attractions or sites, may have an even more direct effect on social cohesion, civic engagement, and building organisational capacity for effective action,

---

118. A pure public good is one that, when supplied to one person, it is supplied to others in such a way that the wellbeing derived by each individual does not detract from the wellbeing obtained by other individuals. For a pure public good, it is not possible to exclude (for example, by pricing) some users and not others (Economics for the Environment Consultancy, 2005, p. 3).

119. Six social effects were derived from participation in heritage projects that, together, enhance cultural citizenship through the 'appropriation of cultural content into the public life of members of society'. These included:
    - Enhancing understanding and capacity for action;
    - Creating and retaining identity;
    - Modifying values and preferences for collective choice;
    - Building social cohesion;
    - Contributing to community development; and
    - Fostering civic participation (Stanley, 2006, p. 1).

than participation in the arts in general. Benefits are not simply derived from participation – the quality of the process and outputs are important (Coalter, 2001, p. 23; Guetzhow, 2002, p. 6; Institute of Public Policy Research, 2003, p. 5; Moffat Centre for Travel & Tourism Business Development, 2005, p. 8; Stanley, 2001, p. 6). This impact results through participating as a member of a team in a heritage project by:

> ...helping to reaffirm a group's identity [which] can help groups gain pride and confidence in their abilities. It can better equip collectives and communities to enter into relationships and cooperate with others as equals. (Coalter, 2001, p. 6; Stanley, 2006, p. 4).

In 2006, fellow Canadian researcher, Douglas Worts, advocated a range of cultural indicators to evaluate the impact of museums and heritage. His Critical Assessment Framework was devised especially to encourage museum professionals to evaluate their cultural impact on their primary stakeholders – individuals, communities, and their institutions – in an endeavour to secure a more sustainable future (2006a, p. 43). He argued strongly for a critical evaluation of the cultural impact of museums, rather than the current reliance on KPIs that measure the institutions as non-profit corporate entities:

> Isn't it odd that museums – one of society's principal institutions dedicated to culture – do not measure their success or impacts in cultural terms? Attendance, revenue, objects accessioned, exhibits mounted, and publications published are some of the measures that museums use to assess their operations. But, it can be argued, none of these are cultural indicators. They do not reflect on the cultural needs, opportunities, or well being of the community, nor do they offer insights into the cultural impacts of museum operations on individuals (Worts, 2006a, p. 41).

Sara Selwood reiterates Worts' concerns in her research on the cultural impact of museums in the United Kingdom:

> Although cultural institutions – including museums – are fundamentally driven by the desire to contribute to the public's cultural experiences, their cultural impact is not always acknowledged in the frameworks designed for government accountability (Sara Selwood, 2010, p. 8).

Worts' argument for using 'three lenses' – individual, community, and the museum, itself, as well as a fourth 'global' lens where applicable – is to ensure that each museum program is responsive to the critical issues of the day, while being grounded in a special relationship to its community 'that helps justify the public funding of cultural organizations' (Worts, 2006a, p. 47).

Previously, the Department of Canadian Heritage developed a Socio-Economic Benefits Framework for the Cultural Sector that was prepared by the Outspan Group in 1999. This was tested on the Canadian Museum of Civilization in 2003.[120] This Framework postulated that all benefits from the arts and culture can be allocated to one of three recipient groups. Indi-

---

120. This analysis revealed 'conceptual and practical problems in applying the Canadian benefits framework' and identified that further research was needed in areas such as 'visitor extra-market benefits (consumer surplus)' (Canadian Heritage, 2003, p. 5).

viduals who derived benefits through their use (direct, indirect, and future) and through their non-use of arts and cultural institutions are the primary stakeholders (Whiting & Outspan Group, 1999, p. iii).

Business is identified as a significant stakeholder because it is the recipient of the net redistribution of commercial activity from outside a defined area to within it, and from attributable spending by stakeholders and producers on management and development (Whiting & Outspan Group, 1999, p. iv).

The Canadian Framework identified a further broader category of societal benefits or 'public good benefits' that cannot be categorised as either personal or business, but 'accrue to society as a whole'. These criteria include: quality of life; national identity; national and international responsibilities; community cohesion; creativity; and health, educational, and scientific benefits (Canadian Heritage, 2003, p. 4; Whiting & Outspan Group, 1999, pp. 20-21). Although the most nebulous of the categories, and probably not quantifiable in monetary terms (and debatable if this is even desirable), the author argued strongly against excluding them from the analytical framework.

A major research undertaking, known as *Our Millennium*[121], investigated the Canadian Millennium projects using four themes – personal empowerment, cultural participation, cultural development and quality of life, and cultural sustainability (Jeannotte, 2006, pp. 118-121). The study demonstrated:

> ...the broad range of activities, both amateur and professional, that come under the rubric of culture; the social and economic value of culture to the life of communities; the intrinsic value of culture to individuals; and finally the understanding, on the part of citizens, that cultural activities constitute an important inheritance for generations to come (Jeannotte, 2006, p. 123).

In contrast to the situation in Canada, there has been only limited research activity in Australia to understand the impact of the arts and cultural industries and identify the key stakeholders.

5.3.7 Valuing arts and culture in the Australian context

The 1975 Pigott Report into Australian museums had limited ongoing impact (see Section 2.9.2). It was not until 1986 that the federal government commenced a review of commonwealth museums and galleries.[122] These reviews were conducted under the auspices of the two departments representing finance and the arts. Not surprisingly, given the different perspectives

121. It investigated 1,800 specific activities that made up the Canadian Millennium Project.

122. The review included major state museums and galleries and other cultural heritage exhibiting institutions to provide a comparison.

of these departments, they found it difficult to agree on the fundamental role of the commonwealth institutions and how to effectively assess their performance.

In 1989, the Department of Finance released its report, *What Price Heritage?*, in which it identified that the main beneficiaries of cultural institutions were middle class participants and the users of cultural institutions, rather than the general public (Department of Finance, 1989, pp. 28-29). It proposed an accountable performance framework, which used similar KPIs to the existing British Public Service Management model, for future commonwealth involvement in museum policy. It included the demand that there be:

> ...a clear move towards financial management improvement with the development of off-budget revenue targets and an environment with enhanced management flexibility and greater incentives for improved performance (Department of Finance, 1989, p. 64).

According to Tony Bennett, the report shows the increasing influence of the treasury's economic rationalism and its wish to extend that influence to the arts and culture portfolios, under the guise of a focus on increasing audience development (Bennett, Emmison, & Frow, 1999, pp. 241-242).

In 1990, the Department of the Arts, Sport, the Environment, Tourism, and Territories (DASETT) issued their response under the title, *What Value Heritage?* It was particularly critical of the Department of Finance's treatment of the research undertaken, and cited serious issues with data reliability and relevance (Department of the Arts, 1990, p. 30). It was also concerned that any analysis of costs should be balanced against the collective benefits, as enunciated by each institution's mission statements. However, it did concur with the treasury that there was a need to address the measurement of performance of museums, including financial performance management (Department of the Arts, 1990, p. 2).

In 1994, the release of *Creative Nation* by the Keating Labor Government in Australia helped elevate the arts and cultural industries to a position where they were seen as an integral component of economic development – paralleling the situation in the United Kingdom. *Creative Nation* saw 'itself unapologetically as being not only a cultural policy, but also an economic policy' (David Throsby, 2006a, p. 14). Creativity was the essential element common to both:

> On the one side artists would generate innovative ideas reflecting our distinctive cultural identity, while on the other side creativity would be fostered as a key resource in the development of the new economy (David Throsby, 2006a, p. 14).

However, this was not universally accepted, even within the arts sector. Typical of the criticism of *Creative Nation* was Donald Horne's concern that the policy represented the ultimate commodification of the arts through its characterisation of the arts as an industry with economic objectives. '*Creative Nation* denied the fundamental *raison d'être* of artistic life' (D. Horne quoted in, David Throsby, 2006a, p. 15).

The recognition of economic outcomes was again manifested in a 1994 study of eighty-nine government-funded community-based arts projects, the vast majority of which were delivered by volunteers. It identified the 'critical link between community, culture and social cohesion' and concluded:

> ...sustainable economic outcomes can be generated when they are supported within a broader cultural development focus incorporating related social and cultural objectives (Williams, 1996, p. 4)

While this debate generated some government interest in the arts and cultural arena, it did not achieve any bipartisan agreement. *Creative Nation* did not survive the election of the Howard Coalition Government in March 1996 and, with its demise, the arts and cultural industries were again relegated to the fringes of government policy concerns.[123]

State governments, however, were still demanding that the arts and cultural industries 'cure a multitude' of societal ills. In Queensland, the state government's 2002 cultural policy, *Creative Queensland,* espoused a vision for Queensland to be 'a culturally dynamic place, rich in diversity and experiences'. While ideas and talent would be supported and artistic and cultural pursuits encouraged for their intrinsic values, the arts and cultural industries were also being viewed as playing a significant role in the economy through the enhancement of excellence in creative innovation (Arts Queensland, 2002, p. 3). This cultural policy document advocated investing in people, communities, places, collections, traditions, and creative enterprise to achieve the government's vision of significant economic, social, and cultural outcomes. It would be able to:

- Promote individual and community wellbeing through participation in the arts and access to arts and cultural events and collections;
- Provide jobs and training opportunities in the cultural and creative industries and foster the creation of local content for knowledge economy enterprises; and
- Strengthen community capacity and our sense of identity, foster social cohesion, and enhance infrastructure and cultural services (Arts Queensland, 2002, p. 3).

---

123. On the national level, the arts played a fairly insignificant role in the 2007 Australian Federal election campaign. The Australian Labor Party did produce an *Arts Discussion Paper* that reiterated some of the intrinsic values it associated with the arts and cultural industries:

> Labor recognises the work that artists produce gives an immeasurable, sustaining dimension to the life of the nation, and that the Arts as a significant field of endeavour are worthy of support in their own right (Garrett, 2007, p. 2).

Although the Australian federal and state governments continued to articulate a broad range of impacts to which the arts and culture industries should aspire, they insisted on using 'generic performance indicators' to assess performance against government policy and programs.[124]

It is only very recently that interest in evaluating the arts in any formal sense in Australia has emerged. During 2007, the Cultural Ministers Council Statistics Working Group (CMCSWG) commissioned a *Cultural Indicators Research Project* to identify internationally comparable indicators that would measure the impact of government funding to the arts sector (Ferres, Adair, Bentley, Messenger, & Kukucka, 2007). Unfortunately, no simple solutions were provided that could assist communities to measure the impact of the arts and cultural heritage services provided by government. Nor was there a framework for assessing cultural production and promotion (Mercer, 2005, p. 14). The final report[125] reinforced the conclusion that government-funded research in this field is looking for measurable indicators of only instrumental values of the arts and culture. The report identified, but did not evaluate or clarify:

> ...[the] plethora of indicators and evolving value frameworks attempting to capture economic, social and civic-democratic impacts of the arts and cultural heritage (Ferres, et al., 2007, p. 1).

An earlier study of the value of the museum and art gallery of the Northern Territory (MAGNT) to its community and economy also failed to include any economic modelling or evaluation of non-market values, such as cultural capital, learning and creativity, social entrepreneurship, and 'trendy frameworks such as the knowledge economy or creative industries' (Tremblay & Carson, 2006, pp. 2-4).

In 2008, the Queensland Museum broadened its mission statements to address its social, cultural, and economic impacts on communities. The museum articulated its intention to 'enrich and enliven Queensland communities'. Its justification for this position was that: 'QM will strengthen social cohesion in Queensland communities and create economic benefit' (Queensland Museum, 2008c, p. 4).

However, in developing more than one hundred KPIs to measure all aspects of its operational plan, the Queensland Museum did not address the issue of measuring its performance against its mission statement. It did, however, identify as its first strategic objective, during 2008–2012, to 'increase awareness of the cultural, social, intellectual and economic value of QM to the State' (Queensland Museum, 2008c, p. 6). The development of

---

124. These were outlined in the 2003 Department of Finance and Deregulation's *Outcomes and Outputs Framework* (Australian Bureau of Statistics, 2008, p. 14).

125. The summary framework includes 'assets/infrastructure', 'investment', 'economic development', and 'reach' (access, but not impact). Only under the headings, 'vibrant cultural sector' and 'quality of life', is there reference to, but no details of, how to assess the priority research question: 'How do communities value the arts and cultural heritage services provided by government?' (Ferres, et al., 2007, p. 19).

the Contingent Valuation Methodology Study to value the Queensland Museum, as discussed in Chapter Six, was a direct outcome of this strategic objective.

While most museums in Australia were slow in adopting a new approach, let alone a post-modern approach, to their mission and operations, there were stronger advocacies for community engagement methodologies overseas. Probably the most vocal campaigner for this new approach was the late Stephen Weil who repeatedly argued for a broader vision for museums and constantly admonished the American museum sector to remember:

> ...the cornerstone on which the whole enterprise rests: to make a positive difference in the quality of people's lives. Museums that do that matter –they matter a great deal (1999, p. 229).

In taking a more business-like approach, it has been argued that the fundamental purpose of a museum is 'value creation', which encompasses customer value, community outreach, and public service (Porter quoted in Neil Kotler, et al., 2008, p. 58). In this value chain framework, museums create social benefits through their unique offerings of collections, exhibitions, program and content development, educational programs, and visitor and outreach services, as well as through hospitality, marketing, and sales (Neil Kotler, et al., 2008, p. 59).

5.3.8 Value to whom?

Before attempting to estimate the benefits that accrue from cultural goods and that subsequently provide some measure of a museum's value, it is necessary to address the question of 'value to whom?' – who are the museum's stakeholders, what benefits do they derive from museums, and what value[126] do they place on their cultural institutions?

John Holden provided one analysis, Douglas Worts provided a second, and the Whiting Group – again from the Canadian perspective – provided a third system for recognising key stakeholders. There are four other frameworks that were identified as useful reference points for formulating a value framework for the Cobb+Co Museum.

The National Trust in the United Kingdom applied Accenture's Public Service Value principles of 'shareholder value' to ascertain the balance between the 'quantification of citizen-focused outcomes with a measure of the cost-effectiveness' with which these are delivered in the Trust's various heritage properties (Accenture, 2006, p. 20). This model shifted the focus to the perspective of the citizen as the investor and key beneficiary stakeholder. Three possible outcomes were identified:

126. 'Value' can be defined as a set of positive characteristics or quantities perceived in cultural objects or sites by certain individuals or groups (de la Torre, 2002, p. 4).

- Optimisation of the user experience (that is, visitors);
- Impact on the local community (that is, the local population); and
- Impact on the wider population (that is, the country as a whole) (Accenture, 2006, p. 20).

Also in the United Kingdom in 2004, the British Broadcasting Commission (BBC) released its strategy, *Building Public Value: Renewing the BBC for a Digital World.* This report identified the BBC's value to three core groups: individuals, society as a whole, and the wider commercial market – its net economic value. It also identified five main drivers, including democratic value, cultural and creative value, educational value, social and community value, and global value, which result from the delivery of high quality broadcasting services, significant project outcomes, and institutional trust (Keaney, 2006, pp. 15,18-19).

As part of her PhD research, Carol Scott developed and tested a topology of museum values in Australia, using four dimensions: use, institutional, instrumental, and intrinsic. She also identified three recipient groups: individuals, communities/society, and economy. Through her primary research with a cohort of museum users and non-users, as well as fellow museum professionals in Australia, she identified useful quantitative and qualitative evidence for her value topology (C. Scott, 2007c). Her conclusion was that museum and gallery professionals need to describe their institutions' worth in terms of value, rather than just instrumental and utilitarian contributions. This led her to develop a 'values toolkit' to assist in seeking evidence (mainly outputs and outcomes) to support identified museum values (C. Scott, 2007b, p. 16). She argued that methodologies employed in assessing value should support the ongoing sustainability of the sector (as does Worts) and be useful for both advocacy purposes and accountability purposes. Frameworks developed to measure value had to be applicable to both 'attraction-saturated publics and accountability-focused bureaucracies' (2007c, p. 7).

In investigating Australian museums, including those in regional settings, Scott's research was useful in evaluating methodologies that might be applicable to use in ascertaining the value of the Cobb+Co Museum to its community. Independent of Scott's research, the Cobb+Co Museum had also identified a three-tier hierarchy of stakeholders.

Stephen Weil frequently argued that a museum 'is expected to return some benefit to the community in exchange for the support that the community provides' (Weil, 2003, p. 28). He quotes Bud Cheit, former Dean of the business school at the University of California, Berkeley. The stakeholders that a not-for-profit organisation must serve were primarily:

> (1) the 'public' (i.e. the members of the community whose needs are to be met); (2) the participants (i.e. the governance, staff, and volunteers of that organisation that will actually be utilized in order to meet those needs); and (3) the 'patrons' (i.e. the donors and grant makers who will supply that organisation with the necessary resources) (Weil, 2003, p. 30).

Table 5.2 compares the stakeholders identified by the seven research projects. It is not surprising that each of the classification systems discussed identified the community (individuals/public) as the primary stakeholders of the arts and cultural industries, including museums. Only five of the systems – the Cobb+Co Museum, Stephen Weil, Carol Scott, the BBC, and the Canadian Socio-economic Benefits Framework – recognised the significance of businesses or economy to the arts and cultural industries. This recognition has been a gradual process, but it is now likely that business will feature more prominently in all future analyses of the stakeholders of cultural institutions.

Table 5.2: Key stakeholders for arts and cultural industries, including museums

		Key stakeholders	Key stakeholders	Key stakeholders
1	**John Holden** *Cultural Players*	**Public**	**Politicians and policy makers**	**Professionals (cultural industry)**
2	**Douglas Worts** *Critical Assessment Framework*	**Individuals**	**Communities**	**Cultural institutions**
3	**Whiting and Outspan Group** *Socio-Economic Benefits Framework*	**Individuals**	**Businesses**	**Society**
4	**Accenture for National Trust, United Kingdom** *Public Service Value Model* **(PSVM)**	**Visitor/user**	**Local community**	**Wider population/country**
5	**British Broadcasting Commission** *Building Public Value*	**Individuals**	**Society as a whole**	**Wider commercial market – its net economic value**
6	**Carol Scott** *Value topology*	**Individuals**	**Communities/society**	**Economy**
7	**Stephen Weil/Bud Cheit**	**Public**	**Participants**	**Patrons**
8	**Cobb+Co Museum** **Toowoomba**	**Community**	**Business and government**	**Tourists**

After identifying the major stakeholders, it is imperative to develop comprehensive and reliable evaluation processes to measure how these stakeholders identify the value of their arts and cultural institutions, including museums. This includes the need for better qualitative and quantitative indicators that can assist in articulating the social, cultural, and economic impacts of the arts and cultural sector as a vehicle for advocacy and accountability (van Schaik, 2002, p. 4).

While serious questions relating to methodology still persist, there have been some positive results emerging from early studies in this field. In particular, the Museums Libraries Archives Partnership (MLA) has attempted to evaluate impacts of its mission:

> To improve people's lives through access to collections and resources – building knowledge, supporting learning, inspiring creativity and celebrating identity (Museums Libraries and Archives Council, 2007).[127]

In its Strategic Statement for 2007–2010, museums, libraries, and archives are described as trusted 'civic places' in which everyone can participate in learning, engagement, and debate. This, in turn, will ensure that these cultural institutions will play a significant role in driving social and economic change (Museums Libraries and Archives Council, 2007, p. 2). To assess this outcome, a major study was conducted by the National Museum Directors' Conference and Museums, Libraries, and Archives Council. This study scrutinised the operations of fifteen major national museums and seven regional museums and galleries in the United Kingdom to determine if they could be promoted as 'catalysts for a new economic and creative age' (Museums Libraries and Archives Council, 2007, p. 2). The study detailed the institutions' capacity to attract huge numbers of visitors and their overall economic impacts[128], civic functions, and contributions to the country's cre-

---

127. In 2007, it outlined this approach in detail.
In pursuing our vision, we embrace and advocate:
  - The intrinsic value of culture;
  - Enriching people's lives through cultural experiences;
  - Ensuring that our artistic activity is world-class;
  - Promoting a society that values knowledge;
  - Encouraging creativity and innovation;
  - Maintaining standards of excellence and quality;
  - Engaging young people;
  - Extending learning opportunities;
  - Celebrating diversity;
  - Connecting communities through culture;
  - Making partnerships central to achieving our goals;
  - Ensuring adequate skills for our sector; and
  - Placing audiences at the centre of what we do (Museums Libraries and Archives Council, 2007).

128. It has been estimated that seven of the top ten visitor attractions in the United Kingdom are publicly-funded museums and galleries and that eighty-five percent of overseas visitors visit the area for the museums and galleries (Museums Libraries and Archives Council, 2007).

ativity and educational performance (Travers, 2006, p. 10). The conclusions drawn from this research focused on the economic benefits of the sector currently and into the future:

> Museums and galleries offer both a major internationally traded service (by generating exports) but also underpin the creativity upon which future high value added economic activity is likely to be based. The storehouses represented by these institutions will encourage people in this country to use their creativity and talent to develop new services, products and even manufactured goods (Travers, 2006, p. 86).

However, much more still needs to be done to overcome the more serious criticisms of methodologies in order to deliver consistent 'robust' results in assessing economic and cultural values for the sector. The only apparent agreement is the realisation that there is no single public value framework that can be applied to all organisations (Keaney, 2006, p. 50). To achieve this goal, it has been necessary for the sector to embrace the discipline of economics.

5.4 The other side of the coin: cultural economics

While museums have only very recently looked at valuing the impact of their institutions and programs, economists have been studying the relationships between economics and the arts for the past thirty to forty years – since the appearance of Baumol and Bowen's research on performing arts, and Mark Blaug's *The Economics of the Arts* a decade later (Baumol & Bowen, 1966; M. Blaug, 1976b; David Throsby, 1994, p. 2). Cultural economics is an emerging discipline that is developed by applying economic thinking to the production, distribution, and consumption of all cultural goods and services and superseded 'economics of the arts' (Towse, 2003, p. 1):

> It is not restricted to financial aspects, such as subsidies and costs, but uses an economic model of human behaviour to understand social aspects of the arts (Frey & Meier, 2006a, p. 398).

In economists' jargon, museums and galleries are 'multi-product producers' (Peacock & Rizzo, 2008, p. 94) that deliver 'economic value', which is expressed in monetary terms, and 'cultural value', which reflects cultural, aesthetic, and artistic significance (Frey, 2005, p. 1). William Baumol insists that the impetus of a 'discipline' of cultural economics emerged not from economists but from the arts seeking justification for their funding in an 'analysis of welfare theory[129], not for themselves, but for the public funding on which they often rely' (Baumol, 2003, p. 20).

---

129. Welfare theory has tried to apply various tools to construct a more solid foundation for public funding besides the merit-goods argument. These include equity of opportunity, beneficial educational externalities, the public-good properties of the arts and cultural products, infant cultural enterprise argument, cultural reputation, and investment in the future (Baumol, 2003, pp. 21-23).

Nevertheless, since the 1970s, a small but growing number of economists have been formulating various socio-economic benefits frameworks for the cultural industries, which are based, in part, on methodologies and concepts derived from studying the public good of parks, recreation facilities, and the preservation of wilderness areas (Kanninen, 2006; D. Throsby, 1982, p. 1). More and more researchers have become convinced that there are many non-market benefit similarities inherent in cultural and environmental products, as well as public recreational use and non-use or 'passive values'[130]:

> In an economic sense, for example, the intangible benefits derived from the preservation of historic buildings and other cultural landmarks have much in common with the benefits derived from preservation of natural landmarks and rare flora and fauna (Papandrea, 2002, p. 3).

It was Blaug who introduced the concept of a public good and who first applied principles of economic modelling to the operations of the Arts Council in the United Kingdom (1976a, p. 146). With regard to museums, it is even more obvious that their collections should be considered 'public assets for the benefit of communities now and for the future' (S. Jones, 2000, p. 15). It has been argued further that:

> ...the cultural and economic value of museum collections identifies them as a public good like other infrastructural goods and services that are supported and managed by government (S. Jones, 2000, p. 15).

The theoretical basis of the arts and culture as public goods has two main characteristics. They are 'non-rival' in that they can be used or consumed by a number of individuals simultaneously without reducing their value for further consumption (up to the level of a venue's capacity). They are also 'non-excludable' in that no one is excluded from consuming them (dependent on payment of an entry fee, at times) (Hesmondhalgh, 2007, p. 21).

Following Blaug's lead, Throsby and Withers studied the performing arts in Australia in 1979 and reiterated their belief that there were significant non-market values associated with the arts as public goods[131]:

> The arts confer general benefits on the community at large, for which members of the community cannot individually be charged through the market, and that this benefit or public good was quite distinct from benefits that indi-

---

130. 'Passive use value' was the term adopted by the U.S.A. Court in 1989 to encompass a number of frequently-used terms, such as 'non-use value', 'existence value', 'bequest value', 'stewardship value', 'intrinsic value', and 'option value' – even though this concept incorporates potential use benefits in the future (Carson, et al., 2001, p. 198).

131. Non-profit arts and cultural organisations need not always be classed as non-market organisations, because their resources are:

> ...identical to resources for all social and cultural activities and are economic resources including funding (or capital) and creative programming which is determined by physical resources (Di Maggio quoted in Rentschler, 2002, p. 43).

> viduals might accrue through individual involvement in the arts 'as consumers, participants or entrepreneurs' (B. J. Thompson, Throsby, & Withers, 1983, p. 4).

Australia's David Throsby has also been at the forefront of this cultural economics movement, specialising in the economics of cultural heritage (David Throsby, 2001, 2005, 2006b, 2008a, 2008b, 2008c). While employing standard economic principles to the question of valuing cultural commodities, Throsby, as well as other academics, insists on regarding economic and cultural values as distinct entities when they are defined for any cultural commodity (David Throsby, 2001, p. 33). He asserts that any cultural good such as a heritage asset:

> Embodies or yields not only economic value through its financial worth and through the economic services it provides, but also cultural value through its historical or aesthetic significance and the cultural experiences it provides for the community (David Throsby, 2006b, p. 6).

In terms of economic value, he postulates both direct use and non-use ('indirect' or 'passive' use) values, which would take into account the asset's 'existence' value, its 'option' or 'future use' value, and its 'bequest' value for future generations.[132] While direct-use value can and generally is measured quantitatively by the generation of admission fees and payments for goods and services in most museums today, non-use values, which do not have a market value, are rarely considered. This is probably because:

> Non-use values are not observable in market transactions, since no market exists on which the rights to them can be exchanged (2006b, p. 8).

While cautioning against overselling the economic importance of the cultural industries, Frey and Meier insist that the *raison d'être* of museums is to provide cultural experience to its visitor, as well as non-user benefits. While museums are generally wealthy, given the value of the collection assets they hold, at the same time they can be economically struggling, because their assets are frozen and their operating costs are growing (Ginsburgh & Throsby, 2006, p. 20). Also, museums will never be major economic generators in their own right because 'museums tend to provide too-high quality at too-low a price, compared to a revenue-maximising firm' (Frey & Meier, 2006b, p. 1028). 'The museum's task is *not* to stimulate the economy.' If that was the intention, one would always build a theme park rather than a museum (Frey & Meier, 2006a, p. 403).

While economic values of the arts can be measured (if only imperfectly) in a quantitative manner, the same cannot be said for cultural values that are 'multi-dimensional, unstable, contested, lacking a common unit of account, frequently containing elements that cannot be easily expressed according

132. Non-use benefits are derived by individuals who gain satisfaction from the knowledge that the arts and culture products/services are available for their possible future use ('options benefits'), that they exist for others to enjoy or provide prestige to the region ('existence benefits'), and that they will continue to exist for future generations to enjoy ('bequest benefits') (Whiting & Outspan Group, 1999, p. iii).

to any quantitative scale' (Hutter & Throsby, 2008, p. 17; David Throsby, 2003, pp. 279-280; 2006b, p. 9). Throsby hypothesises that there are six principal components of cultural value embedded in heritage assets – aesthetic, spiritual, social, historical, symbolic, and authenticity values (David Throsby, 2006b, pp. 9-10; 2006c).[133] However, he insists that despite 'all the ephemeral, shifting, incoherent and even irrational properties' that make up the cultural value of a cultural good, it is cultural values that are:

> ...likely to influence people's decision-making in regard to cultural goods and might therefore affect desirable patterns of resource allocation in this area in ways that cannot be fully captured by standard economic analysis (David Throsby, 2003, p. 282).

Arjo Klamer takes a slightly different stance from Throsby by advocating a cultural economic or 'culturalist' perspective for understanding the value of cultural goods, while not denying the continuing importance of the economic dimension (Klamer, 2004, p. 12). For him there are three dimensions – economic, social, and cultural (Klamer, 2002, pp. 465-467), whereas Throsby incorporates the social dimension within his cultural value matrix. While economic values occupy a significant portion of the value sphere, Klamer advocates that it is social values that preoccupy people more in everyday life. These values operate in the context of interpersonal relationships, groups, communities, and societies and comprise a broad range of values, such as belonging, being members of a group, identity, social distinction, freedom, solidarity, trust, tolerance, responsibility, love, friendship, and so on (Klamer, 2004, p. 7).[134]

Cultural values are defined by Klamer as the qualities above and beyond the economic and the social – 'the power to inspire or to be inspired without regard to social and economic influence' (Klamer, 2004, p. 6):

> It is the inbred, acquired and developed ability to experience the sublime or sacred character of a good, to see its beauty, or to recognise its place in cultural history. Cultural capital then, lends us the ability to realise a meaningful life over and beyond its economic and social dimensions (Klamer, 2004, p. 8).

From the author's perspective of operating a museum for over two decades, it is the potential for education and learning to take place in museum settings that has a strong bearing on both the social and cultural values that the community associates with the institution. However, it could also be argued that this focus on education and learning can, in some cases, actually restrict museum use to a select group within the community. Bourdieu insisted that the community's use of cultural goods (he referred specifically to museum visits) is closely linked to educational levels and social privilege (Bourdieu & Darbel, 1991, p. 14). His social relationships were defined with-

---

133. Not surprisingly, these cultural values have strong resonance with the categories used by museums in the significance assessment for cultural heritage artefacts (Russell & Winkworth, 2001, p. 11).

134. The capacity to deal with social values and adhere to social norms is now called 'social capital' (Klamer, 2004, p. 7).

in a class structure, which had no bearing to gender, race, or ethnicity, but which 'oscillates between a conventional ranking according to relation to economic capital and a stratification by occupation' (Bennett, et al., 1999, p. 12). Bennett's more recent cultural research in an Australian context indicated 'a plurality of scales of value' that emphasised the significance of age, gender, and even regional location, rather than social class, as the dominant determinant of cultural values (Bennett, et al., 1999, p. 269).

Both Klamer (2003) and Throsby (2003) refer to the complex ways in which society values cultural goods – not as individuals, but collectively. As identified in the Rand Report in Section 5.3.3 above, there is a continuum of benefits that are not limited solely to the individual or to society, but are a series of multifaceted private benefits with public spill over that affect both the individual and the community (McCarthy, et al., 2004, p. xiii). This makes reliable measurement of cultural goods more difficult, and methodologies more complex. Though, as most cultural economists would argue, that is no reason to exclude the more difficult components of our understanding of the make-up of cultural goods from any serious evaluation of the arts and cultural industries.

5.5 How to measure value: Choice Modelling and Contingent Valuation Studies

Within the current political agenda in most OECD countries, there is a pressing need for cultural institutions – both for accountability measures and advocacy purposes[135] – to provide statistically reliable information about the ways in which these institutions can have an impact on society. According to John Falk:

> The inability to confidently and objectively justify our existence is the single largest problem facing the museum community today (Falk, 2000, p. 5).

It is generally articulated that museums can make significant contributions to the social, cultural, and economic wellbeing of communities, but impacts from these are moving targets:

> At best we can ever hope for is a series of snapshots, a series of investigations that capture critical junctures in an ever-changing and dynamic system (Falk, 2000, p. 6)

Economic impact analyses attempt to measure value in the arts and cultural industries. These popular instruments try to measure quantitative financial benefits from arts or cultural developments. However, this methodology, together with other techniques that are based on observed behaviour in

---

135. Throsby, however, argues against limiting approaches to advocacy purposes. He indicates that 'poorly-executed studies are particularly likely to arise when the motive is advocacy rather than objective economic analysis' (David Throsby, 2004, p. 1). Advocacy also places emphasis on the benefits of culture, but does not address the cost of culture (Madden, 2005, p. 226).

private markets, can only account for direct-use economic benefits and neglects the important impacts derived from non-market benefits, which include passive-use benefits.

It was interesting to note that the Cobb+Co Museum's National Carriage Factory Appeal Committee consisted of local Toowoomba business people who had mostly never visited the museum prior to their involvement in the project. Neither did they consider their involvement in the development of the National Carriage Factory in terms of being potential direct users of the facility. They provide classic examples of non-users who nevertheless highly value the Cobb+Co Museum in their community.[136] It would be possible to give a monetary non-use value to the considerable time and effort that went into the appeal process by these committee members, including the lobbying of politicians, government officials, friends, and business colleagues – not to mention their direct financial support, of up to five hundred thousand dollars in one case. Throsby acknowledges that:

> ...economic values, both direct and indirect are relatively easy to measure at least in principle, because they can all ultimately be expressed in monetary terms (2006b, p. 9).

A fairly standard procedure to assess economic benefits[137] was employed by CRS Consulting in developing the economic impact assessment for the National Carriage Factory project at the Cobb+Co Museum, in 2006. The consultant's conclusions incorporated both direct and indirect economic impact in terms of employment growth and revenue generation (SCR Consulting, 2006, pp. 21-26).

While such studies are now becoming more common for major infrastructure projects within the arts arena, there is still debate over the economic flow-on assumptions that they employ.[138] In questioning the assumption of the United Kingdom's Department for Culture, Media, and Sports that museums make a significant contribution to regional economies, if not to the national economy, Sara Selwood contends that this might not be the actual situation. Nevertheless, at the very least, by commissioning econom-

---

136. During discussions with the Cobb+Co Museum committee members, the following reasons for their support for the Cobb+Co Museum were frequently suggested: the desire to potentially visit the museum in the future (which many have done – bringing friends and relatives on a number of occasions); their belief in the value of the museum for children and future generations to understand the present; and, most emphatically, the prestige that the museum brings to the city, through creating employment, attracting tourists, and enhancing lifelong learning opportunities. They also agreed that the Cobb+Co Museum 'provides a general socialising effect on the community and provides a leadership role in cultural and economic development' (Martin, 1994, pp. 255-256).

137. Bruce Seaman investigated other methodologies and their potential errors in ascertaining the economic impacts of cultural goods (Seaman, 2003, pp. 224-225).

138. Because an economic impact study is based on the characteristics of the relevant local economy, there is no universally applicable factor for converting a direct impact figure to a value for the total economic impact of an institution's activities (Groves, 2005, p. 2).

ic impact assessments, institutions are engaging in a form of public relations exercise and, as such, are contributing to the construction of the institutions' reputations (Sara Selwood, 2006, p. 70).

It has also been argued that economic impact analyses actually evaluate the arts on an incorrect basis. As the arts are subsidised mainly for cultural and social reasons, it would appear unrealistic and pointless to evaluate them solely for their ability 'to attract tourists and companies and create jobs', as usually occurs in any economic impact analysis. Based on this framework, economic outcomes should be viewed as 'extra gains', not the real aim of the exercise (Billie Hansen, 1995, p. 315).

An alternative methodology for measuring personal economic impacts, which are then accumulated to derive an overall economic position, employs consumer surplus studies. One such study focused on visitors to the Open Air Museum at Beamish in County Durham in the North of England. It aimed to include passive use benefits by identifying the visitor concepts of Value for Money (VFM) or consumer surplus that were derived from visiting the heritage site. The researchers indicated a range of variables that affected VFM but effectively only evaluated 'use' value derived from the heritage site visit (J. Ashworth & Johnson, 1996, p. 68).

This focus on the impact of museums on the local economy addresses only some of the economic consequences of museums, rather than evaluating their primary purpose, which is to enhance enjoyment, learning, and understanding (P. Johnson, 2003, p. 319). Other methodologies need to be used to help measure and value museums' more fundamental benefits.

A broader study of heritage properties was conducted for the National Trust in the United Kingdom, by Accenture who applied their Public Service Value Model (PSVM) to help measure the value of the Heritage Trust's activities across its vast portfolio of heritage properties and services. The PSVM attempts to bridge the gap between the intrinsic value defined for the heritage sector[139] and direct-use economic performance measurement, by combining an assessment of social, economic, and environmental outcomes to ascertain the public value generated by these publicly supported services and assets.

> Its primary strength is that it can balance the quantification of citizen-focused outcomes with a measure of the cost-effectiveness with which these are delivered (Accenture, 2006, p. 20).

In his work, Michael Hanemann identifies a paradigm-shift for economic studies that are now not just seen as a study of markets, but are more generally seen as studies of behavioural relations manifested in human preferences and behaviour (Hanemann, 1994, pp. 37-38). He suggests that a more relevant hypothesis for measuring the value of cultural goods would be to

---

139. The model of value adopted combines the rigour of traditional economically-derived methodologies that are based on use and the sensitivity of the less precise intrinsic values-based approach. This is done in a way that is valuable and meaningful for the heritage sector (Accenture, 2006, p. 19)

capture preferences by asking how much individuals are willing to pay for the particular good, and aggregating the results. This is the basis of 'Choice Modelling' – a useful research tool that represents a family of survey-based methodologies for measuring preference for non-market goods, in which the goods have been described for survey participants in terms of their attributes and the levels of benefit these can produce (Mourato & Mazzanti, 2002, p. 64). This methodology is favoured for analysis of goods of a multidimensional nature, such as cultural heritage. It has been argued that Choice Modelling:

> ...brings together a structured economic theoretical framework, a powerful and detailed capacity of evaluation and a great variety of application possibilities (Mourato & Mazzanti, 2002, pp. 64-65).

There is a general belief that no one methodology can provide 'robust' results across all cultural domains. A combination of methodologies, including Conjoint Analysis and Choice Modelling, are useful in determining what 'bundle of potential benefits' derived from cultural products and services would have the greatest perceived value. Following this, a Contingent Valuation Methodology (CVM) study would be undertaken to determine the perceived value of these previously identified 'bundles of benefits' (Savage & Hall, 2009).

The CVM format has been used extensively in environmental studies and, more recently, in the cultural arena. In essence, contingent valuation uses a survey instrument to encourage respondents to make an economic decision concerning a public good that has both economic values and non-market values that cannot be completely described by economic analysis (Alberini & Kahn, 2006). The respondents are presented with a hypothetical scenario and asked to indicate the maximum amount they would be willing to pay (WTP) for an increase in services, or the maximum amount they would be willing to accept (WTA) as compensation for a reduction in services.[140] Another important feature of CVM studies is their ability 'to derive a total economic value for a public good', incorporating the good's direct-use and passive-use values (Carson, et al., 2001, p. 198; URS Corporation, 2007, p. 5).

Today, Contingent Valuation is probably the most widely used methodology for assessing the passive values associated with heritage goods and services, because it can be used to identify a range of benefits – 'social, cultural, environmental – that are impossible to quantify in market terms' (Cowell, 2004, p. 32). CVM studies also have the added advantages of being 'a form

---

140. WTP is defined as the maximum amount a person would willingly pay – given their current income, current levels of market prices, and other background conditions – to receive a specified increment of a public good (or to avoid a loss). WTA is the minimum amount of compensation a person would willingly accept to forego a proposed increment (or to accept a threatened loss) under similar given conditions (Kling, et al., 2004, p. 2026).

of community engagement and a means of democratising the decision-making process' (2004, p. 32). However, this methodology does have shortfalls. Only hypothetical questions are posed, rather than actual situations and behaviours. This can result in:

> A tendency for respondents to either exaggerate or underestimate the true level of value they may place on a particular good or service when responding to questionnaires, on the basis that they know either they will suffer no direct financial implications themselves or that costs will be shared among a wider group (2004, p. 32).

Throsby, however, defends the use of CVM studies by arguing that there has been a great deal of progress made in recent years to refine the methodology to overcome the difficulties associated with answering hypothetical survey questions (David Throsby, 2003, p. 277).[141]

5.5.1 Contingent Valuation Methodology validity tests

In 1993, there was a real breakthrough in the acceptance of CVM studies as useful techniques for environmental issues (which has been extrapolated to the cultural landscape). A report was commissioned by the U.S.A. National Oceanic and Atmospheric Administration (NOAA) to assess environmental damages from a severe oil spill caused when an oil tanker, the *Exxon Valdez*, crashed into Bligh Reef in Prince William Sound, off the coast of Alaska. After a lengthy submission period and deliberations, a panel of eminent experts, co-chaired by Nobel Laureates, Kenneth Arrow and Robert Solow, concluded that a Contingent Valuation Methodology could produce estimates 'reliable enough to be the starting point of a judicial process of damage assessment including passive-use values' and that such studies can produce a 'reliable benchmark if strict guidelines on the design and administration of the questionnaires are followed' (Arrow et al., 1993, p. 4610).

This provided the green light for the subsequent use of CVM studies. Unfortunately, one of the side-effects of the NOAA assessment, with its stringent guidelines, was that it became very expensive to undertake reliable CVM studies. This has been described as raising the 'price' for 'reliable CV' results above the maximum willingness to pay for the information (V. K. Smith, 2006, p. 22).

Despite this decision, there are still some unresolved issues in the use of CVM studies. Frey, having analysed a number of studies, argues that while WTP surveys 'are useful [they] have a decisive disadvantage in that they are not related to political decisions'. He argues for popular referenda as a more

---

141. A detailed discussion of criticisms levelled at contingent valuation surveys – such as free riding, the embedding problem, and starting-point bias – of willingness to pay (WTP) questions will be discussed in Section 6.2.

relevant and beneficial instrument for cultural decisions, because it combines 'the evaluation of competing alternatives with democratic decisions' (Frey, 1997, p. 243; Frey, 2003, p. 146).[142]

While CVM surveys are used to evaluate non-marketed goods, there are also other methodologies that can also be considered, such as hedonic market and travel cost approaches[143], though neither of these methods were considered relevant for the valuation of the Queensland Museum, with its campus structure and regional program delivery across such a vast area.

More recently, a 'cultural worldview scale'[144] has been proffered as an additional useful methodology in improving the accuracy of economic models relying on stated preference techniques. It has the advantage of being able to segment 'populations according to their attitudinal positions or by providing variables of attitudinal heterogeneity' (Choi, Papandrea, & Bennett, 2006; Choi, et al., 2007, p. 333). Segmenting the population on attitudes to museums was an important consideration in the sampling used in the study to value the Queensland Museum.

Before deciding to use a CVM study to measure the value of the Queensland Museum to its primary stakeholders – the people of Queensland – an analysis of fifteen relevant major CVM studies of cultural goods – not just museums – was undertaken to ascertain the underlying strengths and weaknesses of this methodology and its usefulness in measuring the value of the Queensland Museum.

5.6 CVM studies of cultural goods

Methodological assessments of the individual CVM studies, in which sufficient information regarding the study was available, were undertaken to

---

142. While referenda are more democratic than alternatives, such as CVM studies, they are not free of problems either, and may be inappropriate in countries without the referendum tradition of Switzerland (Frey, 1997).

143. The 'hedonic market approach' derives the values attributed to a cultural object by looking at private markets, which indirectly detect the utility that people enjoy. It assumes that households 'migrate into or out of geographic regions based on tradeoffs between quality of life in those regions and differences in housing prices' (Frey, 1997, p. 234; Snowball, 2008, p. 76).

The 'travel cost approach' measures 'the access costs of users to a specific site or event, i.e. what consumers are willing to pay in travel costs in order to attend for example, an arts festival, a heritage site or a museum'. The underlying assumption is that the object in question must be the only purpose of the trip and that the trip itself does not yield any pleasure (Frey, 1997, p. 235; Snowball, 2008, p. 76).

144. The final version of the CW scale uses nineteen items to categorise respondents into four clusters: 'pro-cultural', 'culture-friendly', 'culture-averse', and 'anti-cultural' (Choi, Papandrea, & Bennett, 2007, pp. 330-332).

understand the benefits and constraints of using this methodology for studies valuing cultural goods and services. These studies were then cross-referenced against the meta-data analysis of sixty-five CVM studies of cultural goods carried out by Douglas Noonan (D. Noonan, S., 2003). Jeanette Snowball's update on Noonan's work was also referenced in assessing the strengths and weaknesses of a number of more recent CVM studies in the cultural arena (Snowball, 2008, pp. 108-110).

As early as 1983, Thompson, Throsby, and Withers pioneered the use of CVM surveys in assessing the benefits of arts institutions in Australia (D. Throsby, 1982, pp. 2-3). In his larger study of the impact of the arts in general, Throsby sought to minimise criticism of WTP survey instruments by performing two pilot studies prior to delivering a final questionnaire. The questionnaire would consist of a range of questions that were either refined or disregarded based on these studies' results.[145] They concluded that the questionnaire, which was delivered to a sample of five hundred and seventy dwellings in Sydney, has to balance the simplicity required for comprehension of the scenario presented and the questions asked, against the theoretical validity required to enable proper testing of the desired hypotheses. This remains an underlying challenge for all CVM studies (B. J. Thompson, et al., 1983, p. 42).

Attributes of this study would be included in the CVM study of the Queensland Museum, including the use of a pilot study to assess the survey questions, and including both negative and positive responses to questions relating to respondents' attitudes to museums in general and the Queensland Museum in particular. However, it was decided not to emulate the study's use of open-ended questions. Instead, it was preferred to provide set monetary amounts and information about the current level of government funding to the museum. These points will be expanded in Section 6.3.2, when discussing the development of the survey instrument.

Billie Hansen's often-quoted study of the Royal Theatre in Copenhagen, in 1993, further developed the methodology used in the earlier study of the arts in Australia. Her study had a twofold purpose: to investigate whether a CVM study could be used to estimate the total value of the Royal

145.Some of the early questions were found to be too complicated, eliciting too many 'don't know' responses, especially those relating to the liability/non-liability distinction and the liability questions based on doubling quantity. This latter issue meant nothing to those unfamiliar with the arts and was confused with quality for those who were aware of the arts. The researchers also disbanded the idea of using set monetary amounts in favour of open-end dollar responses. They also included three possible negative responses out of eight statement options to the first question, which was ascertaining respondents' attitudes to the arts in Australia. Finally, they decided to ask the first 'willingness to pay' questions prior to providing information on the current level of government support for the arts, which is a common complaint for these types of surveys (B. J. Thompson, et al., 1983, pp. 7-10).

Copenhagen Theatre[146] to the Danish population, and to determine whether the theatre's non-market benefits could justify the public grants it receives from the public purse (Bille, 1998, p. 200). Hansen recognised the weaknesses in her study, particularly in regard to the significant differences between the average WTP for respondents who did and did not know the average per capita tax payments. However, she was still able to conclude that the Danish population is willing to pay 'a future options price' of at least the amount the theatre costs in state subsidies (p. 229). The author's final conclusion was that a CVM study is 'well suited to obtain an estimate of the total value of a cultural good which has public good characteristics' and is a suitable starting point for 'decisions pertaining to resource allocation as long as these involved transmission and pure consumption' (Bille, 1998, p. 229; Billie Hansen, 1995, p. 318).

Another Australian study, this time in the broadcasting field, was completed in 1994. Using a face-to-face survey of over two thousand households across Australia, it sought to assess as a priority:

> ...the likely existence of external benefits from the consumption of domestic television programs; and respondents' willingness to pay for the existing mandated level of domestic programming on free-to-air television services (Papandrea, 2002, p. 8).

Results from this project showed that, in the absence of better alternatives, a CVM study 'has considerable merit' when applied carefully and using best practice guidelines, such as those recommended by the NOAA panel (Papandrea, 2002, p. 17).

The growing popularity of CVM studies was demonstrated by the number of case studies presented at the 2002 Contingent Valuation of Culture Conference held at the University of Chicago. One paper of interest was based on the work of Thompson, Throsby, and Withers, and attempted to analyse the value of public places in Kentucky as a '*composite* arts good rather than *specific* arts entities' (E. Thompson, Berger, Blomquist, & Allen, 2002, p. 10). Two separate audiences were surveyed – one was a random sample of six hundred households in Kentucky, and the other was a sample of six hundred households of people that were considered 'arts patrons'. This study provided some insights into the proposed evaluation of the Queensland Museum as a composite entity, and how the specific role of the Cobb+Co Museum within the composite project could be identified.

The second study of interest presented at the conference concerned the five thousand historic shipwrecks off North Carolina's coastline that have earned the region the reputation of being 'the graveyard of the Atlantic'. The researchers in this case used a CVM study to determine whether:

---

146. The Royal Theatre was familiar to all Danes, but few visited it. It could be viewed as one of Denmark's most elitist cultural institutions, with only seven percent of Danes attending a performance in 1992. At the same time, the Royal Theatre annually received over thirty-five percent of the total funding allocated for all seventy-five theatres in Denmark. Eighty percent of the theatre's total funding came from the government (Bille, 1998, p. 200).

> ...there are potentially significant non-market values for managing historic shipwrecks as submerged maritime cultural resources rather than as salvageable market commodities, while at the same time eliciting the residents' WTP to have these shipwrecks protected from treasure hunters (Whitehead & Finney, 2002, p. 2).

The results from this study did not conform to economic theory, because there was little increase in WTP with the increased numbers of historic shipwrecks preserved (Snowball, 2008, p. 98). Referred to as the 'warm glow' hypothesis, or the 'embedding effect', this can prove a shortcoming with some CVM studies. However, it was not applicable in the Queensland Museum study. (see Section 6.2.2).

A number of CVM studies focusing on heritage sites were also analysed for their potential to provide some lessons for the study of the Queensland Museum. These include: the Fort Collins' study in Colorado, which led to the reformulation of the initial government policy regarding the renovation of the old Northern Hotel – a staging stop for horse-drawn coaches (Greffe, 2002; Kling, et al., 2004); a major study in 1998 of the *Napoli Musei Aperti*[147] – a public cultural program provided by the city of Naples to improve neglected areas of a city (Santagata & Signorello, 2000); and the 1997 World Bank study of the advantages of renovating the Medina of Fez in Morocco. This last study surveyed both visitors to Fez and visitors to Morocco who did not go to Fez in an attempt to include both use values and existence values in the research (Greffe, 2002, pp. 57-61).

Heritage assets also abound in the United Kingdom. As both cultural and economic goods, they generate 'flows of human wellbeing' that are positive – that is, heritage contributes to wellbeing and does not detract from it (Economics for the Environment Consultancy, 2005, p. 2). Based on this assumption, CVM evaluations of historic environments in the United Kingdom were undertaken by English Heritage, the Heritage Lottery Fund, DCMS, and the Department of Transport in 2005, and their conclusions provided a number of useful insights. These include the fact that higher income typically leads to a higher WTP for the historic environments; that values held by users of sites (that is, visitors or nearby residents) are typically higher than those of non-users; and that the more trips a given user makes, the more likely they are to have a higher WTP. Non-user benefits are positive, particularly in cases where charismatic or unique heritage resources are under consideration. The fact that there are many more non-users than users means that even if the non-users have lower individual WTP, overall non-users can contribute much more to the total economic value of a site (Economics for the Environment Consultancy, 2005, p. 9).

---

147. *Napoli Musei Aperti* is a cultural network consisting of twenty-nine churches, eight aristocratic palaces, eight historical squares, and one museum. These public cultural goods were previously closed and unrestored and not available to the public. This study aimed to discover the use and passive-use values of these services provided by the city of Naples to its inhabitants (Santagata & Signorello, 2000, p. 183).

Of all the cultural sectors, the library sector has been the most proactive in undertaking impact evaluations, including CVM studies (Poll & Payne, 2006, p. 9; Usherwood, 2001, pp. 2-5). The National Library of New Zealand in 2002 commissioned an economic valuation of its National Bibliographic Database (NBD) and National Union Catalogue (NUC). This was a direct response to the general demand for better accounting of outcomes from government funding allocations. Specifically, the National Library wanted to place both a tangible economic value and an intangible cultural value on the services it provides, the user and client benefits it produces, and its performance relative to its statement of intent (McDermott Miller Ltd, 2002, p. 3).

This study demonstrated the advocacy potential of these types of studies of cultural institutions. It concluded that the benefit-cost ratio of the NBD/NUC is 3.5:1. In other words, the net present value of every dollar expended in providing the NBD/NUC to end users returns a value of $3.50 to them. Also, if the NBD/NUC ceased functioning and all the existing facility was lost, the national economy would lose around one hundred and sixty million dollars (McDermott Miller Ltd, 2002, p. v).

Similarly, the economic impact study of the British Library that was undertaken in 2003 was intended:

> ...to capture a realistic measure of the total economic value of the Library to those who make use of it, to those who may wish to use it in the future, and to those who recognise the benefits that it brings to society even though they do not use it directly (Pung, Clarke, & Patten, 2004, p. 82).

Lord Eastwell, the Chairman of the British Library, reiterated the multiplicity of outcomes that the library delivers:

> The value added by the library takes many forms – economic, cultural, social and intellectual. Second, the British Library, adds value both to those who use our products and services **directly,** and the wider UK population who benefit **indirectly** from the library's existence and the services it provides (The British Library, 2007, pp. 2-3).

In deciding to use a CVM study, the British Library wanted to determine a quantitative measure of its value in order to:

- Be accountable to government and the taxpayer for the annual grant-in-aid (public funding contribution) that it received each year;
- Demonstrate the value that it added to the nation and provide a mandate for continued investment; and
- Focus on the external benefits of what it did in order to sustain and develop its customer-led approach (Pung, et al., 2004, p. 82).

This research is significant as a first attempt to use a CVM study to measure the overall economic impact of a major cultural institution, particularly because it has been able to demonstrate that the British Library generates 4.4 times the value of its annual public funding. The British Government was quick to endorse the report as justification for its continued funding of the institution. Likewise, the British Library used these outcomes as an advocacy tool and to generate publicity for the identified benefits that are accrued by the public.

Borrowing the British Library process, Jura Consultants, working in Edinburgh, undertook a combined CVM study of the municipality of Bolton's cultural facilities. This 2005 study included three museums, fifteen local libraries, and Bolton's central archive service. Only local residents of the government authority area, both users and non-users, were included in the study. The consultants conducted face-to-face interviews, as opposed to telephone interviews. In addition, they organised five focus groups, including a group of school children, to elicit the community and social benefits that were not considered in the survey and/or to verify survey results (Jura Consultants, 2005).

The study's overall result was that the public valued their museums, libraries, and archives at 1.6 times the local government funding to these institutions. It was further able to extrapolate from this study that Bolton's three museums recorded a valuation of 2.48 times their funding allocation (Jura Consultants, 2005, pp. executive summary, 36-42).

There were a number of useful considerations in this research that had direct application to the Queensland Museums CVM study, including the decision not to use telephone interviews because of the difficulty for respondents in comprehending the scenario presented, the inclusion of only local residents in the survey and focus groups, and the inclusion of children as participants.

Also in 2005, Suanhild Aabo was undertaking a large CVM study of the public libraries in Norway. It had three major aims: to provide a better understanding of the libraries total social value – both use and non-use value – expressed in monetary terms; to explore whether or not the citizens found that the benefits they derived from the libraries outweighed the costs to provide them[148]; and to document the value of public libraries to politicians, local authorities, and the general public.

This study used a split sample, with one sub-sample asked about their willingness to accept compensation in the form of a tax rebate for closing the library down, and the other sub-sample asked about their willingness to pay to prevent library closure. Overall, the study found that the benefits to the general public were four times the costs of providing the national library network (Aabo, 2005, pp. 487-488).

In adopting a cautious and conservative approach to the Queensland Museum valuation study, the author rejected the higher potential results from a WTA scenario and limited the investigation to WTP situations.

In recent years, there have been many studies of arts organisations in North America attempting to quantify the value of the social, educational, and (now more frequently) economic outcomes of particular government

---

148.The concept of social value included the social impact of public libraries, in the wide sense, as the individual citizen assesses it (Aabo, 2005, pp. 487-488).

funding programs. These have usually, but not always, been instigated by government agencies. One such study involved an evaluation of the social benefits of the Stan Rogers Folk Festival ('Stanfest') in Canso, Nova Scotia, in July 2002. This study focused on identifying the benefits of cultural activity that stems from the festival's capacity to generate sociability both for participants and locals not attending the festival in that year:

> It identified the *content effect* of exposing festival-goers to new cultural material; the *conviviality effect* or network externalities of consumption; and the *collective-action effect* that might rebound to the benefit of the local community if there are economies of scope in collective action (Dayton-Johnson & King, 2003, pp. 1-2).

The researchers concluded that while they could not provide estimates of most of these non-use and sociability values (except to argue that they are non-negative), their baseline estimate of the festival's net social benefit substantially exceeds the subsidy it receives (Dayton-Johnson & King, 2003, p. 23). They also insisted that social cost-benefit analyses can be applied to publicly-subsidised cultural activity, such as musical festivals, and that these studies are 'superior' to the oft-used impact analyses (Dayton-Johnson & King, 2003, p. 1).

The Museum of World Culture in Gothenburg, one of nineteen state-funded museums in Sweden, provided free entry to visitors when it opened to the public in January 2005. A CVM study was conducted to investigate possible changes in visitor composition associated with the proposed introduction of an entrance fee to the museum. A study of five hundred and sixty-five respondents was conducted prior to the entrance charge being imposed and its results were then compared to the actual situation recorded by three hundred and fifteen respondents after fees were implemented. The study did not focus on regular visitors to museums, but targeted people who were less likely to be frequent visitors, such as men, young people, first- and second-generation migrants, people living in the suburbs, people with lower levels of education, and people with low incomes. The results predicted the actual changed composition of visitors, which led the researchers to conclude that CVM studies are particularly successful when applied to public goods, such as a museum that was familiar to the respondents (Lampi & Orth, 2009, p. 88).

These fifteen CVM studies of cultural goods provided general and specific information about the strengths and weaknesses of this format of Choice Modelling when applied in cultural settings. Each study devised different scenarios in which the survey participants were asked to consider their willingness to pay for added benefits, or their willingness to accept compensation for reduced benefits. The questionnaires were structured differently, the detail and presentation of the information was varied, and some used open-ended questions and others used closed questions, which could be bounded or double-bounded. The selection of survey participants differed and the method of survey delivery varied from face-to-face, mail, or phone. All these considerations were explored in formulating the CVM study of the Queensland Museum that is discussed in Chapter Six.

5.7 Conclusion

Museums have changed considerably over the past thirty to forty years, from being predominately internal collection-focused institutions to having more general awareness of community economic, social, and cultural needs. The major stakeholders of these public institutions have valued the cultural goods and services delivered by museums from different perspectives at different times. Governments, particularly since the 1980s, have sought various economic benefits from their funding of the sector, including individual social and cultural impacts and even the generation of large doses of social cohesion and social capital within communities. It is now more realistic to discuss the arts and cultural industries using a topology of values, including intrinsic, institutional, and instrumental values.

Recently, questions regarding the identity of the stakeholders of arts and cultural institutions have been addressed with more rigour. Of the eight frameworks considered, all nominate the public/individuals/community as the primary stakeholders, even though many museum professionals still assume it is the government/politicians/policymakers who provide the authorising environment for their institutions. This attitude reflects adherence to more traditional museological practices, rather than openness to the ideals of new museology or post-museological thought.

There have also been growing external demands on the arts and cultural industries for accountability measures for their funding allocation. While academics have been studying the economic and cultural value of cultural goods, museum professionals are only just starting to realise that they have little option but to respond seriously to demands for reliable data to assess outcomes from funding allocations. Some institutions have even adopted a more proactive stance, seeing the potential of generating reliable results for advocacy purposes.

Contingent Valuation Methodology studies are assisting by providing 'robust' outcome measurements for valuing cultural goods. This methodology is based on hypothetical scenarios in which the respondent is asked a series of questions relating to his or her willingness to pay for enhanced services, or willingness to accept compensation for removal of services. Modified and enhanced from use in the environmental sector, CVM studies have been used more recently to evaluate the public benefits deriving from libraries, museums, theatres, public broadcasting, heritage attractions, and festivals, as individual organisations; as national, state, or local collections of institutions; and even as the benefits that derive from 'the arts' in general.

The fundamental benefit of the CVM study is its capacity to assess, in financial terms, both the economic and cultural benefits that are derived by the public from exposure to the cultural goods. Fifteen CVM studies undertaken by the cultural sector were investigated to provide a reasonable basis on which to develop a reliable study of the economic, social, and cultural value of the Queensland Museum to the people of Queensland. The ultimate aim of this study, as examined in the following chapter, will be to extrapolate the value of the Cobb+Co Museum to the Toowoomba community.

Chapter 6
Queensland Museum Valuation Project

6.1 Introduction

In 2008, the Queensland Museum commissioned a Contingent Valuation Methodology (CVM) study to determine the public value of the Queensland Museum. This study was undertaken before funding was secured for the National Carriage Factory project. From this study, the value of the Cobb+Co Museum to its local community in its Stage Two iteration was ascertained. It was also intended that this study's results would deliver a new way of valuing the Queensland Museum and would provide a method of demonstrating this in economic terms – a method that could then be used for advocacy purposes to influence key policy and government decisions.

In addition, this project attempted to develop a consistent methodology that could be adopted by arts and cultural institutions in Queensland, thus encouraging maximum impact from individual studies that might be conducted by these institutions. This would allow the development of a shared common language for expressing the value of arts and culture in the state.

In its Strategic Plan for 2007–2008, the Queensland Museum had adopted the aim, as its first strategic objective, 'to increase awareness of the cultural, social, intellectual and economic benefits and value of Queensland Museum to the State' (Queensland Museum, 2008c). This priority was closely aligned to the museum's vision of being 'valued as an innovative, exciting and accessible museum of science, environment and human experience, of international standing' and its mission to 'enrich and enliven Queensland communities' (Queensland Museum, 2008c).

To gauge whether these objectives were being achieved, the museum embraced a methodology that would enable it to measure both the market and non-market benefits of the museum, as perceived by its public – Queensland residents, both users and non-users. Although it would prove a difficult exercise, a Contingent Valuation study was considered the most reliable and valid methodology to elicit Queenslanders' willingness to pay for both existing products and services and a raft of new developments proposed by the Queensland Museum during the next five to seven years (Sarantakos, 2005, pp. 96-99). Besides obtaining economic values expressed in dollar amounts, the CVM study would also investigate a range of non-market values that were important to both users and non-users of the Queensland Museum, as well as providing detailed demographic and psychographic data.

This chapter will begin by providing a brief summary of the Contingent Valuation Methodology and its recent use within the arts and cultural arena. International studies that were reviewed indicated a number of issues that had to be addressed in the development of the survey questionnaire and its administration in order to ensure that the Queensland Museum study would deliver 'robust' results.

The chapter will then outline the procedure undertaken by the Queensland Museum to involve other players in the arts and cultural sector in Queensland. This process involved a public lecture and master class; the appointment of a Steering Committee and Industry Reference Group; the development of a study brief; and the appointment of consultants who worked with the Steering Committee to prepare a draft questionnaire, undertake a pilot study, administer the final questionnaire, and provide the data. The majority of this chapter analyses the five sections of the questionnaire and the results obtained. The overall outcomes of the study and suggestions for further research are discussed in the chapter's conclusion (Tranter, 2009a, 2009b, 2009c).

6.2 Contingent Valuation Methodology validation

As CVM studies are still contested entities – despite the NOAA Report and fifteen years of further use and refinement – the Queensland Museum adopted a cautious approach to the methodology it would apply in developing and administrating its CVM questionnaire. It also took a conservative attitude to interpreting the data collected.[149]

---

149. A consistent point of reference was the general guidelines for CVM studies, as advocated by the NOAA Panel on Contingent Valuation (Arrow, et al., 1993, pp. 4611-4613).

Section 5.6 has already discussed a large number of international CVM studies of a range of cultural goods, including libraries, museums, galleries, historic sites, performance centres, and festivals. From this literature review, there emerged a number of issues that needed to be addressed. These included the sample type and size, minimising non-responses, the form of survey administration (mail, face-to-face, telephone, or web-based), the questionnaire design, the elicitation format, and the scenario descriptions.

Other issues of concern focused on the respondents' approach to the questions relating to willingness to pay for a public good, or, more specifically, their willingness to pay for changes in a public good. Specific concerns related to 'free-riding' and non-revelation of true preferences, the 'embedding' problem, 'starting-point' bias, and discrepancies in outcomes between willingness to pay (WTP) and willingness to accept (WTA).

6.2.1 Free rider problem

The 'free rider' problem in CVM surveys occurs when respondents deliberately over-state their true value of the good in question, in order to ensure that the good is provided, but while knowing that they will not actually have to pay the amount they nominate (Snowball, 2008, p. 87). The detection and control, if possible, of the free rider problem is a major problem for many critics of the preferred preference questionnaire format. The essence of concern is that people might:

> ...misrepresent their willingness to pay especially in the presence of economic incentives to understate preferences when individual payments are related to the response and to overstate preferences when individual payments are not related to the response (Bohm, 1979, p. 144).

Jeanette Snowball summarised a range of previous CVM research studies to try to ascertain the significance of this problem. Her conclusion supports the original findings from Peter Bohm's 1972 study[150] that 'hypothetical bias in properly designed surveys is not likely to be large', especially if the information provided to respondents is controlled and if they have some personal previous experience of the good under consideration (Snowball, 2008, p. 97).

150.Peter Bohr, in 1972, conducted the earliest significant research that identified problems connected with eliciting people's true preferences and the free riding problem. He conducted a series of surveys on five groups of volunteers who were asked to indicate their highest WTP for a new half-hour Swedish television comedy series. Members of five groups were informed that they would be required to pay an amount for the series based on their answers. They might be asked to pay the actual WTP price, a percentage of it, a variable amount, a flat rate, or nothing at all. This study revealed that none of these five approaches gave an average maximum WTP that significantly deviated from that of any other of the approaches. There was no significant variation between those who had to pay nothing and those who had to pay the fee that they indicated in their WTP survey. A sixth group was asked the highest amount they would be prepared to pay if they had been asked an individual admission price (Bohm, 1972, p. 112).

6.2.2 Embedding effects

The 'embedding effect' can relate to a number of different things. The embedding effect has commonly been referred to as 'the warm glow' impact that is often discussed in CVM literature as a serious limitation of CVM studies (Arrow, et al., 1993, pp. 4607-4608). Carson, Flores, and Meade's analysis of Contingent Valuation Methodologies in a large number of environmental studies concluded that altruism in the form of 'moral satisfaction' or 'warm glow' does not present a major difficulty. They do, however, warn that interview bias could be troublesome if the respondent tries to please the interviewer by agreeing (or not agreeing) to pay a particular amount that the respondent might otherwise not have considered (Carson, et al., 2001, p. 177).[151] They concluded that by using well-designed and well-administrated survey instruments, the 'warm glow' effect should not appreciably affect respondents' WTP for a composite good, such as the arts or the environment, and, if it does, it will not vary much with the amount of the specific good in question (Snowball, 2008, p. 98).

6.2.3 Scope and sequencing

Another aspect of the embedding issue refers to the apparent inconsistency between WTP results and what economic theory predicts would happen in the situation. This is especially significant in responses to changing scope and sequencing[152] of the amount of the good being valued. The often-quoted example is of the infamous bird study conducted by Desvousges in 1993. In this study, respondents were asked their willingness to pay to preserve two thousand, twenty thousand, or two hundred thousand waterfowl by covering oil ponds to prevent the birds being killed in the Rocky Mountains. Desvousges discovered that respondents' willingness to pay was much the same, although logic would predict that saving a hundred times the number of birds would elicit a higher WTP. This study is used as evidence that insensitivity to scope suggests that respondents were not valuing the good in an economically rational way, but were merely expressing a positive attitude to the good in question, or 'purchasing moral satisfaction'

---

151. To test the effect of interview bias, a split sample test was conducted by these researchers. In this test, respondents were either asked the WTP question in the standard format or were asked to write down their response and return it in a sealed envelope. The conclusion was that there was no significant difference in the WTP estimates was received (Carson, et al., 2001, p. 177).

152. Scope issues involve comparisons of values for goods that differ in a quantitative or qualitative fashion. Sequence issues involve how the value of a good, changes with the order in which it is valued and the nature of the goods offered before it (Carson & Mitchell, 1993, p. 1263).

from giving to some worthy case[153] (Carson & Mitchell, 1993, p. 1265). According to Hanemann, the majority of findings in CVM literature support the conclusion that variation of willingness to pay is sensitive to scope (Hanemann, 1994, p. 35).

More recent studies by Carlson, Flores, and Meade in 2001[154] indicated that well-designed survey instruments, conducted in accordance with the 1993 National Oceanic and Atmospheric Administration (NOAA) panel guidelines, are showing sensitivity to scope (Carson, et al., 2001, p. 182). For such studies to be valid, they need to avoid vague descriptions of the good; provide a definite provision and/or payment mechanism; and, if possible, to offer the best outcomes for scope sensitivity, the surveys should not be delivered by 'mall intercepts' or short telephone interviews (Arrow, et al., 1993; Snowball, 2008, p. 102).

The CVM study of WTP to preserve shipwrecks off the North Carolina coast from treasure hunters, which was conducted by Whitehead and Finney in 2003, demonstrates the problems encountered when not conforming to some of the NOAA guidelines. In persisting with telephone interviews and offering a choice of only fifty or one hundred shipwrecks to be saved out of a total of more than five thousand (which may not have been perceived as significant), scope insensitivity was highly likely, and could have been avoided with better questionnaire design (Snowball, 2008, pp. 104-105; Whitehead & Finney, 2002). It seems to be the verdict of many researchers that insensitivity to scope is a result of poor survey design, rather than proof that contingent valuation does not conform to economic theory (Carson & Mitchell, 1993, p. 1267).

Sequencing effects are also discussed within the parameters of embedding. Because, at times, the ordering of questions can influence answers, the sequence of questions also needed to be considered in the survey design (Epstein, 2003, p. 273). In the Queensland Museum CVM study, this did not cause any concern, because the second ballot WTP question elicited a higher percentage of support (seventy-five percent) than the first WTP ballot (fifty-two percent).

---

153. Further analysis of this study – undertaken by Carson and Mitchell – provides a totally different perspective. Respondents in the two thousand bird treatment were told that they would be saving much less than one percent of the waterfowls using the flyway. In the twenty thousand bird treatment, respondents were told that they would be saving less than one percent of the waterfowl. And in the two hundred thousand bird treatment, respondents were told that they would be saving about two percent of the waterfowl. If respondents used the percentages – which was likely because the waterfowl under consideration were quite distant from the Atlanta shopping malls in which the surveys were conducted – one might not expect to see large differences in WTA scores (Carson & Mitchell, 1993, p. 1265).

154. The researchers examined thirty-five CVM studies between 1984 and 1997 and found thirty-one of them 'rejected the scope insensitivity hypothesis', while four did not. Since then, major studies that used in-person interviews and well-constructed questionnaires containing extensive visual aids depicting the good to be valued also rejected the hypothesis (Carson, et al., 2001, p. 182).

Finally, within the embedding concept, there is debate over the WTP for a composite change in a group of public goods, such as the Queensland Museum, as an entity, rather than as the sum of four individual components. Research shows that the overall result is likely to be less than the sum of the WTP for individual changes in component parts of the composite good. This could have occurred if four separate surveys discussing the offerings at the individual campuses of the Queensland Museum had been undertaken with different sub-samples and then these figures aggregated to produce the total value for the Queensland Museum (Hanemann, 1994, p. 34). Again, the Queensland Museum CVM study erred on the side of caution by using a single stated-preference valuation.

6.2.4 Willingness to pay versus willingness to accept

More general concerns relating to possible disparities between WTP and WTA and whether to use WTA instead of or in association with a WTP study were also considered. Aabo's investigation of the public library system in Norway offered a good example for the Queensland Museum study. Using a split sample, with one sub-sample asked their WTA compensation in the form of a tax rebate for closing the library down, and the other sub-sample asked their WTP to prevent library closure. His results showed that WTA was five times higher than WTP and that ninety-four percent of respondents felt that they had an inherent right to the cultural good (that is, access to the public library). He concluded that WTP measures will underestimate welfare impacts and will be biased downwards, with the 'true' value being closer to the WTA estimate (Aabo, 2005, p. 492). Kling et al. indicated from their research that disparity between WTP and WTA was greater if the public goods under consideration had high intrinsic values and were not readily substitutable for private goods. This was the case with the Norwegian libraries and with the Queensland Museum (Kling, et al., 2004, p. 2027). In deciding to use only WTP scenarios, as recommended by the NOAA Panel, it was recognised that results from the CVM Study of the Queensland Museum would provide more conservative results than a corresponding study using WTA estimates.[155] A combination study, such as the one Aabo conducted, was also ruled out in favour of the two scenarios used. Any further combination of 'what ifs' was considered too complicated for respondents, given the complex nature of the Queensland Museum structure and service delivery models that had to be digested (Aabo, 2005, p. 492).

It was also recognised that both positive and negative statements of non-market values had to be presented to acknowledge that both positive and negative values could be held by respondents. Epstein explains that not all

155. Any scenario involving closure of a QM venue would not have been a credible situation.

CVM results are always positive[156] (as is often assumed) and, as an example, discusses the ringing of church bells as positive, negative, or neutral, dependant on the distance the respondents live from the source (Epstein, 2003, pp. 269-270).

6.2.5 Elicitation format

The elicitation format used in the WTP questions needed special consideration. The choice was between a dichotomous choice format, with single bound or multiple bound questions using set dollar amounts, or open-ended responses. Proponents argue that presenting respondents set of dollar amounts from which to choose is likely to create anchoring bias with a limited range of values, but using open-ended questions is a difficult task for respondents and often results in a wide spectrum of results that may not be realistic, given the respondents' circumstances (Hanemann, 1994, p. 23). It was eventually agreed for the Queensland Museum study to, again, follow the NOAA Panel's recommendation to present a dichotomous question that asked respondents to vote for or against a particular level of taxation (Arrow, et al., 1993, p. 4612).

Another difficulty with the dichotomous choice format is setting appropriate amounts from which respondents are asked to make a choice. To increase accuracy, this process should be repeated a number of times, during which the WTP amount is adjusted until fifty percent of respondents accept the amount, and fifty percent have rejected it. Unfortunately, time and cost considerations made this an impossible task. The Queensland Museum CVM study instead used three optional WTP dollar amounts, but provided only one option to each respondent.

In analysing the WTP data, there was additional need for caution in distinguishing between average, mean, and marginal values. Again, the Queensland Museum CVM study adopted the conservative approach, as will be discussed when analysing these results (Epstein, 2003; Hanemann, 1994, p. 25; B. J. Thompson, et al., 1983, pp. 7-16; David Throsby, 2003, p. 277).

6.2.6 Information bias

In designing the survey instrument, particular attention was paid to ensure that information bias was minimised due to respondents' previous exposure or otherwise to the Queensland Museum. Deciding on the level of information to provide to respondents is one of the most problematic features of designing a CVM study. On the one hand, Bohm (1972, 1979, 1984) argued

156. He also makes the point that sometimes there might be conflicting values within a good, which are often not considered in CVM studies. As an illustration, he describes a study that focuses on the preservation of redwood trees and asks respondents their WTP for the trees existence value, but neglects to explore how respondents might value the furniture made from redwood timber (Epstein, 2003, p. 271).

strongly for the need for detailed information to be provided so that respondents could express their WTP accurately, while Niewijk, in his 2001 study paper, took an opposing view. Niewijk maintained that CVM studies are supposed to measure pre-existing values. However, if respondents are not directly aware of the existence of a particular good before the survey, the information provided might actually create the value it aims to measure[157] (Snowball, 2008, p. 142). In general, it seems likely that information bias is affected by two things: the quality of the argument for change, and the personal relevance of the good or situation to the respondent (Snowball, 2008, p. 143). The survey design must account for these two attributes to avoid information bias.

As the Queensland Museum is made up of a number of campuses[158] and programs[159], there was a possibility of distorted outcomes resulting from considering individual campuses, as opposed to the Queensland Museum as a whole. Describing the existing Queensland Museum's campuses, programs, services, and the proposed developments in a clear and concise manner was a difficult, but critical task – as was the decision about where this information would appear in the questionnaire.[160] One of the reasons for choosing a web-based questionnaire format was its visual nature and its potential to convey complex information more clearly. The pilot study was seen as crucial in assessing whether respondents understood and could make considered judgements about the scenarios presented.

There was also discussion over the need, or otherwise, to provide some indication of the current level of public support for the Queensland Museum. As the study involved an established policy, it was agreed that re-

---

157. A study of four sites in Pentland Hills Regional Park, on the outskirts of Edinburgh, aimed to test whether the provision of certain types and amounts of information could enable respondents to a CVM survey to reach similar conclusions to experts. It concluded that: 'when the respondents were presented with photographic, textual and ecological information, the public ranked the sites in exactly the same order as the experts. It was argued that the provision of ecological information increased the validity of the public valuation' (Kenyon & Edward-Jones, 1998, p. 471).

158. There are four campuses of the Queensland Museum:
- Queensland Museum South Bank (QMSB) in Brisbane;
- Cobb+Co Museum (Cobb+Co) in Toowoomba;
- The Workshops Rail Museum (TWRM) in Ipswich; and
- Museum of Tropical Queensland (MTQ) in Townsville.

159. Programs include:
- Scientific and Historical Research;
- The Internet;
- Publications ;
- The Inquiry Centre;
- Museum Development Officers; and
- The Education Loans Service.

160. See Appendix One for a copy of the final survey instrument, which shows the wording, the use of a map, and the placement of descriptive information about the Queensland Museum.

spondents would probably want this as 'a point of reference for the framing of their responses', even though this could 'anchor' the results around the given amount and result in a 'starting point' bias (Papandrea, 2002, p. 7).

Despite all these qualifications and concerns, the questionnaire had to be easy to comprehend, had to provide sufficient detail for the respondents to understand the scenarios presented, had to avoid being overly complicated and long, but had to provide 'theoretical validity to enable proper testing of the desired hypotheses' (B. J. Thompson, et al., 1983, p. 41). The CVM study also had to be able to pass various validity and reliability tests[161], such as replication; comparison with estimates from other sources; and comparison with actual behaviour, where possible (Hanemann, 1994, p. 29).

6.2.7 Forms of validation

However, validating a CVM study is not straightforward and requires more analysis. The term 'content validity' is an important underlying determinant of CVM surveys:

> Respondents must (i) clearly understand the characteristics of the good they are being asked to value; (ii) find the CV scenario elements related to the good's provision plausible; and (iii) answer the CV questions in a deliberate and meaningful manner (Carson & Mitchell, 1993, p. 1267).

Other concepts include 'construct validity' in which the results of the CVM study conform to economic theory. These economic theories include: the probability of respondents' WTP decreasing with an increase in price; the notion that direct users of the good are more willing to pay than those who do not use the good; and the fact that income has a positive effect on WTP, age usually has a negative effect, and geographical proximity usually has a positive effect. Negative effects can result if the respondents perceive that the program to provide the good might not be successful, or if they perceive that the payment vehicle might not be appropriate. Most significant are attitudes to the good, itself, which are generally positive predictors of willingness to provide financial support (Carson, et al., 2001, p. 194).

It would appear that ongoing research into the application of Contingent Valuation Methodologies has determined that studies that address the issues discussed above are providing more 'robust' results. One remaining criticism is that to produce a reliable CVM survey is 'neither simple nor inexpensive to implement' (Carson, et al., 2001, p. 196), which was the case in the Queensland Museum CVM study.

---

161. 'Validity' refers to the correspondence between what one wishes to measure and what is actually measured. 'Reliability' refers to the ability of the results to be reproduced by correlating results from different respondents from the same sample, or results from the same respondents at different times (Carson, et al., 2001, pp. 193-195).

6.3 Study methodology

The Queensland Museum adopted the following process to implement its proposed CVM study. In December 2007, the author produced a background briefing paper that articulated a process for the Queensland Museum Board to implement. This included working with The University of Queensland's Museums Study Program and subsequently involving Professor David Throsby from Macquarie University in the process.

Professor Throsby visited Brisbane on 2–3 April 2008 and delivered a public lecture at the Queensland Museum South Bank on the evening of 2 April. This lecture was entitled *How to Value Arts and Culture: Why We should be Proactive in Queensland* (David Throsby, 2008c). More than eighty people attended, including a wide range of industry personnel from Brisbane and nearby regions. During this lecture, Professor Throsby outlined his concept of 'Cultural Capital' by comparing it to 'Natural Capital' and its capacity to incorporate both economic and cultural benefits. He argued that economic benefits could be calculated in monetary terms by the sum of use and non-use benefits, such as existence, optional, and bequest benefits, while cultural values are determined using the significant assessment criteria practised in both the built and moveable cultural heritage domains (David Throsby, 2008c).

On 3 April, Throsby held a master class for twenty-four senior executives from the Queensland Museum, the State Library of Queensland, the Queensland Art Gallery, The Queensland Performing Arts Centre, The Museum of Brisbane, Museum and Gallery Services Queensland, The Queensland Heritage Commission, Arts Queensland, and The University of Queensland. This day-long workshop evaluated the Contingent Valuation process and a number of international case studies and formulated a range of issues that would need to be considered in developing a consultant's brief for a CVM study of the Queensland Museum. The intention was to produce a briefing document that would be general enough for any of the other statutory authorities to adopt for their own purposes, while maintaining a consistent approach. It was hoped that, eventually, similar studies to that proposed for the Queensland Museum would be undertaken by other arts and cultural institutions in Queensland. It was hoped that this would amass a body of consistent data that would be compelling enough to convince government and other stakeholders (Queensland Museum, 2008b).

Following the master class, the Queensland Museum appointed an internal Project Manager who, together with the Manager of Corporate Communications and Marketing and the author, as the Director of Regional Services, formed a small steering committee to conduct the CVM study.

One of this committee's first tasks was to establish an Industry Reference Group (IRG) from among participants in the master class. To have the other major Queensland cultural statutory authorities involved in the whole process was thought to be the best way to encourage an understanding of the CVM process and promote the uptake of similar studies. Invitations were issued to representatives from the Queensland Museum Board, the other Queensland cultural statutory authorities, Arts Queensland, and the Brisbane City Council. Professor Throsby accepted the offer of being the Industry Reference Group's economic advisor. The Industry Reference Group was chaired by the Queensland Museum's Chief Executive Officer, Doctor Ian Galloway.

The steering committee developed the CVM study project brief and advertised for consultants to develop and deliver the questionnaire and provide tables of results and economic analyses of the WTP scenarios.

6.3.1 Appointment of consultants to conduct the CVM study

Assistance was sought from the Office of Economic and Statistical Research at the Queensland Treasury Department and the Corporate Administration Agency (CAA) in devising the brief for the consultancy to undertake the Queensland Museum CVM study.

Issues canvassed during discussions on the development of the brief included the desire to acquire some data from the CVM study that could be used to advocate to the Queensland Government for broader KPIs for museum outputs, which, in turn, could support the Queensland Museum's arguments for additional resources. It was also recognised that Arts Queensland's *Sector Development Plans 2007–2009* did not include reference to the Queensland Museum's scientific research based on its collections, and subsequently did not identify these aspects of the museum's contribution to the state. It was hoped to incorporate a wide range of value criteria in the study, which would include consideration of the museum's scientific research.

A draft project brief was developed and assessed by the Industry Reference Group (IRG). An Invitation to Offer was advertised nationally on 5 July 2008.[162] The purpose of the study was described as follows:

> The Queensland Museum (QM) is seeking proposals from creative agencies to develop and deliver a mechanism to determine the public value of QM incorporating a contingent valuation study. It is intended that the results will deliver a new way of valuing QM and provide a mechanism for demonstrating this in economic terms to be used to influence policy and key government decisions.

---

162. The following timeframe was outlined in the Invitation to Offer:
- The closing date was 28 July 2008;
- The contract would be awarded by 8 August 2008;
- A pilot study would be conducted and the report on outcomes delivered by 30 September;
- The final survey instrument would be approved by 13 October;
- The survey would be completed by 10 November;
- The draft report would be delivered by 5 December; and
- The final report would be completed by 23 January 2009 (Queensland Museum, 2008a).

> The project will also see the development of a consistent methodology that can be adopted by arts and cultural institutions in Queensland to enable the maximum impact from individual studies. This will allow the development of a shared common language for expressing the value of arts and culture in the State.
>
> The project will also provide a detailed report with quantitative and qualitative results analysed (Queensland Museum, 2008a, p. 6).

Considering the complexity of the campus structure and the activities undertaken by the Queensland Museum, there were a number of challenges that had to be considered in devising this project. It was ultimately decided that the study would focus on Queensland residents as users and non-users of Queensland Museum and would also focus on the museum's public interface (the museum's campuses, its regional services activities and its publishing program and website). As the Queensland Museum is a Queensland Government Statutory Authority, it was decided to limit input into the survey to Queensland residents, as it is these residents who effectively provide the bulk of funding for the institution. The study would interview the following sample groups using methodologies that were practical considering the geographical spread of these Queensland residents:

1. Museum visitors to campuses in Brisbane, Ipswich, Townsville, and Toowoomba;
2. Non-visitors in local target areas; and
3. Other Queensland residents.

In summary, the consultants were asked to assess the value the public equates with the Queensland Museum's natural and cultural heritage collections and its public programs (based on research and credibility) and services.

Environmetrics was the successful tender and, on 11 August, Rob Hall, the project consultant, presented the proposed project methodology to the Industry Reference Group at the Queensland Museum in Brisbane. He reiterated that in creating a 'robust' shell for possible later use by other arts institutions, the IRG needed to recognise the limitations in the actual survey instrument that were caused by contextual effects.

He also stressed that while the final dollar value was important and negotiable, 'other values give meaning', and he wanted to build this into the project. Environmetrics had done previous audience evaluation work for Queensland Museum. These studies had identified the Queensland Museum's key audience segments and their attitudes to the institution. These attitudes affect visitors' feelings and, in turn, translate into behavioural patterns, which have strategic value. One of the filters to select survey participants would be their attitude to museums and other cultural offerings, and to the Queensland Museum in particular.

There was some discussion about the proposal to use an online survey[163], even though it meant that the participants were, to some extent, self-recruited, and would be 'paid' ten dollars each for their involvement. In general, the steering committee was happy with the proposed sample size of eight hundred people to be selected from variety of categories (age, gender, location, museum exposure) from a database of over ninety thousand people. The overwhelming cost of using face-to-face interviewing – as a result of the geographical spread of the four survey sites in Queensland – and the bias that can result from this form of survey, precluded it being used in this study. Telephone surveys were canvassed, but it was decided that the dwindling number of landlines used by the population, particularly among younger people, was a limitation. Telephone surveys were also a problem because respondents needed to sight certain information to offer responses to WTP scenarios. The consultant argued that responses to telephone interviews paralleled those of online responses for attitudinal surveys, and that the only marked difference between the two techniques was the purchase arrangements (Discussions with Rob Hall, 11 August 2008). The steering committee was also aware of the increasing Internet usage by Australians and, with this trend showing no sign of change, it was expected that future surveys would be conducted online much more frequently.[164]

The survey methodology precluded children and people under the age of eighteen from participating. This was not considered a major impediment, because most adults respond to questionnaires on behalf of their household, including other adults and children (Discussions with Rob Hall, 11 August 2008). Also, the WTP scenarios with their tax implications, as presented in the survey, would not have been applicable to children and the majority of people under the age of eighteen.

6.3.2 Survey development

The initial draft survey format was discussed with the IRG on Monday 25 August. The main issue for this meeting was the question of: 'what exactly does the Queensland Museum want to value?' The major motivation for this exercise was to formulate a tool to leverage state government funding for new infrastructure projects at the four Queensland Museum campuses, as well as a new website (a fifth 'virtual campus').

---

163. This was to be one of the very early web-based surveys for CVM studies. There was only limited discussion of computer administered surveys in any of the existing literature on CVM studies. These did not provide any evidence to support or otherwise the decision to use a web-based survey (Champ & Welsh, 2006, p. 33).

164. The Australian Communication and Media Authority, in March 2008, indicated that the percentage of households in Australia with broadband access was currently 63.4% and it predicted that this would rise to 76.4% by 2012.

The main purpose for the survey was to establish how much Queenslanders value the Queensland Museum in its current format, and how much they would be willing to pay (or to support a government subsidy) to enhance its offerings. There was considerable debate over the inclusion of some comparative value framework in the survey.[165] It was finally decided to provide information about the average per head subsidy for the Queensland Museum, as well as alternative state government per capita allocation of resources to such services as health, education, prisons, tourism, and transport. To ensure the validity of the survey instrument, there was the need to indicate that for any re-balancing of resources towards the Queensland Museum there would have to be a corollary impact on other state government services. For a CVM survey to be properly formulated, it must remind respondents of their budget constraints and available substitutes (D. Noonan, S., 2004, p. 206). In common with Throsby's earlier Australian study on community benefits from the arts, it was also decided to ask participants to indicate where they think any re-balancing should occur (B. J. Thompson, et al., 1983, p. 3).[166]

Issues relating to how much information should be included in the survey and in what format (photographs and other digital formats) were discussed in relation to the embedded values in any visuals used. It was acknowledged that:

> ...the type, quality and quantity of information provided in a stated choice survey play a crucial role and directly affect the results as respondents base their answers on this information [and] pictures and graphics can go a long way in accurately and efficiently conveying information, provided that they are factually accurate (Mathews, Freeman, & Desvousges, 2006, pp. 111, 130).

It was recognised that respondents' background knowledge of the Queensland Museum would vary greatly, as would their familiarity with the museum's campus structure and its various services and programs. It was subsequently acknowledge that, for a number of respondents, some information about the Queensland Museum would be imperative.

The time devoted by each survey participant was also acknowledged as being closely linked to the participant's interest in the survey presentation and the topic being discussed. In general the IRG agreed that the questionnaire had to be simple, understandable, easy to complete, and theoretically valid, as discussed above (B. J. Thompson, et al., 1983, p. 41).

---

165. There were suggestions that comparisons should be provided with alternative leisure experiences that have well-understood associated costs, such as movie tickets or theme park admission prices. However, the taxation offer was favoured as more realistic.

166. Over eighty percent of respondents indicated they would prefer any increase in funding for the arts to come from reductions in other government spending rather than increased taxes, identifying that they would support reductions in social services and defence, followed by sport and recreation outlays (B. J. Thompson, et al., 1983, p. 3).

It was agreed that pre-testing, which incorporated a process of cognitive interviewing, was essential to ensure the appropriateness and comprehensibility of the information being conveyed and the way it was presented. Pre-testing can also be useful to elicit if any essential information is missing from the survey (Mathews, et al., 2006, p. 123). It was equally important to ensure that the respondents interpreted the survey terminology, instructions, and questions in the way the researchers intended. This can be difficult, considering the hypothetical scenarios involved and the wide spectrum of respondents' educational levels, prior knowledge and experiences, technical backgrounds, and opinions (Mathews, et al., 2006, p. 112).

Other issues canvassed included: the multifaceted experiences and public offerings of the different campuses; the value and public understanding of the Queensland Museum research profile, particularly in the field of biodiversity and geosciences, in contrast to the economic value of this research to commercial operators and government institutions; and the varied opportunities to charge the public for different offerings and experiences.[167]

Finally, the issue of the form of payment was deliberated. The options debated included entry fees, one-off donations, government funding reallocations, and the existing and future travel costs to use Queensland Museum services.

In developing the survey instrument, Environmentrics and the IRG had to address a number of the challenges, which were discussed earlier, that are associated with CVM applications to cultural heritage. These included defining the sampling frame, dealing with respondents unfamiliar with the Queensland Museum (the public good), and eliciting values for complex projects (in this case, component sectors of the Queensland Museum) (Navrud & Ready, 2002, p. 26).

Considerable debate arose over the desire to elicit a current valuation for the Queensland Museum, as well as around asking respondents their WTP for a variety of enhancements. This, to some extent, contradicts the basic premise that:

> In CVM, researchers ask a sample of individuals how much they would be willing to pay for a change in the quantity of a good provided (D. Noonan, S., 2004, p. 206).

At the core of the debate was the issue of respondents' abilities to comprehend the two different scenarios, how they are currently impacted, and how they could be affected by the change. Douglas Noonan alerts the researcher to this limitation of a CVM study, which he describes as the likely:

---

167. The Queensland Museum South Bank has free entry for all visitors, but has a charge for entry to the Sciencentre. The Workshop Rail Museum in Ipswich has a relatively high entry fee, but operates a well patronised membership program. The Cobb+Co Museum in Toowoomba and The Museum of Tropical Queensland in Townsville both have relationships with their regional councils that enable free entry to all local residents.

> ...inability of respondents to formulate preferences under alternative scenario WTP questions, which typically involve respondents comparing their wellbeing in two states of the world, the current and a hypothetical one. Respondents must know what they will want in both states (D. Noonan, S., 2004, p. 208).

The second comparison issue to be tackled was whether to provide the dollar value for the existing public funding for the Queensland Museum. In his review of the thirty- three original CVM studies of arts resources, Noonan makes the following observations:

> An information bias may be present when researchers inform respondents of their current tax liability for the arts; this tends to bias their WTP answers toward that amount. The bias both pushes the average WTP closer to the anchor-point given in the survey and narrows the spread of answers around that anchor (D. Noonan, S., 2004, p. 212).

The consultant's position, based on research done by Rob Hall and corroborated by David Throsby, contradicts Noonan's conclusions. The consultant's believed that a free format field is not advisable because it tends to provide less than robust data. Hall and Throsby's studies found that having definitive selections can remove the outlying responses and subsequently provide a more meaningful result (correspondence with Gillian Savage Environmetrics 29 September 2008). It was agreed to include, in the pilot study, the actual amount of state government funding to the Queensland Museum, of $6.50 per adult Queenslander. This was done to ascertain how this figure would be treated by respondents.

The core of the survey was the WTP questions. It was decided to follow the advice of the NOAA Report and not use an open-ended question format in which respondents could suggest whatever amount they chose. Instead, the so-called 'dichotomous choice' format, with a double bound question, was employed. Initially, respondents were asked if they were in favour of increasing funds to the Queensland Museum (Willis, 2002, p. 312). Each respondent would then be presented with one fixed amount to pay that they can accept or reject and so 'vote' for the amount as reasonable or not.

A very conservative approach was adopted by offering set amounts of one dollar, two dollars, four dollars, and six dollars. This was done because it was thought to be more defensible to have a doubling of funding, as the maximum amount indicated.

Finally, the consultants were adamant that, for a justifiable result, respondents needed to have information available in the survey regarding appropriate changes in other government services, if they were to support any increase in Queensland Museum funding allocations. Consequently, Question Fifteen in the survey identified five specific government services that would be affected by an increase in museum funding. This question asks respondents to rank their preferences for changes in numbers of new hospital beds, classrooms, prison beds, tourism promotional campaigns, and kilometres of new road construction (Environmetrics, 2008a).

6.4 Questionnaire format

The draft survey instrument used the following questionnaire format:

1. **Leisure activities and attitudes to museums and museum visitation** (Questions 1–2)
2. **Attitudes to the QM**
   (a) Campuses (Questions 3–16)
   (b) Products and services (Questions 17–23)
3. **Setting the scenarios – non-market values of QM** (Question 24)
4. **WTP using two scenarios**
   (a) Ongoing WTP for existing products and services (Questions 25–29)
   (b) One-off WTP for increased prescribed products and services (Questions 30–34)
5. **Demographics and some general attitudes, interests, and comments** (Questions 35–44)

6.4.1 Pilot study

The pilot phase was an essential component of the project, because it would enable an early assessment of the questionnaire in terms of any language problems encountered by respondents, potential selection difficulties, cross checking of response categories, and the need for any additional information for interviewers (B. J. Thompson, et al., 1983, p. 42).

It was agreed that pre-testing, which would incorporate a process of cognitive interviewing, was useful to ensure that the level of information being conveyed and the way it was presented was appropriate and understood by respondents.[168] It was equally important to ensure that the respondents interpreted the survey terminology, instructions, and questions as the researchers intended.

The pilot study of twenty-five participants was undertaken in November 2008.[169] It aimed to check respondents' comprehension of the survey and the logic of the survey and to verify the usefulness of the dollar amounts used in the WTP questions. The pre-testing results showed that:

---

168. Pre-testing can also be helpful to elicit what information is lacking in the survey that would assist respondents in making their decisions (Mathews, et al., 2006, p. 123).

169. Of those, five people were given Option A – an increase of one dollar in recurrent funding; seven were given Option B – an increase of two dollars; six were given Option C – an increase of four dollars; and seven were given Option D – an increase of six dollars. The same ratios were used for the WTP for a one-off increase in funding for the proposed developments and service enhancements planned by the Queensland Museum. The values offered in this section were two dollars, four dollars, six dollars, and eight dollars.

- Forty-eight percent of respondents were prepared to pay more for annual recurrent expenses for existing services, with only four percent indicating that they wished to pay less than the existing level of $6.50 per adult per year;
- Seventy-six percent of respondents were prepared to contribute to a one-off payment to enhance the planned services that could cost about twenty-four million dollars;
- Responses were mixed between decreasing other services or increasing taxes to fund the extra museum costs;
- Where people chose to reduce other services, the only services that were earmarked for reduction were prisons and tourism; and
- There was no difference between Options A, B, and C in terms of WTP, which was not surprising because the amounts were small and close to each other in value (Environmetrics, 2008b).

The consultants suggested that the final survey be modified to offer only three options for both scenarios. Option A was to be an extra two dollars in recurrent funding, Option B was to increase to four dollars, and Option C was to increase to eight dollars. These modifications were undertaken to give a stronger indication of the limits of WTP. For the one-off increase option, the values would be: Option A – four dollars; Option B – six dollars; and Option C – twelve dollars. There were three questionnaire formats that used the three option amounts as described above (see Appendix One for the survey using Option B – the middle dollar values). Each respondent would now be presented with one amount chosen at random and, as a result, around one-third of respondents in the final sample, considered each amount when making their choice (see Table 6.21).

6.4.2 Web-based survey

The web-based survey was conducted by McNair Ingenuity, using their online national panel from which samples are recruited for use in a range of government and commercial research. Adult panel members who were residents of Queensland were invited to participate in the survey in return for a standard fee of ten dollars.[170] The survey took place between 5 December 2008 and 15 January 2009, avoiding the Christmas and New Year periods. Table 6.1 provides a summary of the sample and how it was selected.

---

170. Quality checks were in place to ensure that the respondents were who they said they were, that they lived in appropriate areas of Queensland, and that they responded to the survey only once (Environmetrics & McNair Ingenuity, 2009, p. 12).

Table 6.1: Queensland Museum CVM survey sample

Method used	**Sample size**	**Sampling method**	**Population**
Online survey	1174	Purposive to include: - Proportion of residents from Brisbane/Ipswich, Toowoomba, and Townsville; - Museum-goers and non-goers; - Age and gender balance.	Queensland residents recruited from the McNair Ingenuity online panel

6.4.3 Sample representation

While proposing a sample size of eight hundred respondents, it was found that, during the fieldwork stage of the project, there were not sufficient numbers of respondents from the smaller areas of Toowoomba and Townsville. This meant that additional recruiting was conducted, as summarised in Table 6.2. Both Townsville and Toowoomba[171] were eventually oversampled in proportion to the total population. This was to enable closer analysis of the views of people from these centres.

The final survey figures were presented in both unweighted and weighted table formats to account for the over-sampling, as shown in Table 6.2. Where required for a statewide result[172], the weighted sample was used – for example, when estimating the average willingness to increase funding to the Queensland Museum.

Table 6.2: Original geographical spread for the proposed eight hundred respondents, and the final sample of 1,174 completed surveys obtained

Samplesize/ geographical spread	**Proposed sample**	**Obtainedsample**	**Obtainedsample (%)**	**Population%**
Brisbane/Ipswich	300	545	46%	43%
Toowoomba	150	126	11%	3%
Townsville	200	208	18%	3%
Rest of Queensland	150	295	25%	51%
Total	**800**	**1,174**	**100%**	**100%**

171.The final sample for Toowoomba was slightly less than planned (one hundred and twenty-six, compared to one hundred and fifty respondents), but it was still adequate to represent the area for the kinds of analyses necessary for this project (Environmetrics & McNair Ingenuity, 2009, p. 9).

172.For those situations in which the results of this research needed to be expressed in terms of the 'adult residents of Queensland', the obtained sample was weighted by age group, gender, and region. This allowed the overall sample size to remain constant while the proportion of males and females in each broad age group in each of the four geographic regions matched the actual population pattern reflected in the 2006 census.

The final survey sampling results are described in the tables below. The spread of ages was particularly uniform, except for the under twenty-four age group, which represented just over half the number of respondents, compared to the other four categories. Of the respondents in the under twenty-four age group, eighteen percent were from Toowoomba. There were very few respondents aged fifty-five and over in the Toowoomba sample, which was a potential disadvantage. However, this disadvantage did not eventuate, because the results across the age groups were consistent for the whole sample and were not geographically motivated.

Table 6.3: Survey sample showing age distribution using unweighted scores

Age/geographical spread	Obtained sample	Under 24	25–34	35–44	45–54	55 and over
Brisbane/Ipswich	545 46%	60 41%	121 45%	124 44%	100 42%	140 57%
Toowoomba	126 11%	26 18%	38 14%	33 12%	22 9%	7 3%
Townsville	208 18%	31 21%	51 19%	50 18%	51 21%	25 10%
Rest of Queensland	295 25%	29 20%	56 21%	73 26%	65 27%	72 30%
Total	**1,174**	**146**	**266**	**280**	**238**	**244**

Overall, the ratio of females to males was 3:2. However, more than sixty percent of male respondents were from the Brisbane/Ipswich region. There was a more even spread of females across the four geographical regions that were surveyed (refer to Table 6.4).

Table 6.4: Survey sample showing gender distribution using unweighted scores

Gender/ geographical spread	Obtained sample	Male	Female
Brisbane/Ipswich	545 46%	282 60%	262 37%
Toowoomba	126 11%	36 8%	90 13%
Townsville	208 18%	51 11%	156 22%
Rest of Queensland	295 25%	103 22%	191 27%
Total	**1,174**	**472** **40%**	**699** **60%**

6.4.4 Analysis of the data

According to Environmetics, the raw data was captured directly from the website after each respondent finished answering the questions and submitted their response. This data was then checked and edited to remove any spurious respondents – a small number of panel members were no longer living in Queensland and an even smaller number did not complete the full questionnaire.

The data was then input into two software packages: STATA – a data analysis and statistical software package that is well-known in the economic and social research arenas; and MRDC software for market research. This package has extensive applications in commercial marketing research for the efficient production of large numbers of tables derived from survey data. The amounts people were willing to pay for the two scenarios were estimated by Environmetrics using STATA's probit regression to model the outcome variables (Environmetrics & McNair Ingenuity, 2009, p. 14).[173]

6.5 Questionnaire sections

The survey consisted of forty-four questions divided into five main sections. These are analysed in detail below.

6.5.1 Information about leisure activities and attitudes to museums and museum visitation (Questions 1–2)

In addition to age, gender, and geography, the survey also sought to provide a representative sample of respondents with regard to their interest in museums. Two questions were included to allow a comparison with results obtained from other relevant Australian studies. Question One asked how recently, if ever, a respondent had visited any museum or gallery.

Table 6.5 indicates that there was no appreciable difference in the overall effect of using raw scores, rather than weighted scores, for the results to the question – 'When was the last time that you personally visited a museum or gallery in the last six months?'. Using the unweighted percentage, thirty-four percent of respondents indicated they had made such a visit. Using the weighted figures, thirty-six percent of respondents indicated they had made such a visit.

These results, which showed the regularity or otherwise of museum visitation, were comparable to other recent studies that typically also showed that one third of the population were likely to visit a museum or gallery in a six month time frame (Hall, 2005, p. 5; Merriman, 1989, p. 150) (Refer Table 6.5).

173. A more detailed technical description of the analysis was provided by the consultants and is contained in Appendix Two.

Table 6.5: 'When was the last time you personally visited a museum or art gallery?'

Usersand non-users of museums	**Total unweightedscores**	**Total weightedscores**
In the last six months	398 34%	422 36%
Six months to a year ago	263 22%	259 22%
More than a year ago	415 35%	383 33%
Never	66 6%	65 6%
Don't know	32 3%	33 3%
Total	**1,174**	**1162**

The second question addressed the respondent's stated level of interest in museums, and compared these results with exit surveys that were conducted in 2005 at two of the Queensland Museum campuses: Queensland Museum South Bank (QMSB) and The Workshops Rail Museum (TWRM) in Ipswich (refer Table 6.6). It was expected, from previous surveys of random samples of the Australian population using these self-description options, that the proportion of people choosing each option would be approximately equal. The sample for the present study showed more people interested in special exhibits than might be expected in the general population[174], but, importantly, the groups with both 'modest' or 'no' interest formed a substantial portion (fifty percent) of the sample.[175] In contrast, the studies from both QMSB and TWRM show the 'no interest' group making up a consistently low percentage (eight percent) of the sample. However, considering that these surveys were taken by visitors exiting these museums, the low figures are probably understandable. The consultant's conclusion was that:

> Taken together, the patterns of responses to these two questions argue for the sample providing a reasonable representation of general interest in museums across the wider population...[and] was not based simply on people who might be called 'museum enthusiasts' (Environmetrics & McNair Ingenuity, 2009, p. 11).

174. The difference between the other two interest levels across QMSB and TWRM could reflect the specificity of the public programs at TWRM, in contrast to the broader topic range and limited marketing of public programs at QMSB.

175. Interestingly, it would appear that 'the more frequent the visiting, then the more specific the reason for the visit, and the less frequent the visiting, the more likely that it was undertaken for casual reasons not related to the museum's aims' (Merriman, 1989, p. 153).

Table 6.6: Pattern of responses to Question Two about interest in museums, using unweighted figures

Interest in museums	CV	CV weighted	QMSB	TWRM
I keep an eye out for special activities at museums and go when they interest me	50%	51%	20%	66%
I go generally to see what is there; I don't go to see special exhibits or activities	26%	27%	71%	25%
I am not really interested in museums and I don't go very often at all	24%	22%	8%	8%
Sample size	**1174**	**1162**	**1198**	**921**

Again, it was apparent that the weighting had little impact on the results.

There was a more significant variation between respondents' ages and their interest in museums. The youngest respondents (under twenty-four) were less likely to be interested in museums (thirty-three percent), while the oldest group (fifty-five and over) had only eighteen percent. However, each of the five age groups was equally likely to be interested in museums. They rated from forty-eight percent for the youngest group to fifty percent, for those aged 55 and over.[176] So, overall, about fifty percent of each age bracket was interested in museums, and fifty percent only mildly or not really interested, as indicated in Table 6.6.

With regard to gender, fifty-eight percent of women were very interested in museums, compared to only forty-five percent of men.[177] The higher proportion of women respondents could have had a slight impact on the overall results obtained. There was also a slight variation in regional responses to this question. Brisbane/Ipswich recorded fifty-six percent very interested in museums (as could be expected, considering the variety and quality of offerings in the capital city and surrounds), compared to a range from forty-two percent to forty-nine percent in the other three geographical areas.[178]

6.5.2 Attitudes to the QM campuses (Questions 3–16)

A range of questions was designed to elicit information about respondents' knowledge about, use of, and attitudes towards the Queensland Museum. Common with most effective CVM surveys, this section consisted of an introductory section that helped to explain the general concept for the eventual WTP decision to be made and the institutional setting in which the good would be provided.

176. Table 11 weighted survey data QM CVM Study 28/01/09.

177. Table 11 weighted survey data QM CVM Study 28/01/09.

178. Table 11 weighted survey data QM CVM Study 28/01/09.

Each question was repeated four times to enable the respondents to become more familiar with the concept of the Queensland Museum operating on four campuses: QMSB in Brisbane, Cobb+Co in Toowoomba, TWRM in Ipswich, and MTQ in Townsville. These questions sought to discover how well the respondents knew the four campuses of the Queensland Museum; when they had last visited one of them; what the purpose of their visit was; what the experience was like; and what, if anything, they learned during their visit.

Table 6.7: Awareness of each Queensland Museum campus, using weighted scores

Awareness of QM campuses	**QMSB**	**Cobb+Co Museum**	**TWRM**	**MTQ**
Know a lot about it	24%	6%	9%	9%
Know a little about it	53%	21%	35%	17%
Only know the name	18%	31%	32%	23%
Never heard of it	4%	40%	22%	49%
Not sure	1%	2%	1%	2%

These scores indicated that respondents had limited prior knowledge of the museum.

With regard to how well-known the campuses were in their own geographical areas, QMSB registered eighty-nine percent of respondents who knew a lot or a little about it. The same figure was received for Cobb+Co Museum, while MTQ in Townsville recorded ninety-three percent. TWRM in Ipswich recorded only fifty-seven percent, though this is reasonable, since the survey considered both Brisbane and Ipswich residents within the one category. It would not be surprising if this figure was considerably higher if only Ipswich residents were surveyed. The results analysed in Table 6.8 refer to the Cobb+Co Museum, but are indicative of the outcomes across all four campuses. While eighty- nine percent of respondents in the Toowoomba region knew a lot or a little about the Cobb+Co Museum, only twenty-eight percent of respondents across the state would agree, as seen in Table 6.8.

Table 6.8: Recognition of the Cobb+Co Museum in Toowoomba, using unweighted scores

Awarenessof C+C Museum	**Total**	**Brisbaneand Ipswich**	**T'mba**	**T'ville**	**Rest of QLD**
Know a lot about it	92 8%	22 4%	53 42%	1 -%	16 5%
Know a little about it	239 20%	112 21%	59 47%	12 6%	56 19%
Only know the name	353 30%	193 35%	14 11%	61 29%	85 29%
Never heard of it	464 40%	207 38%	- -%	125 60%	132 45%
Not sure	26 2%	11 2%	- -%	9 4%	6 2%
Total	**1,174**	**545**	**126**	**208**	**295**

As expected, recognition of the Cobb+Co Museum was heavily concentrated in the immediate geographical area.

Respondents were next asked: 'When was the last time you personally visited each of the campuses?' Forty-seven percent of Brisbane and Ipswich residents had visited QMSB, while fifty-seven percent of Townsville residents had visited MTQ, in comparison with thirty-one percent of Toowoomba residents having visited Cobb+Co Museum, and only thirteen percent of Brisbane and Ipswich residents having visited TWRM during the past twelve months.[179] Considering the relatively small size of the Cobb+Co campus, compared to the much larger exhibition spaces at the other three, this is probably not a surprising result.

Table 6.9: When was the last time, if ever, that you personally visited the Cobb+Co Museum?'

Cobb+Corecent visitation	**Total**	**Brisbaneand Ipswich**	**T'mba**	**T'ville**	**Rest of QLD**
In the last six months	39 3%	10 2%	24 19%	1 -%	4 1%
Six months to a year ago	36 3%	14 3%	15 12%	1 -%	6 2%
More than a year ago	174 15%	73 13%	55 44%	7 3%	39 13%
Never	894 76%	437 80%	30 24%	194 93%	233 79%
Don't know	31 3%	11 2%	2 2%	5 2%	13 4%
Total	**1,174**	**545**	**126**	**208**	**295**

Within the last twelve months (combining the top two rows), thirty-one percent of local Toowoomba residents using unweighted scores, had visited Cobb+Co Museum.

When asked 'What was the purpose for visiting the campuses?' the results were consistent. The largest identified categories were 'to see the museum in general' and 'to take a child'. QMSB was the only campus to record a significant number of visitors expressing interest in seeing a particular exhibit.[180] Although the sample of respondents was only small, Cobb+Co Museum did show a greater likelihood of visitors accompanying other adults and attending programs (refer Table 6.10 which used unweighted scores).[181]

179. Results for TWRM are considerably skewed, due to the inclusion of Ipswich with Brisbane in a single sampling category.

180. This could relate to the popularity of the Sciencentre and some new exhibits that had recently opened.

181. Cobb+Co is the only campus to offer an extensive range of programs for adults through its heritage trade workshops.

Table 6.10: 'What was the purpose of your most recent visit to the individual campuses?'

Purposefor visit	QMSB	Cobb+Co	TWRM	MTQ
To see a particular exhibit	21%	9%	12%	10%
To see the museum in general	37%	43%	32%	35%
To take a child or children	32%	34%	39%	37%
To accompany other adults	4%	18%	7%	9%
To attend a program or event	2%	12%	3%	7%
To do some research	1%	4%	-%	-%
Other	3%	7%	7%	2%

The survey also investigated how visitors reacted to their museum experiences, because this would probably affect their attitudes to the Queensland Museum and their WTP for services. Respondents were given a list of nine possible experiences and were asked to rate their visits to each of the campuses against each of these experiences, using the criteria: 'very much', 'a little', 'none', or 'don't know'. Table 6.11 records the responses to the 'very much' category for each of the campuses.

Table 6.11: Personal and emotional responses to visiting the campuses, showing the responses of 'very much' to each of the outcomes, using unweighted scores

Personaland emotional responses	QMSB	Cobb+Co	TWRM	MTQ
Connection with the stories of other people's lives and achievements	51%	57%	34%	43%
Sense of spiritual dimensions	17%	16%	12%	16%
New understanding of scientific or technical concepts	35%	19%	29%	36%
Experience of real beauty	40%	29%	15%	36%
Experience of things that are real and not fake	56%	64%	53%	51%
Appreciation of the monetary value of some objects on display	34%	37%	36%	33%
Inspiration to make something yourself	13%	8%	7%	12%
An appreciation of historic events	62%	66%	71%	62%
Pleasure and enjoyment of a stimulating visit	67%	62%	73%	66%
Unweighted sample	**607**	**95**	**59**	**238**

These results show some variations between the campus experiences. QMSB and MTQ recorded similar results, probably because of their fairly comparable exhibition offerings. The Workshop Rail Museum seems to provide a slightly more pleasurable and stimulating visit or experience linked to an appreciation of historic events, while Cobb+Co Museum scored highly on the personal impact categories relating to making connections, developing an appreciation of historical events and authenticity, and deriving pleasure and stimulation from the visit.[182]

182.Cobb+Co did not rate highly on inspiration for personal creativity, but the CVM survey results predate the opening of the National Carriage Factory project.

The survey also sought information about learning outcomes from museum visits, because other studies have shown that this has a large bearing on visitor experience and overall attitude to museums, as discussed in Section 3.7. Environmetrics had developed a series of questions that form the Modes of Learning Inventory (MOLI). These questions have been used in a wide range of collecting institutions and MOLI gives some insights into the pattern of learning outcomes experienced by visitors during a museum visit (Environmetrics & McNair Ingenuity, 2009, p. 30). Table 6.12 compares responses to each of the MOLI questions. The table reports the percentage of respondents who chose the 'yes/somewhat' option.[183]

Table 6.12: Pattern of Perceived Learning Outcomes, using unweighted figures

Learningoutcomes	QMSB	Cobb+Co	TWRM	MTQ
I discovered things I didn't know before	85%	84%	90%	86%
I learnt more about things I already knew about	81%	78%	80%	82%
I remembered things I hadn't thought of for a while	78%	76%	76%	74%
I shared some of my knowledge with other people	62%	48%	51%	52%
I got curious about finding out more about some things	65%	45%	54%	53%
I was reminded of the importance of some issues	75%	66%	71%	76%
I was surprised by some of the things I discovered	78%	66%	69%	76%
I discovered a new perspective on things I already knew about	66%	56%	59%	64%
Some of the things I learnt will be very useful to me	51%	44%	47%	53%
Unweighted sample	**607**	**95**	**59**	**238**

Considering the sample sizes for each campus, the results show a high level of consistency across nearly all the categories. The variations can probably be accounted for as a result of the broader exhibition themes at QMSB and the more limited facilities at Cobb+Co.

6.5.3 Attitudes to QM products and services (Questions 17–23)

The questionnaire then sought information from respondents about the level of their knowledge of other Queensland Museum products and services, including the website, the Museum Development Officers, historical and scientific research, education loan kits for schools, publications, and the Inquiry Centre service where people can ask a museum expert a question.

In general, website awareness was very low across all the campuses, as shown in Table 6.13. As all the respondents were Internet users, it might be expected that these figures would be somewhat higher than for a comparable study using a different survey mechanism.

183. The other two options were 'no/not really' and 'don't know'.

Table 6.13: Website visits by respondents, including campuses and Queensland Museum's corporate website, using unweighted scores

Websitevisits	QMcorporate website	QMSB	Cobb+Co	TWRM	MTQ
In the last six months	59 5%	111 10%	29 3%	56 5%	44 4%
Six months to a year	38 3%	78 7%	17 1%	29 3%	31 3%
More than a year ago	67 6%	109 9%	32 3%	72 6%	35 3%
Never	981 84%	848 73%	1075 92%	994 86%	1043 90%
Don't know	18 2%	15 1%	8 1%	11 1%	10 1%
Total	**1,174**	**1,174**	**1,174**	**1,174**	**1,174**

As expected, the most recently visited website was QMSB, at ten percent. Respondents may have difficulty in distinguishing between QMSB and the corporate site, hence the higher percentage for QMSB, as many people still refer to the South Bank campus as the Queensland Museum.

When asked the purpose for visiting QM websites, 'planning a visit' was consistently indicated as the prime reason for most campuses, followed by 'just browsing' and 'finding information on a topic', as shown in Table 6.14. Cobb+Co rated more highly than the other websites for visitors seeking follow up information.

Table 6.14: Reasons for website visits

Reasonsfor website visits	QMcorporate website	QMSB	Cobb+Co	TWRM	MTQ
To make a booking	-%	4%	12%	4%	-%
To plan a visit to the museum	6%	51%	23%	64%	46%
To follow up a visit to the museum	3%	6%	19%	2%	5%
To find information about a topic	23%	24%	23%	18%	13%
To contact the museum	6%	4%	4%	5%	2%
No specific purpose, just browsing	58%	29%	35%	24%	30%
Other	6%	1%	4%	2%	7%
Total	**31**	**206**	**26**	**55**	**56**

Other Queensland Museum services and programs were also relatively unknown to the vast majority of respondents. Tables 6.15a and 6.15b provide information about six Queensland Museum programs and services. Between one third and one half of the respondents had never heard of any of these six programs. On average, only five percent of respondents knew a lot about any of the programs.

Table 6.15a: Queensland Museum program recognition – MDOs, historical research, and loan kits for schools, using unweighted scores

OtherQM programs	Museum Development Officers (MDOs) working with regional museums	Historical research	Educationkits for schools
Know a lot about it	3%	5%	6%
Know a little about it	17%	37%	31%
Only know the name	17%	23%	25%
Never heard of it	56%	29%	33%
Not sure	7%	6%	6%
Total	**1,174**	**1,174**	**1,174**

Table 6.15b: Queensland Museum program recognition – Inquiry Centre, publications, and scientific research, using unweighted scores

OtherQM Queensland Museum program recognition programs	InquiryCentre – aska scientist	Publications	Scientific research
Know a lot about it	4%	5%	5%
Know a little about it	22%	37%	33%
Only know the name	14%	20%	23%
Never heard of it	53%	32%	32%
Not sure	7%	6%	7%
Total	**1,174**	**1,174**	**1,174**

6.5.4 Setting the scenarios – non-market values of the Queensland Museum (Question 24)

Before proceeding with a series of questions about attitudes to the Queensland Museum as a whole, the respondents were provided with information about the museum's collections and research, venues and outreach programs, and a map of Queensland that showed the museum's spread of activities and services.[184] This proved to be essential, because, as the previous two tables indicated, the respondents often had a very low level of knowledge about the Queensland Museum's programs and services.[185]

The CVM questions in this study were designed to estimate the non-market values of the Queensland Museum from the perspective of both users and non-users. Although a monetary figure was sought, it was realised

184.See Appendix One, survey Question Twenty-four.

185.Familiarity with the good has been described by some researchers as a necessary prerequisite to providing meaningful responses to CVM valuation questions. However, many people purchase goods without a great deal of familiarity with them, especially new products on the market, and would spend little or no time in researching or considering their purchase of non-essential items worth between two dollars and twelve dollars, as is used in this study (Carson, et al., 2001, p. 178).

that respondents' perceptions of non-market values would underpin their decisions about WTP for existing and new services. Consequently, question twenty-four was designed to explore attitudes to the Queensland Museum as a public good. The consumers' surplus estimated by CVM surveys on a specific cultural good, such as the Queensland Museum, is 'a measure of the benefit individuals attribute to that good' (Cuccia, 2003, p. 129). Five of the statements used in Question Twenty-four dealt with general or community public good, while the sixth statement asked about personal relevance.

Table 6.16: Perceptions of the Queensland Museum, using weighted scores

Perceptionsof QM	**Strongly agree**	**Agree**	**Neither**	**Disagree**	**Strongly disagree**	**Don'tknow**
QM does important things for the people of Queensland	43%	49%	4%	-%	-%	3%
QM is not relevant to me and probably never will be	2%	9%	11%	45%	29%	4%
In the future, I might want to visit one of the museums or use one of QM's services	35%	54%	6%	2%	-%	3%
In years to come, people will think that QM achieved very little	3%	6%	13%	46%	27%	6%
I get personal benefit from things QM does	13%	37%	32%	10%	1%	7%
QM will leave an important legacy to future generations	48%	41%	6%	-%	-%	4%

The pattern of these results indicates that respondents read the question carefully – particularly the negative statements. There is a strong correlation of results for the general public good questions, which indicates a high level of bequest, existence, and options benefits associated with the Queensland Museum. However, there was a relatively high level of uncertainty about the extent of personal benefit that is gained from the museum. Almost one-third of the sample (thirty-two percent) chose 'neither agree nor disagree' to the question relating to receiving personal benefit. This is most likely due to respondents' lack of personal contact with the Queensland Museum and its services, as indicated in the previous survey tables.

6.5.5 WTP using two scenarios – ongoing WTP for existing products and services (Questions 25–29)

Questions Twenty-five to Thirty-four were related to the two WTP scenarios. This section, in common with most effective CVM questionnaires, consisted of a detailed description of the good to be offered; the manner in which the good would be paid for; the method by which the survey elicits the respondents' preferences with respect to the good; and the budget implications of WTP decisions (Carson, et al., 2001, p. 179).

For the first scenario – ongoing WTP for existing products and services – each respondent to the survey was asked an initial question to ascertain their interest in changing the current annual amount that the Queensland Museum received from the state government. The following information was provided to respondents before the WTP questions were asked:

> The Queensland Museum is partly funded by revenue earned by the Museum. The remainder of the money comes from the State Government. In 2007, State Government funding for the Queensland Museum and all its operations was $19.5 million, which amounts to $6.50 per Queensland adult per year (Appendix 1 Survey Questionnaire).

The respondents were then asked, in general terms, if they were in favour of increasing, leaving the same, or decreasing funding to the Queensland Museum (see Table 6.17).

Table 6.17: Ongoing funding preference for the Queensland Museum, using weighted scores

WTPfor existing QM services	**Total**	**Brisbane and Ipswich**	**T'mba**	**T'ville**	**Rest of QLD**
Increasing the funds for QM	52%	53%	55%	58%	51%
Keeping the funds at the present for QM	44%	43%	45%	40%	44%
Reducing the funds for QM	4%	3%	-%	2%	5%
Total unweighted row	1174	545	126	208	295
Total weighted row	1162	498	31	36	597

Overall, fifty-two percent of respondents indicated that they would be in favour of increasing the operational budget for the Queensland Museum, while only four percent indicated that they would prefer a reduction in the existing budget. The remaining forty-four percent were content with the present level of funding the museum received from the state government. While these results were consistent across all geographical areas, there was a small variation in gender responses. Fifty-six percent of males were in favour of increasing funding, while this was reduced to forty-nine percent for females. Forty percent of males and forty-seven percent of females wanted the funding levels to remain unchanged.[186]

In line with recommendations from the NOAA Panel that respondents be reminded of substitutes and alternative expenditure possibilities, if a respondent accepted the idea of the Queensland Museum being given additional funds, they were then asked whether they thought the additional funds should come from an increase in taxation or from diverting funds from existing services. Sixty-nine percent preferred to divert funding from

186.Table 120 weighted survey data QM CVM Study 28/01/09.

another government service, while thirty-one percent opted for a tax increase to provide additional funding to the Queensland Museum. In this case, gender results were consistent with the overall figures.[187]

Table 6.18: Payment options to cover hypothetical increased funding for the Queensland Museum

Paymentoptions/ age	**Total**	**Under24**	**25–34**	**35–44**	**45–54**	**55 and over**
Funds to come from reducing some other services	69%	84%	76%	68%	68%	63%
Funds to come from tax increase	31%	16%	24%	32%	32%	37%
Total	**610**	**55**	**96**	**111**	**125**	**223**

The age continuum demonstrated a steady decline, with eighty-four percent of young adults preferring to reduce other services, and sixty-three percent of those aged fifty- five or older indicating this option. Correspondingly, older adults preferred an increase in taxation – perhaps thinking that they would be able to avoid paying any such increase. There was consistency in the responses to this question from the regions surveyed, with the exception of Toowoomba where an overwhelming eighty-one percent preferred a reduction in other services, rather than a tax increase. This could reflect the higher proportion of young participants from the Toowoomba region, which would make Toowoomba's results consistent with the other regions.[188]

The structure of the questionnaire and the wording of the questions were developed to minimise any tendency for a respondent to advocate spending on the Queensland Museum without any consideration of competing interests or personal loss in another sector of public service. The aim was to make clear to the respondent that a trade-off of funding would be necessary. It was also decided to provide actual substitutes (decreases in public services) that might occur if increased funding was provided to the Queensland Museum.

When making their choice, each respondent was given a list of services – health, education, corrective services, tourism, and transport – and for each service there was an estimated reduction in that service that would be caused by diverting the funds to the Queensland Museum. The level of these services varied with the optional value allocated to the questionnaire.[189]

187. Table 121 weighted survey data QM CVM Study 28/01/09.

188. Table 121 weighted survey data QM CVM Study 28/01/09.

189. For example, for Option A – a two dollar increase – there could be sixteen new classrooms built. For Option B – a four dollar increase – there could be thirty-two new classrooms. For Option C – an eight dollar increase – there could be sixty-four new classrooms.

Table 6.19: Actual government services that could possibly be reduced to fund an increase in recurrent funding to the QM

WTPand reductions in other services	Total	Brisbane and Ipswich	T'mba	T'ville	Rest of QLD
Health – 24 new beds	3%	1%	4%	4%	3%
Education – 32 new classrooms	2%	1%	2%	1%	2%
Prisons – 16 new prison beds	41%	46%	59%	38%	36%
Tourism – $12 million tourism promotion	48%	45%	32%	57%	50%
Transport infrastructure – 20 km of new roads	7%	6%	3%	-%	8%

The examples shown in Table 6.19 are in the same order as in the questionnaire for Option B – a four dollar increase in funding. The above figures use weighted scores.

Table 6.19 shows that for respondents favouring a reduction in government services there was an overwhelming preference to curtail tourism promotions and corrective services, rather than cutbacks to education, health, or transport infrastructure.[190] Interestingly, forty-five percent of older adults were more interested in reducing funding to prisons, than younger people, at twenty-eight percent. There were some regional variations, again, with Toowoomba proving the exception, with fifty-nine percent preferring to cut prison funding, but only thirty-two percent preferring a reduction in tourism promotions.[191]

For those who were not in favour of an increase in funds, the questionnaire sought the main reasons for these responses as well. A series of statements was presented, as indicated in Table 6.20.

Table 6.20: Reasons for respondents not in favour of an increase in funds to the Queensland Museum, using weighted scores

Reasonsfor not increasing funds to QM	Total	Brisbane and Ipswich	T'mba	T'ville	Rest of QLD
QM get enough funds at the moment	11%	6%	-%	13%	16%
I value QM but I personally cannot afford/do not want to pay more	24%	24%	12%	43%	23%
I value QM but other services are more important	40%	40%	60%	30%	39%

190. There were a number of comments from respondents relating to this issue. Many of these related to a general desire to express dissatisfaction with money spent on wages for politicians, government marketing campaigns, sporting venues, and sportsmen.

191. Table 123 weighted survey data QM CVM Study 28/01/09.

I don't value QM enough to give it more funds	2%	3%	9%	3%	1%
I don't know enough about it to decide	13%	11%	13%	8%	15%
Other	2%	3%	-%	2%	1%
No response	7%	12%	1%	1%	5%

Overall, the most common motivation was that, although the museum was considered valuable, other services were considered more important. There were some notable variations in responses, particularly from the smaller samples in Toowoomba and Townsville. Age also showed some variance. Not unexpectedly, thirty-five percent of respondents over fifty-five, in contrast to seven percent of those aged between twenty-five and thirty-four, indicated that, while valuing the Queensland Museum, they could not afford or did not want to pay more.[192]

6.5.6 Ballot One – WTP additional amounts for ongoing funding for the Queensland Museum

Of the six hundred and ten respondents (in the weighted sample) who preferred an increase in the current level of funding to the Queensland Museum, each was subsequently presented with one possible increased amount – two dollars, four dollars, or eight dollars – chosen at random. Approximately one third of the sample considered each amount when making their choice, as illustrated in Table 6.21

Table 6.21: Spread of ballot types across geographic regions for the question relating to QM recurrent funding

Spread of ballot types	Obtained sample	Option 1 – $2	Option 2 – $4	Option 3 – $8
Brisbane/Ipswich	545	201	182	162
Toowoomba	126	35	48	43
Townsville	208	52	81	75
Rest of Queensland	295	96	92	107
Total	**1,174**	**384**	**403**	**387**

As the amount of the proposed increase went up from two dollars to four dollars to eight dollars, the interest in paying decreased. This was an important result because it showed consistency with economic theory.[193] However, even at the highest optional amount (eight dollars), the amount was acceptable to the majority of people (seventy-five percent), as indicated in Table 6.22

192. Table 129 weighted survey data QM CVM Study 28/01/09.

193. The percentage of respondents willing to pay a particular price should fall as the price they are asked to pay increases (Carson, et al., 2001, p. 181).

Table 6.22: Increased funding for the Queensland Museum, using weighted scores and three set optional amounts: two dollars, four dollars, and eight dollars

BallotOne increased WTP	**Yes**	**No**	**Numberof respondents**
Option A – an increase of two dollars per adult per year	94%	6%	196
Option B – an increase of four dollars per adult per year	82%	18%	209
Option C – an increase of eight dollars per adult per year	75%	25%	205
Total/overall result	84%	16%	610

Overall results show that eighty-four percent of respondents who had originally indicated their preference to increase ongoing funding to the Queensland Museum above the current $6.50 per adult per annum, accepted the optional additional amount they were allocated in their survey.[194]

It was obvious that the optional amount chosen still underestimated the perceived value of the Queensland Museum to the public of Queensland. There was a commitment to 'play safe' and not set the levels too high, even though these final options had been increased after the results of the pilot study. Professor David Throsby suggested that it is not uncommon for the advocates of studies linked to cultural institutions to under-estimate the perceived value of their institution (Environmetrics & McNair Ingenuity, 2009, p. 15).

The consultants then conducted a probit analysis to model the WTP data collected and to establish the average (mean) and conservative lower-bound (two standard deviations to the left) dollar values. From these results, the total value of increased funding for the Queensland Museum was aggregated from the individual responses.[195]

Although the survey's questions were phrased in terms of per-adult tax increases, there is debate about whether respondents would, in fact, answer on their own behalf or on behalf of their household unit. If museums are

194.Respondents who elected to decrease funding to the Queensland Museum (four percent of the original survey) were also provided with a ballot of the same amounts (two dollars, four dollars, or eight dollars). Overall, eighty-six percent voted 'yes' to the optional amount they were allotted, which demonstrated a very similar pattern to that displayed in Table 6.22.

195.To estimate the point at which the proportion of people agreeing to pay would be equal to the proportion unwilling to pay, it was assumed that the distribution of responses lay on a normal curve around the as-yet-unknown 'true' average amount. From the data, there were three readings linking acceptance to amounts – at two dollars, four dollars, and eight dollars.
These readings were used to establish the overall parameters of the hypothesised normal curve and, as a consequence, identified where the mean/median of the distribution would lie. The mean (or median) in this case was the point at which fifty percent of people were willing to accept the amount (Environmetrics & McNair Ingenuity, 2009, p. 16)

thought of in terms of individual taxation and individual benefit, then the adult figure is probably appropriate to use. If it is assumed that people will make decisions about museums and cultural institutions as a 'household expense', then the per-household analysis is probably better to use. This was the approach adopted in the analysis of the results from this Study.

Table 6.23: Ballot One WTP results for increased recurrent funding for the Queensland Museum, showing both adult population and household figures

Ballot One WTP for increased recurrent funding	**Mean**	**Lower bound**
Estimated increased WTP above $6.50 for existing QM products and services	$12.65	$8.23
Increase WTP ratio above current funding levels	2.9	2.3
Adult population	3,176,068	3,176,068
Total value of increased funding based on adult population	**$40 million**	**$26 million**
Dwellings/households	1,627,600	1,627,600
Total value based on dwellings	**$21 million**	**$13 million**

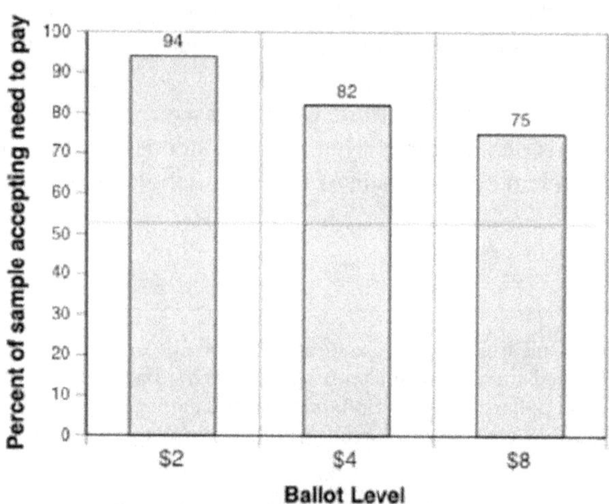

Graph 1: Extent of willingness to pay across ballot amounts

Respondents' WTP for existing services was calculated at between 2.3 and 2.9 times the current levels of funding. The conclusion drawn was that the people of Queensland placed a value on the Queensland Museum that was more than twice the amount reflected in the current government funding for daily operations.[196]

6.5.7 WTP using two scenarios – one-off funding for additional products and services (Questions 30–34)

The second ballot question was related to a once-only levy linked to a program of major infrastructure development at the four existing campuses and a new virtual campus (new website) over the next five to seven years. Each development was described by a single sentence, and the statement that the developments were designed to provide 'better access to collections and research via new displays, innovative learning programs and services and more user-friendly facilities.' The questionnaire included this statement about the development proposed at Cobb+Co Museum: 'The National Carriage Factory at Cobb+Co Museum, featuring new exhibitions and community spaces alongside a unique demonstration and training site for rare heritage trades such as blacksmithing'.

Respondents were asked to consider all the proposed developments – worth an estimated twenty-four million dollars – as a package. To encourage respondents to provide thoughtful responses to the questions, they were told that the information they were providing would be used in the decision-making process (Carson, et al., 2001, p. 180). The respondents were informed that to achieve its vision:

> The Queensland Museum will require more funding and we are seeking your input in identifying how valuable or otherwise these new developments will be (See Appendix 1 Survey questionnaire).

As previously described under Ballot One, respondents were asked the same series of questions. Three quarters of the sample were in favour of increasing funds for the Queensland Museum to provide more services, while twenty-one percent wanted to keep the funding at its present level and not undertake additional development, and four percent registering a nil response. These were remarkable results that demonstrated a very high degree of consistency of responses across gender, geographical region, and ages.[197]

---

196. The study found that Queensland adults would be willing to pay between $14.73 and $19.15 each per annum to support the ongoing operations of the Queensland Museum.

197. Again, as in Table 6.18, adults under twenty-four did not conform to the average results. Only fifty-eight percent of this age group wanted to fund increased services. Thirty-one percent preferred to maintain the existing services at the current funding level, and ten percent made no response. Table 125 weighted survey data QM CVM Study 28/01/09.

Replicating the format above, respondents were then asked how they wanted to fund these one-off donations. The results showed that seventy-two percent of respondents preferred the funds to come from reducing services, rather than a tax increase, with the same variation across ages also being recorded, as for the question for Ballot One. Eighty percent of those aged under twenty-four preferred to see a cut in services. This gradually declined to sixty-three percent for those fifty-five years and older. Again, Toowoomba was slightly different to the other geographical regions, but consistent with its previous results, with a higher propensity to favour reducing services (at eighty percent) rather than tax increases (at twenty percent).[198]

Relating the general preference to see reduced services to actual service delivery cuts, the same response pattern was observed as previously, with an overwhelming proportion of the respondents opting for reduction in prisons and tourism marketing. Table 6.24 uses the order that appeared in questionnaire for Option B – a six dollar increase in funding using weighted scores.

Table 6.24: Actual government services that could possibly be reduced to fund new developments at the QM

WTPand reduction of other services	Total	Brisbane and Ipswich	T'mba	T'ville	Rest of QLD
Health – 36 new beds	2%	3%	-%	2%	1%
Education – 48 new classrooms	1%	1%	2%	-%	1%
Prisons – 24 new prison beds	46%	50%	50%	44%	42%
Tourism – $18 million tourism promotion	47%	43%	46%	53%	51%
Transport infrastructure – 30 km of new roads	4%	4%	2%	1%	5%

6.5.8 Ballot Two – WTP for one-off funding for additional products and services from the Queensland Museum

At this stage in the survey, the second ballot question was proposed. Approximately one third of the respondents who had indicated a WTP a one-off levy so that the Queensland Museum could provide additional services, as previously described, were presented with the choice of paying four dollars, six dollars, or twelve dollars. These optional amounts were distributed similarly to that used for Ballot One.[199]

Question Thirty-two provided additional information about the effect of the allocated four dollar, six dollar, and twelve dollar amounts. For example, a one-off levy of six dollars from every adult in Queensland would

198.Table 126 weighted survey data QM CVM Study 28/01/09.

199.For example, if a respondent was allocated Option A previously – the lowest amount of two dollars – that same respondent would again be only offered Option A, which, for Ballot Two, was the lowest amount of four dollars.

provide twelve million dollars towards the new facilities and services.[200] Table 6.25 uses weighted scores and three set optional amounts – four dollars, six dollars, and twelve dollars.

Table 6.25: One-off funding for the Queensland Museum for new Developments

BallotTwo WTP	**Yes**	**No**	**No of respondents**
Option A – a one-off levy of four dollars per adult	81%	19%	313
Option B – a one-off levy of six dollars per adult	80%	20%	284
Option C – a one-off levy of twelve dollars per adult	70%	30%	280
Total/overall result	**77%**	**23%**	**877**

Although this sample was forty-four percent larger than in Ballot One (eight hundred and seventy-seven respondents, compared to six hundred and ten), there was a slightly reduced number of respondents who were prepared to agree to the optional amount with which they were presented.[201] Again, there was the expected reduction in approval for the optional amount as it increased from four dollars to six dollars to twelve dollars. The most notable variation was the reduction in support for the lowest amount, which was four dollars in this case. In Ballot One, the lowest amount of two dollars was supported by ninety-four percent of respondents, while, this time, only eighty-one percent were willing to pay. Options A and C in Ballot Two actually had doubled amounts, in comparison to Ballot One (two dollars to four dollars, and six dollars to twelve dollars). However, for Option B, the amounts had only changed by fifty percent, from four dollars to six dollars, and the results were much closer for the two ballot questions (eighty-two percent in favour for Ballot One, and eighty percent in favour for Ballot Two).

This data was then subjected to a probit analysis, as previously described, and an aggregated total value was calculated. Again, results were provided for both adults and households and were calculated using both the mean and the lower bound (two standard deviations to the left) figures.

Table 6.26: Ballot Two WTP results for a one-off donation to enhance Queensland Museum's programs and services

Ballot Two – one-off WTP for new QM developments	**Mean**	**Lower bound**
Estimated one-off WTP values	$16.43	$11.47
Adult population	3,176,068	3,176,068
Total value based on adult population	**$52 million**	**$36 million**
Dwellings/households	1,627,600	1,627,600
Total value based on dwellings	**$27 million**	**$19 million**

200. A one-off levy of four dollars would provide six million dollars, while the twelve dollar option would provide $18.5 million.

201. Eighty-four percent were in favour for Ballot One, and seventy-seven percent in favour for Ballot Two (see Table 6.22 for Ballot One and Table 6.25 for Ballot Two results).

The questionnaire had presented a scenario of new developments proposed for the Queensland Museum worth twenty-four million dollars. The more conservative results, as shown in Table 6.26, using households rather than the number of adults, indicated a range of WTP of between nineteen million dollars and twenty-seven million dollars. This would suggest that, even adopting this very cautious approach, the Queensland public would be in favour of funding the new facilities and services proposed by the Queensland Museum to be developed over the next five to seven years.[202]

6.5.9 Demographics and some general attitudes, interests, and comments (Questions 35–44)

Although this CVM study was concerned with estimating the overall dollar value of the Queensland Museum to its communities, it was also interested in how different audiences valued the museum, and, in common with other CVM studies, it collected a set of respondent characteristics, including attitudes and demographic information. One of the overriding reasons for using a CVM study was its potential to include WTP of both users and non-users. The one hundred and forty-six tables of data collected enabled conclusions to be drawn about WTP among various audience groups within the general population. These included:

- People with high or low interest in museums generally;
- People who were recent visitors;
- People with children in their household;
- People of different ages;
- People of different sexes;
- People with different levels of education;
- People in different work situations;
- People who live in each of the geographic areas; and
- People from different lifestyle (psychographic) backgrounds.

6.5.10 WTP and interest in museums

As was expected, the more interested people are in museums, the more likely they are to approve increased funding for using these facilities. However, this study also indicated that fifty-three percent of non-users of the Queensland Museum expressed a WTP to maintain the museum's services, while forty-one percent expressed a WTP more to enhance the Queensland Museum. These respondents were motivated by reasons other

202. 'In other words, if development of the Museum could be achieved for a figure less than these estimates, it would be, from a technical perspective, a "good buy" in that the actual expenditure would be less than the community would be willing to pay' (Environmetrics & McNair Ingenuity, 2009, p. 18).

than the value they gained from actually using the facility and services. Non-users perceive the benefits of museums in communities, which can be a mixture of existence, bequest, and options values. It is significant that only seven percent of non-users advocated a reduction in funding for the Queensland Museum. This means that ninety-three percent of non-users view the Queensland Museum as valuable to themselves or others in their community, now or in the future. One of the respondents to the CVM survey commented:

> I believe the Queensland Museum provides an essential service to the public, although I do not visit regularly it does not mean I do not appreciate the value of the work that the museum undertakes, it needs to be maintained and enhanced for the future generations (QM 2008 CVM Survey).

Table 6.27: WTP across levels of interest in museums, using weighted scores

Interest in museums	**Increase funds**	**Keep as is**	**Reduce funds**	**Total sample**
I keep an eye out for special activities at museums and go when they interest me	59%	38%	3%	597
I go generally to see what is there; I don't go to see special exhibits or activities	48%	48%	4%	311
I am not really interested in museums and I don't go very often at all	41%	53%	7%	253
Sample size	**610**	**507**	**40**	**1162**

6.5.11 WTP among recent visitors

In general, the frequency of respondents' visitations to museums would be expected to positively correlate with their WTP. This was reinforced by the results in this study.[203]

Table 6.28: WTP among visitors to Queensland Museum campuses at least once within the twelve months prior to the present survey, using weighted scores

Recent visitors to campuses	**Increase funds**	**Keep as is**	**Reduce funds**	**Total sample**
Visited QMSB in previous 12 months (Brisbane)	64%	32%	4%	393
Visited TWRM in previous 12 months (Ipswich)	57%	37%	6%	106
Visited Cobb+Co Museum in the previous 12 months (Toowoomba)	58%	41%	1%	57
Visited MTQ in the previous 12 months (Townsville)	65%	33%	2%	129

203. The figures may contain some double-counting, because each campus was treated separately in creating the table.

There appears to be less willingness to pay by recent visitors to both The Workshops Rail Museum in Ipswich and the Cobb+Co Museum in Toowoomba. Both these campuses currently have a single dominant exhibition themes – Queensland railways or horse-drawn vehicles respectively – compared to the more varied exhibition presentations in the other campuses. Environmetrics proposed an alternative opinion:

> It could be that the TWRM appears to some visitors as more like a tourist attraction and thus is thought able to raise funds from commercial activity, while Cobb+Co, being of a more modest scale may not trigger the desire to contribute funds to the same extent (Environmetrics & McNair Ingenuity, 2009, p. 20).

Ironically, the local Toowoomba community has pledged $1.2 million to support the National Carriage Factory Project and redevelopment at the Cobb+Co Museum. This demonstrates a huge actual willingness to pay for new museum services.[204] This actual situation is reflected in a comment made by a survey respondent:

> The Cobb+Co Museum is great value for money and is a very educational and interesting place to take visitors when they are on holidays (QM 2008 CVM survey respondent).

6.5.12 WTP and children in the household

It is significant for museums to try to attract families with children, because it is generally agreed that one of the best indicators of whether an adult will go to a museum is whether he or she was taken to museums by his parents when he or she was a child (Falk, 1998, p. 41).

Thirty-one percent of respondents had indicated the purpose of their most recent visit to one of the campuses was to take a child or children.[205] Consequently, it could be expected that the number and perhaps ages of children in a household might show a positive correlation with WTP.

Table 6.29: WTP and children of different ages in the household using weighted scores

Children in the household	Increase funds	Keep as is	Reduce funds	Total sample
Children aged 0–12 in household	46%	51%	3%	330
Children aged 13–18 in household	48%	49%	3%	205
No children aged 0–12 in household	55%	41%	4%	833
No children aged 13–18 in household	53%	43%	4%	957

204. Of the actual $1.7million raised by the National Carriage Factory Appeal Committee, $1.2million was donated by Toowoomba-based businesses and individuals. On a very rough calculation, this would amount to $12.60 per adult or $24.60 per household in the Toowoomba region.

205. 'Museums are a great way to show our children about things that we couldn't show or teach through just words and pictures' (QM 2008 CVM survey respondent).

Surprisingly, having children in a household shifted the WTP downwards by a moderate extent. Households with children under twelve, whom the Queensland Museum target as a primary audience, were the least willing to pay more for the museum's services. This could, of course, be related to other financial pressures on families with children, rather than being a true reflection of these families' attitudes to the Queensland Museum.

Further analysis was conducted on households with at least one pre-teen resident. These households were distributed across the geographic regions in a similar pattern to the total population reported in the census.

Table 6.30: Age of respondent from households with and without pre-teens, using weighted scores

Pre-teens in household	20–24	25–34	35–44	45–64	65and over	Total
Yes	27%	44%	62%	20%	5%	28%
No	73%	56%	38%	80%	95%	72%

As would be expected, the highest proportion of responses from pre-teen households was provided by a person aged between thirty-five and forty-four. Within pre-teen households, fifty-seven percent of respondents indicated that taking a child or taking children to a campus of the Queensland Museum was their main purpose for visiting[206], in comparison to only twenty percent of non-pre-teen households.

Having a pre-teen in the household may also trigger a modest increase in awareness of museums. In these households, fifty-six percent of respondents claimed to keep an eye out for special activities in museums, in contrast to forty-nine percent of households without a pre-teen. Similarly, it was not unexpected to find that pre-teen households (at eighteen percent) were less likely to record that they were 'not really interested in museums and don't go very often at all', than other households (at twenty-three percent) (Environmetrics & McNair Ingenuity, 2009, p. 21).

6.5.13 WTP for people of different ages

As would be expected from the results of pre-teen households, the age of respondents was also significant in determining WTP, with young adults less likely to vote for increased funding than older adults. The corollary was also true that the youngest age group was most likely to favour a reduction in funding, as shown in Table 6.31.

206. Typical comments in the survey referred to taking children to the museum. An example of such a comment was: 'I think that the Museum of Tropical Queensland in Townsville is fantastic! The kids (aged 3, 5 and 8) love it and we go about 6 times a year. The building and exhibits are well thought out, exhibitions relevant and ambiance excellent' (QM 2008 CVM Study respondent).

Table 6.31: Variation in ongoing funding preferences for the Queensland Museum based on age of respondents using weighted scores

Ages of respondents	Total	Under 24	25–34	35–44	45–54	55 and over
Increasing the funds for QM	52%	37%	46%	49%	62%	59%
Keeping the funds at the present for QM	44%	53%	50%	48%	38%	37%
Reducing the funds for QM	4%	10%	4%	3%	1%	4%
Total weighted row	1162	149	209	226	202	376

6.5.14 WTP based on gender

There was a slight tendency for men to be more supportive of increasing funding to the Queensland Museum, though it is difficult to comment on reasons for this or to infer if the difference was of any real significance.

Table 6.32: Variation in ongoing funding preferences for the Queensland Museum based on gender of respondents using weighted scores

Gender of respondents	Total	Male	Female
Increasing the funds for QM	52%	56%	49%
Keeping the funds at the present for QM	44%	40%	47%
Reducing the funds for QM	4%	5%	3%
Total weighted row	1162	573	589

6.5.15 WTP for people with different levels of education

Education attainment and occupational status had a significant direct bearing on museum attendance:

> Museum visiting increases very strongly with increasing level of education, and is almost exclusively the domain of the cultivated classes (Bennett, 1995b, p. 12; Bourdieu & Darbel, 1991, p. 14).

Consequently, it was highly desirable to achieve an even distribution of educational attainment levels among the survey participants in this study sample. Table 6.33 illustrates that just over one third of the respondents had completed primary or high school, a third had completed a TAFE or college course, and just under a third had attended university.

Table 6.33: Highest education levels and funding preferences, using weighted scores

Education levels	Increase funds	Keep as is	Reduce funds	Sample
Primary/high school	49%	47%	4%	39%
Trade/technical/business college	51%	45%	5%	33%
University – undergraduate degree	61%	35%	4%	20%
University – postgraduate degree	55%	42%	3%	8%

As higher levels of education were attained, WTP for Queensland Museum services also increased, though there is some contradiction in the post-graduate results. This may be an aberration due to the relatively small sample size of this group.

6.5.16 WTP and work status

Respondents' work status provided reasonably consistent WTP results, except for the two categories of 'student' and 'retired'. While the student numbers were low and subsequently require caution in interpreting the results, the retired grouping registered the highest WTP of any category. This was surprising, except when one considers that older members of communities are more likely to express concerns about preserving their heritage for present and future generations. Bequest values associated with the Queensland Museum could be significant to retirees.

Table 6.34: Work status and funding preferences, using weighted scores

Work status	Increase funds	Keep as is	Reduce funds	Sample
Full time work	54%	42%	4%	48%
Part time work	46%	49%	4%	16%
Looking for work	45%	52%	3%	3%
Home duties full time	55%	42%	4%	10%
Student	28%	66%	6%	5%
Retired	60%	36%	4%	19%

6.5.17 WTP in different geographical areas

Respondents from geographical areas were discussed earlier, with reference to Table 6.17. WTP was consistent across all geographical areas of the state. However, using the unweighted scores, which enabled a much larger sample of respondents from Toowoomba and Townsville, there were some modest variations for these two regions, as displayed in Table 6.35.

Table 6.35: WTP in each of the four geographic areas, using unweighted scores

Geographical area	Increase funds	Keep as is	Reduce funds	Total sample
Brisbane/Ipswich	54%	43%	3%	545
Toowoomba	47%	52%	1%	126
Townsville	49%	48%	3%	208
Rest of Queensland	54%	41%	5%	295
Total	**611**	**521**	**40**	**1,174**

6.5.18 WTP and psychographic profile

The questionnaire used for this survey included the self-description questions[207] used by Environmetrics in previous work with the Queensland Museum to sort people into the psychographic groups.[208]

Table 6.36: Recent visitation of any museum or gallery across psychological segments, using weighted scores

Psychological segment	Previous 6 months	6 to 12 months	More than 12 months	Never
Practical and organised	26%	27%	40%	7%
Gregarious out and about	49%	22%	24%	5%
Individualistic out and about	37%	23%	35%	5%
Moderate and unhurried	37%	15%	28%	20%
Discerning and purposeful	42%	27%	27%	4%
Battlers	32%	15%	45%	8%
Conventional suburban	28%	17%	37%	18%
Self-contained, go with the flow	34%	26%	36%	4%
Social pleasure seekers	43%	25%	29%	3%

It is clear from the data in Table 6.36 that some segments are more recent visitors to museums or galleries than others. For example, people from the 'Gregarious out and about' segment are nearly twice as likely to have visited any museum or gallery within the last six months, than people from the 'Practical and organised' segment.

The results displayed in Table 6.28 indicate that more recent museum visitors had a greater propensity for increasing funding to the Queensland Museum. However, interestingly, this does not seem to apply consistently to the psychological segmentation.

Table 6.37: WTP across psychological segments, using weighted scores

Psychological segment	Increase funds	Keep as is	Reduce funds
Practical and organised	60%	37%	3%
Gregarious out and about	44%	50%	6%
Individualistic out and about	52%	43%	5%
Moderate and unhurried	60%	32%	8%
Discerning and purposeful	59%	38%	3%

207.'Psychographics' are the psychological parallel of demographics. The distinction between the two concepts can be characterised by saying that 'demographics' is about the age of a person's head, whereas 'psychographics' is about what is in that head, in terms of attitudes, aspirations, and general views about how to live life (Environmetrics & McNair Ingenuity, 2009, p. 23). See Question Thirty-six in the Survey Questionnaire in Appendix One.

208.See Appendix Three for a more detailed description of each group.

Battlers	49%	51%	0%
Conventional suburban	40%	53%	7%
Self-contained, go with the flow	62%	34%	4%
Social pleasure seekers	34%	66%	0%

Of the three segments that, in Table 6.36, are seen to have been to museums or galleries relatively recently ('Gregarious out and about', 'Discerning and purposeful', and 'Social pleasure seekers'), only the 'Discerning and purposeful' are relatively keen to see the funding for the Queensland Museum increased. While the least recent visitors – the 'Practical and organised'– are the most likely, together with the 'Self- contained, go with the flow' segments and 'Moderate and unhurried', to be willing to pay extra for Queensland Museum services. Environmentics compared these results with their earlier studies and drew some additional conclusions about these behaviour patterns.[209]

In general, WTP across all nine geographic and demographic criteria used in this study revealed that there was a reasonable degree of support for the Queensland Museum across all these groups. Although this is probably not surprising for most of the criteria, it is particularly significant that even those who described themselves as 'not really interested in museums and don't go very often at all' still thought that the Queensland Museum warranted increased funding.

6.6 Final comments

It was decided not to include any debriefing questions at the end of the survey, but to add a 'comments' section to acquire qualitative information regarding the survey instrument, itself, as well as to elicit reasons for particular responses to WTP questions. Most researchers include debriefing questions:

> ...to test whether respondents accepted survey elements or rejected them, and if rejected, whether their vote was affected, and if affected, in what direction (Krupnick & Adamowicz, 2006, p. 54).

209. The 'Self-contained, go with the flow' segment (which previous research has shown as being at the centre of 'friends' activities associated with cultural institutions) is the one most inclined to favour increased funding.
The explanation lies in the observation drawn from previous studies that both the 'Gregarious out and about' and 'Social pleasure seeker' segments are drawn by a sense of 'show' and fashion. They represent the kind of fickle audience that will attend for the champagne opening, but not return for the intellectual content. The 'Individualistic out and about', in contrast, has all the same demographic characteristics as their gregarious and pleasure-seeker cousins, but is much more interested in the content of an exhibition, and may become a regular visitor at museums that tweak their interest (Environmetrics & McNair Ingenuity, 2009, pp. 25-26).

There were a large number of responses – seventy-three in all – to Question Forty-four, which invited respondents to make any final comments. By far, the largest numbers of comments were about the survey itself and, surprisingly, how much people enjoyed completing it. There was only one adverse comment about the format of the survey. This was significant because it helped to validate the questionnaire that was used in this CVM Study. Typical responses to Question Forty-Four included:

- 'I found the questions very interesting';
- 'Enjoyed this survey a lot as it really asked for my opinions'; and
- 'Was an easy survey to complete, easy to understand, used words that everyday people could understand – thanks' (QM 2008 CVM Study Q44 responses).

Many respondents also commented on the Queensland Museum or one of the campuses, or museums in general, as being 'a great place to take kids':

- 'I think the museums are a wonderful place to learn and a valuable asset especially for younger generations'; and
- 'We love the children's activities at the Rail Workshop – thank you' (QM 2008 CVM Study respondents).

There were also many comments about taking grandchildren to the museum, such as:

- 'My grandchildren enjoy visits to the museum as much as I do'; and
- 'Regularly take my grandsons to the Museum of Tropical Queensland; we love it' (QM 2008 CVM Study respondents).

Interestingly, there were a few observations about the appropriateness of the five alternative government services that were presented. These comments suggested options other than the five that were presented, such as reduced funding for elite sportsmen and sports venues in Brisbane, or, as one respondent wrote.

> I thought question 28 was too restrictive in the alternative methods of funding it offered through government cutbacks. There are many other opportunities where Government could reduce funding to increase grants to the museums e.g. grants to individuals and/or organisations that have little or no cultural relevance (QM 2008 CVM Study respondent).

Finally, there were a couple of respondents who felt it necessary to explain their WTP decisions. Surprisingly, these relate to cases in which, despite highly valuing the museum, the respondents decided not to support any increase funding:

> I think museums do wonderful work ...I have enjoyed special exhibitions at the Queensland Museum and thoroughly enjoyed my visit to Cobb+Co for research purposes. I don't believe that everyone shares my positive view of museums however so I can't agree with $12 per person tax (QM 2008 CVM Study respondent).
>
> I think the museums are essential to our culture and way of life. I believe that the Cobb+Co Museum is a vital part of the history of Toowoomba but I think at the moment pouring 24 million into the museums is not viable (QM 2008 CVM Study respondent).

Considering the deteriorating economy when this CVM survey was conducted, more comments like the second one above could have been expected.

6.7 Conclusion

- Results from the CVM study of the Queensland Museum should be regarded as 'robust', because the questionnaire and its administration conformed to the best-practice guidelines outlined by the NOAA Panel and addressed the major criticisms that have been levelled at previous CVM studies. The validity of the survey is based on the following:
- The sample reflected both geographic and demographic characteristics of the population of Queensland, which was identified as the primary stakeholder of the Queensland Museum;
- There was an adequate response rate to the whole survey;
- Respondents demonstrated their understanding of the task in which they were asked to engage, and they spent adequate time – 11.48 minutes on average – completing the survey;
- There were seventy-three unsolicited positive comments about the survey being easy to follow and interesting;
- The nature of the payment for increased funding was clear, as were the alternative choices that detailed budget constraints;
- The questionnaire underwent vigorous analysis and was subjected to a pilot study;
- Participant responses reflected economic theory predictions;
- The results were comparable to more recent United Kingdom, European, and American CVM studies of various cultural public goods, such as libraries, museums, theatres, festivals, and cultural heritage sites; and
- The results reflect the actual situation in the Toowoomba community, where fund-raising has occurred to construct the National Carriage Factory Project at the Cobb+Co Museum.

Although still somewhat contested, the CVM format was chosen for this study because of its ability to estimate non-market values held by both users and non-users, as well as indicating the nature of the non-market value from the respondents' perspectives. WTP, it can be argued, is underpinned by a belief that an institution possesses qualities and attributes that, while not directly reflected in monetary terms, generate perceptions of value (Environmetrics & McNair Ingenuity, 2009, p. 6). It was clear from the results that the Queensland Museum, as a whole, and as the sum of its campuses, which includes the Cobb+Co Museum, is held in high regard by the vast majority of respondents. In general, the respondents believed that the Queensland Museum is important for the people of Queensland and is creating a legacy for the future – though they may be less certain of the personal relevance of the museum in their lives.

In response to the WTP options, there was majority support for both scenarios. For the first scenario, it was concluded that the people of Queensland place a value on the Queensland Museum that is more than twice that reflected in current government funding for day to day operations (see Table 6.23).

The second scenario described a series of new developments proposed for the Queensland Museum, to be developed over the next five to seven years, worth twenty-four million dollars. The results shown in Table 6.26 suggest that even adopting a very cautious approach, the Queensland public would be in favour of funding the level of new facilities and services proposed by the Queensland Museum.

Since the completion of this CVM study, the state government has provided four million dollars to the Cobb+Co Museum for the construction of the National Carriage Factory. This was a direct response to the Toowoomba community's previous efforts in actually raising $1.7 million towards this project.[210] This supports the validity of the CVM survey, because the respondents' WTP was matched by their actual payment for the public good in question.

This CVM study had been commissioned to determine the public value of Queensland Museum. It was always intended that the results would deliver a new way of valuing the Queensland Museum and provide a mechanism for demonstrating this in economic terms to be used to influence policy and key government decisions. The results of this study attest to Queenslanders' commitment to their state museum and their desire to have it adequately resourced to provide better products and services, not just in Brisbane and the South East corner, but across the whole state.

> Museums are important for all the reasons mentioned in this survey, however, for those of us living out of the major centres, distance and equitable access is compromised (QM 2008 CVM Study Q44 final comment).

---

210. Comments made by the Premier, the Honourable Anna Bligh, to the author when making the announcement of the state government's support for the National Carriage Factory at the Cobb+Co Museum, on 17 December 2008.

This comment resonated with the earlier Canadian study in which rural dwellers felt that museums were inaccessible to them for reasons of distance (Dixon, et al., 1974, p. 128).

The CVM study project aimed to develop a methodology that could be adopted by arts and cultural institutions in Queensland to enable a consistent approach from individual studies that might be conducted by these institutions.[211] The questionnaire format and delivery mechanism piloted by the Queensland Museum in this study will be made available to other cultural institutions in Queensland and elsewhere to further research on measuring the public value of museums and other cultural institutions so as to develop a shared common language to give 'voice to these values'.

211. Although, initially, the CVM Study was considered to be of primary importance to other Queensland cultural institutions, many other interstate and national cultural institutions have also expressed interest in this project.

Chapter 7
Conclusion

7.1 Overview

This study has been an attempt to mainstream museological developments in regional Queensland – an area of study that had not previously been identified as having anything significant to contribute to the broader study of museum practices. It has demonstrated that the intersections between the Cobb+Co Museum and its Toowoomba community represent many diverse and fluid possibilities and opportunities that other museums could emulate to share in a creative future with their communities.

Concentrating on the three-phase identity development of the Cobb+Co Museum from 1987 to 2010, it is argued that each transformative stage represents a unique identity for the Cobb+Co Museum. Each stage was marked by a structural change, but each was integrated within the others. These three identities evolved in a considered and directed trajectory that reflected local community responses to specific national and international discourses affecting museums and heritage. Generally, the transformations occurred through accumulative processes that represented both time- and place-specific adaptations to broader trends. The Cobb+Co Museum has subsequently acquired a 'diverse and hybrid identity', embracing each of its three-stage developments with greater or lesser focus, depending on community aspirations and needs (E Hooper-Greenhill, 2007a, p. 372).

The transformative processes undertaken by the Cobb+Co Museum do not represent a paradigm shift, but were rather a result of substantial ongoing changes that proceeded 'on the basis of interrogating and renegotiating earlier practices and philosophies, many of which continue in one form or another to underpin the identity' of the museum today. This renegotiation needs to continue into the future if the museum is to remain relevant to its community (E Hooper-Greenhill, 2007a, p. 368). In 2011, a new brand *Artisans of Life – forging futures,* was developed to direct the Cobb+Co Museum's ongoing relationships with its community.

While exploring the changing dynamics between the museum and its community, this research has assessed the relevance and value of the ongoing developments at Cobb+Co Museum through addressing three questions:

- Has the Cobb+Co Museum's transformation over the period of more than twenty years reflected general changes taking place in museums, or has it been time- and place-specific?
- To what extent are these transformations valued by the community?
- Can the processes enacted by the Cobb+Co Museum in developing and implementing its transformative models act as an exemplar for museums in other regions?

7.2 Summary of Part A – the three-stage transformations of the Cobb+Co Museum

The three-stage transformations experienced by the museum between 1987 and 2010 represent significant identity conversions. From the beginning, however, identity was always somewhat problematic for the Cobb+Co Museum. There was a previous Cobb & Co. Museum in Toowoomba that was operated by Bill Bolton from the mid-1960s until, in 1981, a fire destroyed the building in which the collection was housed. To many residents, the new Cobb+Co Museum was merely a continuation of Bill Bolton's private museum, because both institutions displayed the same horse-drawn vehicle collection.

Of even greater public confusion was the Cobb+Co Museum's dual role of being both a local museum and a branch of the Queensland Museum. It could be argued that this fluctuating dynamic still exists, in which the museum oscillates between a unique Cobb+Co Museum identity and a single component of a 'One QM' brand. As the Cobb+Co Museum's individual characteristics evolved throughout its three-stage transformation, as a result of greater community engagement, its local distinctive identity has emerged, at the expense of the Queensland Museum's overall brand.

Part A of this paper addressed the relationship between the Cobb+Co Museum's three-stage transformation over more than twenty years and developments within museums and heritage practices as identified in academic literature and museological frameworks and operations. Encompassing Chapters Two, Three, and Four, Part A determined that the Cobb+Co Museum's transformations reflected both general changes taking place in museums, as well as being time- and place-specific, responding in unique ways to its community affected by more localised impacts from political, social, cultural and economic changes.

7.2.1 Chapter Two – Stage One summary

Chapter Two investigated the initial Cobb+Co Museum model during its Stage One development, from 1987 until 2001. It analysed the international contexts that enveloped and transformed understandings of the terms 'heritage' and 'museums'. These provided the museological frameworks that underpinned the establishment and operations of the Cobb+Co Museum during its First Stage iteration.

The Museum was founded in 1987 as a branch of the Queensland Museum after the Board accepted a donation of a collection of horse-drawn vehicles that had been the property of a Toowoomba businessman. The new branch inherited the Queensland Museum's traditional museological concern with collections and research, with little or no regard for the community in which it was formed.

One of the few links that was forged between the Cobb+Co Museum and the Toowoomba community in the 1980s was the appointment of the Museum's Advisory Committee, which was made up of community representatives and involved the unusual appointment of a local Toowoomba teacher as the Museum's Manager and, later, its Director. The importance of having stable personnel with educational expertise in strategic leadership roles as well as many local connections and networks would soon become obvious.

The museum's eventual success was a result of these internal attributes, together with the museum's nationally significant collection of horse-drawn vehicles, its location in relation to the TAFE College, and the Advisory Committee's commitment to community 'usefulness'. Gradually, the Cobb+Co Museum adopted a new approach to its community by assuming a leadership role in the regional tourism industry and by providing a significant support role for the community museum movement that had sprung up in regional Queensland in response to a serious decline in traditional rural industries.

Within five years of opening, the Cobb+Co Museum's identity had started to change, as it adopted aspects of new museological practices and gradually shifted its focus towards more client and community responsiveness. These transformations resulted from the changing dynamics that were occurring between the museum and its community.

7.2.2 Chapter Three – Stage Two summary

The museum's traditional identity changed into a social enterprise and community resource centre dedicated to lifelong learning during its Second Stage development, which lasted from 2001 to 2010. During this period, the Cobb+Co Museum developed characteristics of both a community-centred and a client-centred institution – a hybrid place with mixed-use spaces that were available for both internal and community use. Its new features were community focused: new galleries to tell local stories, a central coffee shop as a community meeting place, and extensive public programs geared towards lifelong learning for the very young to senior citizens. A new relationship with the community flourished when the Toowoomba City Council agreed to support free entry for all local residents to the museum.

The Second Stage development, with its social entrepreneurship, multifaceted community roles, and ideological commitment to audience development, rather than content delivery – from back-of-house to front-of-house activities – consistently adhered to the principles underpinning new museological developments.

A three-tier model of stakeholder interests and interactions was espoused, with the local residents, both users and non-users of the museum's services, identified as the primary stakeholders. This naturally led to the museum experimenting with various community engagement strategies and models, which ultimately led to the formulation of the National Carriage Factory community engagement model. While there is capacity in this particular engagement model to support the enhancement of other cultural institutions in regional settings, direct applications to other communities would be difficult without a clear understanding of the underlying strengths of the pre-existing relationships and the internal capacity, capabilities, and history of the Cobb+Co Museum within its Toowoomba community.

7.2.3 Chapter Four – Stage Three summary

Planning for Cobb+Co Museum Stage Three commenced in 2006, when the museum announced the development of the National Carriage Factory (NCF) – a creative-cultural industry construct underpinned by a heritage trade training centre to be established in conjunction with SQIT. From the time of this announcement, there emerged a very different relationship between the community and the museum, which was reflected in the widespread community ownership of the NCF project. Local businesses and individuals donated large sums of money and successfully lobbied the different tiers of government for support. The community's response to the NCF was motivated by different reasons, but was, in part, because the NCF positioned the Cobb+Co Museum as the cultural and educational hub for a new approach to regional community development, based on safeguarding heritage trades, crafts, and skills. The Cobb+Co Museum's Third Stage identity became synonymous with the National Carriage Factory project, which was completed in September 2010.

Chapter Four explored the opportunities for museums to develop into creative-cultural industry hubs that play a significant role in the creative economy. The National Carriage Factory represented a natural progression from the Cobb+Co Museum's first two stage developments, while emphasising the catalytic value of the national carriage collection of horse-drawn vehicles and the museum's international custodianship of the Cobb & Co. coaching legend. The National Carriage Factory was, in essence, an innovative project that sought to embed the safeguarding of heritage trades, crafts, and skills into the community's psyche through becoming the creative-cultural hub for *Hand Made in Country*. This concept was moulded on five international models; creative-cultural industry hubs; the Convention for Safeguarding Intangible Heritage; and new museological developments linked to tourism, including ecomuseums, economuseums, and *HandMade in America*.

Together, Chapters Two to Four illustrated the three-stage identity transformation of the Cobb+Co Museum over more than two decades. These transformative processes undertaken by the Cobb+Co Museum do not represent a complete paradigm shift, but are reflective of substantial ongoing adjustments to earlier practices and philosophies, which resulted from changing community dynamics and changing museum engagement strategies.

Although each of the stages was marked by a building program with new exhibitions and public programs, it was rather the community-related processes and functions that distinguished the Cobb+Co Museum's identity during each of the three stages. These different relationships and their origins are identified in Table 7.1, below.[212]

212. This matrix format was adapted from work undertaken by Cyril Simard relating to economuseology (1991, p. 231).

Table 7.1: Comparison of the three stage developments at the Cobb+Co Museum from 1987–2010

Function/purpose	Stage One (1987–2001) Traditional museum	Stage Two (2001–2010) Social enterprise –community resource centre	Stage Three (2010–) National Carriage Factory – creative-cultural industry hub
Basic purpose	Conservation, display, and research	Displays stimulating public programs and lifelong learning	Conservation to bring out potential of heritage trades and pool of ideas
Focus	The collection	The themes and stories	The trades as intangible heritage and vehicle collection
Attitude to the object	The object for its own sake	The object as stimulus for memories	The object as inspiration for new products
Attitude to community	Operated in isolation to community	Partnership with community members	Embedded in community
Attitude to production techniques	Authenticity and historical exactness	Interpretation of chosen themes to various audiences	Adaptive potential of traditional techniques and profitability
Attitude to site and building	Content more important than site or building	Building as a place for learning	Building as a place-marker and centre of community life and creativity
Main basis of activity	The collection and works displayed	Studies of the main themes as basis for lifelong learning	Technologies of an active workshop and community development through craft activities
Aims of training schemes	For quality restoration and conservation	For understanding techniques, methods, and memories	For updating of techniques and production and sales of quality objects
Types of instruction provided	By museum specialists and graduate volunteers	By educational specialists and volunteers	By craftsmen and at further training level
Staff training	Specialist studies	Specialist studies	Apprenticeships and specialist studies

The Cobb+Co Museum through its transformational processes resulting from its interactions with its community, gradually came to view itself as an agent for positive change, co-creating with its partners and audiences mutually beneficial outcomes in its community. The Advisory Committee took the view that

> We are leaders, not followers. We are well connected, and have our finger on the pulse. We are visionaries that are experimental and ambitious, knowing and learning. We are persistent in tackling major social issues and offering new ideas for wide-scale change (Queensland Museum, 2011).

As seen in the development of the National Carriage Factory project, the Cobb+Co Museum offered some compelling perspectives and solutions that persuaded individuals in the community to work in close partnership with the Museum to create a viable, flourishing community through facilitating social and cultural exchange and economic development.

It has been argued that the museum's three-stage transformations embraced in turn international trends in museums and heritage, social entrepreneurial and creative industry developments, while responding specifically to the local situation existing in Toowoomba and regional Queensland. Each stage also represented a different relationship and value matrix between the museum and its community.

7.3 Summary of Part B – giving 'voice to values'

The question of museums' perceived value was addressed in Part B of this study. This section particularly focused on how to evaluate the relationship and topology of values embraced by the Toowoomba community in regard to the Cobb+Co Museum as the museum underwent its transformational changes.

In working with the Toowoomba community it became obvious that for locals 'one doesn't have to visit to value' the museum, so many traditional methods of measuring support, such as numbers through the door, became irrelevant. In order to ascertain a more reliable measure of the public value of the Cobb+Co Museum and the proposed development of the National Carriage Factory, alternative methodologies were investigated and adapted.

7.3.1 Chapter Five – What value do museums have?

Chapter Five identified the changing character of museums and the reasons they are valued – from intrinsic (cultural), to instrumental (economic and social), to institutional (public good). Of equal significance has been the changing perception of exactly who is or should be assessing museum value and for whom museums should be valuable. Eight models of stakeholder identification were scrutinised, including the Cobb+Co Museum's classification system. While politicians, policy makers, and other museum professionals have traditionally been recognised as the major stakeholders of museums, the framework adopted for assessing the value of museums from their perspectives has been very restrictive. Recognition of the community as the primary stakeholder necessitated a different methodology to effectively gauge a museum's worth.

Reference to cultural economics provided frameworks for recognising the significance of both the economic and cultural values of cultural assets and suggested a range of methodologies to measure both.

Various choice modelling methodologies that had been employed to measure the value of the arts and cultural industries, including museums, were interrogated to find a model that could produce robust results. As the Contingent Valuation Methodology represented the best model for this exercise, a thorough study was undertaken that looked at fifteen previous CMV studies of museums, libraries, galleries, performance centres, heritage sites, and festivals – both stand-alone institutions and those packaged in different formats. Attention was paid to identifying methodological weaknesses ensuring that the CVM model chosen would offer the most valid and reliable results.

7.3.2 Chapter Six – CVM study of the Queensland Museum

Chapter Six was devoted to the development, implementation, and assessment of the Contingent Valuation Methodology (CVM) study, which aimed to value the Queensland Museum, of which the Cobb+Co Museum is a part. This significant study was undertaken in December 2008, prior to funding being announced for the construction of the National Carriage Factory project, and was designed, in part, to develop a platform for the Toowoomba community to provide its own assessment of the Cobb+Co Museum's Stage Two social enterprise iteration.

To fully realise this aim, the museum embraced the potential of a CVM study to measure both the market and non-market benefits of the museum, as perceived by its public users and non-users, who were defined as Queensland residents. Using a detailed survey instrument delivered online to nearly 1200 Queensland residents, the museum sought the participants' willingness to pay in dollar amounts for both existing products and services and for a raft of new developments, including the NCF project, proposed by the Queensland Museum for implementation during the next five to seven years. It also investigated a range of non-market values that were important to both users and non-users of the Queensland Museum, as well as providing detailed demographic and psychographic data.

The survey instrument's design process involved other major cultural institutions in Queensland in the hope that it would have wider application within the industry by providing a robust platform to give a consistent 'voice to values'.

Great attention was paid to the actual survey instrument to ensure it conformed to best-practice international models, based on the guidelines outlined by the NOAA Panel, and that it addressed the major criticisms of previous CVM studies. Its validity rested on achieving nine criteria, as detailed in Section 6.7. The results obtained indicated that the people of Queensland placed a value on the Queensland Museum that was more than twice that reflected in current government funding for day to day operations. The results also demonstrated that the respondents would be in favour of funding the proposed level of new facilities and services, including the NCF project, proposed by the Queensland Museum to be developed over the next five to seven years.

Concomitant with this CVM study the National Carriage Factory Committee was seeking direct support from the residents of Toowoomba. By raising $1.7 million for the National Carriage Factory project from local residents and businesses, it was evident that the CVM study results reflected the actual reality of the situation. The Toowoomba community valued the Cobb+Co Museum very highly and were prepared to contribute significantly to its Stage Three development.

7.4 Questions answered

This study, focusing on the Cobb+Co Museum – a campus of the Queensland Museumin Toowoomba, Queensland – through its three-stage formation between 1987 and 2010, is significant for a number of reasons. Firstly, longitudinal studies investigating identity formation in museums – particularly regional entities – are very rare, so this study filled a recognised void. Secondly, this study contributes to understanding the dynamic processes that operate within communities and the leadership roles that cultural institutions, such as museums, can play to enhance the future of communities and museums, themselves. This study also propagated an innovative community engagement strategy that could have widespread applications for other cultural institutions in other communities. Finally, the major web-based study undertaken in this research program to measure the complexity and interrelationship of museum values from the community's perspective has made a substantial contribution to the international pool of noteworthy valuation studies of arts and cultural institutions.

This research set out to answer three questions about the changing dynamics between the Cobb+Co Museum and its community in Toowoomba, and its applicability to other institutions in other regional settings. The overriding conclusion is that museums need to develop processes for ongoing change if they are to be relevant and valued by communities which themselves are constantly changing. The Cobb+Co Museum case study provides one model of how a museum in a regional setting has been able to achieve this.

In answer to the first question, it has been demonstrated that the Cobb+Co Museum's metamorphosis over a period of twenty-four years has reflected general changes in museum practices that were evident at international, national, state, and local levels, as well as being a reflection of the impacts of new museums models that preference community before collections. The museum has also been affected by new and post-museological aspirations, which enabled the Cobb+Co Museum to more easily adapt social enterprise and creative-cultural industry modelling to its Stage Two and Three iterations. Equally significant has been the museum's involvement in the transformation of the wider domain of heritage, which has become mainstreamed with multiple interfaces embraced by communities as never before.

However, it has also been evident that the Cobb+Co Museum's individual characteristics – including its specific co-location with the TAFE College in Toowoomba, its locally-prized collection of horse-drawn vehicles, the stable community leadership provided by its Advisory Committee and Director, and the Advisory Committee's unswerving belief that museums can, and must take a leadership role in making a difference in their communities – have provided the ingredients that make the Cobb+Co Museum's ongoing transformations unique. However, these specific characteristics of the museum do not preclude the Cobb+Co model from being of both general and particular value for other museums and cultural organisations should they wish to emulate it.

The second question sought to explore the extent to which the Cobb+Co Museum conversions were and are valued by its community. It has been demonstrated that the community values the museum very highly based on the results of the CVM study of the Queensland Museum and on the community's leadership of the National Carriage Factory project, in which Toowoomba residents made significant financial contributions and successfully lobbied governments for support.

Although still somewhat contested, the CVM format was chosen for this study because of its ability to estimate non-market values held by both users and non-users, as well as indicating the nature of the non-market value from the respondents' perspectives. Using a web based survey of nearly 1200 Queenslanders representative of the State's demographic and geographic characteristics, the results indicated very clearly that the Queensland Museum, as a whole, and as the sum of its campuses, which includes the Cobb+Co Museum, is held in high regard by the vast majority of respondents. In general, the respondents believed that the Queensland Museum is important for the people of Queensland and is creating a legacy for the future – though they may be less certain of the personal relevance of the museum in their lives.

In response to the WTP options, there was majority support for both scenarios. For the first scenario, it was concluded that the people of Queensland place a value on the Queensland Museum that is more than twice that reflected in current government funding for day to day operations.

The second scenario described a series of new developments proposed for the Queensland Museum, to be developed over the next five to seven years, worth twenty-four million dollars. These WTP results indicated that the Queensland public would be in favour of funding the level of new facilities and services proposed by the Queensland Museum.

Since the completion of this CVM study, the state government provided four million dollars to the Cobb+Co Museum for the construction of the National Carriage Factory. This was a direct response to the Toowoomba community's previous efforts in actually raising $1.7 million towards this project. This supports the validity of the CVM survey, because the respondents' WTP was matched by their actual payment for the public good in question.

There has been a remarkable transformation in the community's attitude to the Cobb+Co Museum, from viewing it as 'the last stop before the dump' in the late 1980s, to 'owning' it as their special place. Generally referred in the local vernacular now as just 'Cobb+Co', it is no longer identified as a museum (with its traditional connotations of 'old things'), but as a reflection of the community's identity and heritage values, a unique architectural landmark, and a highly valued community and visitor centre. It has been argued that this changed attitude is a direct result of the shifting dynamics between the Cobb+Co Museum and its community.

7.4.1 Three exemplar community processes

Finally, this research project identified three processes enacted by the Cobb+Co Museum in developing and implementing its transformative models, which could act as exemplars for other museums and cultural institutions in other regions.

The first is the community engagement methodology that was used to support the development and ongoing operations of the National Carriage Factory. This strategy and fundraising methodology is generally applicable to other large-scale community projects. The Queensland Museum Foundation's fundraising principles and approaches provide a solid structure for implementation by any well-organised group. However, it needs to be recognised that a major key to success was the ability of the Cobb+Co Museum to leverage off its many years of successful community engagement and service delivery. The museum's brand reputation in its community was enviable. Built upon years of tangible results and emotional 'share of heart' by the community, potential supporters not only believed in the National Carriage Factory project as part of the museum's mission, but also in the museum's capacity to deliver on that mission. The process also relied on the Cobb+Co Museum's strengths in planning, community engagement and leadership, long term media relations, organisational stability, and respected personnel to implement a multifaceted advocacy process to raise the funds required to achieve its objectives.

It has been argued that other cultural organisations with an inspiring vision, comparable characteristics, determination, and a flexible approach to changing economic and political landscapes could successfully replicate the process used to develop the National Carriage Factory for their own significant development projects. The applicability of this model has been recognised and has been embraced by the Empire Theatre Trust in Toowoomba to facilitate its Stage Three development.

The second process is the Contingent Valuation Methodology used to measure the value of the Queensland Museum to the people of Queensland. This CVM study had a specific aim to develop a consistent methodology that could be adopted by arts and cultural institutions in Queensland, thereby encouraging maximum effect from the individual studies that might be conducted by these institutions leading to a common language to express the value of arts and culture within Queensland.

The robust results achieved from the CVM study have delivered a new way of valuing the multifaceted Queensland Museum, of which the Cobb+Co Museum is a part. These results also provide a mechanism for demonstrating the museum's value in economic terms, which could have noteworthy applications for advocacy purposes.

Although this particular study was resource intensive, it has provided a very detailed process that can be emulated by other arts and cultural institutions in Queensland as well as further afield. This in turn should reduce the costs involved for these institutions to a level that they would be willing to pay for the information and advocacy potential that could be derived from similar CVM study outcomes.

The third process is the *Hand Made in Country* regional model for a creative-cultural industry hub based on the heritage trades. This process, which was underpinned by safeguarding heritage trades, crafts, and skills, is now embedded within the Toowoomba tourism region. The broader principles – including public-private partnerships, a focus on formal education and learning, development of creative clusters, emphasis on design and innovation, establishment of standards to ensure authenticity, international perspectives underpinned by a serious research agenda, and strategic marketing and business development, all within a regional tourism concept – are core requirements for the development of any creative industry hub – not just one based on heritage trades. These principles are transferrable to other regions, just as the Cobb+Co Museum adapted various international models for *Hand Made in Country*. During 2011 Tourism Queensland funding has been acquired to undertake further feasibility studies into extending *Hand Made in Country* into the Southern Downs and South Burnett regions adjoining Toowoomba.

In conclusion, It has been demonstrated that cultural institutions, such as the Cobb+Co Museum, that develop the capacity and willingness to play substantial leadership roles in their region can be of seminal importance to their community. This occurs most effectively when relationships become entrenched with shared values that can facilitate social, cultural, and economic benefits for both museums and their communities. The three-stage identity trajectory undertaken by the Cobb+Co Museum is an example of the positive effects that changing dynamics between museums and their communities can initiate, particularly in regional areas. At its optimum, this can result in a relationship that is highly valued and supported by the community. The success of Toowoomba's community-museum relationship was manifested in the community's leadership of and support for the National Carriage Factory project, which was the Third Stage of the Cobb+Co Museum.

Based on evidence to date and the growing confidence in which the museum now interacts with this community tackling more and more serious issues,[213] the Cobb+Co Museum will, and needs to continue, to refine its engagement strategies and partnerships with its community into the future.

By adapting post-museological ideas and practices to solve community needs, the Cobb+Co Museum demonstrates most effectively the wisdom inherent in Su Donghai's statement

For a tree to grow well, the seed can be international,
but the soil must be local

213. These include initiating a community healing process after the devastating floods that occurred in Toowoomba in January 2011.

Appendices

Appendix One

Queensland Museum CVM survey questionnaire Option B (Environmetrics & Ingenuity, 2009).

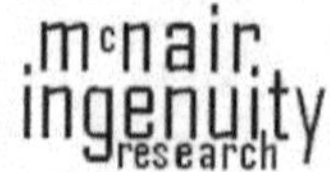

In order to make sure that we are speaking to a broad spectrum of people, we would like to know where you are located.

Please record your four digit postcode.

☐

qm queensland museum

Welcome to this Survey

This survey asks about the Queensland Museum, its network of venues, the services it provides and how you value them.

It will take you approximately 10 minutes to complete.

Your responses will be used for research purposes only and are strictly confidential in accordance with our Privacy Policy.

If you have any questions or problems completing this survey, please call McNair Ingenuity Research on (free call) 1800 669 133.

IMPORTANT: Please take your time and think carefully about the questions in the following survey. We monitor the quality of our data to be sure that everyone is providing thoughtful and attentive responses.

1. **When was the last time that you personally did each of the following for interest or pleasure?**

	In last 6 mon ths	6 mon ths to a year	More than a year ago	Never	Don't know
Attend first-grade or professional sporting event	◯	◯	◯	◯	◯
Eat out at a restaurant	◯	◯	◯	◯	◯
Visit a museum or art gallery	◯	◯	◯	◯	◯
Play sport or do an exercise program	◯	◯	◯	◯	◯
Work on hobbies, painting or music	◯	◯	◯	◯	◯
Go to a nightclub or bar	◯	◯	◯	◯	◯
Go to a concert or play	◯	◯	◯	◯	◯
Make or fix things around the house	◯	◯	◯	◯	◯
Go camping or hiking	◯	◯	◯	◯	◯

Thinking now about museums of all kinds, including small local museums as well as big museums in Australia and overseas…

2. **Which of the following statements best describes you personally in relation to museums?**
   - ◯ I keep an eye out for special activities at museums and go when they interest me
   - ◯ I go generally to see what is there; I don't go to special exhibits or activities
   - ◯ I am not really interested in museums and I don't go very often at all

3. **How well do you know the following museums?**

	Know a lot about it	Know a little about it	Only know the name	Have not heard of it	Not sure
Queensland Museum at South Bank, Brisbane	◯	◯	◯	◯	◯
Cobb and Co Museum in Toowoomba	◯	◯	◯	◯	◯
Workshops Rail Museum in Ipswich	◯	◯	◯	◯	◯
Museum of Tropical Queensland in Townsville	◯	◯	◯	◯	◯

4. **When was the last time, if ever, that you personally visited each of the following museums?**

	In last 6 mon ths	6 mon ths to a year	More than a year ago	Never	Don't know
Queensland Museum at South Bank, Brisbane	◯	◯	◯	◯	◯
Cobb and Co Museum in Toowoomba	◯	◯	◯	◯	◯
Workshops Rail Museum in Ipswich	◯	◯	◯	◯	◯
Museum of Tropical Queensland in Townsville	◯	◯	◯	◯	◯

4.d **Which museum have you visited most recently?**

- ◯ Queensland Museum at South Bank, Brisbane
- ◯ Cobb and Co Museum in Toowoomba
- ◯ Workshops Rail Museum in Ipswich
- ◯ Museum of Tropical Queensland in Townsville

5. **What was the purpose of your most recent visit to Queensland Museum at South Bank, Brisbane?**

- ◯ To see a particular exhibit
- ◯ To see the museum in general
- ◯ To take a child or children
- ◯ To accompany other adults
- ◯ To attend a program or event
- ◯ To do some research
- ◯ Other

(SPECIFY)

6. **What was the purpose of your most recent visit to Cobb and Co Museum in Toowoomba?**

- [ ] To see a particular exhibit
- [ ] To see the museum in general
- [ ] To take a child or children
- [ ] To accompany other adults
- [ ] To attend a program or event
- [ ] To do some research
- [ ] Other

(SPECIFY)

7. **What was the purpose of your most recent visit to Workshops Rail Museum in Ipswich?**

- [ ] To see a particular exhibit
- [ ] To see the museum in general
- [ ] To take a child or children
- [ ] To accompany other adults
- [ ] To attend a program or event
- [ ] To do some research
- [ ] Other

(SPECIFY)

8. **What was the purpose of your most recent visit to Museum of Tropical Queensland in Townsville?**

- [ ] To see a particular exhibit
- [ ] To see the museum in general
- [ ] To take a child or children
- [ ] To accompany other adults
- [ ] To attend a program or event
- [ ] To do some research
- [ ] Other

(SPECIFY)

9. **Thinking about your most recent visit to Queensland Museum at South Bank, Brisbane, to what extent did your visit give you the following experiences.**

	Very much	A little	None	Don't know
Connection with stories of other people's lives and achievements				
A sense of spiritual dimensions				
New understanding of scientific or technical concepts				
An experience of real beauty				
Authentic experience of things that are real and not fake				
Appreciation for the monetary value of some objects on display				
Inspiration to make something yourself				
An appreciation of historic events				
Pleasure and enjoyment of a stimulating visit				

10. **Thinking about your most recent visit to Cobb and Co Museum in Toowoomba, to what extent did your visit give you the following experiences.**

	Very much	A little	Not at all	Don't know
Connection with stories of other people's lives and achievements				
A sense of spiritual dimensions				
New understanding of scientific or technical concepts				
An experience of real beauty				
Authentic experience of things that are real and not fake				
Appreciation for the monetary value of some objects on display				
Inspiration to make something yourself				
An appreciation of historic events				
Pleasure and enjoyment of a stimulating visit				

11. **Thinking about your most recent visit to Workshops Rail Museum in Ipswich, to what extent did your visit give you the following experiences.**

	Very much	A little	Not at all	Don't know
Connection with stories of other people's lives and achievements	○	○	○	○
A sense of spiritual dimensions	○	○	○	○
New understanding of scientific or technical concepts	○	○	○	○
An experience of real beauty	○	○	○	○
Authentic experience of things that are real and not fake	○	○	○	○
Appreciation for the monetary value of some objects on display	○	○	○	○
Inspiration to make something yourself	○	○	○	○
An appreciation of historic events	○	○	○	○
Pleasure and enjoyment of a stimulating visit	○	○	○	○

12. **Thinking about your most recent visit to Museum of Tropical Queensland in Townsville, to what extent did your visit give you the following experiences.**

	Very much	A little	Not at all	Don't know
Connection with stories of other people's lives and achievements	○	○	○	○
A sense of spiritual dimensions	○	○	○	○
New understanding of scientific or technical concepts	○	○	○	○
An experience of real beauty	○	○	○	○
Authentic experience of things that are real and not fake	○	○	○	○
Appreciation for the monetary value of some objects on display	○	○	○	○
Inspiration to make something yourself	○	○	○	○
An appreciation of historic events	○	○	○	○
Pleasure and enjoyment of a stimulating visit	○	○	○	○

13. **Thinking now about learning things. Different people learn things in different ways. Thinking about your most recent visit to Queensland Museum at South Bank, Brisbane, please say whether or not you had each of the following experiences.**

	Yes/somewhat	No/not really	Don't know
I discovered new things that I didn't know before	○	○	○
I learnt more about things I already knew about	○	○	○
I remembered things I hadn't thought of for a while	○	○	○
I shared some of my knowledge with other people	○	○	○
I got curious about finding out more about some things	○	○	○
I was reminded of the importance of some issues	○	○	○
I was surprised by some of the things I discovered	○	○	○
I discovered a new perspective on things I already knew about	○	○	○
Some of the things I learnt will be very useful to me	○	○	○

14. **Thinking now about learning things. Different people learn things in different ways. Thinking about your most recent visit to Coob and Co Museum in Toowoomba, please say whether or not you had each of the following experiences.**

	Yes/somewhat	No/not really	Don't know
I discovered new things that I didn't know before	○	○	○
I learnt more about things I already knew about	○	○	○
I remembered things I hadn't thought of for a while	○	○	○
I shared some of my knowledge with other people	○	○	○
I got curious about finding out more about some things	○	○	○
I was reminded of the importance of some issues	○	○	○
I was surprised by some of the things I discovered	○	○	○
I discovered a new perspective on things I already knew about	○	○	○
Some of the things I learnt will be very useful to me	○	○	○

15. **Thinking now about learning things. Different people learn things in different ways. Thinking about your most recent visit to Workshops Rail Museum in Ipswich, please say whether or not you had each of the following experiences.**

	Yes/somewhat	No/not really	Don't know
I discovered new things that I didn't know before			
I learnt more about things I already knew about			
I remembered things I hadn't thought of for a while			
I shared some of my knowledge with other people			
I got curious about finding out more about some things			
I was reminded of the importance of some issues			
I was surprised by some of the things I discovered			
I discovered a new perspective on things I already knew about			
Some of the things I learnt will be very useful to me			

16. **Thinking now about learning things. Different people learn things in different ways. Thinking about your most recent visit to Museum of Tropical Queensland in Townsville, please say whether or not you had each of the following experiences.**

	Yes/somewhat	No/not really	Don't know
I discovered new things that I didn't know before			
I learnt more about things I already knew about			
I remembered things I hadn't thought of for a while			
I shared some of my knowledge with other people			
I got curious about finding out more about some things			
I was reminded of the importance of some issues			
I was surprised by some of the things I discovered			
I discovered a new perspective on things I already knew about			
Some of the things I learnt will be very useful to me			

17. **When was the last time, if ever, that you personally visited the WEBSITE for each of the following:**

	In last 6 mon ths	6 mon ths to a year	More than a year ago	Never	Don't know
Queensland Museum at South Bank, Brisbane	○	○	○	○	○
Cobb and Co Museum in Toowoomba	○	○	○	○	○
Workshops Rail Museum at Ipswich	○	○	○	○	○
Museum of Tropical Queensland in Townsville	○	○	○	○	○
Main website for the Queensland Museum organisation	○	○	○	○	○

17.e **Which WEBSITE have you visited most recently?**

- ○ Queensland Museum at South Bank, Brisbane
- ○ Cobb and Co Museum in Toowoomba
- ○ Workshops Rail Museum at Ipswich
- ○ Museum of Tropical Queensland in Townsville
- ○ Main website for the Queensland Museum organisation

18. **What was the purpose of your last visit to Queensland Museum at South Bank, Brisbane website?**

- ☐ To make a booking
- ☐ To plan a visit to the Museum
- ☐ To follow up a visit to the Museum
- ☐ To find information about a topic
- ☐ To contact the Museum
- ☐ No specific purpose, just browsing
- ☐ Other

Other **(SPECIFY)**

19. **What was the purpose of your last visit to Cobb and Co Museum in Toowoomba website?**

- ☐ To make a booking
- ☐ To plan a visit to the Museum
- ☐ To follow up a visit to the Museum
- ☐ To find information about a topic
- ☐ To contact the Museum
- ☐ No specific purpose, just browsing
- ☐ Other

Other ***(SPECIFY)***

20. **What was the purpose of your last visit to Workshops Rail Museum at Ipswich website?**

- ☐ To make a booking
- ☐ To plan a visit to the Museum
- ☐ To follow up a visit to the Museum
- ☐ To find information about a topic
- ☐ To contact the Museum
- ☐ No specific purpose, just browsing
- ☐ Other

Other **(SPECIFY)**

21. **What was the purpose of your last visit to Museum of Tropical Queensland in Townsville website?**

- ☐ To make a booking
- ☐ To plan a visit to the Museum
- ☐ To follow up a visit to the Museum
- ☐ To find information about a topic
- ☐ To contact the Museum
- ☐ No specific purpose, just browsing
- ☐ Other

Other **(SPECIFY)**

22. **What was the purpose of your last visit to Main website for the Queensland Museum organisation?**

- ☐ To make a booking
- ☐ To plan a visit to the Museum
- ☐ To follow up a visit to the Museum
- ☐ To find information about a topic
- ☐ To contact the Museum
- ☐ No specific purpose, just browsing
- ☐ Other

Other **(SPECIFY)**

23. **How well do you know the following services provided by the Queensland Museum?**

	Know a lot about it	**Know a little about it**	**Only know the name**	**Have not heard of it**	**Not sure**
Museum Development Officers who offer expertise to regional museums	○	○	○	○	○
Historical research	○	○	○	○	○
Education Kits for Schools	○	○	○	○	○
Inquiry Centre where people can ask a scientist a question	○	○	○	○	○
Publication of books and pocket guides	○	○	○	○	○
Scientific research	○	○	○	○	○

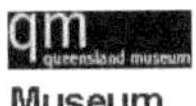

About the Queensland Museum

The Queensland Museum carries out scientific and historical research projects across the State and provides outreach services for small museums statewide. Venues throughout Queensland include:

- Queensland Museum South Bank in Brisbane
- Cobb+Co Museum in Toowoomba
- The Workshops Rail Museum in Ipswich
- Museum of Tropical Queensland in Townsville

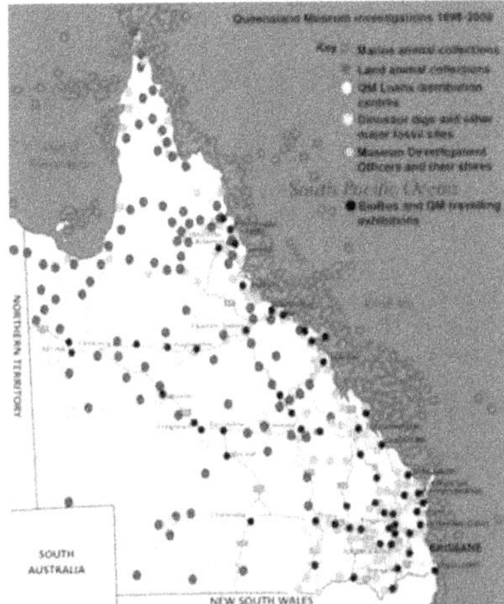

The Museum is the official custodian of Queensland's animal species and cultural & social history. It collects and studies many thousands of objects and specimens that tell the changing story of the State.

Researchers working on Museum collections have helped to protect endangered species, discovered new compounds for drugs and provided information to better understand our changing environment.

Its website and publications help distribute this information to Queenslanders.

24. **To what extent do you agree with the following statements about the Queensland Museum?**

	Stro ngly agre e	Agre e	Neit her	Disa gree	Stro ngly disa gree	Don' t kn ow
The Queensland Museum does important things for the people of Queensland	◌	◌	◌	◌	◌	◌
The Queensland Museum is not relevant to me and probably never will be	◌	◌	◌	◌	◌	◌
In the future, I might want to visit one of the museums or use one of the services of Queensland Museum	◌	◌	◌	◌	◌	◌
In years to come, people will think that the Queensland Museum achieved very little	◌	◌	◌	◌	◌	◌
I get personal benefit from things the Queensland Museum does	◌	◌	◌	◌	◌	◌
The Queensland Museum will leave an important legacy to future generations	◌	◌	◌	◌	◌	◌

The Queensland Museum is partly funded by revenue earned by the Museum. The remainder of the money comes from the State Government. In 2007, State Government funding for the Queensland Museum and all its operations was $19.5 million, which amounts to $6.50 per Queensland adult per year.

25. **In general terms, would you be in favour of:**

- ◌ Increasing the funds for the Queensland Museum
- ◌ Keeping the funds at the present level for the Queensland Museum
- ◌ Reducing the funds for the Queensland Museum

26. **You say that you are in favour of increasing the funds for the Queensland Museum. Would you prefer:**

- ◌ The funds to come from reducing the funding of some other service
- ◌ The funds to come from a tax increase

On average, the amount of state funding that goes to the Museum of Queensland each year amounts to $6.50 per Queensland adult per year.

27. **Would you be in favour of increasing the current funding to the Queensland Museum by an additional $4 per Queensland adult.**

- ◌ Yes
- ◌ No

28. **You said you favour increasing museum funding by reducing the funding of some other government service. Which ONE of the following services would you prefer to see reduced in order to increase funding to the Museum of Queensland?**

- Health (24 new hospital beds)
- Education (32 classrooms)
- Prison (16 new prison beds)
- Tourism ($12 million tourism promotion)
- Transport infrastructure (20 km new roads)

On average, the amount of state funding that goes to the Museum of Queensland each year amounts to $6.50 per Queensland adult per year.

29. **Would you be in favour of decreasing the funding to the Queensland Museum by $4 per Queensland adult.**

- Yes
- No

So that the Queensland Museum can carry out its mission to enrich Queensland communities, it is planning a number of major developments worth $24 million over the next five-seven years.

These developments will provide better access to collections and research via new displays, innovative learning programs and services and more user-friendly facilities.

Developments include:

□ **The redevelopment of Queensland Museum South Bank to manage public overcrowding and access issues, and update current displays and programs to showcase more of the Museum's collection and research.**
□ **The National Carriage Factory at Cobb+Co Museum, featuring new exhibition and community spaces alongside a unique demonstration and training site for rare heritage trades such as blacksmithing**
□ ***Bug Safari* at the Museum of Tropical Queensland, providing an interactive learning experience featuring live insects and exhibits that showcase the Museum's unique collection.**
□ **Further development of The Workshops Rail Museum site providing enhanced access to the North Ipswich Railyard history and heritage, community spaces and public learning opportunities.**
□ **The development of a virtual museum to give people worldwide online access to Museum collections and research.**

To achieve this vision the Queensland Museum will require more funding and we are seeking your input in identifying how valuable or otherwise these new developments will be.

30. **In general terms would you be in favour of -**

- Increasing the funds for the Queensland Museum to provide more services
- Keeping the funds at the present level and not undertaking additional development

31. **You say that you are in favour of increasing the funds for the Queensland Museum. Would you prefer:**

- The funds to come from reducing the funding of some other government service
- The funds to come from a tax increase

32. **Would you be in favour of increasing the funding to the Queensland Museum through a once-only levy of $6 per Queensland adult. This would provide $12 million towards the new facilities and services described above.**

- Yes
- No

33. **You said you favour increasing museum funding by reducing the funding of some other government service. Which ONE of the following services would you prefer to see reduced in order to increase funding to the Queensland Museum?**

- Health (36 new hospital beds)
- Education (48 classrooms)
- Prison (24 new prison beds)
- Tourism ($18 million tourism promotion)
- Transport infrastructure (30 km new roads)

34. **You said you are not in favour of increasing the funds to the Queensland Museum. What is your main reason for saying this?**

- The Museum gets enough funds at the moment
- I value the Museum, but I personally cannot afford/do not want to pay more
- I value the Museum, but other services are more important
- I don't value the Museum enough to give it more funds
- I don't know enough about it to decide
- Other

Other reason (write in)

Finally, some details about you.

35. **Which language do you mostly speak at home?**

[ ]

36. **For each of the following statements, please tell me if you agree or disagree that it describes you personally.**

	Agree	Disagree	Don't know
I am very fashion conscious	○	○	○
I want to achieve a lot	○	○	○
I am really a homebody	○	○	○
I hate getting dressed up	○	○	○
I like to garden and potter around the house at weekends	○	○	○
I would rather watch TV on Saturday night than go out	○	○	○
I thrive on the company of other people	○	○	○
I am interested in abstract ideas	○	○	○
I would rather have a BBQ with friends than eat out at a restaurant	○	○	○

37. **In which year were you born?**

[ ]

38. **Are there any children aged 0-12 years in your home?**

- ○ Yes
- ○ No

39. **Are there any children aged 13-18 years in your home?**

- ○ Yes
- ○ No

40. **Which of the following describes you best?**

- ○ Working full time (35+ hours a week)
- ○ Working part time
- ○ Looking for work
- ○ Home duties full time
- ○ Student
- ○ Retired

41. **What is your highest educational level?**

- Primary/High school
- Trade/technical/business college
- University - Undergraduate degree
- University - Postgraduate degree

42. **Gender**

- Male
- Female

43. **Are you, or a member of your close family, associated with any museums or the cultural industry as employees, volunteers, consultants etc?**

- Yes
- No

44. **Final comments:**

To submit your response, please click on the Submit button below.

This screen will close once your response has been successfully submitted. This may take up to 1 minute, so please do not re-click the submit button or exit the survey during this time.

Thank you for your co-operation. We assure you that your answers are used for statistical purposes only and cannot be identified back to you.

If you have any queries or concerns about this survey, please contact the McNair Ingenuity Research respondent enquiry line on (freecall) 1800 669 133.

Thank you for your time you do not qualify to take part in this survey this time. Please try our next survey.

Appendix Two

Probit Regression (Environmetrics & Ingenuity, 2009, pp34-34).

For both probit regressions, the model is

$$P(\text{Voting yes}) = \Phi(X\beta + \varepsilon)$$

where X contains the dollar amounts of the proposed funding increase and a vector of ones, ε is normally distributed with an unknown variance, and Φ is the cdf of the normal distribution. This model can be fitted using numerical likelihood maximisation.

For the first model, the dependent variable is the probability of supporting a funding increase or decrease; the results are as follows:

Independent variable	Coefficient	Standard error
Dollar amount of funding change	−1.4	0.03
Constant	1.8	0.11

The coefficient on the dollar amount is significant, and has the correct sign. The X^2 statistic for the model is 31.2, which is well above the critical value.

For the second model, the dependent variable is the probability of supporting a tax increase to fund new development; the results are as follows:

Independent variable	Coefficient	Standard error
Dollar amount of tax change	−0.10	0.01
Constant	1.6	0.11

The coefficient on the dollar amount is significant, and has the correct sign. The X^2 statistic for the model is 61.5.

The mean WTP estimates were obtained by numerically estimating the following integral:

$$E(WTP) = \int_{-\infty}^{\infty} x \cdot P(x)dx$$

where x is a dollar amount, and P(x) is the probability that the average person's WTP is less than or equal to x. The value of P(x) for each dollar amount is given by the estimated probit model. For the estimates of the conservative lower bound WTP, we used coefficients that were two standard deviations away from the best estimates, in whatever direction favoured a lower amount.

In estimating the WTP for new developments, we used an unconstrained probit regression for the sake of simplicity. The estimated distribution has about 5% of its mass on WTP values less than zero. Strictly speaking, this effect contradicts our assumption about the minimum WTP, but is small enough not to matter. In particular, given the estimated slope, it does not affect the estimate of the mean WTP.

The scaled-up estimates for the Queensland population used an estimate of the number of adults in Queensland at June 2008 (3,176,068) from ABS cat. 3201.0, and an estimate of the number of households in Queensland (1,627,600) from ABS cat. 3236.0, table 6.19.

Appendix Three

Brief descriptions of the psychographic segments

After extensive research through the 1990's, Environmetrics developed a set of psychographic groupings into which the population can be divided. The groupings are based on the way in which people answer a set of self-description questions.

The nine groups are derived from statistical modelling such that the profile of answers within any group is more similar than is the profile across groups. On average, the groups differ in the kinds of leisure activities they enjoy and, our research has shown, in their responses to cultural institutions (Environmetrics & Ingenuity, 2009, pp36-39).

Practical and organised

Achievement oriented in terms of home projects (will garden and potter).

Enjoy building and making things. Like routine and have an organised approach to life - will write lists of things to do and approach them methodically. Would rather have a BBQ than eat at a restaurant, and would watch TV on a Saturday night rather than go out.

A strong emphasis on their family and immediate residential surroundings. The home and the local neighbourhood are the focal points for much of their life.

Become a museum audience when it is of benefit to their children.

Gregarious, Out and About

Very fashion conscious and like getting dressed up. Like to stand out in a crowd, but also like to feel part of the social group. They enjoy indulging themselves and like to experiment with new things. Want to get somewhere in life: job, money, and material possessions.

Life for them has a strong social component. They measure their own achievements and status against their peers. Very conscious of what is 'in', yet are more likely to be trend followers than setters. Quick to adopt new fashions and ideas, but also quick to move onto the next one.

Attend events to be "where the action is"—indeed they tend to think that they are the action.

Individualistic, Out and About

Also very achievement and socially oriented, but without the fashion consciousness of their Gregarious counterparts. However, still like to get dressed up now and then and will make their presence felt in a crowd.

Like to feel they are different to everyone else. They don't feel they are guided by the latest trends and fashions (although in fact they may be). Generally appreciate life on a more 'cerebral' level. They like to be challenged and to learn and they look for originality in the world around them.

Can be an important part of the repeat audience in museums and galleries if the content interests them.

Moderate and unhurried

Consider themselves to be 'homebodies'. Like to garden and potter around the house. They don't say they want to 'achieve a lot', probably because they tend to be older and are reasonably set in their ways. However, they are content with what they have and still want to enjoy themselves.

They enjoy company, but are also happy being alone. Will watch TV on a Saturday night rather than go out. They do not have extravagant taste. They have a relaxed attitude to life and enjoy comfortable surroundings and the pleasures brought from extended family and friends.

Tend to husband their resources and only come to museums when there is something of an international blockbuster in town. On those occasions, they can be a significant portion of the audience.

Discerning and purposeful

Achievement oriented, enjoy company and appreciate some of the finer things in life. Although they like to potter at home, they wouldn't call themselves a 'homebody'. Like a challenge and are interested in ideas and education.

They enjoy having people around them whether family or friends. Although they like to get out on a Saturday night, having people over for dinner or a BBQ is also a pleasurable pastime for them.

Their strong sense of individualism means they may buy or participate in 'fashionable' things, but they would like to think that their decision to do so is based on good judgment, rather than an urge to follow trends.

They tend to be ABC listeners/viewers and broadsheet readers. Consistent museum patrons and tend to be represented amongst "friends" groups. Likely to use museum resources and libraries for their own research.

Battlers

Battlers claim they have little interest in achievement or experiencing anything new. They claim that they generally 'get by' in life. While they may want more, they perhaps can't see themselves getting much more or are content enough with what they have. They tend to express what they see as the real Australian values – hence "battlers". Many of them are, in fact both wealthy and successful despite protesting that they are just ordinary blokes. John Singleton, Gerry Harvey and Alan Jones might well fit the profile.

They don't like getting dressed up and are not very social in the "interested to meet a lot of new people" sense. Life is focused on their home, circle of friends and specific sporting interests at whatever socioeconomic level they operate within.

Conventional suburban

Call themselves a "homebody", but don't necessarily engage in the more energetic home activities such as gardening or making and fixing things. But they are achievement oriented, possibly on a more material level. They want to get ahead with their job, their income and their lifestyle. They may aspire to a McMansion and a six-cylinder car with a speedboat attached.

They will take an interest in the family and enjoy a BBQ with friends, but also like to get out on a Saturday night.

They are not very interested in abstract ideas and prefer to deal with things that they can see and touch. Given the choice, WRM would probably be more appealing to them than an exhibition on biodiversity (unless it improved their fishing).

Self-contained, go with the flow

While they do enjoy the company of family and friends, this segment doesn't necessarily need company to have a good time. They consider themselves 'homebodies' and enjoy pottering around the house and gardening. They have time on their hands and enjoy some of the simple pleasures of life (reading, walking, cooking). They are 'wanderers' who appreciate and absorb the world gradually. Their hobbies can include painting and music.

They do say they 'want to achieve a lot' and they will try something new, but usually because someone else has recommended it. They enjoy participating in one or two activities that deeply interest them and will persist with an interest over time.

This is why they are often found as volunteer guides in galleries, museums and botanic gardens.

Social pleasure seekers

The group most interested in 'fashion'. Enjoy indulging themselves and like to have other people around (and preferably, like to make their presence felt when in a crowd). Like to potter, but want to get dressed up and either go out with friends or entertain at home. Enjoy going to places to be seen.

They are quite aspirational in their outlook to life - they may be happy with what they have, but are still trying to better themselves and their surroundings. Material acquisitions are often seen as the best way to do this.

They tend also to be "acquisitional tourists" and will travel to see a blockbuster to be able to say they were there. The object they buy in the museum shop will be more important to them than those on display.

References

Environmetrics & Ingenuity, 2009, pp36-39

References

Aabo, S. (2005). Are Public Libraries Worth their Price? A Contingent Valuation Study of Norwegian Public Libraries. *New Library World, 106*(11/12), 487-495.

Accenture. (2006, 25-26 January). *Capturing the public value of heritage: looking beyond the numbers.* Paper presented at the Capturing the Public Value of Heritage, London.

Alberini, A., & Kahn, J. (2006). *Handbook on Contingent Valuation.* Cheltenham, UK: Edward Elgar.

Alexander, E., P., & Alexander, m. (2008). *Museums in Motion: An Introduction to the History and Functions of Museums 2nd ed.* Lanham: AltaMira Press.

Allison, M., & Coalter, F. (2001). Realising the Potential of Cultural Services: the Case for Museums (pp. 1-48). London: Local Government Association.

American Association of Museums. What is a Museum? Retrieved 8 August, 2010, from http://www.aam-us.org/aboutmuseums/whatis.cfm?

American Association of Museums. (2002). *Mastering Civic Engagement: A Challenge to Museums.* Washington DC: American Association of Museums.

Anacostia Community Museum. (2011). Mission and History Retrieved 10 January 2011, from http://anacostia.si.edu/Museum/Mission_History.htm

Anderson, D. (1999). A Common Wealth: Museums in the Learning Age. In Department of Culture Media and Sport (Ed.).

Anderson, G. (Ed.). (2000). *Museum Mission Statements: Building a Distinct Identity*. Washington DC: American Association of Museums.

Anderson, G. (Ed.). (2004). *Reinventing the Museum: Historical and Contemporary Perspectives on the Paradigm Shift*. Walnut Creek: AltaMira Press.

Anderson, M. (Ed.). (1993). *Museums Australia Journal Vols 2-3, 1991-1992*. South Melbourne: Museums Association of Australia.

Anderson, M., & Reeves, A. (1994). Contested Identities: Museums and the Nation in Australia. In F. E. S. Kaplan (Ed.), *Museums and the Making of "Ourselves": The Role of Objects in National Identity* (pp. 79-124). London: Leicester University Press.

Anderson, R. G. W. (1998). is Charging Economic? *Journal of Cultural Economics, 22*, 179-187.

Andrew, C., Gattinger, M., Jeannotte, M. S., & Straw, W. (Eds.). (2005). *Accounting for Culture: Thinking Through Cultural Citizenship*. Ottawa: The University of Ottawa Press.

Archibald, R. R. (1999). *A Place to Remember: Using History to Build Community*. Walnut Creek: AltaMira.

Archibald, R. R. (2004). *The New Town Square: Museums and Communities in Transition*. Walnut Creek: AltaMira Press.

Archibald, R. R. (2006). Real Places in a Virtual World: Museum *of* the City Verses Museum *Representing* the City. *Museum International, 58*(3), 8-14.

Arrow, K., Solow, R., Learner, E., Portney, P., Randner, R., & Schuman, H. (1993). NOAA Panel Report on Contingent Valuation. *National Oceanic and Atmospheric Administration, Federal Register, 58*(10), 4601-4614.

Arts Queensland. (1997). *Queensland Cultural Tourism Strategy: A Framework for Development,*. Brisbane.

Arts Queensland. (2002). Creative Queensland: The Queensland Government Cultural Policy 2002. Brisbane: Queensland Government Arts Queensland.

Arts Queensland. (2007). Queensland Arts industry Creative Communities Sector Development Plan 2007-2009: Queensland Government Arts Queensland.

Arts Queensland. (2009). *Artbeat: Regional Arts and Culture Strategy 2010-2014*. Queensland Government.

Ashoka (Producer). (2006, 4/11/2006). Ashoka: Innovators for the Public. Retrieved from http://www.ashoka.org/social _entrepreneur

Ashworth, G. J., & Graham, B. (Eds.). (2005). *Senses of Place: Senses of Time*. Aldershot: Ashgate.

Ashworth, G. J., & Larkham, P. J. (Eds.). (1994). *Building a New Heritage - Tourism, Culture and Identity in the New Europe*. London: Routledge.

Ashworth, J., & Johnson, P. (1996). Sources of "Value for Money" for Museum Visitors: Some Survey Evidence. *Journal of Cultural Economics, 20*, 67-83.

Australia Council for the Arts. (2005). Australia Council for the Arts Creative Innovation Strategy. Canberra: Australia Council for the Arts and Australian Government.

Australian Bureau of Statistics. (2008). Arts and Cultural Heritage - An Information Development Plan *cat no 4915.0*. Canberra: ABS.

Australian Expert Group in Industries Studies, & Cultural Ministers Council Statistics Working Group. (2004). Social Impacts of Participation in the Arts and Cultural Industries, Stage Two Report. Canberra: Department of Communications, Technology and the Arts.

Bailey, S., & Falconer, P. (1998). Charging for Admission to Museums and Galleries: A framework for Analysing the Impact on Access. *Journal of Cultural Economics, 22*, 167-177.

Bakhshi, H., & Throsby, D. (2010). Culture of Innovation: An Economic Analysis of Innovation in Arts and Cultural Organisations: National Endowment for Science, Technology and the Arts.

Baniotopoulou, E. (2000). Art for Whose Sake? Modern Art Museums and their Role in Transforming Societies: The Case of the Guggenheim Bilbao. *Journal of Conservation and Museum Studies*(7), 1-15.

Barrett, R. (1998). *Liberating the Corporate Soul: Building a Visionary Organisation*. Boston: Butterworth-Heinemann.

Bartholomai, A. (1991). Improving Access to Museum Services in Queensland. *Memoirs of the Queensland Museum, 30*(3), 355-372.

Bartholomai, A. (2005). *Cobb+Co Museum Historical Information*. typed transcript from QM Board Meeting Minutes and annotiations. Queensland Museum.

Batty, P. (2003). *Governing Cultural Difference*. PhD, University of South Australia, Adelaide.

Baumol, W. (2003). Applied Welfare Economics. In R. Towse (Ed.), *A Handbook of Cultural Economics* (pp. 20-31). Cheltenham, UK: Edward Elgar.

Baumol, W., & Bowen, W. (1966). *Performing Arts: The Economic Dilemma*. New York: Twentieth Century Fund.

Belfiore, E. (2002). Arts as a means of Alleviating Social Exclusion: Does it Really Work? A Critique of Instrumental Cultural Policies and Social Impact Studies in the UK. *International Journal of Cultural Policy, 8*(1), 91-106.

Belfiore, E., & Bennett, O. (2007). Rethinking the Social Impacts of the Arts. *International Journal of Cultural Policy, 13*(2), 135-151.

Bennett, T. (1995a). *The Birth of the Museum: History, Theory, Politics*. London: Routledge.

Bennett, T. (1995b, 16-19 March). *That Those Who Run May Read: Museums and Barriers to Access*. Paper presented at the Towards 2000: Evaluation and Visitor Research in Museums, Sydney.

Bennett, T. (2004). *Pasts Beyond Memory: Evolution, Museums, Colonialism*. London: Routledge.

Bennett, T., Emmison, M., & Frow, J. (1999). *Accounting for Tastes; Australian Everyday Cultures*. Cambridge: Cambridge University Press.

Bennett, T., Trotter, R., & McAlear, D. (Eds.). (1996). *Museums and Citizenship: A Resource Book: Memoirs of the Queensland Museum* (Vol. 39:1). Brisbane: Queensland Museum.

Bergdahl, E. (2005). *Ecomuseums in Sweden*. Paper presented at the Communication and Exploration Conference, Guizhou, China.

Bickford, A. (2010). Review of Identity and the Museum Visitor Experience. *Curator, 53*(2), 247-255.

Bille, T. (1998). A Contingent Valuation Study of the Royal Theatre in Copenhagen. In S. Navrud & R. C. Ready (Eds.), *Valuing Cultural Heritage: Applying Environmental Valuation Techniques to Historic Bulidings, Monuments and Artifacts*. Cheltenham: Edward Elgar.

Billie Hansen, T. (1995). Measuring the Value of Culture. *The European Journal of Cultural Policy, 1*(2), 309-322.

Bilton, C. (2007). *Management and Creativity: From Creative Industries to Creative Management*. Malden, MA.: Blackwell Publishing.

Bilton, C., & Leary, R. (2002). What Can Managers Do for Creativity? Brokering Creativity in the Creative Industries. *International Journal of Cultural Policy, 8*(1), 49-64.

Blaug, M. (1976a). Rationalising Social Expenditure - The Arts. In M. Blaug (Ed.), *The Economics of the Arts* (pp. 132-147). London: Martin Robertson & Company.

Blaug, M. (2003). Welfare Economics. In R. Towse (Ed.), *A Handbook of Cultural Economics* (pp. 476-481). Cheltenham, UK: Edward Elgar.

Blaug, M. (Ed.). (1976b). *The Economics of the Arts*. London: Martin Robertson & Company.

Blaug, R., Horner, L., & Lekhi, R. (2006a, 25-26 January). *Heritage, Democracy and Public Value*. Paper presented at the Capturing the Public Value of Heritage, London.

Blaug, R., Horner, L., & Lekhi, R. (2006b). Public Value, Politics and Public Management: A Literature Review. London: The Work Foundation.

Board of the Queensland Museum. (2010). Queensland Museum Annual Report 2009-2010. Brisbane: Queensland Museum.

Bohm, P. (1972). Estimating Demand for Public Goods: An Experiment. *European Economic Review, 3*, 111-130.

Bohm, P. (1979). Estimating Willing to Pay: Why and How? *Scandinavian Journal of Economics, 81*, 143-153.

Bolton, W.R.F. *W.R.F. Bolton Collection*. Cobb+Co Museum.

Boswell, D., & Evans, J. (Eds.). (1999). *Representing the Nation: A Reader: Histories, Heritage and Museums*. London: Routledge.

Bourdieu, P. (1977). *Outline of a Theory of Practice*. Cambridge: Cambridge University Press.

Bourdieu, P. (1990). *In Other Words: Essays Towards a Reflective Sociology*. Cambridge: Polity Press.

Bourdieu, P., & Darbel, A. (1991). *The Love of Art; European Art Museums and Their Public*. Cambridge: Polity Press.

Boylan, P. J. (2006). Museums: Targets or Instruments of Cultural Policies? *Museum International, 58*(4), 8-12.

Boylan, P. J. (Ed.). (2004). *Running a Museum: A Practical Handbook*. Paris: International Council of Museums (ICOM).

Brown, J. (2008, 31 August). Music to Glasgow's Ears, *Sunday Canberra Times*, p. 28.

Bunting, C. (2007). Public Value and the Arts in England: Discussion and Conclusions of the Arts Debate. London: Arts Council England.

Burton, C., & Scott, C. (2003). Museums: Challenges for the 21st Century. *International Journal of Arts Management, 5*(2), 56-68.

Cameron, C. (2006, 25-26 January). *Value and Integrity in Cultural and Natural Heritage: from Parks Canada to World Heritage*. Paper presented at the Capturing the Public Value of Heritage, London.

Canadian Heritage. (2003). Economic Benefits - The Canadian Museum of Civilization - A Case Study Retrieved 2008-07-21, from http://www.patrimoinecanadien.gc.ca/progs/ph/pubs/mcc-cmc/oo_e.cfn

Carey, J. (2006). *What Good Are the Arts*. Oxford: Oxford University Press.

Carmody, K. Biography Retrieved 23 February, 2010, from http://www.kevcarmody.com.au/biography.html

Carson, R., Flores, N., & Meade, N. (2001). Contingent Valuation: Controversies and Evidence. *Environmental and Resource Economics, 19*, 173-210.

Carson, R., & Mitchell, R. (1993). The Issue of Scope in Contingent Valuation Studies. *American Journal of Agricultural Economics, 75*(5), 1263-1268.

Catterall, S. (2005). Public History Review Essay. "Otherness" Plus the Three Cs Minus Orwell: "The Wigan Pier Experience". *Labour history Review, 70*(1), 102-110.

Caves, R. (2000). *Creative Industries: Contracts between Arts and Commerce*. Cambridge: Harvard University Press.

Champ, P. A., & Welsh, M. P. (2006). Survey Methodologies for Stated Choice Studies. In B. Kanninen, J. (Ed.), *Valuing Environmental Amenities Using Stated Choice Studies* (pp. 21-42). Dordrecht, The Netherlands: Springer.

Choi, A. S., Papandrea, F., & Bennett, J. (2006). Valuing Australian Cultural Institutions: Developing a Cultural Worldview Scale *Crawford School of Economics and Governement* Canberra: Australian National University.

Choi, A. S., Papandrea, F., & Bennett, J. (2007). Assessing Cultural Values: Developing an Attitudinal Scale. *Journal of Cultural Economics, 31*, 311-335.

Chung, J., Wilkening, S., & Johnstone, S. (2008). Museums & Society 2034: Trends and Potential Futures: Center for the Future of Museums, American Association of Museums.

Clark, K. (2006, 25-26 January). *Capturing the Public Value of Heritage.* Paper presented at the Capturing the Public Value of Heritage: The Proceedings of the London Conference, London.

Coalter, F. (2001). Realising the Potential of Cultural Services: The Case for the Arts. London: Local Government Association.

Cobb+Co Museum. (1988-2009). Year in Review. Toowoomba: Cobb+Co Museum.

Cobb+Co Museum. (1988-2010). Cobb+Co Museum Advisory Committee Minutes. Toowoomba: Cobb+Co Museum.

Cobb+Co Museum. (2001). Partnership Contract with Toowoomba City Council. Toowoomba.

Cobb+Co Museum. (2005-2006). National Carriage Factory Appeal Planning Committee Minutes. Toowoomba: Cobb+Co Museum.

Cobb+Co Museum. (2006). History Is In Your Hands: Rebuilding the Legend: National Carriage Factory Campaign. Toowoomba: Cobb+Co Museum.

Cobb+Co Museum. (2010). Year in Review 2009-10. Toowoomba: Cobb+Co Museum.

Cobb+Co Museum, & Southern Queensland Institute of TAFE. (2008). Heritage is in Our Hands: A Review of Heritage Trade Training. Toowoomba: Cobb+Co Museum, Southern Queensland Institute of TAFE

Cogo, M. (2005). *Ecomuseums of the Autonomous Provincial Authority of Trento, Italy.* Paper presented at the Communication and Exploration Conference, Guizhou, China.

Collins, J. (2005). *Good to Great and the Social Sectors: Why Business Thinking is Not the Answer.* Boulder Colorado: Jim Collins.

Colp-Hansbury, C. (2009). *Revitalizing a Community: The Potential of a Local Museum in the Public* Doctor of Philosophy, Arizona State University.

Committee of Inquiry into the National Estate. (1974). Report of the National Estate. Canberra: Commonwealth of Australia.

Conwill, K. H., & Roosa, A. M. (2003). Cultivating Community Connections. *Museum News, 82*(3), 41-47.

Coopers & Lybrand Consultants. (1996). Cobb+Co Museum- Joint Venture Carriage Building Factory Feasibility Study. Toowoomba: Cobb+Co Museum.

Cowell, B. (2004). Why Heritage Counts: Researching the Historic Environment. *Cultural Trends, 13*(4), 23-39.

Cowling, J. (Ed.). (2004). *For Art's Sake? Society and the Arts in the 21st Century*. London: Institute for Public Policy Research.

Cox, E. (1995). A Truly Civil Society. Sydney: Australian Broadcasting Corporation.

Crang, M. (1999). Nation, Region and Homeland: History and Tradition in Dalarna Sweden. *Ecumene* Retrieved 30 July 2007, from http://eprints.dur.ac.uk/archive/00000059/01/Crang_nation.pdf

Cuccia, T. (2003). Contingent Valuation. In R. Towse (Ed.), *A Handbook of Cultural Economics* (pp. 119-131). Cheltenham, UK: Edward Elgar.

Cummings, N., & Lewandowska, M. (2000). *The Value of Things*. Basel: Birkhauser.

Cunningham, S. (2002). From Cultural to Creative Industries: Theory, Industry, and Policy Implications. *Media International Australia Incorporating Culture and Policy*(102), 54-65.

Cunningham, S. (2005). Creative Enterprises. In J. Hartley (Ed.), *Creative Industries* (pp. 282-298). Malden MA: Blackwell Publishing.

Cunningham, S. (2006). What Price a Creative Economy. *Platform Papers, Currency House, 9*.

Cunningham, S., & Hearn, G. (2003). Brisbane's Creative Industries. Brisbane: QUT and Brisbane City Council.

Dana, J. C. (1917). The Gloom of the Museum. In G. Anderson (Ed.), *Reinventing the Museum: Historical and Contemporary Persperctives on the Paradigm Shift* (pp. 13-29). Walnut Creek: AltaMira Press.

Darnell, A. (1998). Some Simple Analytics of Access and Revenue Targets. *Journal of Cultural Economics, 22*, 189-196.

Darnell, A., Johnson, P., & Thomas, B. (1998). The Demand for Local Authority Museums: Management Issues and Hard Evidence. *Local Government Studies, 24*(4), 77-94.

Davey, G. (1996). The Moe Folklife Project. Canberra: Department of Communication and the Arts and the National library of Australia.

Davies, S. (2005). Museums and their Visitors 1994-2004. *Cultural Trends, 14*(1), 67-105.

Davis, P. (1999). Place Exploration: Museums, Identity, Community. In S. Watson (Ed.), *Museums and Their Communities* (pp. 53-75). London: Routledge.

Davis, P. (2005). Places, 'Cultural Touchstones' and the Ecomuseum. In G. Corsane (Ed.), *Heritage, Museums and Galleries: An Introductory Reader* (pp. 365-376). London: Routledge.

Davis, P. (2007). Ecomuseums and Sustainability in Italy, Japan and China: Concept Adaptation through Implementation. In S. J. Knell, S. MacLeod & S. Watson (Eds.), *Museum Revolutions: How Museums and Changed and Are Changed* (pp. 198-214). London: Routledge.

Davison, G. (1991). The Meaning of "Heritage". In G. Davison & C. McConville (Eds.), *A Heritage Handbook* (pp. 1-13). Sydney: Allen & Unwin.

Davison, G. (1998). *University and Heritage: an Odd Couple?* Paper presented at the Third International Forum UNESCO: University and Heritage, Melbourne and Geelong.

Dayton-Johnson, J., & King, E. (2003). Subsidising Stan: Measuring the Social Benefits of Cultural Spending: Department of Canadian Heritage.

de la Torre, M. (2002). Assessing the Values of Cultural Heritage (pp. 1-117). Los Angeles: The Getty Conservation Institute

de Varine, H. (2005a). *Ecomuseology and Sustainable Development.* Paper presented at the Communication and Exploration, Guizhou, China.

de Varine, H. (2005b). *The Origins of the New Museology Concept and of the Ecomuseum Word and Concept, in the 1960s and the 1970s.* Paper presented at the Communication and Exploration Conference, Guizhou, China.

de Varine, H. (2008). The Museums as a Social Agent of Development. *ICOM News*(1), 5.

Dees, J. G., Emerson, J., & Economy, P. (2001). *Enterprising Nonprofits: A Toolkit for Social Entrepreneurs.* New York: John Wiley & Sons.

Dees, J. G., Emerson, J., & Economy, P. (2002). *Strategic Tools for Social Entrepreneurs: Enhancing the Performance of your Enterprising Nonprofit.* New York: John Wiley & Sons.

Department for Culture Media and Sport. (1988). A New Cultural Framework London: Department of Culture, Media and Sport.

Department for Culture Media and Sport. (1998). Creative Industries Mapping Document. London: DCMS.

Department for Culture Media and Sport. (2005). Understanding the Future: Museums and the 21st Century Life - The Value of Museums (pp. 1-36). London: Department for Culture, Media and Sport.

Department of Finance. (1989). What Price Heritage? The Museum Review and the Measurement of Museum Performance. Canberra: Commonwealth of Australia.

Department of Sustainability and Environment. (2006). Victoria's Heritage: Strengthening our Communities (pp. 1-66). Melbourne: Department of Sustainability and Environment.

Department of the Arts, S., the Environment, Tourism and Territories,. (1990). What Value Heritage? Issues for Discussion. Canberra: Commonwealth of Australia.

Dicks, A. (1999). 'The View of our Town from the Hill': Communities on Display as Local Heritage *International Journal of Cultural Studies, 2*(3), 349-368.

Dicks, A. (2003). Heritage, Governance and Marketization: A Case Study from Wales. *Museum and Society, 1*(1), 30-44.

DiMaggio, P. (1991). The Museum and the Public. In M. Feldstein (Ed.), *The Economics of Art Museums* (pp. 39-50). Chicago: University of Chicago Press.

Dixon, B., Courtenay, A. E., & Bailey, R. (1974). *The Museum and the Canadian Public*: Arts and Cultural Branch, Department of the Secretary of State, Government of Canada by Culturcan Publications.

Doering, Z. D. (1999). *Strangers, Guests or Clients? Visitor Experiences in Museums.* Paper presented at the Managing the Arts: Performance, Financing, Service, Weimar, Germany.

Donghai, S. (2005). *Chinese Ecomuseums: the Path of Development.* Paper presented at the Communication and Exploration, Guizhou, China

Drucker, P. F. (1990). *Managing the Nonprofit Organisation: Principles and Practices.* New York: HarperCollins.

Economics for the Environment Consultancy. (2005). Valuation of the Historic Environment: The Scope for Using Results of Valuation Studies in the Appraisal and Assessment of Heritage-related Projects and Programmes. London: English Heritage, The Heritage Lottery Fund, DCMS and Department of Transport.

Economuseum Network. What is an Economuseum Retrieved 25 August, 2010, from http://www.economusees.com/whatisaneconomuseum.cfm?

Economuseum Network. (2010). Artisans at Work 2010-2011. Quebec.

Edson, G., & Dean, D. (1994). *The Handbook for Museums.* London: Routledge.

Edwards, J. A., Llurdes i Coit, & Carles, J. (1996). Mines and Quarries: Industrial Heritage Tourism. *Annals of Tourism Research, 23*(2), 341-363.

Ellis, A., Bestwick, D., Smith, C. S., Smith, C., Hytner, N., Hewison, R., et al. (2003, 17 June). *Valuing Culture.* Paper presented at the *Valuing Culture* event organised by Demos on partnershipwith the National Gallery, the National Theatre and aeaConsulting, National Theatre Studio London.

Empire Theatres Pty. Ltd. (2010). Empire Theatres Annual Report 2009-10. Toowoomba: Empire Theatres Pty Ltd.

English Heritage. (2005). Heritage Counts: State of the Historic Environment Report 2005.

Environmetrics. (2008a). Queensland Museum Survey - Draft 4.

Environmetrics. (2008b). Queensland Museum Value Study Pilot Report. Brisbane: Queenland Museum.

Environmetrics, & McNair Ingenuity. (2009). Valuing the Queensland Museum. Brisbane: Queensland Museum.

Epstein, R. (2003). The Regrettable Necessarity of Contingent Valuation. *Journal of Cultural Economics, 27*, 259-274.

Evans, G. (2005). Measure for Measure: Evaluating the Evidence of Culture's Contribution to Regeneration. *Urban Studies, 42*(5/6), 959-983.

Falk, J. H. (1998). Visitors: Who does; Who doesn't and Why. *Museum News, 77*(2), 38-43.

Falk, J. H. (1999). Museums as Institutions for Personal Learning. *Daedalus, 128*(3), 259.

Falk, J. H. (2000). Assessing the Impact of Museums. [Editorial note]. *Curator, 43*(1), 5-7.

Falk, J. H. (2006). An Identity-Centered Approach to Understanding Museum Learning. *Curator the Museum Journal, 49*(2), 151-166.

Falk, J. H. (2009). *Identity and the Museum Visitor Experience.* Walnut Creek, California: Left Coast Press.

Falk, J. H., & Dierking, L. (2002). *Lessons Without Limit: How Free-Choice learning is Transforming Education.* Walnut Creek: AltaMira press.

Falk, J. H., Scott, C., Dierking, L., Rennie, L., & Cohen Johes, M. (2004). Interactives and Visitor Learning. *Curator the Museum Journal, 47*(2), 171-198.

Falk, J. H., & Sheppard, B. K. (2006). *Thriving in the Knowledge Age: New Business Models for Museums and Other Cultural Institutions.* Lanham: AltaMira Press.

Ferres, K., Adair, D., Bentley, R., Messenger, C., & Kukucka, S. (2007). Cultural Indicators Research Project: Literature Review Final Report. Brisbane: Griffith University Centre for Public Culture and Ideas.

Fields, J. (2003). *The Craft heritage Trails of Western North Carolina.* Asheville: Handmade in Country.

Fleming, D. (2006). *The Museum as Social Enterprise.* Paper presented at the The First Stephen E Weil Memorial Lecture INTERCOM Annual Meeting, Taipei.

Flew, T. (2005). Creative Economy. In J. Hartley (Ed.), *Creative Industries* (pp. 344-360). Malden, MA.: Blackwell Publishing.

Florida, R. (2003). *The Rise of the Creative Class.* North Melbourne: Pluto Press.

Florida, R. (2008). *Who's Your City: how the Creative Economy is Making Where to Live the Most Important Decision of Your Life.* New York: Basic Books.

Ford, J. (2009). Setting the Standard: The London Carriage Trade, 1750-1800 In K. Wheeling (Ed.), *World on Wheels: Studies in the Manufacture, History, Use, Conservation and Restoration of Horse-Drawn Vehicles* (pp. 32-64). Lexington, Kentucky: The Carriage Association of America.

Fraser, J. (1992). Joint Venture Feasibility Study Cobb & Co Museum and Toowoomba College of TAFE. Toowoomba: Cobb & Co Museum and Toowoomba College of TAFE.

Frey, B. S. (1997). Evaluating Cultural Property: The Economic Approach. *International Journal of Cultural Property, 6*(2), 231-246.

Frey, B. S. (1998). Superstar Museums: An Economic Analysis. *Journal of Cultural Economics, 22*, 113-125.

Frey, B. S. (2003). *Arts and Economics: Analysis and Cultural Policy* (2nd ed.). Berlin: Springer.

Frey, B. S. (2005). What Values Should Count in the Arts? The Tension between Economic Effects and Cultural Value. *Center for Research in Economices, Management and the Arts Working Paper, 2005*(24), 1-10.

Frey, B. S., & Meier, S. (2006a). Cultural Economics. In S. Macdonald (Ed.), *A Companion to Museum Studies* (pp. 398-414). Malden: Blackwell Publishing.

Frey, B. S., & Meier, S. (2006b). The Economics of Museums. In V. A. Ginsburgh & D. Throsby (Eds.), *Handbook of the Economics of Art and Culture* (Vol. 1, pp. 1017-1047). Amsterdam: Elsevier.

Fulton, W., & Jackson, C. (1999). Charleton Library Anchors Downtown Redevelopment Project. In R. Kemp & M. Trotta (Eds.), *Museums, Libraries and Urban Vitality* (pp. 45-48). Jefferson, North Carolina: McFarland & Company.

Galla, A. (2002). Culture and Heritage in Development: Ha Long Ecomuseum, A Case Study from Vietnam. *Humanities Research, 9*(1), 63-76.

Galla, A. (2004). Museums and Intangible Heritage. *Artery, 9*(1), 11-13.

Galla, A. (2008). The First Voice in Heritage Conservation. *International Journal of Intangible Heritage, 3*, 9-25.

Garfield, D. (Ed.). (1997). *Partners in Tourism: Culture and Commerce*. Washington DC: American Association of Museums.

Garrett, P. (2007). Federal Labor Arts Policy Discussion Paper: Australian Labor Party.

Gathercole, P., & Lowenthal, D. (Eds.). (1990). *The Politics of the Past*. London: Unwin Hyman.

Gernandt, J. (2010). Craft Economies. Asheville, N.C.: HandMade in America.

Gillespie, R., Meehan, C., Nickson, M., & Winchester, S. (2002). Global Trends in Museums - Discussion Notes (pp. 17). Melbourne: Museum Victoria.

Ginsburgh, V. A., & Throsby, D. (Eds.). (2006). *Handbook of the Economics of Art and Culture* (Vol. 1). Amsterdam: Elsevier.

Gleeson, A. (2011). Museum Wins the Award for Best Building in the Region, *The Chronicle*.

Gomez de Blavia, M. (1998). The Museum as Meditor. *Museum International, 50*(4), 21-26.

Goodman, D. (1999). Fear of Circuses:Founding of the Natural Museum of Victoria. In D. Boswell & J. Evans (Eds.), *Representing the Nation: A Reader : Histories, Heritage and Museums*. London: Routledge.

Gorbey, K. (2002). *Organising for Success in the 21st Century: A Challenge for Museum Leadership*. Paper presented at the INTERCOM Conference Leadership in Museums: Are our Core Values Shifting, Dublin, Ireland.

Gray, C. (1998). Hope for the Future? Early Exposure to the Arts and Adult Visits to Art Museums. *Journal of Cultural Economics, 22*, 87-98.

Gray, M. (2006). *Kelvingrove Art Gallery and Museum: Glasgow's Portal to the World*. Glasgow: Glasgow Museums.

Greffe, X. (1994). Is Rural Tourism a Level for Economic Development. *Journal of Sustainable Tourism, 2*(1/2), 22-40.

Greffe, X. (2002). *Arts and Artists from an Economic Perspective*. Paris: UNESCO Publishing and Economica.

Greffe, X. (2004). is Heritage an Asset or a Liability? *Journal of Cultural Heritage, 5*, 301-309.

Greffe, X. (2008a, 14 October 2008). New Business Models for Cultural Companies.

Greffe, X. (2008b, 13 October 2008). Urban Cultural Landscapes.

Grossman, A., & Rangan, V. K. (2001). Managing Multisite Nonprofits. *NonProfit Management & Leadership, 11*(3), 321-337.

Grove, R. (1978). Pioneers in American Museums: John Cotton Dana. *Museum News, 56*(5), 32-39, 86-88.

Groves, I. (2005). Assessing the Economic Impact of Science Centers on their Local Communities. Canberra: Questacon - The National Science and Thechnology Centre.

Guetzhow, J. (2002, 7-8 June). *How the Arts Impact Communities: An Introducation to the Literature on Arts Impact Studies*. Paper presented at the Taking the Measure of Culture Conference, Princeton University Working Paper Series 20.

Gurian, E. H. (1995). A Blurring of the Boundaries. *Curator, 38*(1), 31-37.

Gurian, E. H. (1999). What is the Object of this Exercise? A Meandering Exploration of the Many Meanings of Objects in Museums. *Daedalus, 128*(3), 163.

Gurian, E. H. (2001). Function Follows Form: How Mixed-used Spaces in Museums build Community. *Curator, 44*(1), 97-113.

Gurian, E. H. (2006). *Civilizing the Museum: The Collected Writings of Elaine Heumann Gurian*. London: Routledge.

Gurt, G. A., & Torres, J. M. R. (2007). People Who Don't Go to Museums. *International Journal of Heritage Studies 13*(6), 521-523.

Hall, R. (2005). The "Museum Constant": One-third Plus or Minus a Bit. *Visitor Studies Today, 8*(2), 1-7.

Halpin, M. M. (1997). 'Play It again, Sam': Reflections on a New Museology. In S. Watson (Ed.), *Museums and Their Communities* (pp. 47-52). London: Routledge.

HandMade in America. (2010). *HandMade Institute Training Manual*. HandMade in Country. Asheville.

HandMade Institute. (2005a). AgriCultural Tourism: Asset Building and Marketing. Asheville NC: Handmade in America.

HandMade Institute. (2005b). Building Creative Communities: A Story of American Revival. Asheville: Handmade in America.

HandMade Institute. (2005c). Mapping Creative Economies. Asheville NC: handmade in America.

HandMade Institute. (n.d.). Developing a Regional Trails Guidebook: Connecting People and Places for Authentic Experiences. Asheville: HandMade in America.

Hanemann, M. (1994). Valuing the Environment Through Contingent Valuation. *Journal of Economic Perspectives, 8*(4), 19-43.

Harker, R., Mahar, C., & Wilkes, C. (1990). *An Introduction to the Work of Pierre Bourdieu: The Practice of Theory*. Houndmills, Basingstoke, Hampshire: Macmillan Press Ltd.

Harrison, J. D. (2005). Ideas of Museums in the1990s. In G. Corsane (Ed.), *Heritage, Museums and Galleries: An Introductory Reader* (pp. 38-53). London: Routledge.

Hartley, J. (Ed.). (2005). *The Creative Industries*. Malden, MA: Blackwell Publishing.

Hassard, F. (2009). Intangible Heritage in the UK. In L. Smith & N. Akagawa (Eds.), *Intangible Heritage*. London: Routledge.

Hauenschild, A. (1998). *Claims and Reality of the New Museology: Case Studies in Canada the United States and Mexico.* . Washington DC: Smithsonian Institution.

Hauritz, K. (2010). Handmade in Country: Feasibility Report & Action Plan. Toowoomba: Toowoomba & Golden West Regional Tourist Association.

Hawkes, J. (2001). *The Fourth Pillar of Sustainability: Culture's Essential Role in Public Planning.* : Common Ground Publishing in association with the Cultural Development Network (Vic).

Heal, S., & et.al. (2010). Working Knowledge: Advocacy. *Museum Practice, 10*(49), 39-55.

Hearn, G., Ninan, A., Rogers, I., Cunningham, S., & Luckman, S. (2004). From the Margins to the Mainstream: Creating Value in Queensland's Music Industry. *Media International Australia Incorporating Culture and Policy*(112), 101-114.

Hein, G. (1998). *Learning in the Museum*. London: Routledge.

Hein, H., S. (2000). *The Museum in Transition: A Philosophical Perspective.* Washington: Smithsonian Institution Press.

Hesmondhalgh, D. (2007). *The Cultural Industries* (2nd ed.). Los Angeles: Sage Publications.

Hewison, R. (1987). *The Heritage Industry: Britain in a Climate of Decline.* London: Methuen Paperback.

Hewison, R., & Holden, J. (2006, 25-26 January). *Public Value as a Framework for Analysing the Value of Heritage: the Ideas.* Paper presented at the Capturing the Public Value of Heritage, London.

Higgs, P., & Cunningham, S. (2007). Australia's Creative Economy: Mapping Methodologies. Brisbane: ARC Centre of Excellence for Creative Industries and Innovation.

Holden, J. (2004). Capturing Cultural Value: How Culture has become a tool of Government Policy (pp. 1-65). London: Demos.

Holden, J. (2005). Valuing Culture in the South East. London: DEMOS.

Holden, J. (2006). Cultural Value and the Crisis of Legitimacy: Why Culture Needs a Democratic Mandate. London: DEMOS.

Holden, J. (2007). Publicly-funded Culture and the Creative Industries. London: Arts Council England.

Holden, J., & Hewison, R. (2004). Challenge and Change: HLF and Cultural Value. London: Heritage Lottery Fund.

Hood, M. (1983). Staying Away: Why People choose not to visit Museums. *Museum News, 61*(4), 50-57.

Hood, M. (1995, 16-19 March). *Audience Research Tells Us Why Visitors Come to Museums - And Why They Don't.* Paper presented at the Towards 2000: Evaluation and Visitor Research in Museums, Sydney.

Hooper-Greenhill, E. (1988). Counting Visitors or Visitors who Count? In R. Lumley (Ed.), *The Museum Time-Machine* (pp. 213-232). London: Routledge.

Hooper-Greenhill, E. (2000a). Interpretative Communities, Strategies and Repertoires. In S. Watson (Ed.), *Museums and Their Communities.* London: Routledge.

Hooper-Greenhill, E. (2000b). *Museums and the Interpretation of Visual Culture.* London: Routledge.

Hooper-Greenhill, E. (2004). Measuring Learning Outcomes in Museums, Archives and Libraries: The Learning Impact Research Project (LIRP). *International Journal of Heritage Studies, 10*(2), 151-174.

Hooper-Greenhill, E. (2007a). Education, Postmodernity and the Museum. In S. J. Knell, S. MacLeod & S. Watson (Eds.), *Museum Revolutions: How Museums Change and are Changed* (pp. 367-377). London: Routledge.

Hooper-Greenhill, E. (2007b). Inspiration, Identity, Learning: The Value of Museums Second Study. Leicester: Research Centre for Museums and Galleries.

Howkins, J. (2001). *The Creative Economy: How People Make Money from Ideas.* London: Allen Lane.

Howkins, J. (2002). The Mayor's Commisssion on the Creative Industries. In J. Hartley (Ed.), *Creative Industries* (pp. 117-125). Malden, MA.: Blackwell Publishing.

Hudson, K. (1998). The Museum Refuses to Stand Still. *Museum International, 50*(1), 43-50.

Hutter, M. (1998). Communication productivity: A Major Cause for the Changing Output of Art Museums. *Journal of Cultural Economics, 22*, 99-112.

Hutter, M., & Throsby, D. (Eds.). (2008). *Beyond Price: Value in Culture, Economics, and the Arts.* Cambridge: Cambridge University Press.

Insley, J. (2002). Time Travelling Teens. *Artery, 7*(April), 12.

Institute of Public Policy Research. (2003, 25 June 2003). *Arts and Reconnecting Communities.* Paper presented at the Arts and Reconnecting Communities, Gateshead.

International Council of Museums. (2002). Shanghai Charter *Seventh Regional Assembly of the Asia Pacific Organisation ICOM.* Shanghai: Seventh Regional Assembly of the Asia Pacific Organisation ICOM.

International Council of Museums. (2007). Development of the Museum Definition according to ICOM Statutes (1946-2001). Retrieved from http://icon.museum/hist_def_eng.html

International Movement for a New Museology. Philosophy and History Retrieved 20 December, 2010

Jacobs, J. (1965). *The Death and Life of Great American Cities.* Hammondsworth: Penguin Books.

James, P. (2005). Building a Community-Based Identity at Anacostia Museum. In G. Corsane (Ed.), *Heritage, Museums and Galleries: An Introductory Reader* (pp. 339-356). London: Routledge.

Jamieson, W. (2006). *Community Destination Management in Developing Economies.* New York: Haworth Hospitality Press.

Janes, R. R. (2007a). Museums, Corporatism and the Civil Society. *Curator, 50*(2), 219-237.

Janes, R. R. (2007b). Museums, Social Responsibility and the Future We Desire. In S. J. Knell, S. MacLeod & S. Watson (Eds.), *Museum Revolutions: How Museums Change and Are Changed* (pp. 134-146). London: Routledge.

Janes, R. R. (2009). *Museums in a Troubled World: Renewal, Irrelevance or Collapse?* London: Routledge.

Jeannotte, M. S. (2005). Just Showing Up:Social and Cultural Capital in Everyday Life. In C. Andrew, M. Gattinger, M. S. Jeannotte & W. Straw (Eds.), *Accounting for Culture: Thinking Through Cultural Citizenship* (pp. 124-145). Ottawa: The University of Ottawa Press.

Jeannotte, M. S. (2006). Millennium Dreams: Arts, Culture, and Heritage in the Life of Communities. *Canadian Journal of Communication, 31*, 107-125.

Jensen, J. (2002). *Is Art Good for Us? Belief about High Culture in American Life.* Lanham: Rowman & Littlefield

Johnson, L. (2006). Valuing the Arts: Theorising and Realising Cultural Capital in an Australian City. *Geographical Research, 44*(3), 296-309.

Johnson, N. (2009). Summerlee- the Museum of Scottish Industrial Life, Coatbridge, Lanarkshire. *Museums Journal, 109*(3), 48-49.

Johnson, P. (2003). Museums. In R. Towse (Ed.), *A Handbook of Cultural Economics* (pp. 315-320). Cheltenham, UK: Edward Elgar.

Jones, D., & Keogh, W. (2006). Social Enterprise: A Case of Terminological Ambiguity and Complexity. *Social Enterprise Journal, 2*(1), 11-26.

Jones, S. (2000). Community, Culture and Place. In New South Wales Ministry for the Arts & Local Government and Shires Association of New South Wales (Ed.), (pp. 1-84). Sydney: Museums Studies Unit University of Sydney.

Joubert, A. (2005). *French Ecomuseums.* Paper presented at the Communication and Exploration Conference, Guizhou, China.

Jowell, T. (2004). Government and the Value of Culture. London: Department for Culture, Media and Sport.

Jowell, T. (2005). Better Places to Live: Government, Identity and the Value of the Historic and Built Environment. London: Department for Culture, Media and Sport.

Jura Consultants. (2005). Bolton's Museums, Library and Archive Services: An Economic Valuation. Edinburgh: Bolton Metropolitan Borough Council and MLA North West.

Kanninen, B., J. (Ed.). (2006). *Valuing Environmental Amenities using Stated Choice Studies: A Common Sense Approach to Theory and Practice.* Dordrecht, The Netherlands: Springer.

Kavanagh, G. (2000). *Dream Spaces: Memory and the Museum.* London: Leicester University Press.

Keaney, E. (2006). Public Value and the Arts: Literature Review. London: Arts Council England.

Kelly, L. (2006). *Creating Meaningful Learning Experiences in Cultural Institutions.* report on doctoral study. Australian Museum.

Kemper, C. (2007). Denver Uses Culture to Stimulate Private Development. In R. Kemp & M. Trotta (Eds.), *Museums, Libraries and Urban Vitality* (pp. 58-61). Jefferson, North Carolina: McFarland & Company.

Kenyon, W., & Edward-Jones, G. (1998). What Level of Information Enables the Public to Act Like Experts When Evaluating Ecological Goods? *Journal of Environmental Planning and Management, 41*(4), 463-475.

Kim, W. C., & Mauborgne, R. (2004). Blue Ocean Strategy. *Harvard Business Review, Oct*, 76-84.

Kinnery, T. (2009). Beyond the Builder's Plate: Understanding Brewster through the Manufacturing Evolution. In K. Wheeling (Ed.), *World on Wheels: Studies in the Manufacture, History, Use, Conservation and Restoration of Horse-Drawn Vehicles* (pp. 65-83). Lexington, Kentucky: The Carriage Association of America.

Kinsey, B. J. (2002). *The Economic Impact of Museums and Cultural Attractions: Another Benefit for the Community.* Paper presented at the Annual Meeting of the American Associations of Museums, Dallas, Texas.

Kirshenblatt-Gimblett, B. (1998). *Destination Culture: Tourism, Museums and Heritage.* Berkeley: University of California Press.

Klamer, A. (2002). Accounting for Social and Cultural Values. *De Economist, 150*(4), 453-473.

Klamer, A. (2003). Value of Culture. In R. Towse (Ed.), *A Handbook of Cultural Economics* (pp. 465-469). Cheltenham, UK: Edward Elgar.

Klamer, A. (2004). Social, Cultural and Economic Values of Cultural Goods. Retrieved from http://klamer.nl/articles/culture/art.php

Kling, R., Revier, C., & Sable, K. (2004). Estimating the Public Good Value of Preserving a Local Historic Landmark: The Role of Non-substitutability and Citizen Information. *Urban Studies, 41*(10), 2025-2041.

Koboldt, C. (1997). Optimizing the Use of Cultural Heritage. In M. Hutter & I. Rizzo (Eds.), *Economic Perspectives of Cultural Heritage* (pp. 50-73). London: Macmillan Press.

Kotler, N. (2001). New Ways of Experiencing Culture: the Role of Museums and Marketing Implications. *Museum Management and Curatorship, 19*(4), 417-425.

Kotler, N., & Kotler, P. (2000). Can Museums Be All Things to All People? Missions, Goals, and Marketing Role. In G. Anderson (Ed.), *Reinventing the Museum* (pp. 167-186). Walnut Creek: AltaMira Press.

Kotler, N., Kotler, P., & Kotler, W. (2008). *Museum Marketing and Strategy: Designing Missions, Building Audiences, Generating Revenue and Resources* (2nd ed.). San Francisco: John Wiley & Sons.

Krupnick, A., & Adamowicz, W. L. (2006). Supporting Questions in Stated Choice Studies. In B. Kanninen, J. (Ed.), *Valuing Environmental Amenities Using Stated Choice Studies* (pp. 43-65). Dordrecht, The Netherlands: Springer.

Kurin, R. (2004). Museums and Intangible Heritage: Culture Dead or Alive. *ICOM News, 4*, 7-9.

Kurin, R. (2007). Safeguarding Intangible Cultural Heritage: Key Factors in Implementing the 2003 Convention. *International Journal of Intangible Heritage, 2*, 10-20.

Lampi, E., & Orth, M. (2009). Who Visits the Museums? A Comparison between Stated Preference and Observed Effects of Entrance Fees. *KYKLOS, 62*(1), 85-102.

Landry, C. (2001). London as a Creative City. In J. Hartley (Ed.), *Creative Industries* (pp. 233-243). Malden MA: Blackwell Publishing.

Landry, C. (2003). Culture's Collision Course. *Museum Journal, 103*(1), 16-17,19.

Landry, C. (2009). Intercultural Cities. *Ideas Festival.* Queensland State Library, Brisbane.

Lang, C., Reeve, J., & Woollard, V. (Eds.). (2006). *The Responsive Museum: Working with Audiences in the Twenty-first Century*. Aldershot Ashgate Publishing Ltd.

Laville, J.-L., & Nyssens, M. The Social Enterprise: Towards a Theoritical Socio-Economic Approach (pp. 623-666).

Leadbeater, C. (1999). *Living on Thin Air: The New Economy*. London: Viking.

Leadbeater, C., & Oakley, K. (1999). Why Cultural Entreprenteurs Matter. In J. Hartley (Ed.), *Creative Industries* (pp. 299-311). Malden MA: Blackwell Publishing.

Lennon, J. (1995). Hidden Heritage: A Development Plan for Museums in Queensland 1995-2001. Brisbane: Arts Queensland.

Linett, P. (2006). Civilizing the Museum: The Collected Writings of Elaine Heumann Gurian. [Book Review:]. *Curator the Museum Journal, 49*(2), 265-269.

Lorente, P. (Ed.). (1996). *The Role of Museums and the Arts in the Urban Regeneration of Liverpool.* Leicester: Centre for Urban Studies, University of Leicester.

Lorenze, M., Scott, A. J., & Vang, J. (2008). Editorial: Geography and the Cultural Economy. *Journal of Economic Geography, 8*, 589-592.

Lowenthal, D. (1985). *The Past is a Foreign Country*. Cambridge: Cambridge University Press.

Lowenthal, D. (1996). *The Heritage Crusade and the Spoils of History*. London: Viking.

Lumley, R. (Ed.). (1988). *The Museum Time-Machine: Putting Cultures on Display*. London: Routledge.

Macdonald, R. R. (2006). AAM at 100: And You thought the First Century Was Challenging. *Museum News, 85*(1), 29-31, 60-61.

Macdonald, S. (1998). Exhibitions of Power and Powers of Exhibition: An Introduction to the Politics of Display. In S. Watson (Ed.), *Museums and Their Communities* (pp. 176-196). London: Routledge.

Macdonald, S. (2003). Museums, National, Postnational and Transcultural Identities. *Museum and Society, 1*(1), 1-16.

Madden, C. (2005). Indicators for Arts and Cultural Policy: A Global Perspective. *Cultural Trends, 14*(3), 217-247.

Maggi, M. (2005). *Ecomuseums Worldwide: Converging Routes among Similar Obstacles*. Paper presented at the Communication and Exploration Conference, Guizhou, China.

Markham, S. F., & Richards, H. C. (1933). A Report on the Museums & Art Galleries of Australia. London: The Carnegie Corporation of New York.

Martin, F. (1994). Determining the Size of Museum Subsidies. *Journal of Cultural Economics, 18*, 255-270.

Mason, R. (2005). Museums, Galleries and Heritage: Sites of Meaning-making and Communication. In G. Corsane (Ed.), *Heritage, Museums and Galleries: An Introductory Reader* (pp. 200-214). London: Routledge.

Mastai, J. (2007). "There is No Such Thing as a Visitor". In G. Pollock & J. Zemans (Eds.), *Museums After Modernism* (pp. 173-177). Malden, MA: Blackwell Publishing.

Matarasso, F. (1997). *Use or Ornament? The Social Impact of Participation in the Arts.* Stroud: Comedia.

Mather, P. (Ed.). (1986). *A Time for a Museum: The History of the Queensland Museum 1862-1986.* Brisbane: Queensland Museum.

Mathews, K., Freeman, m., & Desvousges, W. (2006). How and How Much? The Role of Information in Stated Choice Questionnaires. In B. Kanninen, J. (Ed.), *Valuing Environmental Amenities Using Stated Choice Studies* (pp. 111-133). Dordrecht, The Netherlands: Springer.

Mattinson, D. (2006, 25-26 January). *The Value of Heritage - What does the Public Think?* Paper presented at the Capturing the Public Value of Heritage, London.

McBryde, I. (Ed.). (1985). *Who Owns the Past?* Melbourne: Oxford University Press.

McCarthy, K. F., Ondaatje, E. H., Zakaras, L., & Brooks, A. (2004). Gifts of the Muse: Reframing the Debate About the Benefits of the Arts (pp. 104). Santa Monica: Rand: Research in the Arts.

McDermott Miller Ltd. (2002). National Bibliographic Database and National Union Catalogue: Economic Valuation (pp. 35). Wellington: National Library of New Zealand Te Puna Matauranga O Aotearoa.

McIntyre, C. (2010). Designing Museum and Gallery Shops as Integral, Co-creative Retail Spaces within the Overall Visitor Experience. *Musem Management and Curatorship, 25*(2), 181-198.

McManus, R. (1997). Heritage and Tourism in Ireland - An Unholy Alliance? *Irish Geography, 30*(2), 90-98.

McRobbie, A. (2002). Clubs to Companies. In J. Hartley (Ed.), *Creative Industries* (pp. 375-390). Malden, MA.: Blackwell Publishing.

McRobbie, A. (2004). Making a Living in London's Small-Scale Creative Sector. In D. Power & A. J. Scott (Eds.), *Cultural Industries and the Production of Culture* (pp. 130-143). London: Routledge.

Melbourne's Living Museum of the West Inc. (n.d.). About Us Retrieved 28 December 2010, from http://www.livingmuseum.org.au/about-us/index.html

Mercer, C. (2005). From Indicators to Governance to the Mainstream: Tools for Cultural Policy and Citizenship. In C. Andrew, M. Gattinger, M. S. Jeannotte & W. Straw (Eds.), *Accounting for Culture: Thinking Through Cultural Citizenship* (pp. 9-20). Ottawa: The University of Ottawa Press.

Merli, P. (2002). Evaluating the Social Impacts of Participation in Arts Activities: A Critical Review of Francois Matarasso's *Use or Ornament? International Journal of Cultural Policy, 8*(1), 107-118.

Merriman, N. (1989). Museum Visiting as a Cultural Phenomenon. In P. Vergo (Ed.), *The New Museology* (pp. 149-171). London: Reaktion Books.

Merriman, N. (1991). *Beyond the Glass Case: The Past, the Heritage and the Public in Britain.* Leicester: Leicester University Press.

Milne, D. (2006). *Lifelong Learning Discussion paper and Implementation Proposals.* Queensland Museum. Brisbane.

Misztal, B. (2003). Memory Experience: The Forms and Functions of Memory. In S. Watson (Ed.), *Museums and Their Communities* (pp. 379-396). London: Routledge.

Mizzau, L., & Montanari, F. (2008). Cultural Districts and the Challenge of Authenticity: The Case of Piedmont, Italy. *Journal of Economic Geography, 8*, 651-673.

Moffat Centre for Travel & Tourism Business Development. (2005). Realising the True Impact of Museums and Galleries in Scottish Tourism (pp. 1-65). Glasgow: Scottish Museum Council.

Moore, M. H. (1995). *Creating Public Value: Strategic Management in Government.* Cambridge: Harvard University Press.

Moore, M. H., & Williams Moore, G. (2005). Creating Public Value through State Arts Agencies. Minneapolis: Arts Midwest and The Wallace Foundation.

Mourato, S., & Mazzanti, M. (2002). Economic Valuation of Cultural Heritage: Evidence and Prospects. In M. De la Torre (Ed.), *Assessing the Values of Cultural Heritage.* Los Angeles: The Getty Conservation Institute.

Moussouri, T. (2002). A Context for the Development of Learning Outcomes in Museums, Libraries and Archives. Leicester: University of Leicester and The Council for Museums, Archives and Libraries.

Mulvaney, J. (1976). 'The Chain of Connection': The Material Evidence. In N. Peterson (Ed.), *Tribes and Boundaries in Australia* (pp. 72-94). Canberra: Australian Institute of Aboriginal Studies.

Murphy, B. (2005). Memory, History and Museums. *Museum, 57*(3), 70-77.

Museum of English Rural Life. (2008). Rural Crafts Today Retrieved 22 January 2009, from http://ws1000.qm.qld.gov.au/cgi-bin/patience.cgi?id=1b4b22fb-00de-4ffa-b7cd-e5a7f3c3e2c9

Museums Australia. (2002). What is a Museum? Retrieved 29 August, 2010, from http://www.museumsaustralia.org.au/site/what_is_a_museum.php

Museums Libraries and Archives Council. (2004). Investing in Knowledge: A five-year Vision for England's Museums, Libraries and Archives (pp. 1-14). London: Museums, Libraries and Archives Council.

Museums Libraries and Archives Council. (2007). Inspiring Creativity, Celebrating Identity: MLA Partnership Strategic Statement 2007-2010 (pp. 6). London: Museums, Libraries and Archives Council.

Myerscough, J. (1988). *The Economic Importance of the Arts in Britain*. London: Policy Studies Institute.

National Museum Directors' Conference. (2006). Values and Vision: The Contribution of Culture. London: National Museum Directors' Conference.

Navrud, S., & Ready, R. C. (Eds.). (2002). *Valuing Cultural Heritage: Applying Environmental Valuation Techniques to Historic Buildings, Monuments and Artifacts*. Cheltenham: Edward Elgar.

Netzer, D. (2003). Non-profit Organisations. In R. Towse (Ed.), *A Handbook of Cultural Economics* (pp. 331-341). Cheltenham, UK: Edward Elgar.

Nguyen, K., & Falls, M. (Eds.). (2004). *Inside the Minds: The Business of Museums: A Behind the Scenes Look at Curatorship, Management Strategies and Critical Components of Success*. Boston: Aspatore Books.

Noonan, D. (2002). Contingent Valuation Studies in the Arts and Culture: An Annotated Bibliography Retrieved 1 October 2007, from http://harrisschool.uchicago.edu/wp/03-04.html

Noonan, D., S. (2003). Contingent Valuation and Cultural Resources: A Meta-Analytic Review of the Literature. *Journal of Cultural Economics, 27*, 159-176.

Noonan, D., S. (2004). Valuing Arts and Culture: A Research Agenda for Contingent Valuation. *Journal of Arts Management, Law and Society, 34*(3), 205-221.

O'Connor, J. (2004). Cities, Culture and "Transitional Economies": Developing Cultural Industries in St Petersurg. In D. Power & A. J. Scott (Eds.), *Cultural Industries and the Production of Culture* (pp. 37-53). London: Routledge.

O'Neill, M. (2007). Kelvingrove: Telling Stories in a Treasured Old/New Museum. *Curator, 50*(4), 379-399.

Oakley, K. (2004). Developing the Evidence Base for Support of Cultural and Creative Activities in South East England: South East England Cultural Consortium.

Oldenburg, R. (1997). *The Great Good Place* (2nd edition ed.). New York: Marlowe & Company.

Packer, J. (2006). Learning for Fun: The Unique Contribution of Educational Leisure Experiences. *Curator the Museum Journal, 49*(3), 329-344.

Papandrea, F. (2002, 1-2 February). *Contingent Valuation and Cultural Policies: Some Challenges and a Case Study*. Paper presented at the Contingent Valuation of Culture Conference, Chicago

Papeterie-Saint-Gilles. Retrieved 16 December, 2010, from http://www.papeteriesaintgilles.com/papeterie-pages/En/papeterie.Saint-Gilles.premier-economusee_en.html

Peacock, A., & Rizzo, I. (2008). *The Heritage Game: Economics, Policy and Practice*. Oxford: Oxford University press.

Peniston, W. A. (Ed.). (1999). *The New Museum: Selected Writings of John Cotton Dana*. Washington D.C.: Newark Museum and the American Association of Museums.

Pigott, P. H. (1975). Report of the Committee of Inquiry on Museums and National Collections including the Report of the Planning Committee on the Gallery of Aboriginal Australia. Canberra: Australian Government.

Pitman, B. (1999). Muses, Museums, and Memories. (Review). *Daedalus, 128*(3), 8-22.

Plowman, I., Ashkanasy, N. M., Gardner, J., & Letts, M. (2003). Innovation in Rural Queensland: Why do Some Towns Thrive while Others Languish (pp. 1-78). Brisbane: University of Queensland and Department of Primary Industries.

Poll, R., & Payne, P. (2006, 7-9 February). *Impact Measures for Libraries and Information Services*. Paper presented at the Academic Library and Information Services: New Paradigms for the Digital Age, Bielefeld Germany.

Pollard, J. (2004). Manufacturing Culture in Birmingham's Jewelry Quarter. In D. Power & A. J. Scott (Eds.), *Cultural Industries and the Production of Culture*. London: Routledge.

Porter, M. (2000). Local Clusters in a Global Economy. In J. Hartley (Ed.), *Creative Industries* (pp. 259-267). Malden, MA: Blackwell Publishing.

Poulot, D. (1994). Identity as Self-Discovery: The Ecomuseum in France. In D. J. Sherman & I. Rogoff (Eds.), *Museum Culture: Histories, Discourses, Spectacles* (pp. 66-84). Minneapolis: University of Minnesota Press.

Powell, J. (1997). R.S.Colliver Scholarship Research Report into Coachbuilding and Other Heritage Trades in Europe 1996. Toowoomba: Cobb+Co Museum.

Power, D., & Scott, A. J. (Eds.). (2004). *Cultural Industries and the Production of Culture*. London: Routledge.

Pratt, A. (2004). Mapping the Cultural Industries: Regionalisation; the Example of South East England. In D. Power & A. J. Scott (Eds.), (pp. 20-36). London: Routledge.

Prott, L. V., & O'Keefe, P. J. (1992). 'Cultural Heritage' or 'Cultural Property'? *International Journal of Cultural Property 1*, 307-320.

Pung, C., Clarke, A., & Patten, L. (2004). Measuring the Economic Impact of the British Library. *New Review of Academic Librarianship, 10*(1), 79-102.

Putnam, R. D. (2000). *Bowling Alone: The Collapse and Revival of American Community*. New York: Simon & Schuster.

Queensland Government. (1999). Queensland Heritage Trails Network. Brisbane: Queensland Government.

Queensland Government. (2005). Smart State Strategy 2005-2015. Brisbane: Queensland Government.

Queensland Government. (2005). *Engaging Queenslanders: An Introduction to Community Engagement*. Brisbane.

Queensland Government. (2010). Creative Industries, from http://www.export.qld.gov.au/creative-industries.html

Queensland Government: State Development and Innovation. (2005). Creativity is Big Business; A Framework for the Future. Brisbane: Queensland Government.

Queensland Museum. (2005). QM 2010: A Vision for the Queensland Museum in the Smart State. Brisbane: Queensland Museum.

Queensland Museum. (2008a). Invitation to Offer No. QM066/2008: Provision of Audience Research Services. In A. Queensland (Ed.), (Vol. QM066/2008).

Queensland Museum. (2008b). *Minutes of Valuing Arts & Culture Masterclass 3 April*Brisbane: Queensland Museum.

Queensland Museum. (2008c). Queensland Museum Operational Plan 2008-9. Brisbane: Queensland Museum.

Queensland Museum. (2011). Strategic Directions. Brisbane: Queensland Museum.

Queensland Museum Act 1970 (1970 13 April 1970).

Queensland Museum Board of Trustees. (1971 -1979). Report on Activities. Birsbane: Queensland Museum.

Queensland Museum Board of Trustees. (1980 to 2007-8). Queensland Museum Annual Report 1980 to2007-8. Brisbane: Queensland Museum.

Queensland Museum Foundation. (2005). Cobb+Co Museum: *Rebuilding the Legend*: The Campaign Plan. Brisbane: Queensland Museum.

Rasmussen, D. (1981). Praxis and Social Theory (review of *Outline of a Theory of Praxis*). *Human Studies, 4*, 273-278.

Reeves, M. (2001). Measuring the Economic and Social Impact of the Arts: A Review (pp. 1-132). London: Arts Council of England.

Reisinger, Y. (1994). Tourist - Host Contact as a part of Cultural Tourism. *World Leisure and Recreation, 36*(2), 24-28.

Rentschler, R. (2002). *The Entrepreneurial Arts Leader*. Brisbane: University of Queensland Press.

Rifkin, J. (2000). When Markets Give Way to Networks...Everything is a Service. In J. Hartley (Ed.), *Creative Industries* (pp. 361-374). Malden, MA.: Blackwell Publishing.

Rivière, G. H. (1958). *Report*. Paper presented at the UNESCO Regional Seminar on the Educational Role of Museums Rio de Janiero.

Rivière, G. H. (1985). The Ecomuseum - an Evolutive Definition. *Museum, 148*, 182-183.

Rojek, C. (1993). Fatal Attractions. In D. Boswell & J. Evans (Eds.), *Representing the Nation: A Reader; Histories, Heritage and Museums* (pp. 185-207). London: Routledge.

Ross, M. (2004). Interpreting the New Museology. *Museum and Society, 2*(2), 84-103.

Rounds, J. (2004). Strategies for the Curiosity-Driven museum Visitor. *Curator, 47*(4), 389-412.

Rounds, J. (2006). Doing Identity Work in Museums. *Curator the Museum Journal, 49*(2), 133-150.

Russell, R., & Winkworth, K. (2001). Significance: A Guide to Assessing the Significance of Cultural Heritage Objects and Collections (pp. 72). Canberra: Heritage Collections Council.

Saatchi & Saatchi. (2000). Australians and the Arts: What do the Arts mean to Australians? Sydney: The Australia Council.

Saguaro Seminar Report. (2000). Better Together: Report of the Saguaro Seminar on Civic Engagement in America (pp. 1-9). Cambridge, MA: John F. Kennedy Schools of Government, Harvard University.

Samuel, R. (1994). *Theatres of Memory: Past and Present in Contemporary Culture* (Vol. 1). London: Verso.

Sandell, R. (2002). Museums and the Combating of Social Inequality: Roles, Responsibilities, Resistance. In S. Watson (Ed.), *Museums and Their Communities* (pp. 95-113). London: Routledge.

Santagata, W. (2002). Cultural Districts, Property Rights and Sustainable Economic Growth: Working Paper 01/2002: International Centre for Research on the Economics of Culture, Institutions and Creativity, University of Torino, Italy.

Santagata, W., & Signorello, G. (2000). Contingent Valuation of a Cultural Public Good and Policy Design: The Case of "Napoli Musei Aperti". *Journal of Cultural Economics, 24*, 181-204.

Sarantakos, S. (2005). *Social Research* (3rd ed.). Houndsmills, Bassingstoke, Hampshire: Palgrave Macmillan.

Savage, G., & Hall, R. (2009, 17-20 May). *Working Together to make a Case for Funding.* Paper presented at the Work in Progress: Museums Australia National Conference: , Newcastle.

Savitch, H. V., & Kantor, P. (2002). *Cities in the International Marketplace: The Political Economy of Urban Development in North America and Western Europe.* Princeton: Princeton University Press.

Scheiner, T. C. (2005). *Museum, Ecomuseum, Anti-museum: New Approaches to Heritage, Society and Development.* Paper presented at the Communication and Exploration Conference, Guizhou, China.

Scott, A. J. (2004). Cultural-Products Industries and Urban Economic Development: Prospects for Growth and Market Contestation in Global Context. *Urban Affairs Review, 39*(4), 461-490.

Scott, A. J. (2007). Capitalism and Urbanization in a New Key? The Cognitive-Cultural Dimension. *Social Forces, 85*(4), 1465-1482.

Scott, A. J., & Garofoli, G. (Eds.). (2007). *Development on the Ground: Clusters, Networks and Regions in Emerging Economies*. London: Routledge.

Scott, C. (2003). Museums and Impact: How Do we Measure the Impact of Museums? *Curator, 46*(3), 293-310.

Scott, C. (2006). Museums: Impact and Value. *Cultural Trends, 15*(1), 45-75.

Scott, C. (2007a). *Assessing Value: Australian Museums in the 21st Century*. Doctor of Philosophy, The University of Sydney, Sydney.

Scott, C. (2007b, 16 November 2007). *The Values Toolkit: Advocating the Value of Museums and Galleries*. Paper presented at the Museums & Gallery Services Queensland Masterclass, Brisbane.

Scott, C. (2007c, 14-16 September). *What Difference do Museums Make? A Typology of Museum Value*. Paper presented at the Museums & Gallery Services Qld State Conference, Gold Coast.

SCR Consulting. (2006). Economic Impact Analysis National Carriage Factory. Toowoomba: Cobb+Co Museum.

Seaman, B. (2003). Economic Impact of the Arts. In R. Towse (Ed.), *A Handbook of Cultural Economics* (pp. 224-231). Cheltenham, UK: Edward Elgar.

Seligson, J. (2009). The Migratory Museum: Is the Search for Greener Pastures Worth the Risk? *Museum, 88*(6), 42-47.

Selwood, S. (2002). Measuring Culture. Retrieved from http://www.spiked-online.com/Articles/00000006DBAF.htm

Selwood, S. (2004). The Politics of Data Collection: Gathering, Analysing and Using data about the Subsidised Cultural Sector in England. *Cultural Trends, 47*, 13-84.

Selwood, S. (2005). John Holden's Capturing Cultural Value: How Culture has Become a Tool of Government Policy. *Cultural Trends, 14*(1), 113-128.

Selwood, S. (2006). Great Expectations: Museums and Regional Economic Development in England. *Curator, 49*(1), 65-80.

Selwood, S. (2010). Making a Difference: the Cultural Impact of Museums. London: National Museum Directors Conference.

Sheppard, B. K. (2000). Do Museums Make a Difference? Evaluating Programs for Social Change. *Curator, 43*(1), 63-74.

Shorthose, J. (2004). Accounting for Independent Creativity in the New Cultural Economy. *Media International Australia Incorporating Culture and Policy*(112), 150-161.

Silberberg, T. (1995). Cultural Tourism and Business Opportunities for Museums and Heritage Places. *Tourism Management, 16*(5), 361-365.

Simard, C. (1991). 'Economuseology' - a New Term that Pays its Way. *Museum, 43*(172 (4)), 230-233.

Skramstad, H. (1999). An Agenda for American Museums in the Twentieth-First Century. *Daedalus, 128*(3).

Smallbone, D., Evans, M., Ekanem, I., & Butters, S. (2001). Researching Social Enterprise. London: Centre for Enterprise and Economic Development Research.

Smith, L. (2006). *Uses of Heritage*. London: Routledge.

Smith, L., & Akagawa, N. (Eds.). (2009). *Intangible Heritage*. London: Routledge.

Smith, L., & Waterton, E. (Eds.). (2009). *'The Envy of the World': Intangible Heritage in England*. London: Routledge.

Smith, M. (2007). Space, Place and Placelessness in the Culturally Regenerated City. In G. Richards (Ed.), *Cultural Tourism: Global and Local Perspectives* (pp. 91-111). New York: Haworth Press.

Smith, V. K. (2006). Fifty Years of Contingent Valuation. In A. Alberini & J. Kahn (Eds.), *Handbook of Contingent Valuation* (pp. 7-65). Cheltenham, UK: Edward Elgar.

Snowball, J. (2008). *Measuring the Value of Culture: Methods and Examples in Cultural Economics*. verlag Berlin: Springer.

Spock, D. (2006). The Puzzle of Museum Education Practice: A Comment on Rounds and Falk. *Curator 49*(2), 167-180.

Stanley, D. (2001). Beyond Economics: Developing Indicators of the Social Effects of Culture. Quebec: Department of Canadian Heritage.

Stanley, D. (2005). The Three Faces of Culture: Why Culture Is a Strategic Good Requiring Government Policy Attention. In C. Andrew, M. Gattinger, M. S. Jeannotte & W. Straw (Eds.), *Accounting for Culture: Thinking Through Cultural Citizenship*. Ottawa: The University of Ottawa Press.

Stanley, D. (2006). Introduction: The Social Effects of Culture. *Canadian Journal of Communication, 31*(1), 1-7.

Steel, P. (2010). People's Choice. *Museum Journal, 110*(1), 23-26.

Steffen, J. S. (2008). *A Multiple Case Analysis of Museum Participation in Community Visioning: Connecting Civic Engagement and Entrepreneural Social Infrastructure.* Master of Science in Public Horticulture, University of Delaware.

Svensson, T. (2008). The Management of Knowledge of the Intangible Heritage in Connection with Traditional Craftmanship at the Ethnographic Museum of the University of Oslo. *International Journal of Intangible Heritage, 3*, 117-126.

Tait, A. (2010). The Handmade Band. *Australia Today, April/May.*

Taylor Byrne. (1996). Toowoomba and Golden West and Southern Downs Joint Regional Tourism Strategy Toowoomba: Toowoomba and Golden West Regional Tourist Association

The British Library. (2007). Measuring Our Value: Results of an Independent Economic Impact Study Retrieved 10 September 2007

Thompson, B. J., Throsby, D., & Withers, G. A. (1983). Measuring Community Benefits from the Arts. *Macquarie University School of Economics and Financial Studies Research Paper, 261*, 1-69.

Thompson, E., Berger, M., Blomquist, G., & Allen, S. (2002, 1-2 February). *Valuing the Arts: A Contingent Valuation Approach.* Paper presented at the Contingent Valuation of Culture Conference, Chicago.

Throsby, D. (1982). Social and Economic Benefits from Regional Investment in Arts Facilities: Theory and Application. *Journal of Cultural Economics, 6*(1), 1-14.

Throsby, D. (1994). The Production and Consumption of the Arts: A View of Cultural Economics. *Journal of Economic Literature, 32*(March), 1-29.

Throsby, D. (2001). *Economics and Culture.* Cambridge: Cambridge University Press.

Throsby, D. (2002). Cultural Capital and Sustainability Concepts in the Economics of Cultural Heritage. In M. De la Torre (Ed.), *Assessing the Value of Cultural Heritage* (pp. 101-117). Los Angeles: Getty Conservation Institute.

Throsby, D. (2003). Determining the Value of Cultural Goods: How Much (or How Little) Does Contingent Valuation Tell Us? *Journal of Cultural Economics, 27*, 275-285.

Throsby, D. (2004, 12-14 May). *Assessing the Impacts of the Cultural Industry.* Paper presented at the Lasting Effects: Assessing the Future of Economic Impact Analysis of the Arts Conference, University of Chicago.

Throsby, D. (2005). *On the Sustainability of Cultural Capital.* Research Papers Macquarie University Department of Economics.

Throsby, D. (2006a). Does Australia Need a Cultural Policy? *Platform Papers, Currency House, 7.*

Throsby, D. (2006b). *Paying for the Past: Economics, Cultural Heritage and Public Policy.* 51st Fisher Lecture Laureate. Elder Hall, University of Adelaide.

Throsby, D. (2006c, 25-26 January). *The Value of Cultural Heritage: What can Economics Tell Us?* Paper presented at the Capturing the Public Value of Heritage, London.

Throsby, D. (2007, 11-12 January). *Modelling the Creative/Cultural Industries.* Paper presented at the New Directions in Research: Substance, Method and Critique, Royal Society of Edinburgh, Scotland.

Throsby, D. (2008a). *Creative Australia: The Arts and Culture in Australian Work and Leisure.* Canberra: The Academy of the Social Sciences in Australia.

Throsby, D. (2008b, 3 April). *How to Value Arts and Culture: Why We Should be Proactive in Queensland.* Paper presented at the Master class, State Library of Queensland, Brisbane.

Throsby, D. (2008c, 2 April). *How to Value Arts and Culture: Why we should be Proactive in Queensland.* Paper presented at the Public Lecture Queensland Museums, Brisbane.

Throsby, D., & Hollister, V. (2003). Don't Give Up Your Day Job: An Economic Study of Professional Artists in Australia. Sydney: Australia Council.

Toowoomba & Golden West Regional Tourist Association. (2010). *Handmade in Country*. Toowoomba.

Toowoomba City Council. (2008). our Toowoomba towards 2050 Community Plan. Toowoomba: Toowoomba City Council.

Towse, R. (Ed.). (2003). *A Handbook of Cultural Economics*. Cheltenham, UK: Edward Elgar.

Tranter, D. (1988a). Cobb+Co Museum: An Example of Educational Cooperation in the Local Region. *Museum Education Association of Australia Journal, 26*, 10-12.

Tranter, D. (1988b). *Using a Local Museum as a Place for Learning*. Toowoomba: Department of Education.

Tranter, D. (1990). *Cobb & Co: Coaching in Queensland*. Brisbane: Queensland Museum.

Tranter, D. (1992). Cobb & Co: The Great Australian Stage Coaching Company *The American Carriage Journal, 30*(3), 107-111.

Tranter, D. (1993). An Investigation of Wheelwrighting, Coachbuilding and Restoration of Horse-drawn Vehicles in the United States of America: Churchill Fellowship Report. Canberra: The Winston Churchill Merorial Trust of Australia.

Tranter, D. (1997). *Cobb & Co. in Japan*. Toowoomba: Cobb+Co Museum.

Tranter, D. (2002). *Toowoomba Teens 2001*. Paper presented at the *Off the Wall* Regional Galleries of Queensland Seminar Program, Queensland Art Gallery, Brisbane.

Tranter, D. (2006a). *Architect's Brief for Cobb+Co Museum* Cobb+Co Museum. Toowoomba.

Tranter, D. (2006b). *Significance Assessment and Community Identity- What's happening in Regional Queensland?* Paper presented at the Museums Australia National Conference, May 2006, Brisbane.

Tranter, D. (2007). *Conversations between Director and Councillors*.

Tranter, D. (2009a). *Valuing the Queensland Museum: A Contingent Valuation Study*. Paper presented at the International Conference on the Inclusive Museum, Brisbane.

Tranter, D. (2009b). Valuing the Queensland Museum: A Contingent Valuation Study. *The International Journal of the Inclusive Museum, 2*, 159-176.

Tranter, D. (2009c). *Valuing the Queensland Museum: A Contingent Valuation Study 2008*. Brisbane: Queensland Museum.

Tranter, D. (2010a). Safeguarding Australian Heritage Trade Skills. *International Journal of Intangible Heritage, 86-95*.

Tranter, D. (2010b). *Study Tour Report USA 2010*. Cobb+Co Museum. Toowoomba.

Tranter, D., & Douglas, K. (1995). *The Carnival of Flowers: A Case Study in Regional Tourism: An Education Resource Kit*. Toowoomba: Cobb+Co Museum.

Tranter, D., & Douglas, K. (1997). *Toowoomba's Heritage: A Resource Kit*. Toowoomba: Cobb+Co Museum.

Tranter, D., & Powell, j. (1992). *Cobb & Co. Museum - Australia's Finest Collection of Horse-drawn Vehicles*. Brisbane: Queensland Museum.

Travers, T. (2006). Museums and Galleries in Britain: Economic, Social and Creative Impacts (pp. 1-91). London: National Museum Directors' Conference and Museums, Libraries and Archives Council.

Travers, T., & Glaister, S. (2004). Valuing Museums: Impact and Innovation among National Museums. London: National Museum Directors' Conference.

Tremblay, P., & Carson, D. (2006). A Scoping Study on the "Value" of the Museum and Art Gallery of the Northern Territory Community and Economy (pp. 1-84). Darwin: Charles Darwin University - Tourism Research Group.

Trotter, R. (1996). *Touring the Past: A Study of the Relationship between Museums, Heritage and Tourism in Queensland.* Doctor of Philosophy, Griffith University, Brisbane.

UNESCO. (1994). Culture and Development in Africa. Washington DC: World Bank.

UNESCO. (2001). Action Plan for the Safeguarding of the ICH as Approved by the International Experts on the Occasion of the International Round Table on 'Intangible Cultural Heritage - Working Definitions'. Turin.

UNESCO. (2003). *Convention for the Safeguarding of Intangible Cultural Heritage*, Paris.

United Nations and Queensland Government. (2005, 14-17 August 2005). *Brisbane Declaration*. Paper presented at the The International Conference on Engaging Communities, Brisbane.

Urry, J. (1990). Gazing on History. In D. Boswell & J. Evans (Eds.), *Representing the Nation: A Reader; Histories, Heritage and Museums* (pp. 208-232). London: Routledge.

URS Corporation. (2007). Measuring the Value of the Cultural Sector Using Contingent Valuation: A Preliminary Scoping Study (pp. 1-24): West Yorkshire Enterprise Partnership.

Usherwood, B. (2001). Accounting for Outcomes - Demonstrating the Impact of Public Libraries. *2001 Public Libraries Conference*. Retrieved from doi:mhtml:file//C:\data\PhD\research papers\2001 Public Libraries Conference paper.mht

van Schaik, T. (2002). *Social Capital in the European Value Study Surveys*. Paper presented at the OECD-ONS International Conference on Social Capital Measurement London.

Venturelli, S. (2002). Culture and the Creative Economy in the Information Age. In J. Hartley (Ed.), *Creative Industries* (pp. 391-398). Malden, MA.: Blackwell Publishing.

Vergo, P. (Ed.). (1989). *The New Museology*. London: Reaktion Books.

Walker, H. (2005). Museums, Galleries and Tourism: Realising the Potential

Report of the Conference held at the Lighthouse, Glasgow, 14 March 2005 (pp. 1-32): Scottish Museums Council, Visit Scotland and Scottish Enterprise.

Walsh, K. (1992). *The Representation of the Past: Museums and Heritage in the Post-Modern World.* London: Routledge.

Watson, S. (Ed.). (2007). *Museums and Their Communities*. London: Routledge.

Wavell, C., Baxter, G., Johnson, I. & Williams, D. for Robert Gordon University. (2002). Impact Evatuation of Museums, Archives and Libraries: Available Evidence Project: Resource: The Council for Museums, Archives and Libraries.

Weil, S. E. (1983). *Beauty and the Beast - On Museums, Art, the Law and the Market*. Washington D.C.: Smithsonian Institution Press.

Weil, S. E. (1994). Creampuffs and Hardball: Are You Really Worth What You Cost or Just Merely Worthwhile? In G. Anderson (Ed.), *Reinventing the Museum* (pp. 343-347). Walnut Creek: AltaMira Press.

Weil, S. E. (1999). From Being about Something to Being for Somebody: The Outgoing Transformation of the American Museum. (What is emerging is a more entrepreneurial institution). *Daedalus, 128*(3), 229-258.

Weil, S. E. (2002). *Making Museums Matter*. Washington: Smithsonain Institution Press.

Weil, S. E. (2003). 5 Meditations. *Museum News, 82*(1), 26-31, 44-47.

Weisbrod, B. A. (Ed.). (2000). *To Profit or Not to Profit: The Commerical Transformation of the Nonprofit Sector*. Cambridge: Cambridge University Press.

West, B. (1988). The Making of the English Working Past: A Critical View of the Ironbridge Gorge Museum. In R. Lumley (Ed.), *The Museum Time-Machine* (pp. 36-62). London: Routledge.

West, W. R. (2000). Creating the Community-Conscious Museum. *Museum News,* 107.

Whitehead, J., & Finney, S. (2002, 1-2 February). *Willingness to Pay for Submerged Maritime Cultural Resources.* Paper presented at the Contingent Valuation of Culture Conference, Chicago.

Whiting, P. G., & Outspan Group (Producer). (1999). Socio-Economic Benefits Framework for the Cultural Sector Discussion Paper. Retrieved from http://www.creativecity.ca/resources/making-the-case/general/socio-economic-benefits.pdf

Williams, D. (1996). How the Arts Measure Up: Australian Research into Social Impact *The Social Impact of Arts Programs*. London: COMEDIA.

Willis, K. G. (2002). Iterative Bid Design in Contingent Valuation and the Estimation of the Revenue Maximising Price for a Cultural Good. *Journal of Cultural Economics, 26*, 307-324.

Winkworth, K. (2005). *Fixing the Slums of Australian Museums: or Sustaining Heritage Collections in Regional Australia.* Paper presented at the Museums Australia Conference.

Wireman, P. (1997). *Partnerships for Prosperity: Museums and Economic Development.* Washington DC: American Association of Museums.

Witcomb, A. (2003). 'A Place for All of Us'? Museums and Communities. In S. Watson (Ed.), *Museums and Their Communities* (pp. 133-156). London: Routledge.

Worts, D. (2006a). Measuring Museum Meaning: A Critical Assessment Framework. *Journal of Museum Education, 31*(1), 41-48.

Worts, D. (2006b). Transformational Encounters: Reflections on Cultural Participation and Ecomuseology. *Canadian Journal of Communication, 31*, 127-145.

Wright, P. (1982). Trafficking in History. In D. Boswell & J. Evans (Eds.), *Representing the Nation: A Reader: Histories, Heritage and Museums* (pp. 115-150). London: Routledge.

Wright, P. (1985). *On Living in an Old Country: The National Past in Contemporary Britain.* London: Verso.

Yerkovich, S. (2006). Linking the Present with the Past through Intangible Heritage in History Museums. *International Journal of Intangible Heritage, 1*, 44-52.

Yetter, G. H. (1992). *Williamsburg Before and After: The Rebirth of Virginia's Colonial Capitla.* Williamsburg, Virginia: The Colonial Williamsburg Foundation.

www.ingramcontent.com/pod-product-compliance
Lightning Source LLC
LaVergne TN
LVHW020504100826
845148LV00003B/699

* 9 7 8 1 6 1 2 2 9 0 6 7 6 *